MW01030476

CRC SERIES IN
**PRACTICAL ASPECTS OF CRIMINAL
AND FORENSIC INVESTIGATIONS**

VERNON J. GEBERTH, BBA, MPS, FBINA *Series Editor*

Series Editor's Note

This textbook is part of a series entitled *Practical Aspects of Criminal and Forensic Investigation*. This series was created by Vernon J. Geberth, a retired New York City Police Department Lieutenant Commander, who is an author, educator, and consultant to homicide and forensic investigations.

This series has been designed to provide contemporary, comprehensive, and pragmatic information to the practitioner involved in criminal and forensic investigations by authors who are nationally recognized experts in their respective fields.

Stan B. Walters

Principles of
Kinesic Interview
and
Interrogation
Second Edition

CRC PRESS

Boca Raton London New York Washington, D.C.

Library of Congress Cataloging-in-Publication Data

Walters, Stan B.
    Principles of kinesic interview and interrogation / Stan B. Walters — 2nd ed.
        p. cm. — (CRC series in practical aspects of criminal and forensic investigations)
    Includes bibliographical references and index.
    ISBN 0-8493-1071-7
    1. Police questioning. 2. Interviewing in law enforcement. I. Title. II. Series.

HV8073 .W343 2002
363.2'54—dc21
                                                                            2002067405
                                                                            CIP

Visit the CRC Press Web site at www.crcpress.com

© 2003 by CRC Press LLC

No claim to original U.S. Government works
International Standard Book Number 0-8493-1071-7
Library of Congress Card Number 2002067405
Printed in the United States of America 1 2 3 4 5 6 7 8 9 0
Printed on acid-free paper

Table of Contents

Section II
THE PRACTICAL KINESIC
INTERROGATION PHASE

APPENDICES

Editorial Note

I believe that both men and women possess the raw skills necessary to be successful interviewers and interrogators. My study and research have included both gender groups. In addition, the behaviors, personalities, and characteristics described herein have been repeatedly found not to be limited to a single gender group, age bracket, or cultural or ethnic group. However, in the interest of clarity, readability, and sentence structure, I have followed the older form of writing style and used the nonspecific male pronoun when identifying the participants in the interview or interrogation setting.

Preface

Of all the topics taught in law enforcement academies and criminal justice training centers throughout the United States, one of the critical topics that always seems to get poor, little, or even no attention at all is the principles of interview and interrogation. Even in a recent informal survey that I conducted of nearly 1000 investigators in 25 states, I found that the topic is receiving little more than cursory attention in the training curriculums for new officers and investigators. Despite this weakness in their training, we regularly demand that investigators obtain critical information from victims, witnesses, informants, and confessions from suspects.

For more than 25 years, I have had an interest in the dynamics of behavior exhibited in the interview and interrogation environment. My interest led me to a vast collection of articles and a few texts on a wide variety of interview and interrogation theories and techniques. However, I found many of these writings to be abstract, demanding innate comprehension of the material, assuming that the investigators already had the skills to understand the concepts. Some of the writings expected the reader to blindly accept the information presented without any background explanation. Other writings were elementary and provided no real insight, even to the new investigator. I was further frustrated in my learning process as I began to observe methods and techniques used by investigators in various interview and interrogation settings. Many of the interviewers I observed, I considered mature and skilled. When I questioned them as to the nature of their techniques, however, they were unable to provide me with any real guidance or insight as to why they employed certain methods or why one method was chosen over another.

After a few years of frustrated efforts, I was exposed to kinesic interview and interrogation theory, or what was called behavioral analysis. As I began to explore this area in depth, I discovered that many of the ideas being taught were void of much background explanation. Again I began to search for the foundation of this technique and found that there was little or no law enforcement understanding or explanation as to the "whys" and "wherefores." Most of the law enforcement literature I found taught principles to be accepted because "that's just the way people do it."

Returning to the research skills I learned in college, I began to search for the root explanations for the behaviors humans use when communicating with one another. I also searched for explanations as to why we exhibit certain behaviors when we are under stress and, in particular, when being deceptive. I discovered that there was a wealth of information, but only bits and pieces of other larger volumes of research data. The more I explored existing material, the more explanatory background information I found. My goal, then, became to gather this scattered body of information, identify specific behaviors, and attempt to observe them in the interview and interrogation environment. This was my primary objective in the first edition of *Principles of Kinesic Interview and Interrogation*.

The response by the readers of the first edition was overwhelming. I've been contacted by investigative interviewers worldwide who have reported they have renewed excitement and confidence in their interviews and interrogations and that they are seeing much more satisfying results in their efforts. The first edition has received acceptance in the criminal justice education community and has enabled me to become more involved in the study of human deception and the dynamics of interview and interrogation. I was afforded the chance to study my specific areas of interest through the work I did with Johns Hopkins University and even more so in the research with my colleague Dr. Martha Davis at John Jay College in New York. These opportunities have been exciting to me not only as an investigative interviewer, but also, more importantly, as a researcher.

I had several objectives in mind when I began work on this second edition. Anyone who has done any writing knows that even after the initial work is finished, it is never really finished. It wasn't long after the first edition was published that I was already regretting that I didn't have certain research information available prior to the first edition. I also found myself wishing I had taken more time on some topics, and I saw the need to add some new important material. There are three new chapters in the second edition. I have also included results of much of the more recent research in which I have been privileged to participate.

In this edition, I have taken the opportunity to address the issues surrounding false confessions that I believe receive little or no attention in interview and interrogation training curriculum. It is a controversial topic, and claims of false confessions and wrongful convictions are denounced as a threat to our ability to gain confessions and solve cases. I seem to remember the same thing being said about the Miranda Decision years ago. I felt it more important to address the issue head on, examine the findings about false confessions and wrongful convictions, and try to train interviewers to recognize and avoid the pitfalls that could ultimately threaten the admissibility of statements. Although this work may not completely cover the issue, I believe it to be an essential part of the knowledge base of the professional interviewer. Our goal as investigators and interviewers is to find and report the truth so that justice is served — not only in terms of protecting the victim, but also in ensuring that the right subject is identified and prosecuted accordingly.

The first section of this text is The Practical Kinesic Analysis Phase. This is the behavior that assists the diligent interviewer in determining the probable truthful or deceptive symptoms of his subject. My purpose is to identify and classify the behaviors for ready recognition by the interviewer. Where applicable, I have also tried to provide background information as to the reasons such behaviors may or may not appear. This information is the result of years of personal study, research, and observation. I have also updated and expanded every area with new information that I have gleaned from my studies and research. I felt it necessary to add an additional chapter covering the basics of good interview and interrogation skills that I believe that should form the critical foundation of knowledge for the professional investigative interviewer.

The photographic work in Chapter 6, "Nonverbal Behaviors," is part of my effort to isolate and identify some of the behavioral symptoms that I had learned or read about. These photographs were taken from over 900 video-taped interviews of inmates from various correctional facilities around the United States. The reader should know that none of the subjects in the photographs have been "posed," nor were they "coached" to exhibit their behaviors during their interviews. The subjects spontaneously generated all the symptoms I have documented. The inmates' crimes range from simple theft, forgery, burglary, unpaid traffic fines, and disorderly conduct, to rape, arson, murder, child abuse, escape, and including in some cases, multiple and serial offenses. The terms of their incarcerations ranged from a mere two or three days to multiple life sentences. The inmates, who are volunteers, provided waivers for the use of the video and photo work for law enforcement training and educational purposes. I am indebted to these men and women for permitting me to document their behaviors.

Once steps were taken to document various kinesic behaviors in the interview and interrogation environment, I found that my study really began to expand. It was not just enough to identify the relevant behaviors of each person, but to also understand why subjects did or did not confess, why some interviewers were more successful than others, and why some techniques worked only part of the time. Again, conversing with various interviewers and reading law enforcement materials did not give much insight into this area. With the arrival of the FBI's Behavioral Science Unit and the growing interest in "criminal profiling" by other highly qualified law enforcement officers, it was obvious that individual personalities of the interviewer and the subject apparently can come into play. Only a very few interview and interrogation theorists had explored this concept, and fewer still taught this type of information. I, along with this small minority, believe this to be the key to successful interviews and interrogations.

The second section of this text is The Practical Kinesic Tactical Interrogation Phase. It deals with information that I feel is critical to conducting the successful interview and interrogation — the action and interaction of human personalities. Researching the works of Carl Jung, Sigmund Freud, Hans Eysenck, and other recognized personality researchers and theorists, I began to understand why any interview or interrogation came to its particular end. I realized that the stockpiled video work that I had in my possession was a wealth of information regarding personality interaction between the subject and the interviewers. In nearly all the research tapes, there were two interviewers participating in the research and practical exercises. Now I could observe not only the subject's behavior and personality, but also how that personality interacted with the two distinctly different personalities of the interviewers. This section is based on my hands-on observations from numerous interviews and interrogations that I have conducted. In some instances, I have learned a great deal from the active criminal cases that I have been asked to review by criminal justice agencies, courts, and prosecutors from around the country. These experiences, along with my research, study, and interpretations of the works of such great minds as Jung, Freud, Eyesenck, and others have all contributed to an understanding of the dynamics of personality in the interview setting.

The second section relies heavily on observations that I have made according to personality typing and characteristics identified by researchers of personality type. My purpose is to assist the interviewers, first in taking stock of their own behaviors and understanding why they think, act, and respond the way they do. Second, I hope they will learn to understand the significance of personality and appreciate why subjects respond the way they do when being interviewed. Simply put, the goal is for the interviewer to know himself and others. A thorough understanding of such information will assist him in ferreting out and exploiting the idiosyncrasies of an individual who may be reluctant to provide critical information.

By using an inmate population as the group to study behaviors and personalities, I had subjects who demonstrated the extremes in human personality, including various forms of personality disorder, psychoses, and more. This observation gave credence to the criminal-profiling axiom, "Behavior is a reflection of personality." For that reason, I included a short section on schizophrenia, brain disease, clinical depression, and suicidal personalities. I am not trying to create interviewers who are psychologists or psychiatrists; however, these behaviors will often be found during an investigative interview, and therefore, more than a layman's knowledge of this information is essential.

The best interviewers and interrogators are those who have learned to observe and interpret human communication behaviors, are introspective enough to know themselves, have developed a broad-based understanding of other personalities, and have developed the skill to play "the game" in the interview room, and temporarily play the role of any other personality. They also realize that they will never fully understand all aspects of human behavior, communication, and personality, and they perceive every interview as a learning experience. They are the ones who second-guess themselves and critically review their own performances long after the interview is over. Their curiosity about such matters is never fully satisfied. They are what I call "students of human behavior."

This text is not intended to be the final answer to all questions about human communication, deception, and personality. It was written with the information that I have up to this point in time. I request that you accept even the second edition of this text for what it is — a work in progress, for I, too, am striving to be a "student of human behavior."

Dedication

This book is dedicated to
Hilda,
my best friend, wife, and partner for more than 25 years.

To my daughters, Hilary and Allison;
my granddaughter, Jordan;
and to Mom and Dad for their guidance, eternal love,
and constant prayers.

Truth fears nothing but concealment.
The Universal Instructor, 1983
Legal Maxims

Acknowledgments

I am thankful to many people for their support and invaluable assistance. I wish to acknowledge Vernon Geberth, series editor, for his continuing support and work on this series and for his contributions to the field of criminal and forensic investigations and publishing.

I could never say "thank you" enough to my very good friend and business associate Jim Alsup, of the Public Agency Training Council. I have benefited first and foremost from his friendship; as a business associate, I could find no better. We have both grown professionally and personally from not only the successes we've shared, but just as much from the disappointments. Jim and his great staff, national coordinators and my fellow instructors have all been encouraging and supportive and have made contributions to this work in ways they will never realize. I value their friendship.

I will always be a richer man for having known my teaching partner William W. Owens. Bill's wisdom and insights have been invaluable for years. His objective comments and positive reinforcement, and occasionally his "scolding," helped me grow and see the future and determine the direction of my work.

My thirst for knowledge and dreams of real research would never have been possible without the wonderful challenges and opportunities afforded me in the field of scientific research provided by my colleague and friend Dr. Martha Davis. She, along with John Jay College and the City University of New York, have helped to significantly broaden my horizons. I am confident that I will continue to learn and grow professionally as Martha and I continue our research. The sky's the limit!

I have certainly benefited from the experience, knowledge, skills, and insight of Dan Sosnowski. Not only is he my senior instructor, but I am also lucky to have him as my friend. His quiet support and encouragement are greatly appreciated.

I wish to thank Dr. Truett Ricks, former dean of the Eastern Kentucky University College of Law Enforcement. Likewise, my friend and loyal supporter Dr. Brett Scott has made my access to research subjects an easy task. Dr. Dale Olsen of the Applied Physics Lab and Johns Hopkins University has opened the doors to countless opportunities for my growing work.

I owe special thanks to the Commonwealth of Kentucky Corrections Cabinet, the Law Enforcement Training Institute at the University of Missouri, and the Missouri Department of Corrections. Major Bryan Tuma, Lt. Judy Bailey, and Capt. Julie Maaske of the Nebraska State Patrol and the Nebraska Department of Corrections; the Fairfax County, Virginia, Police Academy; the Ohio Department of Corrections; Mississippi Highway Patrol; Mississippi Bureau of Narcotics; and Mississippi Department of Corrections have contributed greatly over the years to the pool of videos that I have developed for research purposes.

To every student in every class I've had the pleasure instructing, for little did they know that I was also learning from them. I am thankful for their input and the contributions they have made to my work by sharing their personal experiences.

Without the patience, encouragement, and direction of my editor, Becky McEldowney, and the great folks at CRC Press, none of my humble efforts would have ever made it this far.

The Author

Stan B. Walters is president of Stan B. Walters & Associates, Inc. He earned a B.S. in Sociology from the University of Louisville and an M.S. in Criminal Justice Administration from Eastern Kentucky University. He is a graduate of the National Crime Prevention Institute. Walters started his 29-plus year career as a civilian employee with the FBI, working for the security division of a Fortune 500 company and as director of security for a commercial bank. His company provides interview and interrogation services and training to business, industry, and law enforcement sectors worldwide.

Stan continues to actively research interview and interrogation behaviors, strategies, and techniques, including hundreds of prison interviews and investigative forensic interviews. His work has received critical acclaim in both the academic and criminal justice communities. He served as subject matter expert on interview and interrogation to Johns Hopkins University in the development of the Mike Simman Interview Training CD for the U.S. Department of Justice. He was a research consultant in a major interview-behavior research project conducted at John Jay College of the City University of New York. Walters and his colleagues are currently conducting continuing research in the area of human behavior and deception and interview and interrogation, and he is the co-author of several articles on these subjects. He has authored numerous training materials, audiotapes, and pocket guides on Practical Kinesic Interview and Interrogation® and other manuals and guides on deception. He frequently serves as a consultant to prosecutors' offices and police departments in criminal investigations.

Walters is an accomplished lecturer, speaker, and instructor, and is in heavy demand worldwide for his informative and dynamic training courses in Practical Kinesic Interview and Interrogation®. He is an adjunct instructor at Eastern Kentucky University, University of Missouri Law Enforcement Training Institute, and for the Department of Defense Polygraph Institute. He is an associate member of the American Polygraph Association and the International Association of Homicide Investigators, and is a professional member of the National Speakers Association.

He has taught in various state, local, and municipal law enforcement academies in over 45 states, as well as for the U.S. Department of Defense;

U.S. Immigration and Naturalization Service; Drug Enforcement Administration; the Texas Rangers; Bureau of Alcohol, Tobacco, and Firearms; U.S. Postal Inspectors; U.S. Probation; U.S. Attorney's Offices; and the Federal Law Enforcement Training Centers in Georgia, Arizona, and New Mexico. Walters has also taught in various U.S. intelligence agencies and numerous other educational, professional, and criminal justice training organizations in the United States, Canada, and East Asia.

Introduction

The primary reason for the existence of any investigator, whether in the criminal, loss prevention, personnel, intelligence, safety, or private investigation field, is to gather information. The success of the investigator is directly related to his ability to conduct effective interviews and interrogations. In 1975, the Rand Corporation conducted a study of the investigative efforts of police agencies, their officers, and detectives in an effort to determine which activities had the greatest impact on the solution of a case. It came as no surprise that the study determined that the two most effective efforts associated with the positive conclusion of a case were the collection and preservation of evidence and the effective interviewing of victims and witnesses (Greenwood, 1979). It is reasonable, therefore, to also conclude that the proper interview and interrogation of possible suspects has an equal, if not greater, effect on the success of an investigation.

Despite the significance that successful interviews and interrogations may have on the solution of criminal cases, the majority of law enforcement training academies provide only token or often no training for officers on this topic during the basic academy process. In addition, once out of the academy, officers receive little or no follow-up training in this topic as part of any in-service training program. The Rand study noted that many departments provide little or no special training when an officer is promoted from patrol to investigations. It is assumed that the necessary skills will be acquired while on the job (Greenwood, 1979). When the training at police academies was reviewed, it was found that more than half of the police departments polled gave their officers no formal training in interview and interrogation (Fisher and Geiselman, 1992).

In an informal written survey, the author queried 1000 officers from various jurisdictions in 25 different states regarding the training they received during their basic academy experience (Walters, 2002). Each was asked about the length of time that he spent in basic training, if he had an interview and interrogation training block, and how much time, if any, was spent on the topic. Although the information is unscientific, it would appear that little has changed in law enforcement training regarding interview and interrogation since the Rand study in 1979. The author found that only approximately 40% of the officers surveyed reported having any training in interview and interrogation during basic academy. Those officers who did get training in the topic reported that the training lasted one day or less. Most officers reported receiving no more than 4 hours of instruction in basic interview and interrogation skills. It was interesting to note that it appeared that military police and federal agencies did spend considerably more time on the topic than other agencies.

Many investigators feel that the concept of interrogation is a skill one is born with and cannot be taught. In reality, reliable interview and interrogation skills can be taught, and officers typically show marked improvement in the effectiveness of their interviews after such training (Fisher and Geiselman, 1992). It would also seem that interview and interrogation is viewed as a method of simply following a list of questions presented in a structured manner with little or no variation. In reviewing texts and articles, both past and present, the new interviewer is led to believe that interview and interrogation is merely an exercise in asking the "who, what, where, when, and how" questions routinely used in reporting. These concepts ignore the fact that human behavior and human interpersonal communication are complex and multifaceted, and that neither can be approached in a restrictive, structured manner.

Traditionally, the study of kinesics focused on the observable outward physical behaviors of the body in order to ascertain the person's current emotional state and the role the body plays in communicating that information. It was quickly learned that by understanding the "vocabulary" of body language, along with the diagnosis of a person's verbal output, an interviewer could more easily assess a person's truthfulness or deception regarding the current issue under discussion. Well-known behavioral scientist B.F. Skinner noted that an individual's speech is not independent from his nonverbal behaviors, indicating that the observation of both mediums is critical to effective communication (Skinner, 1952, 1992). In essence, we can only make an accurate analysis of the content and significance of another individual's communication by observing the whole person rather than just one aspect. To make an analysis of a person's credibility based on a narrow area of observation creates a risk for misinterpretation or may cause the observer to miss the significance of what has been communicated.

Kinesic interview and interrogation is viewed as a multiphase behavioral analysis system used to conduct more effective and efficient interpersonal communications. The foundation of the technique rests on the common everyday behavior of human beings and their diverse communication abilities. Some of these communication skills are learned from a collection of available human behaviors, while other characteristics exist in all humans.

The concepts of advanced kinesic interviewing recognize the complexity of human behavior and communication. These concepts combine not only the principles of basic kinesics in terms of speech and body language, but also those same behaviors exhibited in written statements. They suggest that speech and body language behaviors can give insight into the individual's personality type, indicating the "psychological fingerprint" of that person. By combining the information received through diagnosis of verbal and nonverbal behavior with this psychological fingerprint, an interviewer can conduct an interview and interrogation that is specifically tailored for the subject.

The first portion of the process is the Practical Kinesic Analysis Phase, in which behaviors are observed and decoded to determine the subject's truthful and deceptive behaviors, or at least to determine those areas most sensitive to the subject and, therefore, in need of further attention through verbal inquiry. In this phase, the interviewer gains insight from the subject's verbal and nonverbal behaviors. Practical Kinesic Analysis Phase information is also gained by taking oral or written statements from the subject that are also assessed by recognizing the verbal and nonverbal cues generated at the time the subject renders the statements.

Once the determination has been made that a subject is being deceptive, the interviewer must begin the task of getting him to give an admission of his guilt or deception. During this process, the interviewer cannot depend on a standardized approach to the interrogation that is applied to all deceptive subjects. All individuals are not the same. They do not have the same personalities, nor do they use coping mechanisms in the same way. This approach, if used, can be a frustrating and fruitless process. During interrogation, the interviewer must accurately assess and identify the subject's personality type and his particular use of coping mechanisms. By correctly identifying the personality type, the interviewer can tailor comments on each specific subject for maximum effect.

During interrogation, the interviewer uses the Practical Kinesic Analysis Phase to gather information about a subject's emotional and mental state in response to the interrogation much as a traveler uses a map to determine his current location or which route to take. At the same time, the interviewer develops a profile of the subject that allows him to use a tailored interrogation approach for that subject. This subject-specific approach is referred to as a "Practical Kinesic Interrogation Phase."

The Practical Kinesic Interrogation Phase involves the interviewer determining the subject's frame of mind in response to the interview stress. It also assists the interviewer in determining if the subject is suffering some personality disorder or psychosis that would have an impact on the interviewer's approach. The interviewer determines the subject's personality type, thereby permitting him to understand how the subject thinks, his strengths to be avoided, and weaknesses that can be exploited. Finally, the interviewer must determine the subject's ego-defense mechanisms which keep him from having to face the reality of his actions. The interrogator must identify these mechanisms and disarm each one in order to obtain admission or confession.

By using practical kinesic interview and interrogation as a multidiscipline process of verbal analysis, including statement analysis, nonverbal analysis, stress-response state assessment, and primary dominant personality assessment, an investigator will find he is able to attain more admissions and confessions with less frustration, greater efficiency, and much more positive results.

During our discussions of the various principles of practical kinesic interview and interrogation, we will not be discussing the various legal aspects regarding interview and interrogation. Those discussions are best left to the appropriate law enforcement academies, colleges of law enforcement, and the legal departments of corporations, municipalities, and federal and state attorneys general. Any student of the law knows that the law and its various interpretations change on a weekly, if not daily, basis and from one jurisdiction to another. To write a text on interrogation that attempts to maintain an updated legal section would be futile. By the time the manuscript is written, typeset, published, and distributed, the major elements of a law could change dramatically and the information be outdated before the book was published. We will state, however, that the practical kinesic interview and interrogation technique does not use or teach methodologies that are unethical or illegal, and that the technique abides by accepted legal standards for conducting appropriate interviews and interrogations. In addition, the author does not support or condone such behavior by any professional interviewer and interrogator. Among the several goals of this work, one objective is to assist the investigative interviewer in learning how to get to the truth in any interview and interrogation. The objective of finding the truth and prosecuting the offender should never be done at the expense of the rights of the suspect, nor should it ever be tolerated. To do so is to offend against the victim or victims again and it defames the criminal justice system that is sworn to protect the rights of both the offender and the victim.

Finally, the art of interview and interrogation is a skill that is learned, but not from a single lesson, class, or textbook. It is a skill that is practiced, polished, and honed over time, and the successful interviewer and interrogator is one who knows that the learning process never ends. To be a successful and professional interviewer and interrogator, one must be a committed student of human behavior. To achieve positive results, the professional interviewer and interrogator must study the process, practice his skills, and use his knowledge in pursuit of the truth.

The essential thing is not to find truth, but to investigate and search for it.

Max Nordau
Paradoxes, 1885

I

THE PRACTICAL
KINESIC ANALYSIS
PHASE

Basic Kinesic Principles

1

From smiles to frowns, crying to anger, crossed arms to open palms, the gestures of the human animal have been a constant source of fascination to scientists and the observers of human behavior for centuries. These same groups have argued among themselves as to which behaviors are imprinted, or learned during childhood as part of the socialization process, or are a part of the genetic code handed down from one generation to the next. All do agree, however, that the gestures as well as words speak volumes about our emotions, stresses, and innermost thoughts.

One of the earliest researchers in this field was Dr. Ray L. Birdwhitsell of the University of Louisville. Birdwhitsell is widely credited for coining the word "kinesic" and advancing the study of body motion and communication. His and his associates' research involved the accumulation of a mass of research data demonstrating that body language and verbal behavior are interdependent in the flow of conversation between participants (Birdwhitsell, 1970). Because these mediums of human behavior and communication are so interrelated, he suggested that if human behavior observers knew the vocabulary of body language communication, they should be able to listen to a conversation and know what the body would be doing. Similarly, the observers should be able to watch only the body language of individuals communicating with each other and be able to determine the content of their language.

Historical records and documents exist describing body language behaviors seen during communication. An ancient Hindu writing, *Papyrus Vedas*, from 900 B.C., recorded the historian's observations of a murderer who had killed his victim with poison. "He who gives poison may be recognized. He does not answer questions, or they are evasive answers. He speaks nonsense. He rubs the great toe along the ground and shivers; his face is discolored. He rubs the roots of the hair with the fingers and tries by every means to leave the house" (Trovillo, 1939). In the Old Testament of the Bible, the Book of Proverbs, chapter 6, verses 12 and 13, King Solomon notes the behaviors of guilt and deception: "A naughty person, the wicked man walketh with a forward mouth. He winketh with his eyes and speaketh with his feet and teaches with his fingers." It is interesting to note that both historians described verbal and nonverbal behavior in their observations, indicating the undeniable link between body language and speech that has been more recently noted by Dr. Birdwhitsell and other behavioral scientists.

Sigmund Freud noted that these behaviors are readily observable if we would only watch them. "He that has eyes to see and ears to hear may convince himself that no mortal can keep a secret. If his lips are silent, he chatters with his fingertips: betrayal oozes out of him from every pore."

In the late 19th century, Charles Darwin set out to study the various phenomena associated with human emotions. Among the many things Darwin learned was that these behaviors were consistent no matter what the culture or ethnic group. These results support the belief that many of these behaviors are, in fact, hereditary. A significant result of Darwin's research is interesting in its relationship to kinesic behavior. Darwin determined that "repressed emotion almost always comes to the surface in some form of body motion" (Darwin, 1872; Darwin and Ekman, 1998).

Suppose you are in bed asleep, and late one night you are awakened by unusual sounds in your home. Perhaps, after leaving a late movie or play downtown, you are walking alone on the dark level of a parking garage looking for your car, and you hear movement behind you in the shadows. These types of events create an instinctive response in all of us. Should someone measure the changes in our various physiological systems, they would notice some dramatic changes. Our heart rate, no doubt, would increase along with a temporary increase in our blood pressure. Our muscle tone would change, our eyes would dilate, and our breathing would become rapid and shallow. We may instead feel our hearts skip a beat and possibly find ourselves holding our breaths, and the experience might even leave us with shaking knees.

In any case, we seriously consider our possible response options. Some individuals run from the threat stimulus, trying to put as much distance between themselves and the dangerous situation in the shortest amount of time possible. Others will turn to face down the menace in hope of controlling it or defeating it. Whatever the reaction, these responses are the direct result of our survival instincts. It is these same behaviors that the polygraph examiner is looking for when running charts on a subject. These behaviors are, of course, the result of the "fight or flight" syndrome we learned about in junior high school biology. It is the survival system that all animals experience when confronted with a frightening or threatening situation.

Consider the subject in the interview or interrogation who is questioned about his involvement in a burglary, possession of some stolen property, the presence of fingerprints on a murder weapon, identification as the suspect by a rape victim, and so on. If that subject is guilty, he must now consider a response to the threat. He can either run from the room to get away from the threat presented by the interrogator, or he can stand up and fight the investigator. In both cases, following either path would be unwise, but the subject still feels no less of a threat than the persons in the imaginary scenes described.

When the subject tries to suppress these responses, Darwin's conclusion is made apparent: "Repressed emotion almost always comes to the surface in some form of body motion." Although our subject responds to the threat stimulus through body language signals, these same threats are also assessed on the psychological level. The subject reacts to the fear-provoking question based on his own past personal experiences and the framework of his personality.

In all situations, we respond to our current environment on two levels. We respond emotionally, and we respond cognitively, or mentally. The nature of those responses is based on our past history of experiences and we will apply what we have learned through our successes or failures in those past instances to the current setting in the hope of a favorable out-come. If the situation is familiar or a repeated set of circumstances, we may, to some degree, simply reuse the most productive reactions and avoid any pitfalls from our first experience as our response to the current event. Or, we may combine our knowledge from previous similar events and create what we feel is the most appropriate reaction to a new experience. Whatever the case, our mental and emotional reactions are complementary of each other. The two are in balance and show agreement or are consistent in the message they communicate simultaneously. Deception, on the other hand, requires that we attempt to monitor, edit, suppress, or even censor either our true emotional or our true cognitive response to the present stimulus, and sometimes both.

In anticipation of the possibility that he may have to commit an act of deceit, the liar may try to mentally prepare for that moment when and if it comes. He may script and rehearse the "scene" in his mind numerous times. Of course, in rehearsal, the performance is almost always flawless. The prac-tice sessions may span an extended period of time. What the liar can never really successfully rehearse or anticipate, however, is the type, depth, or strength of the emotion he may experience when that moment finally arrives and he must present the flawless performance. Signs of stress and deception signals occur because the deceptive subject is unable to totally monitor and control his or her emotional and cognitive responses. The mere attempt at monitoring, censoring, or staging the deceptive response creates dissonance between the emotional and cognitive messages, and hence creates the cues that the subject may be engaging in deception.

Since these behaviors and body language symptoms can be readily evident, the interviewer can utilize them to decipher the subject's probable truthfulness or deception. These behaviors, however, are always being generated, so the task is to determine which behaviors are significant and when to discount the insignificant behaviors. Although the task of the investigator is to identify the deceptive subject, to incorrectly identify a truthful subject as deceptive is a greater disservice.

In general, human beings, including investigative interviewers, do a poor job at spotting deception, with the results being little better than chance (Ekman, O'Sullivan, 1991). This failure in the ability of people to accurately identify deception occurs primarily for three reasons, any or all of which might be applicable: 1) judging credibility on the basis of verbal and nonverbal behaviors that are not reliable cues to deception; 2) being unaware of or missing verbal and nonverbal cues that do have a higher rate of occurrence during deception; and 3) making intuitive judgements about a person's credibility that can be prejudiced by the interviewer's preconceptions about the subject's likely credibility.

The pitfalls to accurately diagnosing deception can and must be avoided by the interviewer. First, the observer needs to recognize the failure of popular beliefs regarding the reliable signs of deception. This pitfall can be overcome by learning which verbal and nonverbal elements are more reliable diagnostic tools. Second, establishing a set of disciplined guidelines to follow when making an assessment of each individual person's credibility can reduce errors by drawing conclusions solely on intuitive analysis. We will refer to these guidelines as Basic Practical Kinesic Principles. They will provide us with our framework of analysis, and it is imperative that we abide by them in each analysis we make. To ignore or violate these critical principles can create the possibility of misinterpreting the behavior of the person being questioned.

Basic Practical Kinesic Principles

The first and most important of all the Basic Practical Kinesic Principles is:

No single kinesic behavior, verbal or nonverbal, proves a person is truthful or deceptive.

Despite common beliefs and folk wisdom, there is no single "Pinocchio Syndrome" or universal human-behavior cue that we can rely on solely to determine the possibility that a person is being truthful or deceptive. As sure as we decide that there is one such cue, we will find that for a small part of the human population, that one cue is an exception for every person in that group.

Human behavior is wonderfully diverse, and to assign such significance to a single symptom is foolhardy at best. Take, for example, a person who has been exercising to improve his health. After 20 or 30 minutes of vigorous exercise, the afternoon athlete takes a shower and is relaxing before dinner. He notices some tightness in his chest along with difficult breathing and cold sweats. The person may immediately assume that he is experiencing a heart attack and rush to a nearby hospital emergency room for treatment. The physician enters the room, hears the patient's complaint, listens to the patient's heart sounds with the stethoscope, and promptly announces that heart bypass surgery is needed. The physician quickly sets up a sterile operating field, dons a surgical gown and mask, and begins surgery. Should we be the patient at this point, we would seriously doubt this doctor's professionalism. How could this doctor come to such a precise conclusion based on so little evidence?

Is the interviewer or interrogator any less negligent should a determination of guilt be made based solely on the movement of the eyes, the slightest shift in the torso, or one single verbal cue?

This same scenario can be extended to the next Basic Practical Kinesic Principle:

Behaviors must be relatively consistent when the stimuli are repeated.

Individuals under a variety of conditions can generate random symptoms of all types of behaviors. Among those random behaviors, there can occur symptoms that could be misinterpreted as signs of deception. If the subject we are interviewing repeatedly shows some form of stress reaction each time the interviewer discusses a particular area of inquiry, it can be assumed that the initial response by the subject was not just some random behavior. Repeated reaction to a topic of importance suggests that the particular topic creates some significant emotional or cognitive change in the person. Just because some form of reaction occurs, however, is not by itself confirmation that the person is being deceptive.

The physician will take several diagnostic steps to ensure that his patient does, in fact, have heart trouble. His observations of the patient during these tests should either confirm or refute his diagnosis to assure him that the symptom he initially saw was, in fact, a genuine and not random event. His purpose behind these various tests is to see if he can re-create the conditions that existed when the subject experienced these cardiac events. Should the symptoms reappear under selected conditions, then the physician may now reasonably assume they are the result of a heart problem. We are going to be watching for a subject's symptoms of stress response to investigative inquiry. What makes up those behaviors?

According to most behavioral scientists, our human communication methods are comprised of about 65% body language. For some individuals, that percentage can obviously be higher or lower, depending on their particular communication skills and personality. Approximately 7% can be attributed to verbal content, while the quality of the voice accounts for about 12%. The remaining 16% is a mixture of miscellaneous symptoms, such as chemical changes, odors, and smaller, subtler signals that are difficult to spot. These signals demonstrate our feelings, moods, emotional states, and physiological status. Disruption of these patterns from their normal levels is an indication that the subject is responding to some stress stimulus.

Although we can divide human communication into these four categories, we cannot rely on any one single channel to make an assessment of a person's credibility. There will be times when the only signs of a person's possible deception may originate from the body. At another point in time, a deception signal may be generated from voice content, and then later, the cue may come from the microsignal category. In a research study conducted by the author and his colleague, Dr. Martha Davis, who was the principal researcher, it was determined that the most reliable assessments of deception were made when cues came from at least two separate channels (Davis et al., 2000).

In light of this and other findings regarding behaviors, the next three Basic Practical Kinesic Principles are critical for the investigator to remember.

First,

The interviewer must establish what is the normal, or "constant," of behavior for each subject. Accurate assessment of a person's behavior can be made only after establishing this reference point.

Second,

Once the constant has been established, the observer then looks for changes in the subject's constant of behavior.

Third,

Changes in a subject's behavior are reliable for diagnosing deception only if they appear in clusters.

All individuals do not have exactly the same "constant" behavior patterns. Before we can determine what may be considered a deviation in behavior, we need to establish this particular person's baseline, or constant, in verbal and nonverbal behavior. In this manner, people are primarily judged against themselves, and each person becomes his or her own measuring standard.

The interviewer must consider such things as a person's basic speech patterns in terms of voice quality. Does this person use a lot of gestures when talking, or is there very little gesticulation? Is the subject's speech generally clear and precise, or do we consistently find mumbling, stammering, or other speech dysfunction? If so, then that is the person's baseline behavior, and we should consider changes from these patterns to be indications of stress.

One way we can determine what constitutes an individual's constant of behavior is to ask nonthreatening questions and observe that person's unstressed or relaxed behavior. These nonthreatening questions are those that we use when developing rapport. They include simple questions regarding pedigree, such as full name, date of birth, education, employment, or talking about sports, weather, neighborhood, children, current events — general topics that pose no potential threat. Should we already be generally familiar with this individual and his relaxed behaviors, the rapport-building phase becomes less critical in our subsequent interviews. It is important now to point out that innocent as well as deceptive subjects can be nervous when entering the interview environment. Their apparent nervous reactions for the time being will be their "constant" of behavior, and we should make our assessment based on changes in what might be described as an elevated baseline of behavior (see Figures 1.1 and 1.2).

A common mistake made in assessing a person's credibility is that being nervous is a reliable sign of deception. Stress can be generated in a subject from any number of sources of stimuli. Such general stress is far too common and inconsistent in appearance and occurrence, thus making an assessment of deception highly unreliable (Davis, Connors, and Walters, 1999). In view of this problem and the available information about reliable and unreliable signs of deception, we are going to classify "stress" behaviors into three categories: general stress, incriminating stress, and discriminating stress signals.

The general stress that an individual experiences under various stimulus conditions does seem to present in some pattern. This is what we define as the person's "constant" of behavior. It is a constant in that it is the particular pattern the person uses on a regular basis when dealing with all types of stress. Dr. Martha Davis and the author, as a result of their research, define this type of regularly repeated stress reaction by a person as their "defensive demeanor profile"(Davis et al., 2001; Davis and Walters, 2000).

General stress cues are those that anyone can experience under numerous conditions. This type of stress can occur because we are running late on our way into work due to heavy rush hour traffic. It can be seen on the faces of job applicants waiting for interviews with the director of human resources. The groom may feel a little stress in the hours preceding the wedding, or the

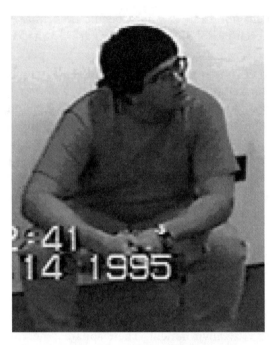

Figure 1.1 Example of a subject's constant and then change in behavior during an interview. Subject was discussing whether he was fully aware or not that he had shot the victim in the head.

newly engaged young woman about to introduce her fiancé to her parents. These signs of stress have little, if any, value in determining a person's credibility. They certainly can be present along with deception signals. In that case, they can help to indicate a great deal of stress associated with the subject's efforts of creating and supporting his deception. At the same time, however, they create a lot of human stress "noise" and can be distracting for the observer trying to decipher whether a person is being honest.

Incriminating stress cues, on the other hand, are those generated by both the truthful as well as the untruthful. They are different from general stress signals in that they occur less frequently in the overall behaviors of both classes of subjects; however, when considering the overall performance of behaviors, deceptive subjects do generate a higher number of these cues than do subjects who are being honest. It is a little more challenging for the observer to isolate these cues and designate them as significant. They tend to be more scattered and nonspecific in their location during a person's behavior. In a sense, they tell the interviewer that there is a significant issue and that the person may be deceptive in this area, which, therefore, warrants more attention by the interviewer. The risk, however, is that analysis of these behaviors borders more on subjective or intuitive analysis and poses a greater risk for misinterpretation. In addition, the observer must make his analysis

Figure 1.2 Example of a subject's constant and then change in behavior during an interview. Subject was discussing whether he was fully aware or not that he had shot the victim in the head.

of deception based on a larger sample of the person's behavior, as opposed to a response to a specific inquiry. We will explore these cues as they appear in verbal and nonverbal form later in this work.

Discriminating signals are those symptoms that appear to occur in direct response to specific points of inquiry or other stimuli. The observation of these signals in clusters suggests that there is a higher probability of deception at this specific point. It is these signals that the author intends to specifically address throughout this work. Familiarization of these signals and correctly identifying them should assist the observer in increasing the degree of reliability in his credibility analysis of the subject's behavior.

Since both truthful and deceptive subjects can present the interviewer with any number of symptoms, we must strongly rely on the Basic Practical Kinesic Principle that requires us to look for behaviors in clusters rather than individually. Just as the physician should not take radical steps to treat our diagnosed cardiac condition based just on a single symptom, neither should we assume guilt based on a single behavior. Should a subject demonstrate two or more behaviors in response to a particular topic, we might infer that the subject has a problem with the question or, for some reason, is sensitive to the issue. It then becomes the duty of the interviewer to make further inquiries into that area in an effort to find why the subject had such a negative reaction. Our cardiologist looks for several abnormal indicators to confirm his suspicions of heart disease. It is the occurrence of several conditions that warrants the final diagnosis and subsequent treatment to intervene in our medical problem.

We have already noted that these kinesic signals can occur either at random or in response to stress areas. We have ruled out random signals, because we know that no single behavior proves anything, and we are looking for clusters of behaviors from which to make our diagnosis. If these statements are true, then when do we start counting the symptoms that make up a cluster and when do we stop counting symptoms? It would appear that we need another Basic Practical Kinesic Principle to deal with this problem:

Behaviors that are significant must be timely.

In other words, what is the stimulus that caused these clusters of symptoms to occur? Was it when a particular fear-provoking question was asked? Was it when the arson investigator approached a specific area of the building when investigating the suspicious fire? If so, the subject's kinesic response is critical to our diagnosis of the presence of stress in that area. In fact, we can generally rely on a rule of diagnosis used by polygraph examiners when reading their charts: the behaviors are worthy of our attention if they occur within a time frame of roughly 3 to 5 seconds of the issue question (Davis, Connors, and Walters, 1999). Some subjects may be slow to react, and their behaviors may more frequently occur at the 5-second end of our time scale, while others may react much sooner. If we have correctly assessed our subject's constant or baseline response rates, we will have probably already established the subject's general response rates.

When considering the timeliness of a subject's behavior, it is important to point out that what may appear to be a cluster of behaviors consistent with a person being deceptive may, in fact, not be. A blanket decision should not be made about the entire interview. The investigative interviewer should not draw a final conclusion about the entire interview based on a single response. Each time the interviewer changes the topic and, ultimately, each question, a unique moment of stimulus is created. Each change in the stimulus by the interviewer, or even other extraneous stimuli in the interview room, can create a response from the subject. The observer should make his analysis based on the behaviors that succeed each new stimulus applied to the subject being interviewed.

If we accept the fact that any subject in the interview room reacts to various forms of stimuli occurring in that environment, we must also acknowledge the fact that the behaviors and demeanor of the interviewer are certainly going to have some form of impact on the subject. Significant stimuli originating from the interviewer can easily overshadow or contaminate the behaviors of the subject, which brings us to our next Basic Practical Kinesic Principle:

The interviewer should monitor his own behaviors in order to avoid contamination of the subject's behavior. The subjects are watching us while we are watching them.

The strongest sources of stimuli in the interview room should be the content of the interviewer's questions or the presentation of physical evidence. They should not be the outward verbal and nonverbal behaviors of the interviewer. Such negative influences can be caused by inappropriate professional behavior from the interviewer, but there can be other, more subtle behavioral phenomena. Leading questions, a loud voice, finger pointing, exaggerated facial expressions, insults, and similar behaviors often create reactions from a subject. These usually occur when the interviewer has already developed some preconceptions regarding the subject and his credibility. Some of the causes of this type of behavior range from the interviewer being unprepared for the interview because of a lack of training, having some personal agenda, or generally being indifferent to the fact that his own behavior is extremely important in an interview.

All interviewers have had that feeling in the pit of their stomachs when they have left an interview that the person they just talked to may have been deceptive. People have varying levels of subconscious skills. Why shouldn't the subject sense that the interviewer is unprepared, distracted, bluffing, may be on a fishing expedition, or just doesn't want to hear what the subject has to say? The interviewer has just had his kinesic signals read by the subject.

It may be obvious at this point that interviewing is not merely the simple task of asking questions. In fact, there are many myths about what investigative interviewing really is. It is not just asking a list of prepared questions: who, what, where, when, how, or why. It is not a game of domination (Hess, 1989). Each interview has specific objectives, and the dynamics of the subject, the interviewer's personality, physical evidence, the decision-making process, and more must be taken into account. It is, in fact, an enormous mental battle that cannot be taken lightly. Our next Basic Practical Kinesic Principle states:

Observing and interpreting behaviors is hard work.

Even the best of interviewers will comment that there have been many times when they have left the interview and interrogation room feeling mentally drained. It is a process that takes a great deal of concentration and mental discipline. To delay an important interview because it is an inconvenience or until we really have to do it is an injustice to the victim, the witnesses, and even the suspect, not to mention the disservice we have done to ourselves. No interview should be taken lightly. All information is critical and is worthy of our full attention. Note that this Basic Practical Kinesic Principle indicates that "observing" and "interpreting" is hard work. That means watching, listening, and diagnosing the significance of the subject's kinesic behaviors.

Practical Kinesic Interview and Interrogation is by no means an absolute science, and therefore does not teach any ironclad rules. It is best described as a behavioral science. It is subjective to a large degree and heavily dependent on the skill of the interviewer. Dr. Paul Ekman in his text, *Telling Lies: Clues to Deceit in the Marketplace, Politics, and Marriage*, indicates that the ability to successfully decipher deceptive behavior is based on the skill of the "lie catcher." This author has noted in *The Truth About Lying: How to Spot a Lie and Protect Yourself From Deception* that lies only succeed if the target of the lie believes the lie (Walters, 2001).

There are situations in which the quality of information gleaned by decoding kinesic symptoms may be less than desired or suspect in reliability; thus the next Basic Practical Kinesic Principle states:

Kinesic interviewing is not as reliable with some groups as with the general population.

Certain subject types , including the mentally deficient, children at adolescence, psychotics, and subjects under the debilitating influence of drugs or alcohol at the time of the interview respond differently than the general population.

Mentally deficient subjects are those who fall into an Intelligence Quotient of about 70. These individuals are easily led by those with stronger, more stable, and mature mental abilities. Frequently, individuals in this category make statements that are not necessarily the truth, but the answer that they feel the interviewer wants to hear and that will please the interviewer. The mere tone of the interview can lead to these subjects' providing incorrect information even to the point of confessing to crimes they did not commit. This can be due to an overwhelming desire to escape the pressure of the interview room, to be allowed to go home or return to the safety and comfort of their families, to gain approval from the adults present, and more. There is a high risk of false confession from this subject population, and great efforts should be made to protect them. These considerations are in addition to the normal legal complications regarding subjects of diminished capacity being aware of their actions and the significance of the interview.

Adolescents are included in this group of subjects requiring special consideration because they are experiencing dramatic hormonal changes and, as a result, may generate a great deal of random body language as well as personality changes. It is not unheard of for a teenager to convince himself that it is morally acceptable to stick by his deceptions due to some assumed loyalty or code of conduct within a particular peer group. This, by no means, suggests that all children consistantly lie, but they do warrant special care.

A review of the research studies of children and teenagers in investigative interviews dispels many of the misconceptions about their ability to perform in an interview. Children and teenagers do not lie any more often than adults do, despite the beliefs of many investigators that they are consumed by rampant fantasies (Johnson and Foley, 1984). Children are no more susceptible to misleading questions than adults during an interview or interrogation.

There are some elements of an investigative interview that can affect the quality of information gained from children and adolescents. Repeating the same question at different points in the interview affects the accuracy of the child's answer. These subjects may respond to the repeated questioning as a sign that the first answer was wrong, and will try different responses to get the correct answer (Moston, 1987). Second, a lot of what any person, including children and teenagers, recalls depends on that person's ability to recognize that the event is of importance and "encodes" the memory initially. Then, once the person has encoded that memory, retrieving, or "decoding," the memory depends on the person's skills at retrieving his memory details. The child or teenager may not have developed the advanced skills necessary to know how to store and retrieve memory (Loftus and Davies, 1984). Another factor that critically affects the quality of information gained from the child or teenage interview subject is the behavior of the interviewer (Goodman, 1984). Should the investigator encounter problems with an adolescent's interview, it may be advisable to request the assistance of a child psychologist or a veteran juvenile officer. These professionals will be keenly aware of the dramatic effect the adolescent mental, physical, and socialization processes can have on a juvenile interview.

Recent research regarding the interview of children indicates that successful, productive interviews of children can be accomplished. Results of research by R. Edward Geiselman, Gail Bornstein, and Karen J. Saywitz of the University of California, Los Angeles showed that accuracy ratings of 84 to 89% could be obtained from children when using a cognitive-type interview.

Psychotics comprise a group of people who often fall outside the abilities of the kinesic interviewer. By definition, psychotics are not in touch with reality and are principally unaware of their actions and the consequences of those actions. The origin of these disorders is psychogenic in nature, that is, their point of origin lies in the psychological make-up of the person. The information gained from such individuals may by suspect because it may be contaminated with their delusions, paranoia, and hallucinations, either audio or visual in nature. It is interesting to note that this particular group comprises approximately 1% of the U.S. population, yet makes up as much as 10% of the criminal justice population (Monahan, 1996).

On the other hand, subjects who suffer from some form of brain disease or physiological or neurological disorder create significant problems in the investigative interviewer's ability to glean reliable information from them. The afflictions of these subjects may be the result of chemical abuse, physical trauma to the brain, or psychological disorder. The complicating factor in the quality of information gained from these subjects is the fact that they may suffer from spatial or temporal dysfunction. Later in this text, we will discuss the outward characteristics of subjects who are suffering the moderate to severe effects of these types of disorders and the difficulties of interviewing them.

Finally, a group of people on whom the technique should not be used is those who are under the severe or moderate effects of drugs or alcohol. The two primary reasons for this are: first, the legal problem of diminished capacity caused by intoxication; and second, the effects that drugs and alcohol cause on the brain in terms of clear recall, the compression and expansion of time, and similar phenomena.

The Five Stress–Response States

As we go through the day-to-day routine of our lives, we regularly encounter various stress-creating events. These may include everything from being late to work because of traffic or car problems, to learning about the loss of our job, an argument with a spouse or friend, or learning of a serious illness. We react to each of these anxiety-filled situations in one of five stress–response behaviors. The subject in the interview room, when presented with the case facts or their individual liability in the situation, responds within the same framework of these responses. Four of these stress responses are negative and therefore represent general rejection of the situation or event. The fifth response indicates his acknowledgment of the dilemma or his role or responsibility, if any.

The four negative responses are anger, depression, denial, and bargaining, while the fifth response, acknowledgment, is the state in which confession occurs. All of the specific verbal cues and nonverbal symptoms we will discuss in this text are indications of the presence of at least one of these response states. The recognition of each of these states and an understanding of their functions enables the interviewer to determine the subject's current psychological response to the stress stimulus. By being able to recognize each state and understanding its purpose, the interviewer can either disable his subject's efforts at dissent or capitalize on his acknowledgment response, thereby gaining an admission or confession. The five response states are much like road signs to the interviewer. Each identifies the next turn to take during an interview just as road signs and route markers indicate to the traveler which turns to take in order to reach his final destination.

Later in this text, we will discuss in greater detail the specific characteristics of each of these states and what the presence of each represents to the subject and to the interviewer. For the time being, however, we will concern ourselves with the outwardly readable verbal and nonverbal symptoms we will use to diagnose the subject's stress response, along with a general definition of each.

The negative-response state of anger is best described as a state of dominance that a person uses to try to gain or maintain control through some form of aggression. The anger response is regarded as the most destructive of all the response states. In this condition, the subject is in mental closure and will probably not comprehend, much less listen to, more than a small percentage of the interviewer's comments. Just as an intimate couple or a pair of good friends, when having an argument, are not really hearing what the other is saying. Each has his own agenda and cares little about the needs or concerns of the other. It should be obvious at this point that the interviewer cannot allow a subject to remain in a state of anger because to do so means little chance of any form of admission or confession, much less cooperation. Later, we will discuss techniques the interviewer can use to diffuse an anger response from the subject.

The second negative-response condition, depression, is akin to the first in that it has the common characteristic of aggression. The difference between the two is that depression is aggression that is focused inward. Instead of attacking outwardly, the subjects experiencing depression are, more literally, attacking themselves; they are being consumed internally by their aggression.

If anger is the most destructive of all the responses, then depression is the most emotionally debilitating. The subject is expending more energy on himself than on the interviewer. Although many interviewers believe otherwise, full admission or confession does not come from a subject who is experiencing depression. It is possible that the subject may slip in making some incriminating remark, but that behavior is not deliberate. In fact, as we will discuss later, many interviewers incorrectly identify depression as acceptance because of the outward physical behaviors the two responses have in common.

The largest and most prevalent of all the negative-response states is denial. The subject who is responding with denial is rejecting reality and by doing so is lying to himself as well as to others. The lion's share of deception that is committed by the subject in the interview room is done in the denial state. In fact, probably at least 90% of the subject's deceptive behavior is denial. Continuing denial by subjects creates the single largest barrier for the interviewer to overcome on the way to gaining a subject's confession and, therefore, consumes the largest amount of time and effort on the part of the interviewer.

The fourth negative-response state is bargaining, which is the mood of transition. This is the weakest of all the negative reactions. In this state, the subject is disguising reality. The subject is attempting to alter the listener's opinion of the subject, the situation, the victim, or the true nature of the crime. It is a negotiating effort, with the subject constantly jockeying for the best position for himself. The ultimate risk of bargaining for the interviewer is if the interviewer is taken in and makes the unfortunate decision to accept any portion of the subject's flawed view of himself and the crime, thereby validating the subject's position.

The subject who is responding to the situation with acceptance has prepared himself to take responsibility for his actions. The interviewer will find the subject to be quite submissive to the interviewer's questions and requests. In this state of response, admissions and confessions are obtained. These statements will be obtained only if the interviewer correctly diagnoses the response state as acceptance and can seize the opportunity to gain the confession without inhibiting the subject by continuing to talk or failing to ask the right question.

Conclusion

We have now built the basic foundation upon which we construct the Kinesic Interview process. Some basic rules and guidelines have been established for proper application, and we have outlined the general framework upon which the subject's responses to the interview are predicated.

Should the interviewer forget to apply these important rules and follow the guidelines, he takes the risk of making an incorrect or flawed diagnosis of the subject. If the concepts are ignored during the interrogation process, the interviewer will be subject to constant error, miscalculation, and most likely a complicating or destructive interrogation approach. Disciplined adherence to these and other rules that we will establish increases the prospect of successful interviews and interrogations.

Fundamentals of Productive Interviewing

2

The effective and successful investigative interviewer possesses a wide range of skills and talents, centered on the four most important aspects of criminal investigation. The investigator's knowledge includes an understanding of what evidence of importance may be found at a crime scene, what should be collected, and why it should be preserved; the physical sciences used by forensic experts in analyzing the collected evidence; human behavior and how the actions of the person during the commission of the crime — either as a victim, witness, or suspect — reflect and predict personality type; and interview and interrogation theory and the practical skills needed to effectively interview victims, witnesses, informants, and subsequently suspects to gain additional information, admissions, and confessions.

These essential skills are not inherent or easy to come by. They are not a "gift" with which the investigator is endowed when he or she is first called an investigator. They are developed after extensive training, retraining, practice, and most of all, experience. It is said that a good investigator does not necessarily make a good interviewer, nor does being a good interviewer mean that the person is a good investigator. A solid foundation in these essential skills is a must, however, for a successful and productive criminal investigator. All too often in law enforcement, the critical skills necessary to successfully investigate and prepare cases for prosecution are not being adequately taught in all basic police training academies. In many cases, the officer is expected to acquire these skills merely through on-the-job training once he is assigned to an investigations unit. The officer often experiences little or no in-service training covering the specific investigative skills he needs to develop in order to handle his job assignments (Greenwood, 1979). These conditions similarly apply to interview and interrogation training.

This is not to say that interviewing skills are the most important of the essential skills, nor are they the least significant. Interview and interrogation skills are merely one tool out of many. To believe that interviewing skills alone represent the only real instrument by which any criminal case can be solved is a gross misuse of this tool. As with any tool an artisan may possess, it may be used a great deal on successive projects and then not used extensively for a period of time, only to be sorely needed again to complete a future task. On the other hand, to ignore the critical importance of good interviewing skills is to flirt with disaster.

As we have stated previously, two of the elements most essential in obtaining a conviction in a criminal case involve the investigative interview: the quality of the interviews and information gained from witnesses, and the ability to secure the cooperation of those witnesses for the prosecution of the case (Greenwood, 1979). Despite the significant impact that interviewing has on the outcome of criminal cases, it receives marginal focus, at best, in too many training academies (Fisher and Geiselman, 1992). There are obviously exceptions to this in some academies, and it would be safe to assume that a measurable difference would be found in the quality of the interviews conducted by the officers in academies that focus on this, and the cases brought forward for prosecution. In such cases, we should try to determine what those academies and officers are doing to produce such quality results and attempt to duplicate the teaching of those skills.

Acknowledging the importance of interviewing in relation to all the other skills a professional investigator must have is the first step toward being able to conduct complete and accurate interviews. The next step is to be exposed to a learning experience that teaches the correct theories and concepts of interviewing. The professional investigative interviewer must understand that the study of interviewing is an ongoing process; the investigative interviewer becomes a student of human behavior. Practicing whenever possible is critical to learning how to use those skills with any level of efficiency. And finally, the interviewer must use the learned and practiced skills as often as possible and add all those experiences gained from each interview to the arsenal of weapons needed to uncover the truth.

Principles of Successful Investigative Interviewing

Any learning process must start with good basic principles and theory. There are many different styles of interviewing and just as many techniques. Of all the approaches to interviewing, no single theory or technique can satisfactorily cover all the possible situations in which the investigative interviewer may find himself (Gudjonsson, 1992). A broad knowledge of the various methods and styles of interviewing provides an interviewer with the specific tools needed to meet the demands of each unique interview.

Interviewing theory assists the investigator in planning and carrying out the interview of the victim, witness, complainant, or suspect, but certain practical skills are required for interpreting and dealing with all the factors that can inhibit or facilitate the flow of information (Gordon, 1975). Practical skills come from continued practice and information passed on from the experienced investigator to the rookie. The information handed down, however, is not always reliable. In fact, most current interviewing theories rely on erroneous assumptions based solely on experience and little on valid scientific study and research (Gudjonsson, 1992). Unfortunately, nearly half the information written in training manuals and materials and taught in courses on interviewing is also misleading and does not agree with empirical studies on detection of deception and interviewing (Ekman, 1992). Personal experience is no doubt a valuable teaching tool, but bad habits and techniques are passed along with the proverbial axiom, "That's the way we've always done it." One police officer described the interviewing approach as, "You just ask them what, where, why, when, and how" (Fisher and Geilselman, 1992).

Extensive research into human behavior developed and relied upon by social scientists, psychologists, and criminologists is the basis of the productive efforts of criminal investigators and profilers, such as those in the FBI's Behavioral Science Unit and similar units in local and state departments throughout the United States. The very same behavioral science gives insight into the most effective methods of interviewing and is based on quality scientific study and research. The most successful interviewers are those who realize that different methods and approaches are necessary for the different types of individuals who are interviewed. They recognize that a static, universal approach to all subjects in all interviews in all settings is not always productive (Gudjonsson, 1992). In this manual, we will address interviewing theory and practice based on reliable behavioral science study and empirical information. We will also attempt to identify the counterproductive errors that are repeatedly made in the interview room and how to avoid them.

Fundamentals of the Productive Interview

As noted earlier, no single theory of interview and interrogation will satisfactorily meet all the needs of every possible situation. Therefore, the best interviewer is one who is knowledgeable in several techniques. Although many techniques are available, they should all be based on four common, fundamental phases. Successful interviewers are those who know these four fundamental phases and their objectives, and successfully accomplish those objectives in every interview. The four principle phases to a productive interview include:

Phase 1: Orientation
Phase 2: Narration
Phase 3: Cross-examination
Phase 4: Resolution

During orientation, the interviewer must accomplish four basic tasks. The first of those tasks is to clearly establish the purpose, topic, and goals of the interview. Obviously, those goals will be subtly different if you are interviewing the victim, suspect, witness, complainant, and so on. This task is accomplished primarily by advising the subject of the general purpose of the interview and the role each individual is expected to play in the process. This is not going to be a pronouncement that "You, sir, are the suspect and I am the interrogator, and you are going to tell me what you did to that poor woman in the parking lot outside the grocery store last week." It will be more along the lines of informing the subject that the issue to be discussed is the incident involving the assault of Ms. Anderson in the parking lot last week. As the investigator, your job is to get to the truth about the circumstances concerning the incident. If it is Ms. Anderson who is being interviewed, then she would be informed that the investigator has been assigned the case and that he is going to do whatever is necessary to help find the person who attacked her. It is also the time to take the opportunity to assure her that he will keep her informed of the progress of the case and that he is very concerned about what has happened to her. At this point, he needs her to help him collect the information necessary to determine what happened in order to solve the case. For a witness, the dialogue is obviously going to be a little different. The end goal is to reinforce to the witness the importance of cooperating and the fact that he or she may have important information that is critical to solving the case and preventing any further such attacks by the subject.

The second objective of the orientation process is to formally identify each of the individuals involved in the interview. The interviewer will relate to the subject being interviewed his formal status in the case as the case officer or agent, polygraph examiner, juvenile officer, counselor, court-appointed probation or parole officer, or whatever his status may be. The interviewer will then also take the steps necessary to attempt to formally identify the person being interviewed. This will involve gaining essential background information, such as full name, address, date of birth, social security number (or similar formal government identifying number), workplace, education, etc. If necessary, this may be the point to determine ownership of any vehicles, homes, weapons, or other issues critical to the case. It would also be the appropriate time to determine if the subject is capable of reading and writing the particular language in which the interview is being conducted.

During the orientation phase, it is necessary to complete any legal requirements regarding the purpose, content, or subject's participation in the interview. This includes the advice of rights under the Miranda decision for criminal interviews and interrogations conducted in the U.S. If the interview is being conducted by professionals in the private or corporate sector, it may be necessary to advise the subject of any rights provided by his employment contract, union contract, union arbitration, requirements stated in the employee manuals, and so forth. Under this same heading, it may be necessary to advise the person being interviewed of any electronic recording of the interview, if required by state statutes, department policy, or policies established by the employer.

The final objective of the orientation process is one of the most critical, and this is the establishment of rapport with the subject. The successful interviewer is one who has developed the skills necessary to utilize communication in order to obtain information from other people. A crucial part of that skill is the ability to facilitate a free flow of conversation between himself and the subject of the interview (Fisher and Geilselman, 1992). The interviewer can accomplish this by drawing the subject into a general, nonthreatening conversation by discussing such topics as a spouse, boyfriend or girlfriend, school, sports, the weather, etc., or just get the subject to talk about himself. On the surface, this may appear to be time-consuming and wasteful, but it has a critical purpose; that is, to allow the interviewer to establish the "constants" in the subject's normal behavior. When attempting to make an assessment regarding the credibility of a subject's responses and diagnosing the subject's truthful and deceptive behaviors, the interviewer must look for changes from the normal behavior pattern. If the interviewer needs to make a decision about deception or honesty, the time of contact with a person must be long enough to observe those constants of behavior for that individual.

Also of paramount importance is the fact that the more the subject admires or respects the person attempting to spot deception, the stronger that person's emotional response will be to lying. The stronger the subject's emotional response to lying, the greater the chance of detecting deception by the interviewer-observer (Ekman, 1992; DeTurk and Miller, 1985). The interviewer is well advised to also remember that the admiration and respect of another person is earned and not demanded. It is not embodied in a badge, credentials, or the name of an agency, but is based on face-to-face contact from the first meeting through all subsequent meetings.

There will be times when rapport will not be established; i.e., the ability of the interviewer and the subject to identify common interests or backgrounds. In such cases, the interviewer and subject may do nothing more than engage in conversation that is strained at best. In this case, the interviewer will have to be satisfied with establishing this frame of behavior as the subject's baseline, or constant, of behavior and look for changes in the pattern. Such a condition will also exist with hostile or uncooperative witnesses and, at times, even victims. It may also be that the subject being interviewed is already under severe stress, and the interviewer may find it difficult to alleviate that tension in the subject at the beginning of the interview. Although it may not be the ideal establishment of a constant for that subject, it may be all that the interviewer has to work with. Readings of significant changes in behavior based on this can be made.

The narration phase may be labeled the "listening phase," because the subject is, or at least should be, doing most of the talking, and the interviewer should do the majority of the listening. The main task is to get the subject to give a general narrative of the sequence of events. With a suspect, this information is going to be his alibi. The interviewer should ask simple, open-ended questions: e.g., "Can you tell me what happened?" "Where were you when it happened?" "Can you tell me what you have heard?" "What do you know about…?" Questions in this form suggest to the subject that he is in charge of the conversation and is going to be permitted to express what he feels is the most important information to him that he wishes to share. If the subject is not forthcoming with his comments, the interviewer can encourage the subject to continue giving more details with such questions as, "And then what happened?" or "What did you do then?" to stimulate the subject to continue the narration. In the case of a suspect, the questions may be in the form of, "Where were you when it happened?" "What do you think happened?" "How would you explain what went on?" "What have you heard about…?" In this case, the suspect is allowed to present his story or explanation and make the choice either to tell the truth or to engage in deception. It is during the process of narration that the interviewer begins the behavioral analysis process. The information gained at this point is used to formulate more specific questions for later use in the interview.

During the next phase, cross-examination, the interviewer asks specific questions regarding statements made by the subject in the narration phase. The interviewer now has the opportunity to explore what he perceives as possibly important points in greater depth and detail. These may be areas of the subject's statement on which interviewer feels he needs to stimulate the subject to give additional information or fill in missing pieces of the story. It is possible that the cooperative subject or witness has overlooked the relative importance of this information. The interviewer, recognizing the significance of these details, will need to focus the subject's attention on these issues. His objective is to get the subject to understand how critical the information may be and to focus more conscious attention on trying to relate the missing details. In the case of the deceptive subject, he has obviously glossed over these issues because of their incriminating nature. Focusing on these issues forces the evasive subject to address the information. It will also impress upon the subject that the interviewer is listening and can increase the stress experienced by the suspect when he makes further attempts at evasion or outright deception. A focus attack on such issues wears down and can eventually destroy the subject's confidence in his ability to maintain his attempts at deception.

After listening to the subject during narration, the interviewer may find that he needs to return to key issues to verify specific pieces of information that may later be critical, or to clarify his interpretation of the subject's remarks. This type of information may be vital at some future point to pin the subject down in terms of his responsibility or personal involvement in the case. Obtaining such information, self-incriminating or otherwise, is necessary to emphasize or point out any previous contradictory statements. This type of information permits the interviewer to gain control of the pace, flow, and focus of the interview.

Investigative interviewers frequently confuse the two critical phases of narration and cross-examination. Some interview and interrogation training and literature instructs the interviewer to immediately confront the subject at the first contact or at the moment the first deception occurs; this should be reserved for the cross-examination phase. This accusatorial approach significantly denies the interviewer the benefits of establishing rapport and determining the subject's baseline behavior. More importantly, it greatly reduces the amount of information gathered and diminishes the interviewer's ability to gain additional useful information from the subject. Another risk is the increased possibility of generating a false confession (Gudjonsson and Lebeque, 1989) or falsely accusing an innocent person (Ekman, 1992). We will discuss these interviewing approaches later in this chapter.

The goal of the final phase, resolution, is to get the subject to accept the established truths or exposed deceptions of his statements, as well as ownership of those statements, or, in the case of a suspect, responsibility for his actions. This is the admission or confession stage.

Good Interviewing Habits

Interview Approach

Studies have shown that there are two main strategies for exposing deception: accusatorial and inquisitorial (Moston, 1991; Irving, 1980). Although the latter approach has consistently proven to be far more productive, it is the one that interviewers generally use the least. The inquisitorial approach is aimed more at information gathering at the beginning of the interview. It typically is far more productive in establishing the rapport aspect of the interview, which allows the interviewer a more accurate picture of the subject's baseline, or constant, of behavior. A grasp of the constant of the subject's behaviors, therefore, improves the interviewer's ability to recognize changes in the subject's behaviors that may highlight deception. The inquisitorial interview and interrogation strategy generally uses more open-ended questions and fewer closed question types (e.g., selection, identification, yes–no).

The accusatorial approach is characterized as a direct, confrontational style that focuses solely on the purpose of getting a confession. It also produces the lowest yield in information (Moston, 1995; Irving, 1980). This approach is more likely to generate a greater number of closed questions as well as leading questions. The presence of this interrogation style nearly always indicates that the interviewer has already developed some assumptions, expectations, or biases before entering the interview. The dangers of such an approach will be discussed later.

Determinants

The extreme importance that the interview of a victim, witness, complainant, or subject has on the outcome of any investigation cannot be overstated. A Rand Corporation (Greenwood, 1979) study found that in any investigative process, the single most important determinant of whether a case will be satisfactorily resolved is the information gained from the interview of the witness or victim of a crime. With so much resting on the interview process, the investigative interviewer must develop good interviewing habits that enhance his ability to gain information that is accurate, complete, and reliable. To accomplish this goal, the interviewer must understand how to correctly phrase questions, when to employ each type of question, and how to recognize which actions to take or avoid to increase the quantity and quality of information gained.

The factors that help create conditions that are conducive to the productive flow of information between the subject and the interviewer can be divided into two general categories: the interviewer's personal actions, behaviors, or activities, and the formulation and structure of the questions asked by the interviewer.

Interviewer Behaviors

Research has shown that a good interviewer must learn to avoid four activities when conducting an interview. The first, and one that so many new interviewers seem particularly susceptible to, is the taking of copious notes. This habit most likely develops because of the inexperienced interviewer's desire to include every single piece of information and turn in that perfect interview report. In reality, however, research has consistently shown that giving so much importance to taking notes creates an atmosphere that resembles secretarial dictation rather than one in which crucial information is gained (Moston, 1990; Gudjonsson, 1992). It has also been determined that cumbersome note taking destroys the interviewer's ability to maintain the control and flow of the interview (Irving and McKenzie, 1989).

If an interrogation is expected to generate a large volume of information, and if the information is expected to be critical, arrangements should be made to record the interview by means other than note taking. The obvious option is some form of electronic recording; other options include the use of a stenographer or court reporter. The interviewer should not take these actions upon himself without first consulting with a supervisor, department legal counsel, or prosecuting authority. Some jurisdictions, departments, and agencies have specific guidelines or restrictions about the use of any of the various means of documenting the contents of interviews. Another option is to have a second interviewer present in the room whose job is to maintain the interview notes. A further advantage to this choice is that now the interviewer has another set of eyes and ears in the room to provide confirmation of any critical verbal and nonverbal signals generated by the subject.

The remaining three actions that a productive interviewer must learn to avoid are those that have been found to hinder a person's normal memory-retrieval process, namely, frequently interrupting the subject, asking too many questions that evoke short answers, and asking questions in an inappropriate sequence or at the wrong time. We will discuss these issues in greater length later in this text.

Frequent interruption by the interviewer is particularly detrimental when a witness or victim is attempting to concentrate on important mental images. In addition, the subject begins to expect the interruptions and will give only superficial responses with little of the collateral information that would keep the interview productive and flowing.

Although asking direct questions that require short, specific answers can be a productive method of gaining precise information from the interview subject, this action has two drawbacks. First, this technique, because it is specific, does not draw out a great deal of information. Second, the wide use of short-answer questions creates a narrowing effect, i.e., the range of topics and important peripheral data is decreased, and areas that may require further exploration can go unexposed (Fisher, Geilselman, and Raymond, 1987).

The third habit, and one of the major problems that every interviewer must learn to overcome, is asking questions in an inappropriate sequence or at the wrong time (Fisher, Geilselman, and Raymond, 1989). Asking follow-up questions in response to a subject's remarks is certainly appropriate, but they should be the "correct" questions. Unfortunately, some interviewers have developed such an intense train of thought about what they want to discover that they worry more about the entire "list" of questions they need answered, and will ask those questions as if they were conducting a survey (Fisher, Geilselman, and Raymond, 1989; Hess, 1989). The interviewer will also ask

what may in fact be an important question, but at the wrong time during
the interview — an action that also interrupts the smooth flow of information. The only question that the interviewer should be concerned with is the
next question to be asked in the next 30 seconds, which should be based
solely on what the subject has said in the preceding 30 seconds.

The Structure of the Questions

A common myth about the process of interviewing is that it is nothing more
than simply asking a person a list of questions (Hess, 1989). However, some
question types are less productive than others; some are good, but only when
used at the appropriate moment, and some are always best avoided. Interview
question types fall into two general categories — "open and closed" and
"leading." All investigative interviews should be nonstandardized and individualized because the interviewer does not always know in advance all the
information that needs to be sought, and many questions will be developed
as the interview progresses (Gudjonsson, 1992).

Open questions are most often used in the orientation and narration
phases; for example, "What happened to you last night?" "What have you
heard about…?" "What did you do at the lake yesterday?" These questions,
by their very nature, indicate to the subject that an extended and informative
response is anticipated. Such questions are certainly essential when interviewing witnesses and victims, and their value when questioning a suspect
should not be overlooked. Again, they give the observer an opportunity to
identify the subject's constants of behavior for comparison with subsequent
behaviors. They also permit the subject to make the decision to be deceptive
or truthful. As the investigative interviewer listens to the subject's remarks,
he should be on the lookout for those clues to possible deception.

Closed questions, on the other hand, are those that the subject can answer
with a minimum of words. These include identification questions, selection
questions, and yes–no types of questions. Although all three types are important, they tend to be limited and produce little progression from one topic
to the next. Too many such questions will cause the interview to "run down"
quickly.

Identification questions require the subject to identify a person, group,
object, date, time, location, etc. Examples include, "What time did you get
off work Tuesday?" "When was the last time you saw your brother Robert
alive?" "Who was at the party when you got there?" "Which days were you
off sick last week?" These types of questions can be critical in obtaining any
missing or important information.

Selection-oriented questions limit the subject to a small set of options
that are usually embedded in the question. "Did he have the gun in his pocket
or was it visible?" "Was he wearing a jacket or was it a sweatshirt?" "Was the

car gray or dark blue?" The obvious problem with these questions is that the correct answers may not be made available to the subject, or the interviewer may give the subject information that he previously did not have. Subjects have also been known to respond with a guess merely because they feel compelled to answer. Selection-oriented questions should be used sparingly and worded carefully to avoid generating misleading responses.

Yes–no type questions are narrow, but they do have an important place in the interview process. A question such as, "Did you take the money?" has only two possible answers. A response other than yes or no may indicate that the subject is being deceptive. Such questions also provide a method for pinning the subject down with a specific response that later may be used to impeach the person and prove that he in fact was being deceptive. The drawback to yes–no questions are the results that may occur when dealing with subjects who are mentally or emotionally weak. Such subjects may respond with answers that they believe the interviewer "wants" to hear, thereby possibly resulting in a false confession.

Leading questions rarely, if ever, should be used within the interview environment. Their use indicates that the interviewer has already violated one of our Basic Practical Kinesic Principles; that is, that the interviewer has apparently developed some preconceptions regarding the subject being interviewed or the outcome of the interview. The use of leading questions indicates that the interviewer has already developed "expectations" and indicates that he has in mind a "premise" as to how events occurred. This leads the interviewer to ask only those questions that support or lend credibility to his personal premise or theory (Gudjonsson, 1992; Moston, 1989; Baldwin, 1993; Irving, 1989).

Examples of leading questions include, "Did you hit him once or several times with your fist?" "Did the subject fire one or two shots into the ceiling when he walked into the bank?" "Was he carrying a knife in his left hand?" "You weren't already drinking before you got to the party, were you?" "Do you still beat your wife?" These types of questions have been shown to seriously distort the information gained from the subject. A question like, "How fast was the car going when it smashed into your car?" will generate a totally different response than, "How fast was the car going when it collided with your car?" It should be obvious that the answers to these two questions can differ dramatically because of the way the questions were formulated.

Practical Kinesic Principle

The investigative interviewer should never enter the interview room with any preconceptions about the subject or the interview.

Investigative interviewing has a far different purpose than does a general conversation between two individuals. In an everyday conversation, the mutual exchange of information should flow in two directions. On the other hand, in an investigative interview, the information flows more in one direction than the other. The investigator asks the questions, and the subject provides the answers (Trankell, 1972). Because of the nature of this exchange, the interviewer has already approached the conversation with some tentative assumptions, expectations, and hypotheses about the incident in question. The danger exists that the strengths of those biases may be so strong as to skew the interviewer's objectivity. When such a condition occurs, the observer may become the victim of his own biases and ask only those questions that support the biases or only "hear" the answers that he wants to hear. Any responses, remarks, or evidence that may be contradictory to his beliefs or assumptions can be too easily dismissed; any that are not congruent with those assumptions and beliefs may be erroneously classified as evasion, defensiveness, or simply lies (Gudjonsson, 1992; Moston, 1990; Irving, 1980). The interviewer then runs the risk of the gravest of all errors: *not believing the truthful person.*

Verbal Quality

3

The human voice has the unique capability of communicating a wide range of information on several different levels. It communicates the emotional state of the individual, the strength and depth of the emotion or mood being experienced, and an endless stream of psychological information, both on an audible level as well as on a subconscious plane, which is the subject's conversation with himself. The interviewer's ability to decode this multichanneled information generated by a subject is essential for a productive interview.

The first point regarding speech cues of which the investigative interviewer needs to be keenly aware is that, in large part, verbal cues do not occur in a vacuum. What was the source of the stimulus that triggered the subject's verbal reaction? The source may be the interviewer's question or the interviewer's behavior as observed by the subject. The subject might find that stimulus significant enough to make some form of verbal response. The form of verbal response in terms of voice quality indicates the strength of emotions the person is experiencing at the time of his verbal output (Skinner, 1952, 1992).

The verbal cues we generate provide the listener with a wealth of information. The voice is our most efficient means of self expression (Darwin, 1872; Darwin and Ekman, 1992). As a result, if we wish to deceive, we constantly measure our comments to ensure that we communicate only as much as necessary to provide understanding of an idea. Mentally, we constantly censor our speech for meaning and content, attempting to protect ourselves from verbal mistakes and any possible punishment that may occur either because of either the verbal remarks or the information disclosed by those remarks. We do not, however, give the same level of attention to the body language symptoms of stress that we may be generating at the same time. Our next Basic Practical Kinesic Principle addresses this issue:

People are better able to control their verbal kinesic signals than they are able to control their nonverbal kinesic signals.

This presents an interesting paradox for the interviewer. Subjects more aware of their speech than their body language generate more body language symptoms than speech symptoms. The trade-off, however, is a diluted value of some body language cues because there can be so many nonverbal messages. As a result, important nonverbal cues can be buried within a stream of seemingly random physical behaviors. At the same time, because there are a smaller number of verbal deception cues, those signals that a subject does generate are of greater value to the listener. The interviewer needs to bear in mind the following Basic Practical Kinesic Principle regarding verbal cues:

> **Verbal signals are usually the most productive kinesic cues and are the easiest for the interviewer to identify, but they occur less frequently.**

The observer must understand several important elements. The most important is that although speech cues can be outnumbered by nonverbal cues, speech is not independent from the nonverbal behaviors of the subject (Skinner, 1952, 1992). When the messages broadcast from verbal cues and nonverbal cues are incongruent with each other, there is a strong possibility of deception on the part of the speaker. These may be combinations in which one verbal cue is incongruent with another verbal cue, or when the voice is in disagreement with a body language cue. The following Practical Kinesic Principle deals with these conflicting signals:

> **The observer should watch for contradictions in the subject's behavior, as these are strong indicators of possible deception.**

In this chapter, we are going to discuss the quality of the voice and its significance to the listening interviewer. Voice quality consists of our voice and speech patterns, which include pitch, volume, rate of speech, and clarity. Voice-quality characteristics should not be considered as indicators of deception, but rather as indicators of the strength and depth of the particular emotion the subject is experiencing. When voice-quality symptoms are coupled with the symptoms apparent in voice content, the interviewer can make a more specific diagnosis regarding the degree of stress experienced by the subject and any possible deception. If nothing else, the observer will at least be able to isolate the most significant areas in a subject's responses, as indicated by his general stress reaction. Once the interviewer has gained some sense of the subject's constant of voice quality, then any timely changes that occur become significant. The question to be answered by the observer is what the significance is to the stimulus that caused the change in the subject's behavior (Skinner, 1952, 1992).

Pitch, Volume, and Rate of Speech

The presence of tension or stress in a subject is often revealed by a change in the pitch of the voice. The interviewer should already have assessed the subject's normal speech quality prior to asking any possibly fear-provoking questions. If, at the stress-stimulus question, the subject's pitch changes, we can reasonably assume that the person has had a strong reaction to the question. The type of change identified indicates what type of internal, emotional, and possibly cognitive elements are at work. When the pitch rises, we can assume that the subject most likely is experiencing anger or is in a highly excited state of stress. Research has determined that an increase in pitch often accompanies a moment of deception by the subject (Darwin, 1872; Darwin and Ekman, 1992). We are not to conclude, however, that every time we hear an increase in the pitch of the voice of an individual we can assume that the statement has been a lie. On other occasions, the pitch of the voice may drop. In this case, the subject's emotional energy has dropped significantly, and he may be experiencing some form of withdrawal into depression, or at least some degree of emotional isolation. In some cases of extreme fear, the voice will become deep and husky, while the words may become less distinct and hard for the listener to decode. In some cases of such fear, the voice may even fail altogether (Darwin, 1872; Darwin and Ekman, 1992).

For most individuals, the pitch of the voice will rise when the person speaking is under significant stress. We all have laughed at Deputy Barney Fife on *The Andy Griffith Show*. Barney, with his infinite, but flawed, law enforcement knowledge, is always ready to enlighten any listener with his wisdom. When "Ol' Barn" is in a pinch, his voice almost always rises to a new octave, indicating severe stress for our hapless hero.

There is probably not a law enforcement agency around that does not have at least one officer on staff whose voice is normally deep and rich during everyday conversations. The same officer, when involved in a high-speed pursuit, a foot race with a perpetrator, or in desperate need of backup, can be heard over the radio sounding a lot like "Ol' Barn." The humorous side of the situation is when tapes of that officer's radio transmissions are played back and he adamantly swears that it is not his voice, or that the department's equipment is defective and always makes his voice sound that way. The officer's obvious change of voice is explained by this Practical Kinesic Principle:

Tension can cause a change in the pitch of the voice, as well as in the volume and rate of speech.

The volume of the voice can take on one of two characteristics for a subject suffering the effects of stress. The most common response is for the subject to increase his volume. Just think back to the last time you and your spouse, friend, or supervisor had a spirited disagreement. As the discussion continued, one or both of you quite likely began to raise your voices, a sure sign that there was some stress involved in the conversation. Such increases in volume accompany those moments when the subject needs to express that he is confident in his remarks and in himself. Increases in volume also occur in moments when the subject feels the need to demonstrate some form of dominance or control over the listener.

For some individuals, however, a marked drop in the volume of the voice demonstrates the presence of stress. In this case, it may suggest that the subject is moving more toward the emotional withdrawal associated with a depression-like state. It may also indicate that the person has little interest in the topic and thus, very little energy is being expended by the person as he addresses the issue at hand. Because of this drop in energy level by the speaker, the words may sound muttered or whispered (Skinner, 1952, 1992). The interviewer may feel that he is losing his hearing because of the decreased volume. It is as if the person psychologically wants to disappear or, at least, shrink in size in the face of the threatening inquiry. Once again, it is obvious that the speaker recognizes that what he is saying puts him at risk for some form of negative sanctions by the person or persons to whom he is addressing his comments.

A change in the rate of speech is directly related to the status of the subject's mental processing rate. People from different areas of the U.S., as well as from different cultural groups within this and other countries, have at least slight variations in their general rate of speech. Therefore, it is critical to ascertain the constant that is unique for each individual and not necessarily assign a standard rate of speech for all speakers. When the subject is in a low-stress situation, the listener should find the individual's speech to be repetitive and patterned. This pattern has a certain rhythm, and it is the break in this rhythm for which we are looking.

Should the subject's rate decrease, we can correctly assume that the subject is carefully weighing his words. It is as if he has an acting coach or a speech coach within his head. This "coach" is, in fact, editing or censoring the subject's words before he speaks. The job of this coach is to review the script before the subject begins to express himself, and thereby reduce any possible risk of punishment by the listener. This slow rate of speech helps reduce any buildup of the negative effects of the statements and, as such, lessens the overall impact of any negative or damaging remarks (Skinner, 1952, 1992). If the internal coach finds that any portion of the script could create such difficulties for the speaker, which would increase the risk of discovery, the coach's job is to edit and rewrite those lines of the subject's "play," or even create a possible lie before the subject recites his "part." This editing process is one of the primary reasons why there are fewer verbal cues than nonverbal symptoms and why they are of greater value.

Each one of us as a juvenile committed some act that we knew was wrong. Once we committed that act, we consciously began to prepare for the fateful moment when we believed someone would ask us what happened. To protect ourselves from what many of us felt was the inevitable inquiry, we began to create our alibi. The problem, however, was not the questions we prepared for, but the questions that we had not anticipated.

When a subject is confronted with questions he has anticipated, his rate of speech often increases. This increase in the rate of speech suggests that what is being said is an important point in the mind of the speaker (Skinner, 1952, 1992). It is a significant thought the person has developed, possibly over time, and is not merely a fleeting thought. This also usually occurs because it may be a practiced portion of his alibi in response to the anticipated inquiries, so there is little need for him to prepare a spontaneous answer. To the subject, neither the question nor the answer was spontaneous. At the same time, the subject is most likely quite energetic about proving his innocence and may spring at the opportunity to verbalize such, increasing his speech rate markedly above normal.

Speech Dysfunction

Linguists describe speech dysfunction as "speech dysfluency" or speech errors. No matter how it is labeled, speech dysfunction represents uncharacteristic flaws in the subject's speech indicating the presence of stress. The investigative interviewer will, over time, observe that all subjects, both truthful and deceptive, can generate many symptoms of speech dysfluency (Zuckerman, DePaulo, and Rosenthal, 1992). He should not conclude, however, that these are solely definitive clues that an individual is being deceptive. In fact, studies of these phenomena have shown that they are often misinterpreted as reliable signs of deception and contribute to the misdiagnosis of deception (Ekman, 1992). Upon comparing the overall behaviors of deceptive subjects vs. subjects who are being truthful we will find that deceptive subjects do generate a greater number of these behaviors. These cues, therefore, can represent what we call "incriminating stress" signals that suggest there may, in fact, be some form of evasion present in the subject's response. It would then be the duty of the interviewer to identify the most significant topic areas in which the dysfluencies occurred and explore those issues at greater length with the subject. This extended exploration by the interviewer should then help him locate, or at least narrow down, areas of likely deception through "discriminating signals" of probable deception that may be observed during the more specific inquiry. Our next Practical Kinesic Principle addresses this phenomenon as noted not only by interviewers, but also by linguists:

Deceptive subjects demonstrate more speech dysfunction than truthful subjects do.

Before we discuss these particular speech symptoms, we should explain why they occur. Let us return to the idea of our personal "acting coach" who edits our speech to keep us from making any incriminating statements to the listener. With the presence of stress and the large amount of communication information that needs to be addressed and appropriately edited mentally, the subject may find that the editing or censoring process becomes too burdensome or overwhelming, and the result is flawed speech. The subject now finds it difficult to keep clear in his mind what he really does or does not want to say. This dilemma is the focus of the following Practical Kinesic Principle:

Speech dysfunction symptoms occur because the subject is being hit with relevant questions and does not have a clear "thought line."

The continuing, or at least frequently occurring, incidences of a subject being unable to maintain a clear thought line results in a greater number of speech errors, often recognized as slurring words or stammering. Research shows that the existence of this phenomenon, when it is not the normal pattern for the subject, indicates approximately a 90% probability of deception (Davis, Connors, and Walters, 1999; Davis et al., 2000; Davis et al., 1999). The deception may be either in the form of omission of truthful information or of misleading embellishment.

Speech dysfunction is classified into two general forms. The first form is best described as nonspeech sounds or paralinguistic cues. The most frequently used of these nonspeech sounds are "ah," "err," "um," and "uh." Not only do these sounds indicate stress on the part of the speaker, but they also are great stalling mechanisms. Most of us have heard an inexperienced public speaker floundering in front of a group of people during a speech. We have all sat uncomfortably through a veritable blizzard of "ah," "err," "um," and "uh" as the flustered speaker tried in vain to express his thoughts. The reason we all feel so uncomfortable for the speaker is most likely because we ourselves have been through the same frightening event as novice orators.

Additional paralinguistic sounds include grunts, groans, growls, moans, whistles, and other similar sounds. These sounds may, in some cases, be an incomplete start to some thought the subject considered expressing. Initially, the sound was part of a full expression used in other stress situations on a regular basis. These same emotions, previously experienced, have once again been triggered in the strong emotion-evoking situation of the interview (Darwin, 1872; Darwin and Ekman, 1992; DeTurk and Miller, 1985; Zuckerman, DePaulo, and Rosenthal, 1992). The subject may be interrupting that reaction with these stalling sounds for fear of the context in which the reaction may be diagnosed.

Heavy gulping or swallowing and gasping for breath on the part of a subject are also common signs observed when the subject is under significant stress. These signs can indicate when a person is being deceptive, and are frequently found in the company of deception cues. The gulping reflex almost appears to be a "speech reset" function. The subject's speech has been getting out of sequence, and with stress building up, a brief moment of reset is required. This comes in the form of a gulp. The same may be true of the gasp. Under stress, breathing becomes more labored, and the interviewer may observe the subject taking in large quantities of air by gasping. In some cases, gasping and gulping include an almost convulsive or involuntary motion of the lips and quivering of the cheeks (Darwin, 1872; Darwin and Ekman, 1992).

Stammering and stuttering are also included as possible speech dysfunction behaviors. The delivery of these two speech symptoms is apparently the result of two different phenomena. Stammering occurs because the subject may be trying to verbalize a large or important thought line at a faster rate than the mouth and other associated speech organs can function to form speech. Stuttering occurs because the person hasn't made up his mind before he speaks as to how he is going to express an idea. In both cases, the speaker is concerned about the content of the message he wishes to transmit and its interpretation by the listener. Poorly chosen words could bring negative sanctions from the listener, either for what has been said or for what the speech content has actually exposed (Skinner, 1952, 1992). Again, these changes are only significant signs of stress if the speaker has not demonstrated some form of preexisting speech pathology.

Pausing in speech presents an interesting focus point for the interviewer. Generally, in a conversation between two people, a pause signals one of two things. First, it is a momentary break that is silently asking if the listener is comprehending what is being said and allows time for the absorption of an important point. Second, it is a signal that the person talking has finished and it is now time for the other person to respond.

A break in the pattern of pausing during a conversation between the interviewer and the subject may suggest other issues at work in the conversation. One variable is when the subject interrupts the interviewer with a response. This usually indicates that it is a significant issue that the subject has already considered and feels a need to respond to quickly. This may be done as a way to stop the inquiry from moving into a critical area and to divert the interviewer away from the topic. It may also be due to the stress of the subject having anticipated the inquiry into a problem area. Under the buildup of stress caused by expectation of this significant moment, the subject practically blurts out his response. These pauses should not be considered definitive clues of deception, but they do have significant incriminating value. In particular, if the interviewer recognizes that, when considering the overall verbal behaviors of the subject, there appears to be a significant number of pauses — especially long pauses — these can be critical markers suggesting extensive speech monitoring. Deception may be at work — at least in the form of evasion. The subject has been unable to work out his thoughts ahead of time when considering possible exploration of this topic of conversation (Ekman, 1992).

By themselves, paralinguistic cues are not reliable signs of deception, but they are significant indicators of stress on the part of the speaker. The speaker may rely on these cues, however, as tools for stalling so he can fully prepare the deceptive message he wants to articulate. In this case, the observer needs to be able to discern whether the cues are the result of the stress of speaking while under observation or are a symptom of the development of deceptive communication. The significant presence of these cues when the person is discussing a critical topic would warrant further exploration of that topic by the interviewer. This effort by the interviewer is likely to consistently trigger deception cues in clusters, which should help confirm whether the subject is withholding information. The alternative is that the interviewer can dispel his suspicions by getting the subject to discuss the topic at greater length, thus enabling the interviewer to determine the reason for the subject's heightened stress symptoms.

Two sounds need additional explanation: the sigh and the laugh. The sigh has two possible meanings that should be of concern to the interviewer. The first sigh symptom involves continuous sighing, which is an indication that the subject is possibly feeling sorry for himself or, more accurately, that he is experiencing some degree of depression. We will deal more with depression later on in this text. The second form of sighing is a deep, single, almost lung-cleansing sigh. This sigh usually occurs when the subject is in the mood of acceptance, and is one of several preparatory signals suggesting that the subject may be ready to confess. He is in a state of submission or resignation to the reality of the situation or the information presented by the interviewer. We will also discuss acceptance or preconfession behaviors later in this text.

The nervous laugh provides interesting benefits to the subject during the interview. One use of the laugh can be an obvious display that the subject is neither feeling any stress with the issue at hand or the objectives of the interviewer, nor is he perceiving any real threat from the interviewer. In this case, the laugh is an aggressive behavior associated with some attempt to control the interview and the interviewer. It is more or less a laugh of disdain. The correct diagnosis by the interviewer is, in fact, that the subject is using it as a control or "anger" mechanism over the interviewer, and most likely the laugh is being used as a stalling tactic. We will discuss the significance of stalling tactics later in the chapter covering speech content. In brief, extensive use of stalling tactics is seen in subjects who are very likely engaged in some form of deception.

The nervous laugh is an interesting sign of stress for several reasons. First, of all human expressions, it is the easiest human expression for a person to "fake," if necessary. By using the fake smile I can, to some extent, lower any threat potential in an interaction between the other person and myself. In a sense, it takes the "edge" off of what may be a tense situation and helps lower the other person's suspicions.

Second, a nervous laugh is an efficient reliever of internal stress for the subject. Acting as a pressure-relief valve, the "laugher" finds it as a reassurance that everything will eventually turn out all right no matter how bleak the current outlook. However, the most important key to understanding about laughing during an interview is that the laugher recognizes that the rest of his response to a question or inquiry involves a great risk of negative reinforcement from the listener. Whether the response by the laugher is coming in the form of verbal or nonverbal behavior, the listener can perceive it in an extremely negative light. Consciously adding a laugh to the response, but more likely subconsciously, is a message to the listener that should the statement or action be interpreted negatively by the listener, the punishment should be less severe because the response was delivered with something less than truly malicious intent by the speaker (Skinner, 1952, 1992).

The second form of dysfunction presents itself in terms of errors in speech form, or what we are going to label an "unclear thought line." Exploration into these speech dysfunctions has showed that there is a connection between these symptoms and deception. They are frequent markers that deception has occurred (Davis, Connors, and Walters, 1999; Davis, et al., 2000). This special class of speech dysfunction may signal to the observer that the subject is, at that moment, creating the deception. The speech content by the subject may be recognized overall by the listener, but it is presented by the subject in an incorrect or flawed format.

One example of an unclear thought line is the omission of words from the person's speech. In some cases, these speech symptoms include the deletion of small or article words from sentences, such as "the," "and," "or," "as," or "is." Apparently, the speaker is intent on controlling speech output and inadvertently deletes more than he intends. This same condition most likely also exists when a subject begins to omit suffixes, such as "ing," "ed," "es," "s," or even "tion." In other cases, the observer may recognize that an entire word, or even several words, appear to be missing from a sentence or short response. This symptom may also be the result of rushed or hurried speech because of the subject's desire to get the alibi or excuse verbalized as soon as possible. In either case, it represents an attempt to control speech output.

The interviewer may hear the subject begin to correct his choice of words in mid-sentence in a form of spontaneous editing. It is as if doubts arise about a selected word or term, and the subject attempts to choose a more appropriate, less suspicious term. The speaker may become concerned about his choice of words and fears that they will be taken in the wrong context and generate a negative response from the listener (Skinner, 1952, 1992). This same type of doubt may also result in word clipping, in which the person doubts his word choice in the middle of the word, as evidenced by halting or choppy word pronunciation. In this case, the words may be spoken in a staccato fashion, as if the speaker is verbally "punching" each word for added emphasis.

A subject under stress attempting to control his speech may also demonstrate some speech repetition. The subject begins to make a comment or express an idea, then repeats the same phrases or words within the same sentence. It is as if the speaker needs to orally reassure himself, as well as the listener, that the correct phrase or word has been chosen to express a particular idea. This repetition indicates the significant strength of the issue in the mind of the speaker.

A similar phenomenon that the author has observed on several occasions and that is currently studied for its significance is the repetition of a previous portion of the subject's story. The repeated points are generally out of sequence from the rest of the events described by the subject. It appears that these repeated elements are extremely important to the subject (Skinner, 1952, 1992). He may not be satisfied with his previous "performance" and needs another opportunity to restate the comment in a more convincing performance. These repeated elements also seem to be associated with significant elements of the overall events and, as such, are hard for the subject to deal with, mentally or emotionally, or both. It is almost as if the subject is "drawn" back to this critical area and is seeking to relieve some severe stress associated with the particular element by repeating the information. This type of behavior can also be described as a "fixation of thought." The issue is so significant that all the subject's thoughts are absorbed with this one issue.

Case Study

A young couple contacted the local police early one morning to report that their infant daughter had apparently been kidnapped from their home. The parents reported that they might have left the back door to their apartment unlocked. The eight-month-old child had been left asleep on the living room floor for the night, a practice that the parents indicated had never occurred before. Upon arising the next morning, they found the back door ajar and the child missing. In a police interview with the father, he mentioned numerous times out of context that on separate and multiple occasions, he had fed the little girl and that his wife fed the child in a short four-to-five-hour period. It was apparent to the author during the police interview that there was some relevant issue regarding the child and food. It was recommended that the issue of the child's eating habits and food be emphasized in the follow-up interview along with the parents' discovery of the child being missing. The kidnapping was exposed as a false report to cover up the child's death. While the father was away on military maneuvers for two weeks, his wife had neglected the child and she had died of complications from malnutrition and starvation. The father had found the child dead upon his return. He disposed of the child's body in a pond on the military post during the night, and then he and the child's mother concocted the story of the kidnapping.

Some of the mental symptoms of continuing stress and anxiety have been identified as "flight of thought." Flight of thought is experienced by a stressed individual when there are so many important issues at hand that each is vying for immediate attention on his mental stage, thus preventing him from appropriately addressing each of the issues. The observer can recognize the impact of this mental stress in two forms. In one case, the subject will have several incomplete sentences. It is as if the ideas are running so fast that the subject is unable to complete one thought before jumping to the next. This behavior could be compared with a record or CD that is experiencing "skip" while being played. The subject is literally "rethinking" his statements in mid-sentence and is starting another two, three, or even four or more thoughts.

A similar flight of thought symptom is what we will label "indirect ideas." In this case, the interviewer may be discussing a specific topic, but the subject's response addresses a distant and often unrelated topic. The subject has not really heard the interviewer and diverts to an unrelated topic. There may appear to be little or no connection between the question asked and the response given. The subject's response may be incoherent, in a form of avoidance.

As a result of the division of the subject's attention among several developing lines of thought, he may generate some incoherent words. Consider the idea that for speech to occur, several different parts of the body, or speech centers, must function in a synchronized fashion. Those speech centers are the lips, jaw, tongue, larynx, and diaphragm. For coherent words to be spoken, these speech centers must all perform in a carefully coordinated sequence. Different words and expressions require a different "firing sequence." Under stress, the subject's single-channel line of thought is being bombarded with multiple lines of thought. In mid-sentence, the subject may change the intended message, causing an abrupt change in the firing sequence already in progress, and start a new sequence. This change in sequence has started too late to stop some of the action by parts of the speech centers that are now being asked to articulate a totally different word or idea. The result can be some rather strange-sounding words or utterances.

Conclusion

In this chapter, we have discussed the general character of the subject's voice, which is represented by its pitch, volume, and rate of speech. We have noted that the quality of the voice indicates a change in the speaker's emotional status and that the level of the quality changes indicates the strength of the emotion felt by the subject. It is important to remember, however, that these are not cues to deception. They are more accurately identified as the "noise" of human stress and can be found in both truthful and deceptive subjects.

The occurrence of speech dysfunction generally indicates that a subject is having problems with mental clarity as a result of the stress condition in which the subject finds himself. Within the category of speech dysfunction, we have found a category rich in deception diagnosis — that being the expression of the unclear thought line. Those discriminating cues include word clipping, sentence editing, incomplete sentences, indirect ideas, slurred speech, extensive pausing, and the omission of words.

Speech symptoms are not only the easiest for the subject to control, but also are the most important cues the interviewer must accurately diagnose. It is also important to remember that speech cues rarely occur by accident. They are frequently important because the presence of a speech symptom tells us that the subject has found a connection with some stimulus. What the person says in terms of content tells us what the connection is. The quality of the speaker's voice tells us about the emotion associated with the issue and how strongly the person is experiencing the particular emotion.

Verbal Content

4

The content of our speech is the direct link in communication between our thoughts and the individual receiving the speech message. Speech is also our most efficient method of communication (Skinner, 1952, 1992). In most non-stress situations, we do quite well in preventing the receiver from gaining insight into the true thoughts and feelings we may be experiencing. When we are under stress due to conflict or anxiety, the normally quiet internal conversation we have with ourselves becomes strong and loud, and slips past our efforts at self-censorship. When this happens, the receiver begins to hear our true thoughts and feelings. If that receiver is skilled at decoding that information, he is capable of becoming an intimate partner in our thoughts.

For the interviewer or interrogator, success depends on his ability to accurately decode speech characteristics indicating the current stress response of the victim, witness, or especially the suspect. As mentioned previously, those stress responses are anger, depression, denial, bargaining, and acceptance. Each of these responses will be discussed in greater detail as to their purposes and functions. For now, we will concern ourselves with the concept that these responses give the interviewer an indication of the subject's immediate reaction to the issue at hand and generate cues of truth or deception. It is important to remember two of our Practical Kinesic Principles, which tell us that there is no single symptom that suggests deception, and that clusters of symptoms permit a more reliable analysis. These responses are important to the interrogator because they suggest the appropriate response that the interrogator should make.

Anger

As noted earlier, the rejection response of anger is a mood of dominance in which the subject is trying to gain or maintain control through some form of aggression. The use of anger is a mental form of fight known as the "fight or flight" animal response. When an animal is trapped and has no other means of survival, it will attack the immediate threat to its safety. Anger is presented to the interviewer in one of three forms: focused, covert, or rage, each of which has its own unique characteristics. Remember that anger by itself is not a sign of deception. Any subject, truthful or deceptive, is capable of demonstrating anger during the discussion of any issue.

Focused Anger

Focused anger is the most easily recognizable of the three forms. There are few interviewers and interrogators who have missed the demonstration of focused anger by a subject. Focused anger is an open, frontal attack on the interviewer, victim, or witness. It often elicits an anger response from the person against whom it is directed. To respond to anger with anger can be self defeating, and we will learn later how such situations can be avoided. For the present, we will focus on recognizing the verbal symptoms of focused anger.

A common and readily identifiable anger response is seen when the subject verbally attacks the interviewer. The subject resorts to this type of behavior in an attempt to bully or intimidate the investigator. This can include threatening to sue the investigator, taking his house, car, and even his pension. The subject may say he has already contacted an attorney and that he's the best attorney in town. The subject might say that this attorney is known for his ability to ruin the careers of overzealous investigators or is good at suing companies whose security departments harasss employees or good customers. The subject may indicate that he will make sure that the interviewer loses his job, be severely reprimanded or suspended, or have his work performance brought under public scrutiny. The public agency inter-viewer may be reminded that the subject "pays your salary." The subject may also threaten to go to the press and expose the actions of the investigator or his department.

As a variation of attacking the interviewer, the subject may attack the interviewer's department or agency. The department may be accused of using quotas to meet performance expectations. There may be accusations of mis-conduct or harassment based on economic status, age, social group, or polit-ical affiliation. If the cops knew that he was doing burglaries and didn't stop him, they are just as guilty as he is for not stopping him.

The interviewer may also hear about officers or investigators who were caught in some form of wrongdoing, were behaving in a less-than-profes-sional manner, or who are generally incompetent. This form of anger is reminiscent of rival teams "bad-mouthing" their competition. By attacking and degrading the interviewer and the represented department, the subject feels that he can improve his position of control in the interview room.

Another target of attack by a suspect is the victim of the crime, whether it is an individual, business, agency, or government entity. All too frequently, investigators have been told that the rape victim is at fault because of the way she was dressed or the way she acted, that the victim was a crook himself, or that he shouldn't have been around the location in the first place and was taking a big risk by even being there at that particular time of the day. The suspect may blame his employer for making it so easy to embezzle or commit other acts of fraud. The suspect may feel that the employer cheated him or did not keep promises, thereby placing responsibility for the crime on the victim.

It should not surprise the interviewer that witnesses are not immune to the subject's verbal attacks. Witnesses, along with the interviewer, are accused of prejudice, incompetence, or ignorance. The subject might say that the witness had no business even being around, or that he should have been minding his own business. Perhaps the witness was really up to no good himself, and this is a way to draw attention away from whatever he was doing. Witnesses will be attacked for poor eyesight, bad hearing, or even unwarranted interference in matters that are of no concern to them. The investigator may also be "assured" by the suspect that the witness is lying and will be sued along with everyone else on the suspect's shopping list of planned legal action.

Covert Anger

Covert anger is a far more subtle use of aggression by the subject. This clandestine attack is conducted on an intellectual level and is often overlooked by the interviewer. Though covert anger does not have the same level of displayed energy, it is still an attack and must be recognized and treated as an anger response.

One of the most common methods of displaying covert anger is for the subject to attack case facts. The subject attempts to find some evidentiary aspect of the case against him and tries to discount its ability to implicate him. What is interesting about this type of response is that the subject may, in fact, not deny that the crime occurred, but respond to the allegation with a "prove it" attitude. If the subject can somehow successfully discredit the evidence, then he can no longer be proven guilty. Subjects have been known to take this approach even in the face of extremely reliable, high-quality scientific evidence. Other attacks may be as simple as, "She was alive when I left her."

A subject may find it necessary to complain to the interviewer. He may complain about how he has been inconvenienced by the entire investigation, but state that he is willing to help. He has decided to assist even though his work and private schedules have been totally disrupted. The interviewer is also told that he is wasting time by focusing his attention on the subject; the subject could not possibly have had anything to do with the crime.

Intelligent, well-educated, or professional subjects are also in the group of subjects who use covert anger. These subjects are experts at putting the investigative interviewer in his "intellectual place." They remind investigators about how important they are because of their titles, positions, degrees, or intellect.

When working the economic crime, the subject might remind the investigator that he has a degree in accounting or is even a certified public accountant, thus suggesting that the interviewer is out of his league. The electronic data processing professional may attempt to overwhelm the interrogator by using complicated computer terms. Physicians, attorneys, or pharmacists remind the investigator that they have many more years of college or public recognition than the investigator. Company chief executive officers, chief financial officers, board members, or administrative assistants can find exactly the right moment to bring up the topic of how they hold such important or trusted positions or how important they are. This same type of behavior is used by the production foreman, the tenured professor, the company junior partner, the accountant, the public employee, and an endless list of individuals immersed in their own self-importance, no matter who they are. This, again, demonstrates the use of anger in a covert form.

As children, it did not take us long to learn when we were in trouble with our parents. One way we knew that our parents were upset was by the quality of their voices when they called our names. We discussed voice changes earlier when we addressed voice quality. Another indicator of impending childhood doom was being called by our first, middle, and last names. At that point, there was little doubt in our minds that we were in serious trouble.

Listen to two friends involved in an emotional discussion, or to an intimate couple in a heated disagreement. Pay particular attention when they begin to address each other with an emphasis on a different name or a formal title. The occurrence of this phenomenon indicates that the two participants have reached an impasse. From that point on, there will be little quality communication between them on the topic at hand. This phenomenon is called a "change in the form of address," and is a sign of covert anger suggesting a widening gap between the participants, with any form of agreement becoming a remote possibility. The interviewer will recognize a change in the form of address when the subject suddenly starts referring to him as Officer Wilson, Sergeant Page, Mr. Walters, Ms. Flowers, etc., whereas previously he had been calling the interviewer by his first name or conversing with the interviewer without using the interviewer's name at all. The pattern of change in the form of address usually moves from an informal address to one that is formal.

A deceptive subject may also use another form of covert anger in which he tries to make an issue out of a non-issue. The subject may find it necessary to bring up how he was treated the last time he was in the interview room. He may mention that he had to hang around for hours before anyone talked to him or told him what was going on. You may be challenged as to why you are asking so many personal questions that the subject feels have little bearing on the investigation. The goal of this type of covert anger is to throw up a barrage of issues to complicate the information-gathering process. The subject turns what would have been a simple task into an exercise in futility.

The same type of result is accomplished by the person who questions trivial details and argues about minor items in the case. The subject may try to make it appear that the real issue is not that a burglary occurred, but that the victim never really had anything near the value he claimed to be missing. The vehicle spotted leaving the hit-and-run accident could not have negotiated a particular turn at more than 20 miles per hour because the angle of the turn is too severe for anyone to drive through it at a higher rate of speed. You may be questioned as to how a 65-year-old woman could know that the subject was about 6 feet tall and weighed nearly 185 pounds when she wears glasses and claims to have seen the subject just before dusk. What should be apparent to the interviewer in these cases is that the subject is trying to create a cloud of confusion by arguing about issues that are not relevant to the offense.

We should never assume that only a guilty person would become angry in an interview environment. An innocent person can also show anger. There appears to be, however, a difference in the patterns of how anger is demonstrated by truthful and deceptive individuals. Deceptive subjects tend to demonstrate their hostility at the beginning of the interview, oftentimes even before any form of accusation has been leveled at them. Their attempts at demonstrating anger or indignation are designed to throw the interviewer or interrogator off balance, forcing him to be more cautious in his questioning. Once that has been accomplished, the subject may appear to be cooperative until another sensitive issue is raised, resulting in another aggressive display. The key to helping the investigative interviewer identify possible deception in the use of anger is to determine if the person is using anger along with avoidance. This combination of behaviors can be an "incriminating stress" cue and suggests that the person wishes to avoid some issue (Walters, 2000) and, therefore, deception may be involved.

Truthful persons generally appear to be cooperative and open to the interviewer's comments. In general, the interviewer will have little difficulty directing the subject's attention to various topics. The subject gives the interviewer little or no resistance to most topic areas. Any resistance that is encountered is usually in some form of guilty knowledge. The subject is unsure about the accuracy of his observations or information and would prefer not to make comments about something he isn't sure of. If the interview proceeds to the point, however, in which the truthful person realizes that he is not believed and is being wrongfully accused, the level of aggression will increase. In many cases, the truthful person doesn't easily forget or readily forgive the interviewer for the wrong accusation. Recovering respect and cooperation after incidents of wrongful accusation may be difficult for the interviewer.

Depression

Anger and depression are often viewed as being at opposite ends of the behavior- or conflict-response continuum when, in fact, the two have a strong common bond: the presence of aggression. In anger, it is obvious that the aggression is focused outward. In depression, the aggression is focused inward onto the depressed person. Depressed persons are, thereby, attacking themselves. This form of depression results in the isolation of subjects from others. Anger, on the other hand, forces others to isolate themselves from the angry person. The depression described here is not to be confused with clinical depression. The form of depression we are discussing is a stress response or a mood that one can experience on a temporary basis. We will deal with clinical depression later in the text.

It is important for the investigative interviewer to remember that just because a person is in depression does not mean that he has been or is going to be deceptive. Subjects in this emotional state of mind are difficult to gain information from, and an open communication exchange is difficult to establish. The isolation from reality and from others causes the subject to focus almost entirely upon himself and his problems. The concerns of the interviewer are of little or no importance. There are responses and steps the interviewer must take to deal with a subject's depression and establish a dialogue. Such tactics are discussed later in this text.

The most common form of depression demonstrated by the subject includes negative comments, all focused by the subject on himself. The subject may state that he is depressed about the entire situation; that he really gets "down" when he thinks about all that has been happening. He may indicate that he has spent hours in self-imposed isolation and doesn't want to talk to anybody or doesn't really want to get out and go anywhere. The interviewer may be told how the subject's life has been ruined; that he feels as if he can no longer show his face in public or that everyone is talking about him behind his back.

Depressed subjects discuss all forms of physical ailments that they have suffered, such as headaches or chest pains. There may be descriptions of severe tension, stiff neck, ringing in the ears, or increased blood pressure. You may hear that they have not eaten well in several days or that they are experiencing problems with an ulcer. Subjects may inform the interviewer that they are unable to keep food down or are suffering from an intestinal disorder caused by stress. The investigator may also be told that a subject's sleep patterns have been totally disrupted, with hours of tossing and turning in bed, fitful sleep periods, or dreams and nightmares about this problem.

Countless interviewers have been informed that the subject's reputation has been forever ruined. Any possible chances he may have had for a great career have been shattered. In fact, his entire family has been traumatized, with family members now arguing among themselves, or the subject has become the family outcast.

The third form of depression is rage. Rage has three components: fear, pain, and aggression. This is the most intense state of depression that the interviewer will encounter. The subject is now in pure "survival" mode. This response is usually triggered because of what the subject perceives as extreme threats. Those threats, in the subject's mind, may be the location of the interview, the intervention by the investigative entity, or the behavior of the interviewer. In all cases, the subject's reactions have been contaminated from external sources and compounded by his severe internal stress. The interviewer will find the subject explosive, yet withdrawn. Any attempts at conversation or other interaction will be met aggressively. The interviewer should take careful stock of the situation and try to change some of the dynamics that are causing this enraged survival response.

One of the keys to correctly identifying these types of comments as true depression is to listen for the subject to indicate that all these symptoms are a direct result, or are at least in some form associated with, the crime, crisis event, or the case in which the subject is involved. Subjects often use these same types of comments, but only for the purpose of attracting sympathy from the listener. This type of behavior is a bargaining behavior and is dealt with differently from depression. When a subject is in genuine depression, the interviewer will be able to identify the cues on three levels. First, he will hear the depression in the subject's voice. The voice is often softer in pitch and lower in volume and possibly less distinct. The way in which the subject expresses his thoughts has already been outlined. Second, the interviewer will see it in the subject's body language, through slow movements, slumped body, heavily furrowed brow, or other facial expressions. Third, the interviewer will feel the person's depression on an intuitive level. He will "sense" the emotional pain the person is suffering.

The depressed individual may also make suicidal comments. These can range from open, easily identifiable statements about self-destruction, to camouflaged comments, such as "I wish I had never been born," "If only I could end all of this," or "I don't think I can face this thing anymore." Responses to these and other types of depression statements are discussed in the section on how to deal with mood-response statements.

Investigative interviewers often make two common mistakes when diagnosing a subject as experiencing the stress–response state of depression. The first involves the diagnosis of body language. The body language of depression has many of the same characteristics as the body language of confession. The same basic body slump, drooping shoulders, chin in the chest, crying for the first time, as well as other confession body behaviors, are also evident when the person is in depression. Both acceptance and depression are low emotional-energy states.

The second error is assuming that subjects give confessions when they are in depression. This erroneous assumption is made because the body language symptoms appear to be the same. The distinction to be made is that when in depression, the subject makes some form of verbal attack on himself. In depression, the subject is isolating himself from the realities of the situation. When in confession, however, the subject has ceased his attack on himself and accepts the reality of his error or crime. Acceptance is the acknowledgment of and submission to reality. Depression and acceptance are two different mental states with different verbal cues. The existence of the possibility of making an error in diagnosis warrants another Practical Kinesic Principle:

Do not misinterpret depression as acceptance. Listen for the verbal output and proceed with caution.

Denial

The stress–response state of denial is the subject's effort to reject reality. Fully 90% or more of the subject's deceptive behavior will present itself to the investigative interviewer in the form of denial (Davis, Connors, et al., 1999; Davis, Walters, et al., 2000; Walters, 2000). Denial also serves as the main support system of the other three rejection behaviors: anger, depression, and bargaining. The successful attack on, and the dismantling of, denial normally results in the collapse of the other three rejection responses. Failure to correctly diagnose and respond to denial allows subjects to use this form of rejection to strengthen their resolve against making a confession or admission.

Memory Lapses

A common, but troublesome, method of denial used by deceptive subjects is a memory lapse. Deceptive memory lapses occur because the subject has been put in a position where an answer must be given, but at great risk to the subject (Skinner, 1952, 1992). In reality, the subject is unable to explain or discredit the evidence against him. The easiest way for an individual to avoid incriminating himself is to state that he does not recall. Conversely, the individual may indicate that he has an extremely good memory or even an exact recall of the event; this may suggest that the person has practiced or memorized his story. This leads us to the next Practical Kinesic Principle:

> **When discussing critical areas, deceptive subjects experience more frequent occurrences of memory failure than do truthful subjects.**

The functions and operations of human memory are complex, but research has revealed interesting information that can be of use to the interviewer. First, it is important for the interviewer to know how information is catalogued for storage and retrieval from the memory. The three different kinds of memory are: procedural, semantic, and episodic.

Procedural memory is in use when we remember how to drive, ride a bike, or throw a good curve ball. These are functions we have learned to do in the past and are capable of repeating with little or no thought. Some of the activities are simple to learn and execute, while others are complex and require frequent practice or study.

Semantic memory is used to assist us in communicating ideas and concepts. The semantic process enables us to assign words to concepts and mental images. For example, the word "cat" immediately conjures up images of feline creatures that catch mice. Within the preceding sentence, we have been using semantic memory to understand what the writer is trying to communicate, such as, what is a mouse, what does feline mean, and what is meant by the concept of "capture?"

Although procedural and semantic memories do come into play during an interview or interrogation, episodic memory has the greatest significance to the interviewer. Episodic memory is defined as the memory of events stored for recall. An interview with a victim, witness, or suspect requires the specific application of episodic recall functions. Even with episodic memory, however, critical systems are at work, of which an interviewer should be aware, and upon which he can capitalize.

Realistically, we cannot remember everything that happens to us in our lives. To do so would clutter our brains with a lot of trivial data and memories that would eventually interfere with our ability to think. To reuse a previous example, the little "censor" inside our head is constantly weighing the possible value of all our sensory input and is deciding the possible future need of that information. Some of the data is deemed trivial and may be tossed into a "junk memory closet," only to be swept away with time. This is referred to as "memory degradation." Other pieces of sensory input are more important and may be marked, catalogued, and meticulously stored for later retrieval. For example, what you had for lunch on Tuesday of last week may already be forgotten because it was of little or no importance. If lunch last Tuesday was with the President, or with a movie star you have always fantasized about, you can bet that your memory of it will be strong, and a great amount of detail will be recoverable. Those memories have been deemed important and have been labeled for easy retrieval.

The sorting process of critical events is done through the use of labeling criteria. The information is labeled in such a fashion as to facilitate recovering the memory, and retrieval is dependent upon the identifying label. Successful retrieval depends on "cues," "moods," or "states." Each labeling system identifies specific memory-triggering keys.

Cue-dependent memory uses specific pieces of data for storage and recovery of information. For those individuals who are old enough to remember the date November 22, 1963, they will recall specific memories: first, the assassination of President John F. Kennedy; and second, where they were when they heard the news. The name Christa McAuliffe brings back memories of the teacher astronaut who died in the explosion of the Space Shuttle *Challenger*. September 11, 2001, brings back the memories and images of the terrorist attack on the World Trade Center in New York City. "Never eat soggy wieners" is how my children learned to remember the cardinal points on a compass. School children remember, "In 1492, Columbus sailed the ocean blue." All of these are examples of data that are stored and retrieved through "cues."

State- or mood-dependent memory information is stored on the basis of the person's mood or emotional state or the levels of impact the event had on how the individual felt at the time of the incident. For example, those of us who played football in high school or college still get that feeling of dread in late August when the ground is hard and dusty and the heat is almost intolerable, just as we did years ago when two-a-day football practice began. The same feelings arise in the spring at about the time track practice, tennis practice, or baseball tryouts start. Those memories are triggered because the environmental conditions are closely related to the event and the sensory feelings or emotions we were experiencing at that time. We have the same type of response when we hear that special song from the old days that reminds us of our first love and that very first, special kiss. The same memories or emotions can come flooding back when we visit the Vietnam

Memorial or review photographs of our children when they were just born or photographs of loved ones who have passed away.

An interview or interrogation is, in actuality, an attempt to get an individual to recall information regarding past events. That recall is enhanced by the interviewer's efforts to identify and stimulate cue- and mood-dependent stored data. The interviewer may ask the subject when was the last time he saw his wife alive. If that subject was responsible for the death of his wife, the last time he saw his wife alive may have been moments before he wrapped his hands around her throat in order to strangle her. The memory of that moment will be strong and, therefore, difficult for the killer to ignore. An arsonist may be asked about how and where the fire started in the office building while at the same time standing in the room where the burn patterns were found. That subject's thoughts will immediately address that scene when the paint thinner was poured on the files and the match was struck. Constantly reminding an individual of specific events, particularly those that involve wrongful behavior, can create a great deal of stress for the individual. When confronted with the reality of his behavior, the individual responds with one of the five stress–response states. To avoid incrimination by admitting the misdeed, the subject may resort to a memory lapse, which is a form of denial.

There is a high probability of deception on the part of the subject who responds to an important question with "I don't remember," "I don't recall," "Not that I can think of," or a similar response. To be assured of an accurate diagnosis, the interviewer must be sure that the question is an "important" one. Does the inquiry involve a significant piece of cue-dependent or mood-dependent data that should easily assist the subject in recalling critical information? "Did you assault the old woman?" "Were you driving the car that was seen last night at the liquor store?" "Did you see Ralph holding the gun?" "Did you cause the death of the child?" A response of "I can't remember" to these types of questions makes it hard to believe that the person is unable to answer with a direct "yes" or "no."

Memory lapses can be classified into three types, with each serving a specific purpose. The most common form, which we discussed earlier, involves "memory degradation." Certain pieces of information may be of little or no significance, or possibly may not even have been fully observed or identified. Those tidbits of information wind up being lumped together with other small bits of information that begin to disintegrate over time.

Another form of memory lapse is due to repression. An event or incident may be so upsetting, traumatizing, or emotionally disturbing that the individual may not be able to handle all the harsh cue-dependent and state-dependent information. Our minds are designed with an overload system for such a situation. When these types of situations arise, the mind locks the memory away, hiding it from us until we are mentally and emotionally able to handle the details of the event. This is, for example, the reason why we do not feel the pain of the event itself, but can remember not to put ourselves in the same situation again, if possible. This explains why some rape or incest victims may not remember their victimization until some later time. This type of repressed memory currently has the medical, psychological, and victim-assistance communities at odds with each other over whether some of the victimizations are real or have been suggested during therapy.

The form of memory lapse most frequently encountered by an interviewer is referred to as the "motivated," or "selective," memory lapse. This is a purposeful effort on the part of the deceptive person to avoid admitting knowledge of information. The memory lapse occurs because the subject consciously chooses not to recall in an effort to protect himself and avoid incrimination. This memory lapse has nothing to do with emotional or mental trauma or misplaced minor details.

No matter which form of memory failure the subject is experiencing, the interviewer can be assured that something significant has happened. If, in fact, the question involves significant information that cannot be overlooked or forgotten by a subject, the interviewer can be confident that one of two reasons remain as to why a subject cannot remember a piece of information. Either the subject has been traumatized by the event, which should indicate that it did occur, or the subject is using selective memory and chooses not to discuss the issue. This should also indicate to the interviewer that the subject, in some fashion, is aware of the event.

When we discuss statement analysis later in this text, methods of attacking memory lapses or extraordinary memory will be discussed. For the time being, it is recommended that the interviewer respond to memory lapses as indications that the subject is not sharp enough to create a good lie and is unable to respond with a direct yes or no answer. The interviewer should pin the subject down about the reason he is unable to recall important information and illustrate to the subject why a memory failure is unlikely. The interviewer should continue probing in this sensitive area until he makes some progress with the subject.

One interview approach that should be avoided is the practice of suggesting to the subject that he may have committed the act but forgotten that he has done so. The development of a false confession using this technique is high. There are situations in which a subject can be convinced to doubt his own memory and will confess to acts that he did not commit. These false confessions are the result of a phenomenon known as "memory distrust syndrome" (Gudjonsson and MacKeith, 1982). These subjects will have no actual memory of a crime, but will still give a confession. These "coerced-internalized false confessions" (Ofshe, 1989) are usually obtained from subjects who have high rates of suggestibility. These subjects can include the mentally deficient, those who suffer from some form of organic brain disease, severe alcoholics, those who abuse drugs, older subjects who may be suffering from senility or possibly early stages of Alzheimer's disease, and in some cases, young children. It is strongly recommended that an investigative interviewer never use this approach to interview or interrogate. There are times in which a subject may fall into the category of being highly suggestible, and the interviewer may not be aware of the possibility. It is safer to allow the subject to broach the topic and then work on the memory lapse by focusing attention on the details before and after the crime that the subject does recall in order to prove the case facts and the subject's frame of mind and intent.

Denial-Flag Expressions

Each one of us knows about "war stories" and have more than likely told several. "War stories" involve a little bit of truth with a whole lot of embellishment. The interesting thing about them is listening to how those stories begin. There are some characteristic words and phrases commonly used to preface these special stories (Nierenberg and Calero, 1973). By using these phrases, the speaker is alerting the listener, as if to say, "You may not believe anything else I've told you, but it is important for you to believe this." Most of the time, these special words and phrases are at the beginning of a statement. In other cases, they are found at the end of a comment in order to add emphasis and reinforce to the listener that the statement was important in the overall content of the subject's statement. The "flag" characteristic of these phrases is that they typically "flag," or "mark," a critical point in the subject's statement. The easiest way to describe denial-flag expressions is to provide some examples:

"Really, Mr. Walters. I couldn't do something like that."
"I couldn't lie to you."
"Honestly. I didn't do it."
"I didn't forge the signature, believe me!"
"To tell you the truth, I didn't know he was in there."
"I have absolutely no reason to lie."
"Frankly, I didn't believe anyone would do that."
"To be 100% honest with you…"
"I've never even thought of doing something like that, seriously!"
"I'm being as serious as a heart attack."
"Just between me and you…"
"I'm being as straightforward as I can on this."
"I'm being straight up with you."
"Truthfully speaking, I don't know where the fire would have started."

"Frankly speaking, I can't tell you what really happened."
"This ain't no _____ !"
"To be totally truthful with you, I never saw that before."
"To the best of my knowledge, I've never met her before."

These are but a few examples of the use of denial-flag expressions. The list changes constantly as individuals create new methods of trying to convince others of their truthfulness. As a part of denial, these expressions have a strong link to deception (Davis, Connors, et al., 1999; Davis, Walters, et al., 2000; Walters, 2000). Remember, do not base your diagnosis on any individual symptom. "No single behavior by itself proves anything" was one of our first Practical Kinesic Principles. Another important principle we established at the beginning of this book was to interpret deceptive behaviors in clusters rather than individually.

Weighted Expressions

A subcategory of denial-flag expressions is the use of a weighted expression. Weighted expressions are used when the subject needs to address an important issue without calling attention to his concern over the issue. It is as if the subject is trying to camouflage the serious nature of the topic being mentioned. The internal thought process of the subject is to bring up an issue that the listener would typically expect the subject to avoid because of its sensitive nature. The speaker reasons that if it is a topic that would most reasonably be avoided by a guilty person, then by mentioning that topic openly, it will prove he is not guilty of any deception (Ekman, 1992). The television character Lieutenant Columbo, played by Peter Falk, is adept at using this tactic. One of Columbo's trademarks is the weighted expression, "Just one more thing, sir." Columbo then asks the question that eventually implicates the subject at the end of the episode. Subjects use these verbal behaviors in the same way. You may hear, "By the way, did you find anything when you checked the telephone records?" "By the way, did they discover any blood in the car?" "Incidentally, were there any witnesses found in the neighborhood?"

Whatever follows comments such as "by the way," "incidentally," or "one more thing" tells the listening interviewer that the issue is important to the individual. Occasionally, weighted expressions may also be silent expressions, such as, "Oh, uh, did you happen to find any flammable stuff in the closet?" The weighted interest is there, but is expressed silently. If it is so important for the subject to bring up these topics in such a camouflaged manner, the interviewer should give them his full attention.

Modifiers

A modifier used by a subject suggests that any portion of the comment that has just been made is subject to change or qualification (Nierenberg and Calero, 1973). The use of a modifier in a comment acts like an intellectual eraser, permitting the subject to change his stand easily if the need arises. It "disqualifies" the person's response, but allows the response to still be made. The two most commonly used modifiers are the words "but" and "however." "You may not believe this, but… " or "I know this sounds incredible, however.…" Then the subject presents the qualified response that leaves room for escaping from his answer. These are some examples of commonly used modifiers:

> "**Ordinarily**, I don't get involved in things like that."
> "I **almost** did something I knew I would regret."
> "**Most of the time**, I don't lose my temper."
> "She is **generally** very good about that kind of thing."
> "I am **essentially** a very patient and tolerant person."
> "**Basically**, I try to avoid that kind of situation at work."
> "I **may have** done it sometime."
> "I don't **usually** make the deposit that late."
> "I **hardly ever** have that much to drink after dinner."
> "I **may have possibly** touched her there."
> "**Actually**, it didn't happen that way."
> "He **rarely** does that kind of thing at work."

In these examples, notice how the bold-faced words left a particular amount of uncertainty in the subject's answer, providing an opening for adjustment, if necessary.

Guilt Phrases

Guilt phrases are "signature statements" that are triggered due to the stress of guilt, or at least guilty knowledge, on the part of the subject. The interesting aspect of guilt phrases is that they are unsolicited comments the individual makes that are detrimental and self-derogatory. In some ways, they are similar to "Freudian slips." They are statements the subject makes that are mental "slips of the tongue" and that are not necessarily in his best interest. For example, an individual may voluntarily tell you about previous contacts that he has already had with the police or investigators on other issues. You may hear that the person has been investigated or accused of a similar situation in the past.

Case Study

A female clerk was robbed at gunpoint at a convenience store at approximately 1:30 A.M. Upon arriving at the scene, the police officer inquired as to the physical condition of the victim and then asked if anyone else was injured. After determining that the scene was secure, the officer indicated that he needed to interview the clerk and ask her some questions about the robbery. The clerk responded, "Okay. Just remember, I'm the victim, not the suspect." Further investigation determined that the clerk had falsified the armed robbery report to cover her embezzlement. It was learned later that she had perpetrated the same scheme at three other convenience stores in two other states.

Subjects are notorious for saying that interviewers have already made up their minds that the subjects are guilty, and that nothing the subjects say will convince the interviewers otherwise. In fact, the subjects may state, they are generally disliked and picked on by everyone around them and are always blamed for everything.

Some subjects agree with their identification as possible suspects in an investigation. They indicate that if they were the investigator, they would be questioning someone like them, too. You may even hear that they can understand how it looks as if they had every reason in the world to commit the crime.

An extremely interesting statement made by subjects, which also has a high deception-probability rating, is what is referred to as a "third person" comment. These comments almost always sound like theoretical inquiries about hypothetical situations. In reality, what the individual is doing is attempting to address the issue, but from a personally removed or safe position. "What if I had this friend who" indicates a lot more personal involvement than the question suggests. "Let's just say for instance" suggests some knowledge of the event. These types of statements are the strongest guilt phrases a subject could use. If this person is not involved, he at least has some guilty knowledge.

Blocking Statements

A subject makes a blocking statement as a form of quick defense against a strong allegation. The interviewer has presented an apparently convincing piece of proof against the subject. The subject, however, turns that same piece of damaging evidence into an argument that it is actually proof that he would never do such a thing. Blocking statements are also used as a method of eliciting information from the accuser or determining the strength of the evidence presented. These statements usually come in the form of a question, and frequently contain the word "why." Some examples include:

"Why would I risk embarrassing myself and my family by doing something like that?"

"If I took the money, why didn't I use it to pay some of my bills?"

"Do you actually think I would steal the money and put it back into my own checking account?"

"Why would I burn my own car? The insurance still wouldn't cover the loan."

"Do you actually think I would rob my own store? I'd just be stealing from myself."

"Why would I start doing something like that now? I could've done it a long time ago if I really wanted to."

Case Study

During the interview of a subject who was accused of molesting two of his common-law wife's children, the subject indicated that he had only had a "few incidents" with the police that, in fact, were 43 arrests. Among the arrests were five charges for child abuse and molestation. The subject made the comment to the interrogator, "Why would I do something like this? It usually starts back when you are young." The subject was 23 years old.

Bridging Phrases

When a subject is describing his involvement in a sequence of events, he may find it necessary to omit some of the elements in order to reduce apparent involvement. In order to maintain a fluid transition from one moment to the next while omitting this data, the subject resorts to using unnecessary connecting phrases (Rudacille, 1994). These "bridging phrases" may sound innocent enough. However, they often hide critical information and conceal problems for the person. "I had just started eating lunch, and the next thing I knew … ," "I worked at the office most of the afternoon and had a meeting with John later on that afternoon … ," "He was telling me to do exactly what he said, and then after a little while … ," "I went to the garage to check on the car, and then the next thing I realized the house was full of smoke." When a subject uses these types of bridges, the interviewer should be sure to take the subject back and try to get him to reconstruct the events that have been conveniently passed over. Examples of bridging phrases include:

"After awhile … "
"The next thing I knew … "

"All of a sudden … "
"Before too long …
"Out of nowhere … "
" … for awhile … "
"After a little bit … "

Vocabulary Shifting

Each of us has a base vocabulary, which is common to most people. We also carry a personalized dictionary that is unique to each of us. That "dictionary" contains vocabulary that is indicative of our personal life, personality characteristics, education, intelligence, and personal history (Skinner, 1952, 1992). At particularly stress-filled moments, notice when an individual changes out of that personal dictionary and begins to insert new words into his conversation. For example, the "argument" may suddenly be described as the "confrontation." The "people" at the party may become the "principals" involved. "Yelling at the supervisor" may become "adamantly registering discontent." These changes most often involve the use of nouns, verbs, and adjectives, and are used most frequently by more intelligent subjects. Such vocabulary shifts are used as a form of mentally or intellectually separating oneself from the critical situation described.

Vocabulary shifting particularly applies to pronouns. A subject may initially use singular pronouns, such as "he" or "she," but may, within a short time frame, use "they" or "them," indicating the existence of more than one person. Shifting from singular to plural pronouns is the most frequently occurring phenomenon, although shifts from plural to singular do occur. The interviewer should suspect that these shifts represent a truer picture of the participant in the event being described.

Shifting of verbs is not limited to changing the choice of verb, but also to changing the tense used (Skinner, 1952, 1992; Nierenberg and Calero, 1973; Rudacille, 1994.). If an individual is describing what happened in a historical sense, the verb usage should be past tense. Should the subject, however, make a comment about past behavior or conditions and use a present-tense verb, the implication is that the individual is making up the information as he goes along and thus is most likely being deceptive. Although shifting from past to present tense is far more frequent in occurrence, present to past tense changes can also be noted. If, for example, the investigative interviewer asks an individual to describe or reenact how he performs a routine function, the verbal description of the activity would probably be in present-tense form. If the subject lets down his mental guard and begins to describe actions in past-tense form, the possibility exists that the individual has now inadvertently given a description of events in which he has participated.

Displacement

The use of displacement terms by a subject is an attempt to depersonalize his participation in an event. This is marked by an increase in the use of terms describing others (Hocking, Baucher, et al., 1979; Rubin, 1984; Skinner, 1952, 1992). By using third-person terms, the event sounds more as if it is a fantasy and the participant or participants anonymous in nature. The interviewer may hear how "everybody knew it would happen sooner or later." "Anyone could have made the same mistake." "What they did was really unusual for them." "All of the people in the area knew about it." Displacement terms include "they," "them," "those people," or "others." A remarkable use of displacement occurs when a person makes comments using "he" or "she" when no name has been given or inferred during previous conversations.

Case Study

> The investigation of the disappearance of a grade-school girl turned up several possible leads, including the description of a vehicle seen near the bus stop where the child was last observed. Witness accounts, however, did not include anything about a possible suspect. During news reports about the child's disappearance, the child's mother and stepfather often referred to the individual responsible for taking the child as "he." Both parents even described how "he" was probably jealous and how they did not understand how "he" could take their child. The stepfather of the child later confessed to his therapist that he was responsible for the disappearance and subsequent death of the child.

Stalling Maneuvers

Deceptive subjects often employ a simple method of denial known as a "stalling mechanism." The use of stalling behavior by a deceptive subject accomplishes two primary goals. First, stalling gives an individual time to organize his thoughts, or to attain a "clear thought line." The purpose of that organizing effort is to assess the threat of the posed question and then decide, "Do I lie or tell the truth?" Second, if the subject decides he will attempt to deceive the listener, how big is the story he is going to tell and can he tell it without getting caught? When we speak, we are always monitoring our speech for fear of making remarks that might put us at risk of punishment or negative reinforcement from the listener. To ensure that we have enough time to review and edit our remarks before they are spoken, we develop subtle ways to delay the words for pre-speech analysis (Skinner, 1952, 1992). Stalling maneuvers are overt methods of helping us accomplish the goal of edited speech.

Stalling behavior occurs more frequently with deceptive subjects than with truthful ones. The exception, of course, is individuals who are affected by some form of speech pathology. The first form of the stalling mechanism is the use of non-speech behaviors. Once a question is asked, the interviewer may notice that the subject is silent for several seconds before he responds.

Case Study

During the investigation of a religious figure accused of molesting several children within the church, it was learned that some of the members of the church's governing body were aware of the suspect's inappropriate sexual contact with the children. Although these individuals were aware of the sexual abuse, the minister was moved to another position within the church and was put in charge of a group of children. One of the administrators was confronted with this information, questioned about the wisdom of the governing body's actions, and asked why the parents of the victimized children were not notified of the minister's behavior. The administrator took nearly 27 seconds before he gave an answer designed to protect himself.

Other non-speech stalling maneuvers include laughing before answering the question, particularly if the laughter is inappropriate. Laughing, as previously mentioned, is a way of relieving the stress of the moment and also of lowering the risk of punishment or negative reinforcement for the statement being made. For example, suppose a man is asked if he killed his mother-in-law by strangling her and stuffing her body into a freezer located in a self-service storage facility. If he responds with a laugh and then says, "Why would I put her body in a storage facility that I was paying rent for?" it could be considered quite inappropriate.

Stalling behavior using non-speech symptoms might include a cough or clearing of the throat before the response is given. Similar behaviors include a quick intake of air before responding, or a long exhalation. The subject may also stall by grunting, groaning, whistling, moaning, growling, or even taking a huge swallow before giving a verbal response. These symptoms include the speech-disturbance cues discussed earlier. This shows how subjects may combine two or more mechanisms when being deceptive. As mentioned, these combined behaviors are called "clusters."

The other forms of stalling are more verbally organized methods. These include answering a question with another question:

Interviewer: "Did you take the classified documents out of the building?"
Subject: "Do you actually think I'd do something like that?

Another stalling method is to repeat the question back to the interviewer:

Interviewer: "Are you using any illegal drugs before competition?"
Subject: "Am I using any illegal drugs before competition?"

Answering the question with a question can include the subject rephrasing the question:

Interviewer: "Did you report all your past employment on your application?"
Subject: "Have I withheld anything from my application?"

The subject may direct the interviewer back to a previous question after being asked an interview question:

Interviewer: "Have you ever been questioned about the robbery at the furniture store?"
Subject: "Well, what did you mean awhile ago when you asked if I've ever owned a hunting knife?"

All these forms of stalling maneuvers permit the subject to deal with the stress of the question and allow him time to organize the least damaging response possible.

Specific or "Surgical" Denials

Subjects often play word games with their interviewers. This is most evident when they begin to deny in specifics. For example, should the interviewer ask, "Were you in the research lab when the computer system went down last night?" it would appear to most people that the interviewer is asking about the subject's general location at the time of the computer failure. The subject, however, interprets the question literally and may respond, "No, I was not in the computer room when the computer went down." The subject reasons that because he was, in fact, in the computer control room and not in the room with the computer, a negative response can be justified. "Were you in the kitchen with Mike when he was looking at the body?" A response of "No, I was not in the kitchen with Mike when he was looking at the body" could suggest to the interviewer that there might be some error in the question that the subject has recognized.

Denial in specifics by a subject occurs in two formats. The first concerns the examples demonstrated above. The subject determines that one or more parts of the interviewer's question have an error and responds specifically to the error. The deceptive subject might respond to the question, "Did you put the coat hanger wire around the child's neck?" with, "No, I did not put a coat hanger wire around the child's neck." This may, in fact, indicate that the subject did not wrap a coat hanger around the child's neck, but avoid the fact that, in reality, it was another type of wire. The subject will focus his response only on the error in the interviewer's comments. Truthful subjects respond to the allegation or deny the crime in general.

The second form of denial in specifics is demonstrated when a subject discusses information relevant to an event or situation that may have occurred long ago. If a long period of time has passed since the occurrence of an event, the interviewer should be suspicious of a subject who seems extremely gifted in the ability to recall exact pieces of information. The information that the subject recalls is often the minutia that most individuals would probably forget after only a short period of time. For example, a subject may demonstrate the ability to remember the time to the exact minute when the phone rang, telling him of his business partner's death. The subject may be able to recall the exact words spoken by the supervisor during a brief conversation out on the floor of the assembly line. A passenger in a vehicle implicated in a drive-by shooting may recall the exact location of the vehicle in the street when the shots were fired. The variations on this theme are endless and could include such things as exact amounts, distances, and physical locations, as well as the exact content of a lengthy conversation, including specific quotes or even physical actions taken by an individual. At this point, two additional Practical Kinesic Principles are worth mentioning:

> The liar will only admit to what can be proven to him, then will always refuse to admit to items of the case that cannot be proved.
> Liars frequently give less factual information that can be substantiated in order to control information.

Deceptive "Yes" or "No" Responses

Of all the forms of denial that a subject can use, the simplest method is to say "no." It would seem that there would be little kinesic information available for the interviewer to glean from this simple two-letter response. The same also applies to the "yes" response. In reality, there is a wealth of information generated when a person responds in the negative and is suspected of lying.

When diagnosing a deceptive "yes" or "no" answer, the interviewer must be certain to employ some previously stated Practical Kinesic Principles. The principles of greatest importance in this case are that we must identify signals in "clusters" and that it is a change in a previously established pattern of saying "no" that is of concern. In this case, it is not merely the word "yes" or "no," but the difference in how the words are verbally, as well as nonverbally, articulated and demonstrated. It is also important to remember that this different form of "yes" or "no" is a timely response to a stress question.

An interesting characteristic about the description of each deceptive "yes" or "no" is how often an accompanying body language symptom completes the deceptive cluster. For example, there is the "yes" or "no" that is said while subjects are crossing their arms or legs. When body language symptoms are discussed later in this text, crossing behaviors are shown as general symptoms of defensiveness.

Other body language-assisted "yes" or "no" responses include saying "yes" or "no" while at the same time shaking the entire body to add emphasis. These types of responses can be classified as "performance cues," in that the subject is literally "performing" the answer to prove conviction in his response (Davis, Connors, et al., 1999; Davis, Walters, et al., 2000; Walters, 2000). The subject may respond with a "yes" or "no" while simultaneously breaking eye contact with the interviewer by either covering the eyes with the hands or some other object, closing his eyes, or looking off in another direction. The nonverbal element is a form of aversion and can be a significant sign of deception (Davis, Connors, et al., 1999; Davis, Walters, et al., 2000; Walters, 2000).

Subjects have been known to respond with a "no" while nodding their heads "yes." This can be a significant cue to deception. In this case, there is a dramatic contradiction between the verbal and nonverbal cues. One communication channel is giving one message, while another channel is sending a conflicting cue. Though rare, these tend to be significant moments of deception on the part of the subject (Davis, Connors, et al., 1999; Davis, Walters, et al., 2000; Walters, 2000).

Facial expressions that accompany the "no" answer may be indicative of deception. A blank, empty look on a subject's face when stating "no" can be a sign of possible deception. This is a form of "control" behavior associated with deception in which the subject is attempting to suppress his normal facial expression to prevent it from being read by the observer (Davis, Connors, et al., 1999; Davis, Walters, et al., 2000; Walters, 2000). A "no" spoken in conjunction with a cold, hard stare can be deceptive in that the subject is using the stare as an aggression response, almost daring the observer to take issue with the answer. Another staged or "performed" response is a "yes" or "no" spoken with a confused facial expression, as if the person doesn't understand the reason for the question. A "yes" or "no" answer with a casual facial expression can be deceptive if it is obvious the subject has had significant open facial messages throughout the previous portions of the interview. It is even more significant if the question is important and the conversation is serious. The interviewer may make the same assumption if the subject inappropriately laughs while answering "yes" or "no" to a serious inquiry.

An interviewer may suspect that a subject is undergoing significant stress and could be deceptive if he notices that the quality of the subject's voice shows some form of change when the subject says "yes" or "no." The "yes" or "no" may be different from any other because the subject may elongate the enunciation. The subject may do this to add emotional emphasis to his response. On the other hand, a deceptive person may respond with a series of "no's" spoken in rapid-fire, staccato fashion: "No, no, no, no, no!"

Case Study

A small-town police chief was under investigation by a grand jury for illegal activities in which he had participated. As his stress mounted during the investigation, he became short-tempered and easily agitated. During a verbal disagreement with one of his officers, the chief physically assaulted the officer, and the officer promptly filed criminal charges. At a press conference at which the chief announced his resignation, he was asked if his resignation had anything to do with the grand jury investigation or the assault charges that had been filed against him. The chief responded, "Oh no, no, no, no! That had nothing to do with it. I resigned on my own accord. That had nothing to do with it."

Other "no" answers rendered with a change in voice quality include those that have a change in the response time. You may notice that a subject hesitates before he answers, when all his other responses have been coming out in a timely pattern. A reverse situation may occur when the subject almost cuts the interviewer's question off by answering "yes" or "no" before the question has been completed. Most likely, this is an example of a situation in which the suspect has anticipated the question and is in a hurry to make his response.

Sometimes a "yes" or "no" doesn't even sound like a "yes" or "no." There is a silent "yes" or "no" in which you may see the person's lips move as he mouths the word, but no sound is made. The other altered "yes" or "no" form sounds like a hummingbird as the person answers with his lips closed.

Deceptive subjects can also respond with a "yes" or "no" answer that sounds, more like a question than an answer. The interviewer could get the impression that the person is guessing at the answer rather than being convinced of his response. A subject's "yes" or "no" response may sound as if he is really pathetically pleading in the answer. A "yes" or "no" from the subject may be followed by a thoughtful appearance, as if the subject is giving his answer a little more consideration.

Bargaining

A subject responding to a stress situation with a bargaining-response mechanism is attempting to disguise reality. This is the weakest of all the rejection behaviors, leaving the subject open for manipulation by the interviewer. Bargaining is more a form of evasion than outright deception, as seen in denial. Evasion also tends to be more common than all-out deception (Dais, Connors, et al., 1999; Davis, Walters, et al., 2000; Walters, 2000; Ekman, 1992). The response state of bargaining does not generate a full confession from the subject, but only permits the selling of substitute solutions.

When responding with bargaining, the subject is making an attempt to get the listener to agree with his perceptions of himself or the conditions surrounding the issue at hand. This attempt to get the listener to agree or bond with him on the issue is flawed, however, because the image he is selling and the characteristics of the situation are tainted and are a distortion of the true reality.

Complaining for Sympathy

A common bargaining method used by some subjects is complaining in order to gain the interviewer's sympathy. The complaining usually focuses on some kind of misfortune that has befallen the suspect. It is almost as if, just because the event in question has occurred, any possible suspect will fall victim to some form of adversity. It is amazing to learn how often the adversity has something to do with the person's immediate health or the health of someone close to him.

One of the author's close friends has been a college professor for almost 30 years. This professor contends that he has disrupted more lives, created enormous emotional and financial burdens, brought sickness and plague to hundreds of people, and is singularly responsible for more deaths than several serial killers put together. This man of education knows that, without a doubt, when he announces the assignment of a term paper or the date of an exam, calamity is sure to follow. He has made note of the numerous catastrophes that have befallen his students because of such cold-hearted statements as, "The midterm exam will cover … ," or "Your 25-page research paper is due." He has caused the deaths of numerous grandparents, aunts, uncles, cousins, and other family members. Homes have burned and cars have thrown trans-missions, blown engines, or had flat tires. Illness has stricken many students the day of an exam or the night before the term paper is due. Students have lost jobs, been forced to work overtime, and suffered even more, with uncanny timing. Alarm clocks and clock radios have stopped functioning, and watches have been stolen. The thefts of textbooks, research notes, lab notes, class notes, and even completed papers have increased at alarming rates. This academic knows the carnage will persist as long as he continues to be a university professor who insists on giving tests and requiring research papers from his students.

We have all entertained the use of such excuses to protect ourselves from our lack of planning and self-discipline. Our goal is to put off the inevitable and give us a little more time to throw together that research paper. By using these transparent ruses, we hope that our teacher or professor will have a little pity on us and allow us to better prepare for our assigned duties, and yet not condemn us for our procrastination.

Subjects of investigative interviews use complaining behaviors for almost exactly the same reasons as the students described above, and with these we are all intimately familiar. Deceptive subjects may indicate that they are currently ill, have been ill, or feel as if they are now coming down with some malady. This is usually a direct attempt by the subject to garner the interviewer's sympathy, hoping the interviewer will find it in his heart to go a little easier on the subject.

Subjects have been known to bring physician's notes or medic alert tags to an interview in an attempt to stay the interrogator's inquiries. They may be sure to mention several times to the interviewer that they are under a physician or psychiatrist's care for some physical or emotional problem. They may present medicine bottles and even take medication at critical moments during the interview.

Complaining behavior is in no way limited to deceptive individuals. Innocent subjects may also have something to complain about now and then. If complaining can occur with both truthful and deceptive subjects, then how is the interviewer to differentiate between the two? In this regard, there are separate patterns to the complaining behaviors. First of all, deceptive subjects generally complain in order to interrupt the interview, and they start complaining almost from the moment they walk into the room or are introduced to the investigator. Truthful subjects hold their complaints until after the completion of the critical portion of the interview.

Another significant difference in the complaining behavior of truthful and deceptive subjects is that truthful subjects complain to convey information to the interviewer. The information presented is often to correct a mistake in facts that the interviewer has made. Furthermore, the truthful person's complaints are legitimate and can be verified.

Case Study

A local district judge was hearing a complaint of probation violation filed against a female defendant who he had previously sentenced for possession of stolen property. After hearing testimony from the investigating officer and the report of the probation officer, the judge was ready to revoke the defendant's probation. The judge asked the woman to stand for sentencing and then asked her if she had any statement to make before he passed sentence. The defendant promptly told the judge that he could not send her to jail. The judge, unruffled, asked her why he couldn't do so. The defendant responded that she was ill and, therefore, could not go to jail. The judge asked her about the illness she was suffering. She responded, "Judge, I have cirrhosis of the brain." The judge responded, above the courtroom snickering, "You mean cirrhosis of the liver, don't you?" "No, the doctor said I've cirrhosis of the brain and it's serious." The judge responded, "I imagine that it is. I'm going to see that you get around-the-clock care for your problem. The defendant is remanded to the custody of the sheriff to serve 1 year."

Substitute Words

Not all the phenomena that we are discussing are limited to deceptive subjects. Many people often use the same behaviors. One of the crossover behaviors is the use of "soft" words or substitute words to describe our actions. We often use these substitute words when describing our behaviors to other people in order to ensure that they sound more palatable. Deceptive subjects use these same substitute descriptions in a desire to avoid the harsh reality of their inappropriate activities. Psychologically, the process is called "minimization;" to minimize one's behaviors or the realities of an uncomfortable situation (Strachey, 1976).

In the last several years, we have heard about many politicians being accused of lying to their constituencies. In response to these allegations, we have heard our political leaders denying that they have lied, but indicating that they may have "misspoken" or that they have been "quoted out of context" or "misquoted." Erroneous comments have been explained away as the result of "political spin." President Nixon, in his autobiography, indicated that he did not lie to the American public about his role in the Watergate scandal, but he did admit that he "dissembled" the truth (Nixon, 1979).

The use of substitute terminology by subjects includes referring to embezzlement as "borrowing." Rape might be referred to as "hurt." Sexual contact with another person has been described as a "relationship" or being "involved" with that person. A child molester or incest suspect may describe his inappropriate contact with a child as "teaching the child," "playing," "sex education," or "tickling." During an interview of a subject regarding his molestation of two girls, ages seven and five, he stated that he did not put himself into their "pee pee holes." Subjects have described arrests as "accidents with the police" or "contact with the law." A driver stopped for suspicion of driving under the influence may respond that he has only had the proverbial "two beers," is just "tired," "on medication," "drowsy," or that he just has a "buzz." Discrepancies on tax forms, expense vouchers, or billing may be called "cost overruns" or "math errors." The person just had to use "fudge factors" or "creative accounting."

Whatever the situation in which these types of euphemisms are used, the interviewer needs to recognize the subject's current psychological image of his behavior. This is not a denial of the crime, but an attempt at a disguise of its reality. As noted earlier in the brief description of bargaining, this is a transition state, in which the subject is open to some manipulation by the interviewer. The interviewer should respond to the subject on the same level until he gains some agreement with the subject. Once this common ground has been established, the interviewer should "help" the subject move toward a more accurate and full description of his behavior. In a sense, the interviewer may find that he has to "get sick," or empathize, with the subject before a healing admission or confession can be obtained.

Gray Statements

Another form of bargaining behavior by the subject is represented by the use of value statements when responding to a question. These "gray answers" are also described as "value statements;" they are deliberately vague responses from a subject. These have little or no boundaries or clear answers, and they leave a lot of room for anyone listening to assume whatever they want. Most of us remember the axiom regarding "assume:" "it makes an ASS outta U and ME." This openness to gray interpretation is exactly what the subject wants to occur.

An example of a gray answer might be seen when an employee is asked if he has ever used cocaine. A response of "Yes, but that was a long time ago," should trigger an inquiry from the interviewer as to how long ago it might have been. If an assault suspect indicates that he didn't hit a woman that hard, the interviewer might need to know how big his back swing was. The child abuser might respond that he really only lost his temper a few times with the child. This should make us suspicious as to just how many times he did lose his temper, just as we may be suspicious of the dentist or doctor who tells us that "this is going to sting a little bit" or "this might hurt a little."

Case Study

During the interview of a male nurse's aide who admitted that he had poisoned a patient with cyanide, the interviewer asked him if this had ever happened before. He responded, "I can't really say." The interviewer's response was "Okay." There was no further follow-up to the suspect's answer. It was later learned by the television press and through subsequent confessions by the suspect that he was responsible for over 80 homicides in a 16-year period. He has been sentenced for 37 of those deaths.

The interviewer should never let the interview end without clarifying a subject's "gray answer." It is critically important to make a subject be specific and give details concerning any such response.

Religious Statements

A frequently used bargaining tactic is the use of a religious statement in an attempt to add the appearance of credibility. This behavior does not include those individuals recognized as devoutly religious people who may regularly make religious comments. The difference between the two is that deceptive subjects invoke religion only at the most critical moments when they desperately need to have someone believe them.

There are three types of religious statements that a deceptive person may choose to employ. The first is the swearing of some religious oath. You may hear the subject state, "I swear to God," or to some other religious deity or figure, as well as "I'll swear on a stack of Bibles" or "I swear on my mother's grave." This swearing of oaths does not necessarily have to include a direct religious reference, as illustrated in the last statement. "On my dead children's eyes" and "on the life of my father" are other examples of oaths without deity references.

The second form of religious-oriented statement is when a deceptive subject brings a religious or beloved object into the interview room. This may be done for two possible reasons. The subject may be, in some fashion, attempting to provide himself with some form of visible or tangible moral support, or it may be done solely for the benefit of the interviewer's observation.

The list of religious or beloved objects that may be displayed in the interview room is enormous as well as interesting. For example: Bibles; prayer books; rosary beads; prayer beads; crucifixes; photographs or statues of Christ, the Virgin Mary, or any of the saints or apostles; pictures of Mohammed, the Dahli Lama, Malcolm X, Martin Luther King, Jr., Ferdinand or Imelda Marcos; the subject's children or grandchildren; satanic symbols or other ritual symbols; medicine bags; and so on. Just about the time you think you have seen everything, someone shows up for an interrogation with a new twist on the same theme.

Interviewers often find themselves being preached to or having the subject inquire about the destination of the soul in the hereafter. Holy Scriptures or writings may be read or quoted to the interviewer. Subjects may pause for prayer or pray for divine intervention. These prayers are often done aloud, and the interviewer can be assured that the person's plight will be mentioned along with the interrogator's name.

Suspects have also arrived for interviews, lineups, or polygraph examinations with their ministers, rabbis, spiritual advisors, deacons, elders, Sunday school teachers, or prayer partners. In one federal court proceeding, the defendant arrived for his sentencing with the entire church choir in tow. The choir members filled up the back two rows of the courtroom, all wearing their choir robes.

The interviewer is reminded not to become overwhelmed by such displays of religious dedication. These displays are primarily done for the express purpose of deflecting the interrogator's accusations and allegations. Be reminded that truly religious or faithful people don't normally demonstrate this type of behavior. When the display of religion is used, consider the circumstances. It may simply be an ostentatious display that is deliberately presented at the outset and emerges again at critical stress points during your interview, much to the benefit and at the convenience of the subject.

Personal Moral Statement

A phenomenon that also arises in the interview which is quite similar to that of religious statements, is that of comments from the subject regarding his high personal code of conduct. When a subject wishes to divert suspicion from himself, he may make profound statements regarding his own moral standards. You may hear how the subject was brought up in a strict home with parents who would not tolerate inappropriate behavior from their children, and who especially would not put up with anything like what he is now accused or suspected of doing.

The listener may be informed of the specific lessons of life regarding acceptable and unacceptable behavior that the subject has experienced. He may make references to professional associations that demand certain ethical standards of their members to which this person has always adhered. He may name famous persons, either real or fictional, with high standards of moral conduct, and insist that he has tried to model his own life after these heroes.

Comments from a deceptive individual may also include how he has been an honest, hard-working, law-abiding citizen for years, without so much as a traffic citation. The interviewer may be told that the subject has been an employee with the company for so many years, has received the highest achievement award, or has been nominated so many times as employee of the year. The subject may also elaborate about the number of years of service he has given to the community as a member of a service organization, as a Scout leader, local community leader, or member of the PTA. Without a doubt, the interviewer will be advised that he has just encountered "the" model citizen, who is, therefore, totally above reproach or suspicion.

Overly Courteous

An interesting method subjects have of utilizing bargaining behavior is to be overly polite to the interviewer. The subject theorizes that if he is extremely friendly and polite to his possible accuser, the interviewer may be amicable or overlook him as the suspect. These displays of cordial behavior, which are sometimes taken to the extreme, are specifically designed to "con" or "butter up" the interviewer.

An early television character perfected one of the finest examples of this type of behavior. Every parent cringed at the thought of this character, and other children despised him. The endless artificial compliments rendered by the character Eddie Haskel on *Leave It To Beaver* are legendary in the mind of any 1960s television viewer. Many deceptive subjects have attempted similar Eddie Haskel "maneuvering" to insulate themselves from suspicion.

Think how you would respond if you were wrongfully accused of a crime you did not commit. You might find that it is difficult to insult the guilty subject.

Name Dropping

It is truly amazing how many important people a deceptive person can name when he enters an interview room. Investigative interviewers are well within reason to be suspicious of a subject who goes to great lengths to stand up when the interviewer walks into the room and who possibly crosses the room to give the interviewer a vigorous handshake. The next thing that will often occur is a listing of important people. You might find that the subject is a friend of the Chief of Police or a council member, or an attaché to a highly placed political figure. The list mentioned by this "well-connected" suspect may run from the payroll clerk at City Hall to someone who has worked at one time on the staff of the President of the United States.

There is no limit to the number of names a subject may drop, just as long as they are mentioned. This is done in hopes that the name may strike fear or respect in the mind of the interviewer. The goal is to cause the interviewer to question his motives and maybe even his case facts. If the interrogator hesitates in the attack, holds back when it may be appropriate to be more forceful, or even suspends an accusatory tone, the suspect has succeeded in achieving his goal.

Acceptance

A subject who is in the state of acceptance has reached the point where he can no longer deny the reality of events. His efforts at denying or disguising reality have failed, and his use of anger or depression has presented him with no relief from the stress and anxiety he is experiencing. At this point, the subject is open to the suggestions of the interviewer. This window of opportunity, however, may not remain open long. The wrong stimulus, overstimulation, or even an overly energetic response from the interviewer could cause the window to close. The key to an appropriate response by the interviewer to a subject in acceptance is first to accurately diagnose that the state exists, and second, to correctly handle the response once it has been identified.

There are three types of statements from a subject that indicate he may be open to the suggestion of confession. These three verbal cues of acceptance include "debt service" statements, fantasy–reality or "third person" statements, and "punishment" statements. In the future, other types of statements indicative of the acceptance response may be defined further. At this point, however, we will deal with those types of responses that have been identified to date.

"Debt Service" Statements

"Debt service" statements made by a subject have within their content some form of indication that the suspect would like to be able to buy his way out of the problem. The subject is hoping that an alternative exists that has, more or less, a monetary price tag or some other rate of exchange attached to it. If that price is paid, the issue will be resolved. A comment by the subject suggesting that he may be prepared to make that payment indicates that the subject is moving into an acceptance state and is open to suggestions that result in admissions or confessions.

Some examples of "debt service" statements are:

"I didn't steal it, but I would be willing to pay it back just to get this over with."

"I'll just drop my claim on my policy and take the loss for the fire."

"Why don't I just pay you and the department for your time on this case, and we'll drop my complaint?"

"I know my kid wouldn't do something like this, but divide the total cost and I'll pay his share."

"I don't know where that piece of equipment could be, but I'll help pay for a replacement."

"I would never hurt those kids in any way, but I'd like to help pay for their treatment or counseling."

Case Study

Two juveniles were suspected in the vandalism and arson of a neighbor's car. The state fire marshal's office initiated an investigation that quickly identified the two suspects. Once identified, one suspect immediately joined the service. The other suspect wrote a letter to the vehicle owner stating, "_____ and I probably weren't involved in the damage to your car, but we don't remember because of alcohol. We will pay for the repairs, but _____ is in the Army now and can't be reached. Please give us more time." (Notice the references to memory failure due to alcohol and the use of the word "probably.")

When a subject makes comments indicating that he is moving into the acceptance phase, the interviewer needs to make the appropriate response. Each of the different types of acceptance responses requires the correct reaction by the interviewer to facilitate the admission or confession.

Once a suspect makes some form of "debt service" comment, the interviewer should first act to secure the subject's desire to pay for the "cost" of the problem. This is done for two reasons. First, it acknowledges the person's desire to pay the costs. The interviewer should not agree to drop the issue at this point, stop prosecution, or "go lightly" on the subject based on this agreement. This is done to assure the subject that his comment has been heard and that future statements will also be heard and responded to by the interviewer.

The second reason for responding to the suspect's agreement to pay is that this commitment creates a set of "psychological handcuffs" for the suspect. Once the comment has been made and agreed to, it is nearly impossible for the suspect to take back his words. This "handcuffed" psychological state will play to the interviewer's advantage in the subsequent steps of the interviewer's response.

After obtaining the subject's commitment to "pay back" the losses, create a hypothetical situation similar to the incident currently under discussion, and identify a smaller number of similar incidents or a smaller amount of loss, but use only round figures. The interviewer should avoid giving specific numbers if possible. Once this scenario of a similar incident has been thoroughly described, ask the subject to do you, himself, and everyone else a favor and also pay for the loss that resulted from this incident. One of several reactions is likely to occur.

If the subject agrees to repay the losses suffered in this similar incident, there is a good possibility that you have not yet discovered all the related incidents and that there are more losses than you have previously uncovered. If that is the case, you need to address all these incidents in greater detail in order to uncover the full magnitude of the suspect's activities. If, however, you are able to fictionalize similar incidents in such a fashion that you know for certain that the suspect could not be involved, you may have uncovered a person with a guilt complex who needs to be the center of attention and will confess to anything. This may also occur if you have a subject who is mentally deficient and is trying to "please" the interviewer or is confused.

On the other hand, if you offer the suspect the opportunity to pay for other "incidents," he may flatly refuse to pay. Should this occur, ask the subject why he is willing to agree to the payment. You may hear some form of comment in which the person claims no responsibility for that incident or loss, or is not going to take responsibility for the incident or loss. The interviewer should then remind the subject of the agreement to pay for the first incident for which they weren't responsible, and that it only seems logical that he could pay for this one also. The subject should, at this point, realize the position into which he has just placed himself. The "handcuffs" have just snapped shut.

Fantasy–Reality or "Third Person" Statements

Fantasy–reality, or "third person," statements are comments made by subjects indicating that they are accepting the reality that the event or crime has indeed occurred. Their remarks are designed, however, to hold on to that one last thread of hope that they can solve the problem without making the final remark that labels them as guilty.

Third person or fantasy–reality statements made by subjects indicate a psychological desire to address their problems from a third-person perspective. This is done in order to displace the guilt feelings that they are experiencing. Subjects reason that acknowledging the event without accepting guilt will be sufficient to satisfy the interrogator and put an end to the uncomfortable situation in which they find themselves.

Some examples of fantasy–reality statements include:

"Do you want me to lie to you and tell you I did it even though I didn't?"
"I didn't do it, but I'll say I did if you really want me to."
"Would it make you happy if I just confess to this?"
"If I told you I did it, I'd be making something up on myself."
"I can't admit to something I haven't done."
"I don't remember doing it, but if you say I did it, then I probably did."

Note that by the content of these sample statements, the suspects are not denying the crime. However, neither are they totally prepared to verbally acknowledge that they were involved. The interrogator's response should be to explore the entire sequence of events in as much detail as possible. In this manner, the subjects implicate themselves because of their extensive knowledge of key evidentiary information. Although the interrogator does wish to explore the facts that subjects are ready to acknowledge, he must proceed carefully with the inquiry so as not to push subjects into accepting personal responsibility until the time is right.

The nature of the subject's comment can be a trap for the interrogator should he make the wrong response. Any comment by the interviewer, such as "No, I don't want you to lie," "I don't want you to confess to something you didn't do," or "I only want you to tell me the truth" is a response that tells the subject not to confess. Conversely, any positive answer that suggests that the subject should lie to the interviewer may have just annulled the validity of his eventual confession. The subject will also be aware that you may be setting a trap for him and may move out of the acceptance response.

When a subject makes a fantasy–reality based statement, the interviewer should assist him in explaining why he apparently has such an intimate knowledge of case information. The interviewer can suggest that the reason this situation exists is possibly because he may have overheard someone talking about the case, or because he may have even been directly involved in the conversation. The interrogator can then ask the subject to relate the contents of those conversations. This concept may seem rather simple or farfetched, but the interrogator needs to remember that the subject is already in the state of acceptance. He is at the point where he has acknowledged the crime and is on the brink of admitting his involvement. The interrogator is providing the subject a way to deal with the anxiety about the reality of his behavior and gives him a way out of this dilemma while still saving face.

Other ways of dealing with fantasy–reality remarks may be to suggest that the subject put himself in the shoes of the real suspect and have him predict what the subject was thinking. The subject may be asked to hypothesize about why the suspect made certain mistakes or if there were any mistakes made. The subject can be asked why he thinks the suspect took certain actions or carried out specific types of behaviors. Note that in each of these scenarios, the investigator has not suggested that the subject committed the crime, but is simply allowing the subject to remain in this state of displacement as he deals with his own guilt. The subject is frequently the person who makes that final statement indicating his guilt. The subject may also carry his explanation of the crime to its final conclusion, and the interrogator then need only respond with a question about the subject's personal involvement.

"That's why it happened, isn't it, John?"

"It wasn't supposed to really happen like that, was it, Helen?"

"Shirley, was this the first time it happened?"

"Mike, what you have just told me is why all the evidence points to you, isn't it?"

"Kevin, the only way anyone would know all this information is if he or she was there when it happened, isn't it?"

Other ideas for responses to this form of acceptance statement include having the subject imagine that he was present when the offense occurred, and then have him describe the sequence of events he would have seen. You may suggest to the person that he found videotape of the event and have him review what he would see on the videotape. The subject could be presented with the idea that he was looking through a hole in the roof or from a vantage point above the scene, and have him describe the sequence of events as they would have unfolded.

You may also find it helpful to have the subject play the role of the victim or the imaginary perpetrator and elaborate on that person's point of view during the crime. An excellent approach is to have the subject describe the suspect's or victim's emotions when the offense occurred, what the victim would have said to the suspect, or what scared the victim the most. Have the subject tell if he would have been scared.

The creative interviewer may suggest that the subject relate what he would read if he found someone's diary describing the crime. The subject could be asked to consider what he would have heard if he were listening in on an electronic bug. Success in getting a confession in such situations can also be found in suggesting that since the subject knows the victim intimately and knows how that person would behave in a situation that he described, what he thinks the victim would have said or done.

The goal of the interviewer responding to a fantasy–reality-based acceptance statement is to keep the subject talking and allow him to respond in the third person. The interviewer should also ask questions that permit the subject to speak in the third person. As noted earlier, the subject has not made that final step in conceding that he is guilty. The types of replies that the interrogator can give the subject are limited only by the interrogator's imagination.

Punishment Statements

These are statements made by the subject that address the issue of punishment. The subject is inquiring about the nature of the penalty or punishment that is usually imposed on someone who has committed the type of act the interrogator is questioning. Samples of these types of statements include:

"What could happen to somebody who did something like this?"
"What am I going to be charged with?"
"Could I be fired?"
"Has anyone ever been suspended from school for something like this?"
"What if this whole thing was just an accident?"
"What does the book say a person could get for doing this?"
"How long before I would see the judge?"
"Is the bond or bail pretty high in these types of cases?"
"Could I just talk to my kids one more time?"
"Would I be able to get some counseling or psychiatric help?"
"Could they just get me into some kind of therapy?"

"Is this going to be on the news?"
"Does my wife have to hear about this?"
"Is my father going to find out?"

In all of these cases, the subject has, in his mind, accepted his guilt in the incident and is now concerned about the sanctions that will be taken against him. The biggest part of the interviewer's battle is over. He must be careful in replying not to shock the subject out of his acceptance state by describing punishment in the most intimate and gruesome details.

In many cases, the investigator does not know exactly what the punishment will be. The interrogator can respond in a vague manner, suggesting the real outcome may still be in the hands of the subject, depending on his future actions. Sample responses to a subject include:

"I don't know, Mike, but I'll be glad to talk to the prosecutor and tell him your side of the story."
"That depends on the people on the jury. It would be better if they heard the whole story from you and not from someone else."
"I'll be glad to talk to your wife for you if you want me to tell her what happened."
"I'm sure your boss will understand if you just trust him and tell him about it."
"It would be better if we talk about this first before everyone else learns about it."

The interrogator's objective is to minimize the possible severity of the punishment the subject may have to endure. This is not to suggest that the interrogator indicate to the subject that he can make a deal for him or can personally assure him of leniency if he confesses. In fact, the interrogator should go to the lengths necessary to make the subject aware of this fact. The interviewer does want the subject to understand that the best possible course of action is to be open and honest and discuss his personal problems.

When the investigator recognizes that the subject is in the state of acceptance, he has only a limited period of time to respond. The interviewer has three things that must be done in order to facilitate the subject's confession. The interrogator must show the subject that he is in acceptance, provide an atmosphere conducive for the subject to confess, and avoid applying too much pressure.

The interrogator must imitate many of the subject's characteristics during the interview, as well as control the subject's negative-response states by diverting his behaviors. When the subject is responding with acceptance, the interrogator must also show that he is in acceptance. If the subject determines that the interrogator is shocked, dismayed, or feels contempt for him because of his action, the interrogator has erected a barrier to confession. The interrogator must be in the state of acceptance and show that he is mentally and intellectually open to the subject's dilemma.

Second, the interrogator should learn that this is the most critical moment of the interview — the time for the interrogator to stop talking and start listening. Too much speaking can actually talk the subject out of a confession. Sales professionals refer to this as "buying the product back." Getting overanxious and trying to "help" the subject choose the correct confession response is extremely detrimental. The interrogator needs to realize that he has made his point and the subject has accepted it.

Finally, the interrogator needs to leave the subject a way to save face. The subject's ego-defense protection system is still at work. The interrogator cannot totally demoralize and crush his opponent. As shown with each response to the three types of acceptance remarks, the suspect is offered a method by which he can confess while still holding on to some form of dignity.

There is no magic comment, secret phrase, or clever tactic to get a subject to give a confession or admission. The interrogator simply must ask for the confession, give the subject a palatable method by which to do it, and then remain in acceptance, which will provide the opportunity for the subject to confess. The following Practical Kinesic Principle will serve the interrogator well:

When the subject is demonstrating that he is in acceptance, the interrogator should stop talking and start listening.

Practical Kinesic Information Recovery and Statement — Credibility Assessment

5

If the investigative interviewer intends to make some form of assessment regarding the credibility of a person's statements or remarks, there needs to be a method by which he obtains the most complete and least contaminated information possible. The optimum is for the interviewer to conduct the interview and make an assessment regarding the credibility of the statement at the same time. However, there are times when the investigator is forced to rely on the initial interviewing efforts of other investigators, counselors, victim advocates, and so forth. In such cases, a full analysis of these statements may not be possible, although all is not lost. A dedicated investigator realizes that no interview is ever wasted, because if he works at it and diligently reviews a statement, there is always information that has some value to the investigation.

One of the most persistent problems with interviewing subjects — even those who are cooperative with the investigator — is that many of the interviewer's methods and even his own behaviors tend to contaminate the process (Fisher, Geiselman, et al., 1987; Fisher and Geiselman, 1992). The interviewer's approach to the interview and the methods by which he asks for information tend to be counterproductive, and in many cases, can disrupt the normal process of memory recall. In some cases, the training most investigative interviewers receive at the academy or basic-training level is quite limited (Fisher and Geiselman, 1992; Walters, 1997) and often contains major scientific errors. The greatest majority of the skills acquired by interviewers is through on-the-job training (Fisher and Geiselman, 1992; Greenwood, 1979) or by watching an experienced interviewer. However, the experienced interviewer often received no better training at the basic level than did the new investigator. There is no real assurance that senior investigators' interviewing skills are better-than-adequate. For many investigators, the interview is simply a matter of asking who, what, where, when, and how (Fisher and Geiselman, 1992; Hess, 1989; Mullaney, 1977) or following some other list of formalized questions. Thus, this approach of the junior officer watching the senior detective interview subjects may perpetuate bad habits and poor

interviewing and listening techniques through each generation of new officers. This section is designed to help teach the basic principles of eliciting
information from subjects.

This section addresses the process of recovering information from victims, witnesses, and subjects, and how to identify factors that either increase
or decrease the overall credibility of the statement. This is accomplished by
extracting information from the mind of the victim, witness, suspect, or
informant using methods that will not contaminate the statements, and is
based on the principles of cognition and memory. The result is that cooperative subjects gain confidence in themselves, their memories, and the amount
of information they provide. We are subtly teaching this subject to probe his
memories and recover larger and more accurate blocks of information. For
the person who intends to be deceptive, however, his initial efforts at deception eventually create serious cognitive problems in trying to maintain this
deception. They also create emotional arousal at the fear of being caught in
his deception, which, in turn, tends to stimulate stress and deception signals
at those points in his statement that are most suspicious. Once the interviewer
identifies those areas during which the subject demonstrated some form of
cognitive disruption or emotional arousal, those become the focus of the
interviewer's follow-up questions.

Basic Theory

The first objective in the information retrieval process is to draw out details
regarding an event from the deeper recesses of the subject's mind into the
conscious level of the subject's awareness. For the cooperative subject, we are
creating an atmosphere that is conducive to retrieving information stored in
his memory. The methods used are designed to facilitate the subject's best
use of his own memory and to do so more efficiently and effectively. By
assisting the subject in the retrieval process, we help him gather critical
information and details. This is conducted in a narrative-based interview
atmosphere that has been shown to successfully produce more information
in terms of volume and quality. At the same time, it is least likely to contaminate the subject providing the statement.

While we are creating this narrative-based interview atmosphere, we are
going to reduce the risk of contamination of a suspect's statement due to the
interviewer's preconceptions. This also helps reduce the amount of erroneous
or misleading information, as well as false confessions. The deceptive subject
will resist this process and avoid providing any damaging or incriminating
details. The deceptive subject also finds ways to merge nonthreatening
information with truth. He must find a way to make the link between the

two as smooth and believable as possible in order to avoid detection of his deception.

Our analysis of the subject's statement to determine credibility involves the isolation of various verbal, nonverbal, and behavioral cues. The more of these cues that are identified, the lower the credibility. It is essential at this point to emphasize that there is no time at which the subject has "failed" the analysis. Our primary objective is to obtain as much reliable information from each subject as efficiently as possible and with the least amount of contamination from the interviewer. When we find clusters of cues suggesting poor credibility, our efforts during the cross-examination, or follow-up, phase of the interview will be focused on these areas. In other words, these clusters are "markers" for the interviewer that identify where the subject has experienced significant cognitive and emotional changes that need further attention to determine why these symptoms occurred during the discussion of that particular issue. For the truthful subject, these cues could indicate embarrassment, uncertainty, guilty knowledge, or similar phenomena that are not malicious in nature, but warrant further attention.

First, we should address the situations during which the results of the analysis process are going to be marginal. We are not going to be able to gather consistently reliable information from subjects who are mentally ill. By definition, individuals with mental illness are at times unable to distinguish between fantasy and reality. The information we gain in statements from such subjects is too easily tainted with their hallucinations, delusions, and paranoia. The best we may be able to ascertain from their statements will be the nature and severity of their mental disorder and the disordered thoughts that drive their behaviors.

Our information retrieval and analysis process is also not going to be productive when it is used on subjects who suffer physiogenic disorders — more commonly referred to as brain-diseased. Our analysis process relies heavily on a person's ability to operate on some form of time continuum and to identify people, places, items, etc. Unfortunately, for the brain-diseased subject, this is at the heart of his disorder in that he invariably has a great deal of trouble accurately sorting and identifying spatial and temporal information. These subjects frequently become frustrated with their memory problems and are known at times to make up information in order to give any answer so as not to be looked upon unfavorably by the interviewer. In some severe cases of brain disease, these subjects have also been reported to suffer from hallucinations. They often have a hard time focusing their attention over long periods of time or when dealing with multitask projects.

Subjects who are classified as mentally deficient can also present symptoms that make it difficult for us to conduct some form of productive analysis. Of concern is whether the subject has been previously interviewed regarding the same topic. In these cases, the subject may believe that he performed poorly or inaccurately the first time and may change his responses in an effort to give the "right answer" or in an effort to please the interviewer. Multitask projects can also be a problem due to his inability to stay focused on more than one issue at a time. These subjects have not developed adequate free-recall memory skills, basic memory retrieval, or rehearsal skills, which are vital in performing our analysis.

The use of this process on children is strongly discouraged. A normal, fully developed mind has, to some degree, mastered the ability to organize information based on time, similarity, and function, make intuitive connections between ideas, and develop memory retention and retrieval schemes. These skills are still, in many respects, elusive for a child, depending on his age, social skills, and cognitive development. It is not unheard of for a child to omit critical information because he did not encode the information when initially exposed to the stimulus, or failed to connect the significance of the information with the question asked by the interviewer. Children are also extremely vulnerable to negative feedback behavior from the interviewer. A question that is asked a second time, even though it may be in a different format, is seen as a sign of failing in the first response. Typically, when a child's statement is diagnosed as less than credible, it is due to the adult who conducted the interview and the methods used (McGough and Warren, 1994).

There is little argument that the results of such analysis may not be productive when interviewing subjects who are under the influence of drugs or alcohol at the time of the interview. The type of drugs used, amount of alcohol consumed, and length and degree of any continuing abuse of such chemicals by the subject leaves the credibility of his statements in doubt. Cognitive functions are, without a doubt, impaired, as are the issues of time and emotional status when the individual was exposed to the events in question. Our ability to acquire information depends heavily on the ability of our senses to capture the information and the brain's ability to recognize the significance of the event and encode or store the information correctly for later retrieval.

Trying to conduct the interview using some form of language interpretation can also complicate the statement process. There are terms, words, or ideas that do not translate the same from one language or culture to another. Should the interviewer be conducting an oral interview, it may be difficult to recognize the correct timing of the subject's reactions to a specific point in the question or to identify what nonverbal cue was associated with which verbal response. There are also situations in which a seemingly normal behavior for one culture is a form of insult in another. What the interviewer may identify as an innocent remark may, in fact, be important to the culture of the subject. It is also not unheard of to have the translator, due to boredom, lack of understanding, or ignorance, provide a general rather than literal translation. It would be advantageous for any investigative agency to take the time to identify several different translators in their community and work with them in advance of any and all interpreter-assisted interviews. With advanced discussion, training, and planning, these types of pitfalls can be avoided.

Eliciting the Statement

Human memory and its development is a complex process that cannot be adequately discussed in this short treatise on recovering and assessing statements. We do want to take a few moments, however, to get a general grasp of this complex process so we can understand why we are taking certain steps and certain times during this analysis.

Our memories are an intricate web of complex interactions between all the events that occur within the range of our five senses, the context in which those events have occurred and our role in those events, and our mental status at the time of the event (Fisher and Geiselman, 1992). We first must be present at the event and then be aware of how important the event may have been to us at that time. Our frame of mind and emotions at the time we were exposed to the stimulus have a direct impact on what was stored, and how it was stored, in our memory reserves. The information is then encoded by interlacing all the emotional, cognitive, and sensory elements, and we use all these cues as a means of retrieving this information at a later time.

We will use the analogy of a CD that has information stored on it. This CD has seven different tracks on which different types of data are stored. On one track, all the visual data is stored. On another, sounds; the third contains taste data. Touch is on the fourth track, and smell is on the fifth — in other words, all our five senses are on these five tracks. There are two other significant tracks of data that are also critical to this process. On one track is stored our emotions and thoughts that occurred at the time of the event. The final track is the one that keeps all the information synchronized with the event and holds it in place, and that will be a time continuum, creating a network of associated information. These CDs of our memories are further sorted based on their significance, the impact they may have had on our lives, and if they are classified as episodic, procedural, or semantic memories, which we have discussed previously.

Any time we attempt to call up memories, we search for them using the cue-dependent and state-dependent labeling system discussed earlier. When we search for memories, we are working through this complex grid of inter-related information. As each point begins to intersect other pieces of data, the memory is retrieved (Gudjonsson, 1992). Understanding that this is basically how memory is encoded, stored, and retrieved, we are going to employ methods that take advantage of this process and streamline the infor-mation-recovery process when interviewing subjects. In addition, we are going to use the narrative-based interview process discussed earlier, as well as follow our four-step format for productive interviews: orientation, narra-tion, cross-examination, and resolution.

Statement Samples

We are going to review the information-retrieval process as taking a statement sample. In a sense, we are "sampling" the subject's memory. We're going to divide the analysis process into three levels. As we progress, notice that the degree of difficulty increases. Initially, the process is easy for subjects, both truthful and deceptive, but as we progress, the demands on the deceptive subject to keep the stories connected and accurate without giving away any emotional or cognitive cues of deception become more difficult. On the other hand, the truthful subject will gain confidence in his progress, and as a result end up providing more and better-quality details.

The first sampling is a "narrative sample." We are going to assume at this point that the interviewer has already spent at least some time with the subject getting typical pedigree information, answering the subject's general ques-tions, and identifying his role as well as the role of the subject and the objective of the interview. In doing so, the interviewer should have already been able to identify the "constants" in the subject's behavior.

In the narrative sample, the subject is given the opportunity to tell the interviewer what he thinks are the most important elements of his memory. The interviewer stimulates the subject to begin talking by using open-ended questions. Appropriate questions are: "Tell me what happened last night when you were robbed." "What have you heard about …" "Please tell me about …." As further encouragement, the interviewer might say, "Tell me everything that happened, and please don't leave anything out and don't make anything up if you don't know." Questions should be phrased in this form to encourage the subject to take the floor and begin his own effort at recalling the necessary elements of the critical event.

If applicable to the case, try to get the subject to start his recitation about two hours before the event occurred. In fact, this is a good response to a subject who asks, "Where do you want me to start?" Let's assume you are discussing the robbery of a convenience store at 3:00 a.m. Ask the victim to start his story from when he first got to work at 11:00 p.m. Or maybe ask the rape victim about her usual routine when she goes to the health club for aerobics on Thursday nights. There are several reasons for doing this. First, as the person's recollection progresses, he will find himself developing the same emotions and thoughts that occurred when he experienced the event the first time. This facilitates the recall process, because it was under the same conditions that the event was experienced and the memory stored in the first place. Second, it helps the observer get a better grasp on the mental capabilities of the subject, as well as further identify his constant of verbal and nonverbal behaviors. Third, in some cases, subjects have leaked information that helped disclose the fact that they may not have been totally passive during the event and provided clearer details as to their real level of involvement.

During this initial narrative phase, do not interrupt the subject. If the subject appears to be lost in the story or acts as if he is not sure you are following his train of thought, he can be encouraged to continue with comments such as "Go on," or "Then what happened?" or "What did you do next?"

Should you immediately identify what appears to be deception during this narrative phase, it is critical that you do not attack the deception at this time. Even though the subject may have lied, we want him to continue the process because we may get more deceptive clues. We do not want to alert him to the fact that we have spotted deception and immediately create a hostile interview situation. We must also take into account the fact that we may have misdiagnosed the behavior as deceptive when, in fact, it may not be deception at all. By waiting for an opportunity to follow up on the issue, we may again see deception, and then we can be assured that what we saw was genuine and not a random behavior.

An important reason for not attacking immediately is that innocent subjects may at times withhold information from the interviewer. They do this because they may be embarrassed about the topic or about some act that they feel was foolish on their part. They will withhold information if they have some suspicions, but are not quite ready to confide those suspicions with another person in case they may be wrong. Innocent subjects may also withhold or omit critical information if they are still not quite sure about the interviewer's future intentions and what will be done with the information. Should we make an immediate attack on an innocent person, we are likely to alienate what was a cooperative person who would later have given us a great deal of critical data. The opportunity for "attacking" the deception will come later at a more appropriate time.

In this first level, all subjects are at low risk. This level of the interview allows subjects to focus on the information they feel is the most critical. An atmosphere is created for the cooperative or truthful subject to feel at ease in sharing information, and the reactions and assistance of the interviewer assure the subject that the interviewer is paying attention to what he is saying.

Should the subject be deceptive, this same atmosphere allows the subject to feel as if he is in control, at least for the time being. It gives him the opportunity to decide whether to be deceptive or truthful and which topics to be deceptive about. It permits the deceptive subject to at least once give the statement that he has most likely rehearsed several times before the interview. The comfort level for the deceptive subject, however, quickly disappears. Before long, the deceptive subject realizes that at least portions of his lie may have been uncovered, and now he has four choices. He has the option to continue to be deceptive, when at this point, it is going to become obvious that his credibility is taking a serious nosedive. He can create a new series of lies, but the subject also realizes the increased risk of disclosing that his first statement was deceptive and that subsequent deceptive statements may also be identified. The subject can refuse to give any more information, but this means that the only information he has given up to this point may already have been identified as deceptive, and it will be the only statement he has given. Finally, the subject may choose to tell the truth, which is what we, as the investigative interviewer, are really after in the first place. The bonus to this process is that the subject has put himself in this predicament with little effort on our part. We just provide an environment free of interference for the subject to make his own choice about telling the truth or to attempt to deceive us. Remember, your objectives at this point are to first, get as much information as possible, and second, determine whether the subject is truthful about the information he has provided.

After we have obtained the initial "narrative sample," we can move on to the "cross-examination" sample process. We now have the subject review his statement and retrieve information from more specific and narrower points of view. We do this by having the subject focus only on one "track" of information at a time. We can have the subject focus only on sights, sounds, touch, time, and so forth.

To accomplish this successfully, the subject must have some form of information stored on those tracks. Should the information that we are trying to obtain be incriminating or damaging to his case, he is going to have to find ways to circumvent our efforts at gathering this information. It is during his efforts to accomplish this game of misdirection that the deceptive subject is more likely to show signs of emotional arousal and cognitive disruption. These clusters of deceptive cues should coincide with the same point in the story during the narrative phase in which the subject generated similar reactions.

Interestingly, this same process recovers more details and with greater accuracy from the truthful person. He will find himself capable of generating quality information, and typically does a better job than he did on the narrative phase of the interview. Once again, the subject is made to feel as if the interviewer is genuinely listening and is assisting him in retrieving vital information (Fisher and Geiselman, 1992).

We can get the subject to focus on these individual tracks of information by asking him to describe only limited or specific types of data. The stimulus questions one might use are: "Mike, you've heard robbers tend to use the same approach for all their robberies. This is very important. I want you to think a moment just about their voices. Describe what each voice sounded like to you. I want you to repeat as best you can the exact words that each person said. If someone had been back in the bathroom and heard the robbery, what sounds would have been the loudest? What would they hear going on out by the front register?" We could ask similar questions about sounds that an engine made or peculiar noises from the car door, noises heard right before the smoke alarm went off, or even the noises heard during the crash.

For retrieving information from the sight track, the interviewer might ask which door the robber ran out when he left the bar: "When he ran past you, which part of his body did you see? In your mind's eye, stop him right there in front of you and describe him to me from the top of his head all the way down." "What color were the flames that you saw coming out of the corner of the building? How high was the smoke? How would you describe the smoke?" Ask questions that force the person to isolate only selected bits of detail. The interviewer can use the same type of questioning for smell, touch, and taste.

An additional track that one can "sample" is the time continuum. This track keeps all the others synchronized. The subject can be directed to the details oriented around time through a couple of methods. One effective method is to have the subject describe parts of the event in reverse order. This is not done by announcing to the subject, "All right. Tell me your story again, but this time tell it to me backwards." It is more effectively done by saying, for example, "Okay, Matt. There are parts of your story that I'm a little confused about. Can you go back to the part where Thomas hit Sharon? What was everybody doing and where were they standing just before that part happened?" "Allan, go back to the part when you were arguing with Nathan. What were you doing right before Lester came up to you, and go through that part again."

The results of this approach are often rewarding. Subjects who have chosen to rehearse or extensively memorize their story can't seem to keep the story straight when they do this, most likely because they have memorized the fictitious events in forward order. Yet apply the same approach to a cooperative person, and he is capable of maintaining the story line and including more specific details.

Case Study

While working on a case, the author was asked to interview a prisoner who had made a remark about a missing teenager. After spending a short period of time with the subject, during which he admitted making the statement, he eluded to the fact that he might know where the victim was located. After the subject told the story each time, the author would have the subject reverse small segments of his statement, and each time he would inadvertently give up small pieces of additional incriminating information. After a period of questioning, it was learned that the suspect and his friend owed the victim money for drugs. The victim kept demanding payment, and the two suspects kept putting him off. Eventually, the other suspect convinced the interviewed subject that they could get rid of the victim, hide his body, and no one would know what happened to him. The interviewed subject eventually revealed details of the beating death of the victim, including his participation in cleaning up the crime scene and digging the victim's grave near a flooded creek bank. Bits and pieces of the critical details had been gained by carefully reversing time-sequence elements of the subject's statements and pointing out the mistakes and inconsistencies each time.

At this point, if the interviewer feels he has enough information, he may want to proceed with the interrogation and progress to the next analysis statement. In that case, he uses the details gained from the narrative and cross-examination samples and makes an interrogation attack based on the subject's personality type. We will discuss the interrogation process and the development of the subject-specific interrogation later in this work.

The next statement samples to be obtained are those that focus on the cognitive and emotional tracks of the subject's memory. This phase is demanding, not only on the subject, but also on the interviewer. The interviewer must be confident that he can accomplish this approach and that he has considerable knowledge of the case. At this level, the subject will most likely be overconfident and feel that he has full control over the interview, as well as the interviewer. This particular approach works well on subjects who are highly intelligent and have a strong ego. In reality, these two characteristics work against the subject in the analysis level because ego and intelligence can be capitalized on by the interviewer, to the disadvantage of the subject.

The following two methods should be used only after the first two steps have been followed. They should never be used on subjects of low mental abilities, because this approach tends to give those subjects the impression that they are permitted to fantasize or make up stories about the crime, and that is not our objective. This approach can be used with caution if the interviewer realizes at some point in an interview with a mentally deficient subject that the subject is in the correct frame of mind to carry out this analysis.

This is described as the "third person" approach. The subject is asked about the thoughts and emotions of either the victim or the suspect at the time of the incident. Questions include: "What do you think she had in mind when she went to his house?" "Do you think he would have planned it that way?" "What should he have done differently?" "I know you weren't there, but you've known Craig for several years and you know what he's like. What would he do when he was mad?" "Children learn their behaviors from watching their parents and siblings. How would your son act around other adults? Was he outgoing?" "You worked with Shirley a long time. Would she ever leave the office at that time of day? Where do you think she was going?"

The interviewer wants to get the subject focused on the emotions and thoughts of the person or persons involved. We talk about things that are common to us and what we have experienced in the past. Pay close attention to details that only a person who was on the scene or involved in the incident would know.

Using the same approach, ask the subject to provide insight into what he predicts each person involved thought the other individuals were feeling. "Do you think he really knew how she felt?" "What did she think he was probably going to do?" "You have as much insight into what happened as the rest of us. Did Fred intend for Glenn to get there before him? Why? Why not?" This approach works extremely well on egotistical subjects. In this case, the interviewer should play down his knowledge, skills, and intelligence and feed the ego of the subject. It is as if the interviewer is paying deference to the subject's intelligence and insight, and he, as the lowly interviewer, has come to the fountain of knowledge to learn from the "wise man." The Ego Dominate subjects discussed later play into this approach quite well.

The Analysis

It is important to reiterate that no one "fails" this type of analysis. There is no breaking point at which we say anyone with a score above this point is truthful and anyone below this score is lying. Each analysis stands on its own merits. We are making an assessment of the overall credibility of the subject's statements based on the presence of clusters of cues generated during his response to our structured inquiry.

In this type of analysis, a cluster is defined as two or more symptoms per sentence or response. Once these clusters are identified, they will be the points on which we will focus our follow-up questions during the cross-examination phase of the interview. At that time, we can determine if the clusters are signs of deliberate deception or just an issue of guilty knowledge, embarrassment, or so forth.

If the interviewer notices that the statement seems to have a large number of "clusters" in the range of four or more throughout the statement, he should suspect that these "clusters" are not just minor occurrences. One or two random clusters — even in a truthful statement — are probably not unusual for the reasons already noted. However, growing numbers of clusters of four or more suggest that the subject is withholding a large amount of information for some significant reason. In this case, when the time comes for the investigator to consider the overall credibility of the statement, he would be best advised to work through the entire statement with the subject and not just the individual "cluster" sites. The subject, for some reason, is making a much more concerted effort to withhold information from the interviewer, and the reasons for such behavior need to be identified.

One of the main reasons for using this information retrieval and analysis process is to gain information of greater quantity and quality. It also provides an adaptable platform from which the investigator can conduct interviews of various types of subjects for different purposes. One of the habits that all interviewers tend to fall into is always conducting interviews from the same approach, using a single method every time. The results from these types of interviews are usually marginal because such a narrow approach has been used. It is recommended that for the best results, the interviewer try to obtain at least two statement samples from at least two different statement categories. It would be even more advantageous to get three samples, if possible. For example, we must get two narrative samples and one third person sample, or perhaps one of each: a narrative, cross-examination, and third person sample. The reason for alternating is to try and gain as much information as possible using different levels of retrieval. Using the same approach two or more times with the same subject has diminishing results. Using a varied approach challenges the subject's memory on several levels and elicits more-specific data from a broader range of information.

Documenting the Statements

The next issue to address is how we intend to document the statements the subjects generate. As noted earlier, there are times when the investigator has no choice as to the form in which he initially receives the statement because someone else conducted the initial interview. Depending on the subject's willingness to cooperate, we may not get the opportunity to conduct any follow-up interview. In that case, we have to settle for someone else's interview notes, the subject's previously prepared statement, or, if we are lucky, an audio recording or videotape of the interview.

The optimum choice for documenting any interview is to videotape the entire proceeding, conditions permitting. Videotaping provides future observers, such as in a court proceeding, to observe the actual conditions in the interview room, the interviewer's behavior, and the subject's entire verbal and nonverbal behaviors. There are presently few jurisdictions that use videotaping in their interview rooms (Geller, 1993). In some cases, after the subject has confessed, the subject will recap his confession on tape. Some agencies tape only felonies, while others tape entire interviews. The overwhelming evidence, however, is that videotaping provides protection, not only for the suspect, but also for the interviewer. It has also proven extremely valuable for the prosecution in preparing for trial and defending how voluntary the confession, the lack of true remorse on the part of the defendant, or during any plea-bargaining negotiations.

Other options for documenting the statements include the use of audiotaped or handwritten notes. Though audiotaping is quite valuable, it is not on the same par with videotaping because it cannot show the subject's physical demeanor, the interview setting, or the behavior of the interviewer. Another drawback is the case in which transcripts must be prepared. That can be a labor-intensive process, especially if the audio recording is of poor quality.

One of the least effective methods of documenting the interview is the interviewer taking handwritten notes. First, the practice becomes more of a process of dictation as opposed to the free exchange of information between the two parties (Moston, 1995; Gudjonsson, 1992; Walters, 1997). At the same time, the subject ends up having more control over the flow of the interview than does the interviewer (Irving and McKenzie, 1989; Gudjonsson, 1992). Most critical is that large amounts of significant information may never be recorded in the interview notes, or the topics most critical to the investigation get little and sometimes no attention at all.

Other interviewing habits have been identified in past studies of investigative interviewing and should be diligently avoided (Fisher and Geiselman, 1992). These include frequently interrupting the subject, asking too many short-answer questions, asking for information out of order from the sequence of events, and failing to follow up on any incomplete answers. We discussed the effects of negative interviewing habits earlier in this text.

Negative Credibility Cues

It is important to remember that the subject cannot "fail" our analysis. We are making a general assessment about the possible degree of the statement's credibility. The more cues we see in clusters, the more the statement drops in its level of credibility. No single cue or cluster carries more weight than another. Our goal is to generate as much information as possible from the subject and isolate any deception clusters for more direct cross-examination.

The negative-credibility cues are divided into four categories: procedural, verbal and nonverbal, written, and behavioral. The more cues from each category that are generated by the subject, the more the credibility of his statement diminishes.

Procedural cues are associated with the subject's overall attitude and response to the interview process in general.

1. Uncooperative — Does the subject make the interview process as difficult as possible? Perhaps he argues over the meaning of the Miranda Warning or argues that signing or not signing is a sure sign of guilt or innocence. The subject finds ways to be belligerent with the interviewer at every opportunity possible.

2. Won't follow instructions — The subject never wants to abide by any of the interviewer's requests. Symptoms include failing to show up at the time scheduled for the interview. He may refuse to start the discussion at a particular point on the timeline in the cross-examination statement. He may refuse to conduct the interview at a specific location or refuse to bring requested documents, papers, or other pertinent items.

3. Asks lots of questions — The subject tries to control the interview by asking lots of questions, such as how long the process will take. Does everyone else have to do the same thing? Who is going to see or hear this statement? Why do you want him to go through a portion of the statement again?

4. Stalling or delaying during the initial statements — Does the subject try to find ways to put off starting his statement? Does he give a lot of superfluous information first? Does he try to divert you from taking the statement?

An additional area to consider with regard to procedural cues is to pay attention to what the subject addresses as the main issue. A main issue is the crime, crime scene, or the subject's alibi. Which area does the subject start with, and what appears to be the most important issue to him? Normally, in an armed robbery , for example, the most important thing the clerk discusses right away is seeing the gun and being immediately afraid. For the rape victim, it might the moment that the assailant approached her outside her car in the parking lot. What does your subject think is the most important thing for you to hear initially?

1. Repeating the alibi — Is the most important point in your subject's initial response the alibi? Does he get it out as soon as possible and then keep repeating it like a broken record? It is as if he repeats it long enough and often enough, the whole case, and his possible involvement in it, will just go away.

2. Never discusses any main issue — Does the subject avoid the main issue completely? Is he more interested in talking about useless or insignificant minor details while time totally avoiding the crime or important crime scene elements?

3. Uses a numbering system to recall information — Some subjects utilize a form of sequence structure to keep their stories straight. You will find highly visible references to exact times, days, dates, locations, room numbers, and similar numbering systems to help them remember exact sequences (See Figure 5.1).

4. Memory compression — Does the subject compress several hours or even days of activity into brief phrases with few details when the opposite should be true?

5. Memory circumlocution — Does the subject describe what would normally be about 10 minutes of activity, but takes an inordinately long time to explain it?

We have already spent time on the identifiable verbal cues that subjects generate during their responses. It is exactly these types of clusters of cues that we are looking for in the content of the subject's statement. Some clusters of cues identify the high probability of deception, such as the section covering

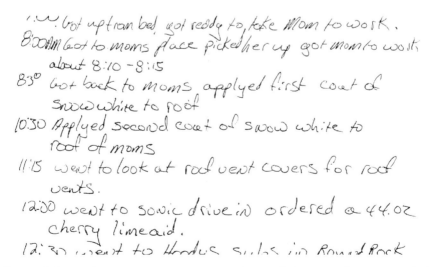

Figure 5.1 A subject's written statement that includes specific times to help establish his alibi and keep memorized events in order.

denial. Other sections, such as anger and depression, are of value in determining the subject's emotional reaction to the events and his current frame of mind. Some anger cues have incriminating value, but do not isolate specific points of deception. The same applies for the section on bargaining. Bargaining is the "disguising of reality," and these cues also have incriminating value to them.

Speech Dysfunctions:

1. Non-speech sounds: ah, er, um, uh, grunts, groans, growls, moans, whistles, sighs, or laughs.
2. Unclear thought line: omission of words, slurred words, clipped words, incomplete sentences, repetition of thoughts, sentence editing, halting speech, indirect ideas, stammering, stuttering, pausing.

Anger:

1. Attacks case facts.
2. Attacks the victim or witnesses.
3. Attacks the interviewer
4. Formal name changes.
5. Attacks minor details.
6. Attacks false issues.
7. Attacks your department or agency.
8. Uses sarcasm or profanity in the extreme.

Depression:

1. Speaks of feeling depressed.
2. Discusses health problems.
3. Mentions sleeping problems.
4. Mentions troubles with his personal life.
5. Discusses mental problems and worries.
6. Defames himself or makes derogatory comments about himself.
7. Mentions suicide.
8. Blames the issue at hand for causing his problems.

Denial:

1. Memory lapses: cannot recall, does not remember, too drunk or stoned to remember, etc. when discussing major points.
2. Denial-flag expressions: trust me, believe me, to tell the truth, honestly, etc.

3. Modifiers: basically, most of the time, hardly ever, almost, but, however, etc.
4. Circumlocution: long, wandering statements with little or no substance.
5. Weighted expressions: by the way, one more thing, incidentally.
6. Guilt phrases: I always get blamed. You have already made up your mind I'm guilty. Talks in third person. Do you want me to lie to you? Suppose I had this friend…?
7. Blocking statements: why would I do something like that? If I took the money, why didn't I pay my bills with it?
8. Vocabulary shifts: Verb tense is incorrect, changes language, uses different vocabulary other than his normal one.
9. Displacement: everybody, somebody, everyone, those people, them, they, someone, etc.
10. Stalling maneuvers: answers questions with a question, repeats questions, long pauses before answering, etc.
11. Surgical denial: narrow responses to only part of a question.
12. Deceptive "yes" or "no" response clusters.
13. Never discusses the crime scene.
14. Focuses his comments on minor details.
15. Leaves out or adds major information between statements.
16. Repeats previous portions of the statement events out of sequence.

Bargaining:

1. Complaining for sympathy: claims illness, alcoholism, drug abuse, on medication, just came from the doctor, etc.
2. Minimizing: deliberate downplay of behaviors, such as "borrowed" the money, "hurt," "misspoke," and other "soft" words.
3. Gray answers: only took a "few" of them, it has been "awhile" back, not very many.
4. Religious remarks: wants to pray with you, claims to be very religious, swearing of an oath, swearing on a grave, brings a Bible, etc.
5. Personal moral code: I was raised better that that. I'm a former Boy Scout. I'm a good mother. I'm a loyal employee.
6. Overly courteous: extremely cooperative, overdoes the "sir" or "ma'am," extremely complimentary, etc.
7. Name dropping: mentions the names of people you may both know as a character reference. Professes to know one of your family members or close associate, etc.

There are times when the only way the investigator can get a statement from a subject is in the written form. Another investigator may have already obtained the statement or someone else has already conducted an initial interview. Although neither of these are ideal situations, there is no need to despair, because all is not lost. The same words and phrases we use when we speak are also present in the content of our writing. An advantage for the interviewer and a disadvantage for the subject is the fact that the subject has more time to try to edit his writings. That extra time can, in fact, be the undoing of the subject's attempts at protecting himself from discovery. His efforts at editing his remarks show up in obvious writing cues (Skinner, 1952, 1992).

It is critical for the person making the credibility analysis of a written statement to remember that these writing cues are not signs of deception. In and of themselves, they will not discriminate between truthful and deceptive statements nor truthful or deceptive writers. These writing cues are more specific as to the emotional change that is occurring in the subject at the time of the writings. The writer is reacting to his own writings in anticipation of how the reader is going to interpret the writings (Skinner, 1952, 1992).

An analogy we can use to help explain this change is to think of the task of the writer of a Sunday newspaper comic strip. If the cartoonist wants the reader to get the impression that the character he has drawn is yelling, the letters in the conversation balloon above the character's head are in large type and bold print. If the character is to be portrayed as whispering, the opposite would be true — the letters are small and in fine print. If the character is speaking like a Shakespearean actor, the font selected for the words might be Old English or Book Antigua. All these types of changes in writing are ways of expressing different emotions, emphasis, and speaking styles. Do not over-value these cues, however, for they are nothing more than representations of subconscious emotional and cognitive changes in your subject. For the most part, the subject is not fully aware of why he is writing differently. There is no value in pointing out these changes to the subject in hopes of increasing pressure on him to acknowledge that he is being deceptive or that the changes are significant.

Written Cues

1. Switching from cursive to block printing or from block printing to cursive. This is seen when a specific word or phrase is important (see Figure 5.2).
2. Capital letters: pay particular attention to words and phrases in which the subject has chosen to capitalize all the letters in each word. Inappropriate capitalization of the first letter of a word is not significant. Only if all the letters in a word or all the letters in all the words in a phrase or sentence are capitalized is this significant. This issue is important, and the subject needs for it to stand out from the rest of the writings around it (see Figures 5.2 and 5.3).

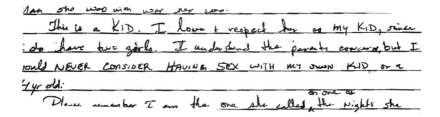

Figure 5.2 The subject started writing in cursive, but changed to block printing, and then back to cursive. Notice the topic areas that are in block printing. Also notice that the block printing is all in capital letters.

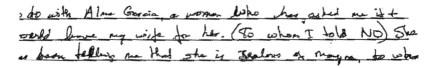

Figure 5.3 The subject started writing in cursive, but at one point used capital block letters to write "NO" as if to shout the word to the reader.

3. Underlining passages: this is done to call the reader's attention to what the writer considers important. He does not want you to overlook this issue or take it lightly.

4. Retracing letters or words: occasionally, during his self-editing, the writer questions his own choice of words. He will retrace a word or phrase to put it in darker or bolder print. Retracing also happens when the writer inadvertently starts a word with the wrong letter. This may be due to oversight or a subtle slip in self-editing.

5. Erasing or scratching out sections of the statement: these are usually incidents of major editing cues on the part of the subject (see Figures 5.4 and 5.5).

6. Tearing up statements and starting over: another form of significant self-editing. If this occurs in your interview room and you have an opportunity, retrieve the destroyed statement. Review the contents, and compare the "draft" version with the final version, and notice the distinct differences.

7. Noticeable changes in writing pressure: changes in writing pressure with the writing instrument suggest significant changes in the subject's emotional status and the strength of that emotional change. Pay particular attention to what was being written when the writing style changed. This includes changes in the slant of the letters and the speed at which the section was written (see Figure 5.6).

8. Shifts in letter size: as in the example of the cartoonist, notice when the subject's written characters change size. Larger size is to be noticed, as if the subject is shouting the information. Small characters suggest an attempt at lighter emphasis and an attempt to avoid calling attention to the content.

9. Adding words or phrases in the margins: an editing attempt on the part of the subject. The subject has all the time in the world to think about his writings. Why, after having written a section, would he think it necessary to go back and add details? Once again, the writer is concerned about the interpretations that are going to be made by the reader (see Figure 5.7).

There is a class of behaviors in which some subjects engage that are hard to classify and, frankly, that would be hard to study scientifically. The

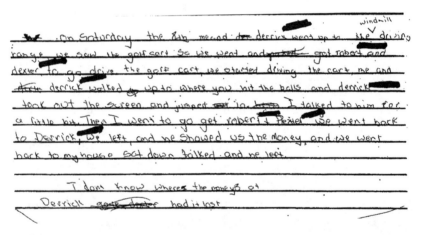

Figure 5.4 In this statement, the subject continually scratches out the name "Dexter." Perhaps the writer is protecting Dexter or is fearful of retribution from Dexter.

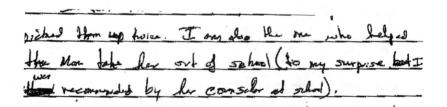

Figure 5.5 The subject writing this statement scratched out a couple of points in the parentheses. This is a form of editing that may suggest concern over the initially chosen word or words.

behaviors do not have a direct link to the content of the interview nor to the content of the subject's statements. They are merely behavior phenomenon that cast a shadow over the person's overall appearance of credibility.

Behavioral Cues:

1. Subject asks for a copy of the statement: perhaps this is to remember what he told you so he can keep it straight the next time. This would exclude situations in which state "sunshine laws" apply to different types of government hearings. It also would not apply to union settings during the grievance process, when copies of hearings or disciplinary interviews are the right of the employee.
2. Subject asks for a list of questions in advance: it makes you think he wants the "test questions" ahead of time so he can study for the "final exam."

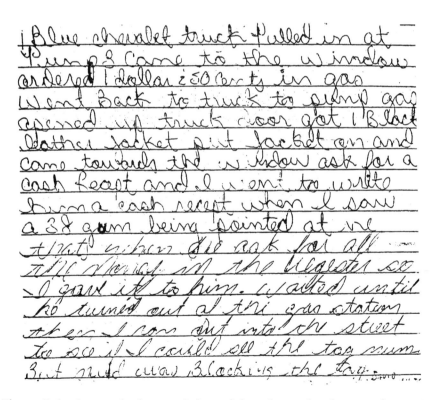

Figure 5.6 Observe the form and slant of the subject's handwriting, but notice the change in form and slant when he discusses the money exchange with the robber. This was a false robbery report.

3. Subject wants to read previous statements: this could be his previous statements or the statements of other subjects or witnesses. He wants a chance to adjust his statement or to discredit negative information made about him in other statements.

4. Brings friends or witnesses: suspicion is frequently aroused when the subject brings along his own character witnesses or a friend to sit in on the interview and support him. It might be to receive counseling advice from that friend or to act on his behalf later when the interview itself may be called into question. Again, this does not apply to employees protected under specific union rules.

5. Brings family members: subjects show up with parents, siblings, or spouses. Perhaps today the baby sitter couldn't take care of the toddler, and the toddler becomes the perfect distraction or even the excuse to end the interview early.

6. Brings a tape recorder: subjects do this to help remember their statements later or to intimidate the interviewer. Whether or not to allow the subject to tape the interview is up to the interviewer.

7. Takes notes during the interview: this is another version of having a tape recorder. In some cases, subjects have brought along a friend or spouse to take notes for them (see items 4 and 5).

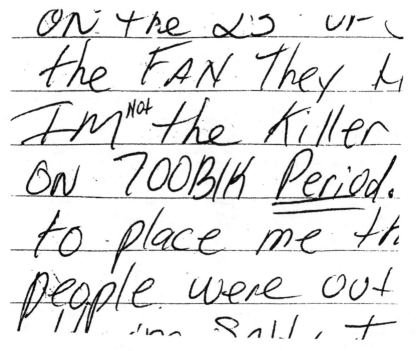

Figure 5.7 Oops! This subject forgot to write "no" in the middle of his statement "I'm not the killer." He added it after he caught his mistake.

8. Brings papers and documents: subjects may show up with their evidence file filled with worthless documents as their form of proof. These include phone bills, television grids, schematic drawings or sketches, pay stubs, employee manuals, insurance documents, weather reports, and newspaper articles. In some cases, the subjects are even energetic enough to research local laws or court decisions and bring copies along to support their arguments.

9. Brings a prepared statement: these prepared statements may be ones they have prepared in advance or statements someone else has written in advance. Some subjects even take the time to get the statements notarized to prove their integrity. The interviewer is well advised to take the statement from the subject, but then reinterview the subject without a statement to which he can refer.

10. Mails the statement: excellent way to avoid having to come in and do a face-to-face interview. "I'm too busy. I'll prepare one and send it to you to save each of us some time." Don't be surprised if it comes express delivery, special courier, or overnight express courier.

11. Faxed or e-mailed statement: the objective here is the same as in item 10. This way, the subject doesn't have to talk to the interviewer face-to-face.

12. Multiple suspects with duplicate statements: it would not necessarily be unusual for two or three people who have witnessed the same event to have similar descriptions of that event. It would not be unusual if they quoted the same phrases that a suspect spoke or described similar actions. What would be unusual is if the statements had major sentences, phrases, or even paragraphs that were almost identical to each other when the response for each subject should be unique. It appears that the subjects have memorized or rehearsed exactly what each was going to say, down to almost the exact same lines.

13. Memory reanimation: this is a form of nonverbal "illustrator" that will be discussed in the section covering body language. When a subject is discussing a particularly significant event, notice when the subject reenacts some of the physical actions. He will re-create actions; draw virtual maps with his hands; demonstrate the use of weapons; and demonstrate the size, shape, or location of weapons, cars, buildings, or people by using the hands, arms, or the rest of the body. These are not signs of deception, but it is an extremely interesting human memory phenomenon to watch. Typically, these movements are done at just below the conscious awareness of the subject. There are times when the subject may make inadvertent reenactments that don't match his verbal descriptions.

Conclusion

The purpose of the Practical Kinesic Information Recovery and Statement Credibility Assessment is to provide the interviewer with a template to following during the interview. It is designed to assist the interviewer in retrieving statements and information from each subject in an organized fashion and in a form that is conducive to further assessment for credibility. At the same time, it has a low-impact approach to the interview, in that, being narrative-based, it is least likely to contaminate a subject's statement. It will prove more productive in gaining larger amounts of information and details from all interview subjects, from which the investigator can develop essential follow-up leads.

The best way to master the process is to practice. One ideal form of practice is to pull out some old cases and review any documented statements made during the investigation using the tools described in this chapter. What will be of great help is the fact that the case has been resolved, and the investigator will be able to validate the results of his review with the outcome of the case. He will find that there may have been critical information that was developed early in the case, but was overlooked because its significance was not identified at the time.

Nonverbal Behaviors

6

Nonverbal behavior is a direct visual representation indicating the development of the fight-or-flight survival response in the subject. If our verbal behaviors give the observer cues to our thoughts, then our body language gives away our emotions, any stress we may be experiencing, and the degree of that stress. The stronger the emotional or stress response we are experiencing, the harder it is for us to censor it from the view of an observer (Darwin, 1872; Darwin and Ekman, 1998). As a result of this connection between emotions and nonverbal behavior, observation of body language changes and clusters is a relatively more accurate source for determining deception with regards to emotion. The stress response is demonstrated through the four stress–response states of anger, depression, denial, and bargaining, or by the absence of fight-or-flight, which is evidence of acceptance.

In reviewing the different levels of stress that subjects generate during their responses and as they react to the interviewer and the interview environment, you will recall that we classified some behaviors as falling under the heading of "general stress." These are typically the types of behaviors that we all generate under stress situations. They tend to be prevalent, but have little value individually as markers of possible deception. Each of us has our own range of stress-reaction behaviors. If someone were to watch our behaviors over an extended period of time, he would find that our reactions are fairly consistent. This consistent pattern of stress response on the individual level is what is referred to as a "defensive demeanor profile" (Davis, Walters, et al., 2000; Davis, Walters, et al., 1999). We generate these cues, for example, when we are caught in a traffic jam and running late for an appointment, concerned about an upcoming job interview, or that the store is going to close before we get that anniversary present. These are the general reactions we have to everyday stress-creating events. As investigative interviewers, we see them frequently in interviews. We may see these cues when taking a statement from the rape victim, the store clerk who has been robbed, the witness to the fatal accident, and so forth. They are good for determining the general level of stress the person is experiencing and which emotional and intellectual mechanisms may be at work as the person tries to cope with the problem. These cues are also frequently seen in the company of deception signals. The problem with these general stress cues, however, is that they tend to be distracting. As they occur, they may draw our attention away from the more reliable cues to deception.

The second form of stress signals indicates "incriminating stress." These are cues that both truthful and deceptive people are capable of generating. However, when we do a side-by-side comparison of the performance of truthful and deceptive subjects, we find that deceptive subjects have a higher rate of occurrence of these cues, which appear more as signs of "evasion" than outright deception (Davis, Connors, et al., 1999; Walters, 2000). When these symptoms occur, it should suggest to us that there is something important about the issue in general. It would be well worth our time and energy to explore the topic at greater length and in more detail with the subject. During this exploration, we need to focus our attention on the subject's responses, looking and listening for the more reliable cues to deception — the "discriminators."

The "discriminators," or discriminating stress cues, is our third category. The observance of these cues in clusters suggests there is a high probability that the subject is being deceptive. When observed in the scientific setting, these cues show a high occurrence rate with moments of deception (Davis, Connors, et al., 1999; Walters, 2000). These cues are significant when they occur while the subject is responding to some inquiry or similar stimulus from the interviewer. The nonverbal forms of these discriminators include aversion, negation, performance, contradictions, and control cues.

Aversion cues are body movements that indicate an "away" reaction, such as the body markedly moving away from the interviewer in some form during the subject's response. It also includes aggressive movements, gestures, and similar actions. Negation behaviors are any form of covering or blocking of the mouth, eyes, or other parts of the head, and other "covering" signs. Performance cues are those in which the subject appears to be "putting on" or "acting" or, more appropriately, "overacting" his response in an attempt to "sell" his reaction to the observer. Performance cues tend to be a little more complex and at times hard to decipher. They are also at the low end in the range of reliable behaviors of deception. Contradiction behaviors are also less frequent, but are significant in locating a less-than-truthful response. Contradiction behaviors are verbal and nonverbal cues that are in conflict with each other, in that one cue reports one type of response or emotion, while another cue generated at the same times indicates a totally different meaning. Control cues indicate significant moments when a subject attempts to suppress some form of nonverbal reaction, such as hanging on tightly to the arms of the chair, or a deliberate "frozen" body position when the subject had been moving freely previous to the critical question.

It is important to put the correct amount of weight on the value of body language signals. There are many cases in which interviewers have claimed that they do not need to observe or diagnose the verbal behaviors of a subject because body language will tell them everything they need to know about a person's credibility. In reality, however, there are times when a person is deceptive and there may not be any discernible body language cues of deception (Davis, Connors, et al., 1999; Walters, 2000). Verbal and nonverbal cues are interdependent upon each other. When observing body language, the observer needs to remember that it is not the body movement itself that is important; it is what the movement means. In other words, what is the meaning and purpose behind the behavior that the subject has generated (Skinner, 1953, 1992)? "Meaning" is not a property of the nonverbal action, but the conditions under which the behavior has occurred. This is what is important to understand and diagnose. A deceptive person is not what causes the signals that we see and hopefully identify correctly, but it is involved with various emotional processes that influence our behaviors (Zuckerman, DePaulo, et al., 1981). The main process is the arousal of the person under stress and his attempts to control his symptoms, along with any feelings of guilt, anxiety, and in some cases, pleasure over the deception event.

Nonverbal behaviors, or body language symptoms, generated by subjects are often abundant. We noted earlier that possibly as much as 65% of human communication is nonverbal. In comparison, the total amount of verbal cues reach only 20%. The primary reason for this phenomenon is because subjects are, in general, not as vigilant in their efforts to control body language symptoms as they are to conceal verbal cues. We innately recognize that our verbal behavior is more efficient for personal communication and is going to be regarded more carefully by those listening to us. Our next Practical Kinesic Principle addresses this phenomenon:

A person is better able to control verbal signals than to conceal and monitor nonverbal symptoms.

Due to this awareness of verbal behavior and lack of focus on controlling nonverbal behavior, there is a trade-off in the amount of cues generated from both systems. Subjects tend to generate fewer verbal cues, but those cues that are generated are important in analyzing that person's credibility. On the other hand, because we do not monitor our body language as diligently, there tends to be a lot of body language. This, however, creates a unique situation for the observer. First, the person may generate a lot of "uncensored" nonverbal information that is important in assessing the subject's emotional responses and stress reactions to each issue. The drawback, however, is that there are a large number of nonverbal cues that have nothing to do with deception. As a result of this "nonverbal static," the observer can be distracted trying to watch all the nonverbal behavior and still, at the same time, miss a significant nonverbal cue when it does occur.

Although there may be a large number of body language symptoms from a particular subject, individually, these symptoms, at times, may not have the same value as individual verbal cues. Yet there are other times when a nonverbal cue may be extremely important because it appears at one of those unguarded moments, and the subject may leak some important nonverbal cues that are a contradiction to his verbal message, indicating a high probability of deception. When this happens, we must look for the multiple-symptom phenomenon called a "cluster." Amidst all the information seen in a nonverbal cluster, some of the individual cues may be nothing more than stress reactions and emotional behavior. Yet these stress- and emotional-behavior cues can be wrapped around a deception signal.

A body language cluster that is of significance to the interviewer tends to be larger than a verbal cluster. Verbal clusters often contain several general-stress cues alongside nonverbal cues of deception. The interviewer must accurately identify those significant behaviors while dismissing symptoms of little importance, also remembering that the symptoms must be timely. Such nonverbal reactions should also occur consistently when the interviewer carries the conversation into problem areas.

Recent research on body language and deception confirm what earlier studies have concluded: there is not a single body language symptom that conclusively indicates deceptive behavior (Davis, Connors, et al., 1999; Davis, Walters, et al., 1999; Walters, 2000; Davis, Walters, et al., 2000; Ekman, 1992). Body language is best considered as a means of confirming the symptoms and information generated verbally and alongside other nonverbal cues. When verbal and nonverbal cues are incongruent, there is strong probability of deception on the part of the subject. By the same measure, there is a strong possibility of deception if the person generates body language cues that are incongruent when compared to each other. We have referred to these types of conflicting signals as "contradictions."

Body language symptoms are like the gauges and dials on the dashboard of an automobile. The gauges inform the driver about the vehicle's speed, distance traveled, fuel level, water temperature, and so on. In short, the gauges tell the driver how the car is functioning.

So, too, does the body tell the interviewer how the subject is functioning. By accurately reading the body's gauges and comparing their readouts to the verbal output, the observer can improve his diagnosis of the subject's emotional, mental, and psychological states. In keeping with the analogy that the body is providing a visual readout, we will divide the body into four primary gauges, using the acronym, "HEAL," which stands for head, eyes, arms, and legs. Seeing the body as generating information through these four "gauges" streamlines the decoding procedure. When these four gauges are incongruent with each other or with the verbal cues generated by the subject, there is a high probability of deception.

The Head

The head is generally the easiest part of the body for a person to control. The features of the head and face can be regarded as our main communication center. We are more conscious of the symptoms we generate from the head than from the rest of the body (Ekman and Friesen, 1974). We are less likely, for example, to be aware that our legs and feet are generating a great deal of information about our internal status.

Through various forms of expressions, eye contact, etc., we provide feedback information to the listener, as well as using the behaviors as an enhancement to our verbal expressions (Knapp, 1978). In the same context, as the speaker, we look for return expressions from the person with whom we are communicating to discern his reaction to our message. His expressions tell us if he is receiving our message and if he believes its content. We also watch the listener's reaction to determine if there is any negative reinforcement for our behaviors and comments. As a result of our inability to control all of our nonverbal symptoms, some of them may begin to percolate through our defensive efforts. As this "emotional seepage" occurs, the observer will notice an imbalance in our overall body language.

Head Positions

A person listening to and interested in comments made by another often tilts the head to one side or the other (Darwin, 1872; Darwin and Ekman, 1998). In some cases, you may notice that the person's hand is open and flat against the side of the face. For the interviewer, this is a positive sign, because it indicates that the subject is listening. Our minimum goal is to get the subject to at least listen to us as we try to dismantle his efforts at denial and other negative reactions. We have all, at one time or another, been amused by the young dog or cat that tilts its head and twitches its ears upon hearing a new sound. These actions indicate that the animal is listening and trying to evaluate this interesting sound. The implication is the same for the subject.

A negative state is indicated when the subject's head remains straight, with no tilt to either side. Such a subject, in fact, may be in the state of anger. A review of other facial expressions and body language may confirm this. In particular, if the interviewer notices that the side of the jaw is twitching or flexing, there is a high probability of at least suppressed anger. This twitching or flexing is noticed at a position on one or both sides of the face, in front of or below the ear.

If the observer notices that the subject appears to be thrusting his chin up or out while facing the interviewer, the interviewer can assume that the subject is hostile regarding the issue or even the interviewer. The fists might also be clenched; there might be aggressive finger-pointing, and the chest may even be puffed up or thrust outward.

If the subject's head sinks down onto the chest, with the chin nearly resting on the sternum, and if the eyes are also lowered, this may be indicative of either depression or acceptance, and is a symptom typical of resignation (see Figure 6.1). When deciphering signs of acceptance or depression, it is imperative for the interviewer to remember that the body language symptoms of both acceptance and depression have the same appearance. The best way to distinguish between the two is to pay close attention to the verbal cues the

Figure 6.1 An example of resignation or "submission behavior" from a subject. Notice the bowed head and rounded shoulders.

subject generates. As discussed earlier, verbal cues of depression and acceptance are quite different from each other and represent totally different states
of mind.

If the subject appears to have dropped his head onto the chest, but his
eyes are focused on the interviewer, the subject is not experiencing either
depression or acceptance. Most likely, the subject's eyes will be either looking
over the rims of glasses or through the eyebrows. The chin has not really
"dropped" so much as the person has tucked the chin in towards the neck.
This "chin tuck" posture can be a variation of an aversion behavior (see
Figure 6.2). Instead of the subject turning the head away from the interviewer
in a typical rejection behavior, the subject is drawing the head back. In this
case, during the subject's response, the subject's behavior is likely to be
deceptive. If this behavior is noticed while the interviewer is talking, the
subject is most likely in an aggressive- or anger-response state.

Figure 6.2 Subject demonstrating "chin tuck" head behavior. Notice the subject
is making hard eye contact with interviewer to his right.

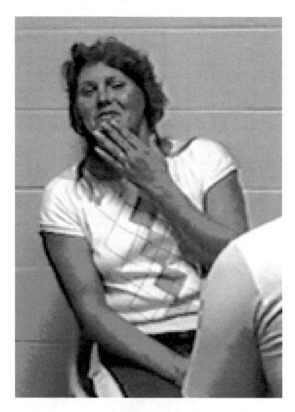

Figure 6.3 Female subject showing head "aversion" behavior. At the same time, she is covering her mouth and laughing.

A significant cue to possible deception is aversion behavior as it relates to changes in the position of the head. In this case, the subject turns his entire head or face away from the interviewer at the moment of response (see Figures 6.3 and 6.4). The head may rotate on the neck, with the face turning away. Another variation is the head leaning away from the interviewer, with or without the face turning away from the observer as well. Frequently, the upper torso and sometimes a large portion of the trunk of the subject's body leans away also. The interviewer should be sure to mentally document other verbal and nonverbal cues of deception to confirm that there has been a deception cluster, and not make his diagnosis on any single cue.

Facial Color

There are times when, despite our best efforts, our body telegraphs the presence of stress. Dramatic changes in facial color are one of those indications (Darwin, 1872; Darwin and Ekman, 1998). At stress points, the interviewer may notice the subject's face and the sides of his neck turn chalky white. This

Figure 6.4 Male subject showing "aversion" behavior. Notice the subject is laughing and that body is generally leaning away from the interviewer.

is due to the reduction of blood to the cutaneous capillaries just below the surface of the skin.

In fight-or-flight situations, the body's response systems often cause the cutaneous capillaries to constrict. This is done to force the blood into the deep muscle tissue and into the core of the body. Since blood in the cutaneous capillaries contributes to our skin tone, to remove one of these color pigments causes the skin to appear lighter. A similar response also occurs when, due to the shock impact of the question or statement, the subject's blood pressure drops quickly. It may appear that the subject is going to faint — another good sign of stress.

A converse reaction may also occur. At "hot" questions, the interrogator may notice the subject's face and neck turning red. The same cutaneous capillaries are now dilated, allowing a greater blood flow. The investigator may see the red develop in blotches on the face and neck, or the color may literally "crawl" up the neck toward the head. The whites of the eyes may get red, and, in some cases, red may appear inside the ears. Subjects presenting these reactions are likely more oriented toward the "fight" side of the stress–response spectrum.

Under severe stress, the interviewer may see the skin around the subject's eyes or mouth turn dark. The color can be black, blue, or dark brown. This means that the blood is under high demand for oxygen and the nutrients necessary to maintain the increased metabolic rate the body experiences during a fight-or-flight situation. The suspect may appear to be suffering from cyanosis similar to that experienced by heart attack or stroke victims.

Facial Expressions

No single facial expression indicates guilt on the part of the subject, but facial expressions can help the interviewer identify the subject's emotional-response status (Ekman and Friesen, 1975; Knapp, 1978). The primary reading and also the easiest one for the observer to decipher is which emotion the subject is currently experiencing. These are usually basic expressions and those that the speaker is either not trying to hide or not fully aware that he is generating. These tend to be fairly accurate measures of the subject's current emotional state.

The next element of the expression that can be observed is the degree to which the person is experiencing a particular emotion. The strength of the emotion is evident by the "depth" of the expression lines created by the facial muscles (Ekman and Friesen, 1972; Ekman, 1969; Ekman, 1992). In other words, the more the facial muscles are involved in the expression and the deeper the expression lines on the face, the greater the intensity of the emotion being experienced. In this manner, we can determine that the person is not only angry, but very angry. Perhaps he is just not sad, but very depressed, and so forth. Those expressions that are usually strong are accompanied by both other body language cues and straightforward verbal cues.

At the moment that the subject is faced with an accusation, the interrogator may see what appears to be a look of pleasure with a defiantly challenging overtone. The response status of the subject is anger. The negative-reaction state of anger also exists when the subject responds to a question with a cold, hard stare. The intensity level of this anger is greater than in the previous example. A cluster of behaviors indicating denial includes facial expression as well as signs from the arms and legs. At the accusatory question, the subject may have a facial expression of defiance along with crossed arms protecting the torso and crossed legs protecting the genitals. Crossing behaviors of the arms and legs will be explored in a later section.

If a subject is aware that his facial expressions can be deciphered by a skilled observer, he may try to suppress his expressions. As a result, other facial symptoms may appear instead. For example, the interrogator may spot what can be called a "stone face." The subject may try to freeze an expression on his face. This is a type of "performance" cue in that the subject is trying to deliberately project a particular emotional response in an effort to control or manipulate the interviewer. Should the interrogator observe the "stone face" on his subject, he should interpret the expression as being false. Most often, the facial expression demonstrated is opposite of what the suspect is really experiencing internally.

During conversation, the facial expressions of the participants often change. These changes occur as the speaker attempts to add visual representation to the emotions attached to his words. The listener's expressions change as he inputs and responds to the speaker's comments. Periods of time without these characteristic changes suggest that either the listener is not really hearing what is being said or is suppressing his true mental and emotional reactions. This is a form of nonverbal control, or "concealment," and suggests possible deception, in that for some reason he feels the need to conceal his true emotions from the interviewer.

Another interesting nonverbal cluster involves a facial expression along with an incongruent level of arm and leg activity. Take note of a calm expression on the face while there is a remarkable increase in the movements of the arms and legs (see Figures 6.5 and 6.6). The subject, through attempts to control his kinesic signals, may be able to inhibit symptoms generated from the face, but emotional seepage occurs because of inability to control signals from other areas of the body. These are the types of inconsistent body language clusters that strongly suggest deception on the part of a subject.

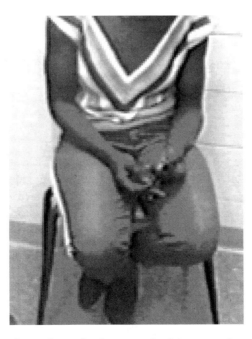

Figure 6.5 This subject showed calm upper body posture, but demonstrated she was experiencing significant stress by wringing her hands constantly.

Figure 6.6 This subject is showing general stress behavior as he picks at his fingers and fingernails during his interview.

Facial Tics

Facial tics take the form of grossly exaggerated muscle spasms on the sides of the face and neck, although they can sometimes include the arms and legs. A high percentage of the time, they are strong signs of stress and possible deception. These facial tics last between one-fourth to one-half of a second. They are uncontrollable responses to fight-or-flight situations, and are the result of the facial and skeletal nerves misfiring because of the dramatic chemical changes occurring in the body. Tics around the face are often incomplete or suppressed muscle movements.

Another form of inconsistent facial expression occurs when the interviewer identifies what appear to be two different emotional expressions on the face (Ekman and Friesen, 1975; Knapp, 1978; Ekman, 1992). These are described as "blended expressions." They are an extended form of a facial tic. For example, the mouth may demonstrate what appears to be an attempt at a smile, but the eyes show strong aggression. Similarly, the person could try to appear happy, but demonstrate a subtle "depression" or "emotional pain" signal with the eyebrows. In each of these cases and similar configurations, there is a strong emotional response occurring within the subject, but for fear of negative reinforcement or even possibly anticipated eventual punishment from the listener, the speaker tries to mask the strong emotion with the performance of a contrary nonverbal expression. The strength of the felt emotion overrides the "performed" response and bleeds through, creating a blended expression.

The Nose

The nose is the most stress-sensitive part of the body. There is delicate erectile tissue in the nose that engorges with blood when an increase in blood pressure occurs. This same tissue constricts as blood pressure drops.

As previously discussed, the fight-or-flight response creates numerous physiological changes, including changes in heart rate and blood pressure. The constant mental and emotional fluctuations that occur during interviews play havoc with the erectile tissue in the nose. The result is a stimulation of the nasal membranes that requires relief by touching, scratching, pinching, or massaging. In the high-stress areas of an interview, watch for an increase in the number of times the subject's hands move to the head. When these incidents occur, watch for more than 50% of the touching to occur in an area referred to as the "facial touch target." As with covering the eyes, this is a form of "negation" that has a significant association with deception (see Figures 6.7 through 6.10).

The purpose of negation behavior by a subject is a subconscious intent to hide "leaks" of emotion from the face. Although, as the speaker, we are not as keenly aware of our body language as we are of our verbal cues, we are most aware of the head and face as compared to the rest of the body. In that our speech and responses to inquiries from others may create the risk of triggering negative responses or even sanctions from the listener, we may want to guard some of our expressions from the observer's view. Negation behaviors act like a filter, and by partially hiding the nonverbal facial expressions, we may be less likely to bring punishment or other rejection sanctions upon ourselves. The covering of the nose as a negation cue may be a less obvious behavior than completely covering or blocking the mouth. Therefore, touching or covering the nose may be a detour or diversion on the way to covering the mouth.

The Practical Kinesic Principle involved here is:

**Deceptive subjects tend to have a greater number of touches
to the head than do truthful subjects.**

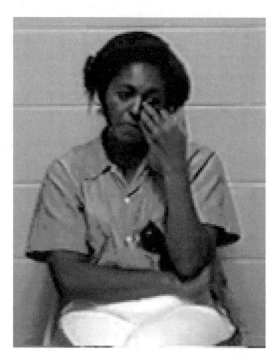

Figure 6.7 Subject showing negation behavior of covering the face by playing with her nose.

The primary facial-touch target is an area that extends from halfway down the nose to the middle of the chin, or just below the bridge of the nose to just below the bottom lip. The outside edges of this "circle" extend about one-fourth to one-half inch outside the corners of the lips.

If you have ever noticed someone pinching his nose shut, your immediate interpretation is that the individual has gotten a strong whiff of an unpleasant odor. The nonverbal implication is that "this stinks." Think of the same analogy if you see nose-touching behaviors in the interview room.

If you are talking about specific aspects of your investigation or particular evidence that is damaging to the suspect, look for an increase in activity around the facial-touch target. The interpretation is that the subject does not like the information and is going through stress trying to deal with it. In other words, the subject is nonverbally telling you that your statements "stink" and he doesn't like them.

If the subject is making verbal statements to the interviewer about how he is not involved or he is giving an alibi or similar statements, an increase in activity in the facial-touch target now has a slightly different meaning. The subject's movements in the facial-touch target now indicate that he is aware his statements are false and are probably unbelievable. In other words: "I know my own comments stink."

Figure 6.8 Negation behavior by a subject who is pinching his nose between his fingers.

The Mouth

Verbal signals are the most productive, as well as the easiest symptoms for the interviewer to spot and decode. As a result, the subject is more aware of his verbal cues than of his nonverbal cues and therefore tends to be more vigilant in controlling verbal cues. However, there are various mechanical, or nonverbal, cues that the mouth can give.

In the previous section covering verbal cues, we reviewed bargaining behavior. One of the bargaining-response cues discussed was that of the subject being entirely too friendly or helpful to the interviewer. This is done to gain acceptance from the interviewer in hopes that the interviewer will go easy on the subject (Skinner, 1952, 1992). A body language sign of bargaining that may accompany the friendly verbal behavior is the use of the "false smile." This "false smile" is a "performance" behavior suggesting that the person is putting on an expression to mislead the other person. A true smile engages the facial muscles differently than does a "false smile." True smiles involve the cheeks, lips, and eyes. During a true smile, the lips tend to be fuller and

Figure 6.9 The subject is rubbing the side of his nose with his hand and partially blocking the face in a negation behavior.

the corners of the mouth turn up, while in a false smile, the lips become thin, retracting tightly against clenched teeth (Darwin, 1872; Darwin and Ekman, 1998; Ekman, 1992). During a true smile, the person's cheeks tend to rise and the eyes often take on the appearance of a smile (Darwin, 1872; Darwin and Ekman, 1998; Ekman, 1992). The "false smile" is that large, toothy grin the subject may give the interviewer when he is attempting to be overly friendly. The "false smile" is frequently characterized by a wide smile with only the upper teeth and gum showing. In particular, the eyeteeth or the canine teeth are prominently displayed. These are considered the flesh-tearing teeth. In the animal kingdom, this expression is considered to be a defensive sign (Gray, 1971). It signals to other animals that the subject animal will not attack, but will vigorously defend itself from any perceived attack.

When a subject is demonstrating bargaining through verbal cues and nonverbal facial expressions, the interviewer should scan the rest of the subject's body for other symptoms, particularly the other features of the face, such as the eyes and jaw. Quite often, you will spot other signals being generated that are contradictory to the bargaining behavior the subject is displaying on the surface.

Figure 6.10 The subject is covering the face by rubbing his nose during negation. Notice that the subject also has his head turned down and away from the interviewer.

An interesting behavior involving the mouth is the yawn that occurs during periods of slight to moderate fear or stress (Darwin, 1872; Darwin and Ekman, 1998; Gray, 1971). Yawning occurs when there is a lack of oxygen in the blood. This oxygen deprivation occurs due to the body's increased metabolic demands. As mentioned, the metabolic rate is increased during fight-or-flight situations. More significant, however, is that along with the increased intake of oxygen, the yawn is part of an overall physiological response that also triggers the release of a neural stimulant into the bloodstream (Gray, 1971). This stimulant triggers the body into a higher level of readiness, as if to prepare for some form of unknown threat or attack. Therefore, yawning can be an excellent sign of stress. Although we have noted that yawning occurs because of the body's demand for oxygen and the release of a neural stimulant, it is not always a sign of deception. Yawning can also occur because of fatigue, drowsiness, or boredom. The interviewer's task is to accurately interpret the yawning behavior.

Deceptive yawning is most often observed in subjects who are around 25 years of age and younger. There is no real scientific reason for this other than it appears to be due to a lack of maturity on the part of these subjects. It is also probably due to the lack of advanced skills by the younger subject in trying to control deceptive cues that emanate from the body (Gray, 1971).

Deceptive yawning has several characteristics. If the interrogator notices continuous yawning throughout the interview, there is a high probability of deception on the part of the subject, provided that the interrogator knows of no reason why the subject should be suffering from any real fatigue. If the interrogator notices that yawning only occurs during relevant questions, the yawning may be a sign of a speech disturbance on the part of the subject. Speech disturbances occur because the subject is unable to attain or maintain a clear mental line of thought. This is a good sign of stress and possible deception.

Another condition that may exist with yawning is stalling. The subject may use frequent yawning as a way to fake boredom. Yawning may also be used to show a lack of respect for the interviewer. In other words, it is a subtle form of anger that we previously described as veiled anger.

Gulping or frequent swallowing is another characteristic sign of stress (Darwin, 1872; Darwin and Ekman, 1998; Ekman, 1992), and is stimulated by changes in the autonomic nervous system. The chemical changes that occur in the body during fight-or-flight situations also affect the production of saliva in the throat and mouth to the point that salivation may even cease. In some individuals, the result is a dry throat and mouth, requiring the person to swallow more frequently. In other situations, the normal swallowing reflex is interrupted, and the person experiences a buildup of saliva, requiring large swallows to clear the mouth and throat.

There are two other characteristics indicating a dry mouth. First, the interrogator may hear a clicking sound emanating from the mouth. This occurs because the tongue and cheeks are sticking to the dry teeth, and the tongue is also sticking to the roof of the dry mouth. The result is a clicking sound as the person is forming words with the tongue and lips. The second indication of a dry mouth is dry lips. You may see the subject constantly licking dry lips, yet the lips still remain dry (see Figures 6.11 through 6.13). In extreme cases, the interviewer may see the lips chap and even crack from dryness the longer the interview progresses.

The interviewer may notice some subjects with spittle or white foam in one or both corners of the mouth (Gray, 1971). A change in saliva production often includes a change in its composition, which results in a thick, milky secretion. This substance appears as a white foam or stringy deposit at the corners of the mouth. This can be a significant sign of stress. There are other conditions, however, in which the interviewer may see white foam at the

Figure 6.11 Female subject exhibiting the stress behavior of lip licking. Usually due to a dry mouth, but it can also be a stalling behavior. Notice the subject smiling at the same time.

Figure 6.12 Subject showing the results of stress by licking his lips.

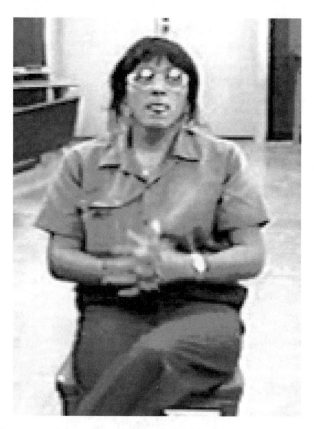

Figure 6.13 Subject demonstrates stress by licking her lips. Notice that her hands also appear to be busy as a result of her stress.

corners of the mouth. The same condition has been observed in individuals suffering from post-traumatic stress disorder; alcoholic delirium tremors; abuse of cocaine, crack, methamphetamines, or other chemical abuse; and the use of some medications, particularly for the heart. It is also frequently seen in subjects who are mentally unstable or mentally ill.

Lip Behaviors

Since we are aware that our verbal symptoms can be damaging to us, we are quite diligent at controlling most verbal symptoms (Skinner, 1952, 1992). As a backup system, however, we may rely on mechanical, or nonverbal, means to control some of those same verbal slips. Many of us have said such things as: "I could just bite my tongue for saying that." "It was all I could do to hold my tongue." "I nearly bit a hole in my cheek to keep from telling her what I really thought." "I had to cover my mouth to keep from giving her a piece of my mind." All of these comments are verbalizations of mechanical

Figure 6.14 Biting of the lips as a form of controlling speech.

speech suppression. This aspect of behavior warrants another Practical Kinesic Principle:

Any obstruction of speech, whether physical or symbolic, is a sign of stress and possible deception.

The interviewer should watch for an array of mouth- or lip-obstructing behaviors (Skinner, 1952, 1992). For example, watch for subjects that bite or gnaw on their lips during stress areas (see Figure 6.14). This negation behavior is an obvious attempt at suppressing speech and has sometimes been so pronounced that subjects have chewed or gnawed on their lips to the point that their lips bleed.

In keeping with our earlier Practical Kinesic Principle about the facial-touch target, the interviewer should watch for any negation behavior that involves the hand covering or blocking the mouth (Skinner, 1952, 1992; Davis, Connors, et al., 1999; Davis, Walters, et al., 2000). This may be as obvious as the whole hand over the lips, or it may be as simple as one finger placed vertically over both lips or horizontally across the top lip. The inference is the same in either case (see Figures 6.15 through 6.18).

Other means of blocking the lips include chewing on fingernails, pipe stems, ear pieces of glasses, pens, pencils, paper clips, or similar objects.

Subjects have been known to place purse straps in their mouths as well as shirt collars, the ends of long hair, cigars, cigarettes, key rings, the corners of documents, file folders, or papers (see Figures 6.19 and 6.20). During one interview, the author noticed a juvenile who took the strings from his hooded jacket and stuffed them into his mouth and then tried to talk with his mouth

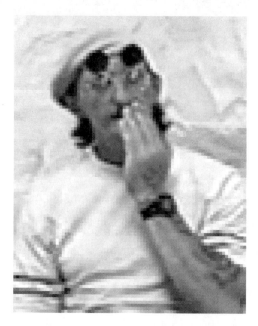

Figure 6.15 This subject is blocking the mouth in a negation behavior by playing with his mustache.

Figure 6.16 Negation behavior by subject who is partially covering the mouth with his hand.

full of string. In another case, a subject pulled the collar of his undershirt from beneath his sweatshirt and chewed on the collar of his undershirt. The list of objects placed in the mouth is endless, but the goal is simple — stop the mouth from getting the subject into trouble.

Another signal from the lips is the squeezing of the lips together, or pursing the lips (see Figures 6.21 and 6.22). The objective is once again to control speech, but there is a secondary implication. Very tight or thin lips suggest the development of the anger response. In this case, the lips tighten into a thin line (Darwin, 1872; Darwin and Ekman, 1998; Ekman, 1992). Licking the lips, on the other hand, is associated with general stress, and in some cases, can be a habit of the subject. The dryness of the mouth sometimes experienced by the speaker can also apply to the lips. Other than general stress, we cannot consistently infer anything about the truthfulness of the subject at that time.

Smoking Behavior

Whether a subject should be allowed to smoke in the interview room has been debated for a long time and will undoubtedly be the subject of future debate. Permitting the subject to smoke is probably best left up to the interviewer, and the decision should be based on each individual situation.

Figure 6.17 Female subject partially blocking her mouth in negation by using her finger to wipe her top lip.

Figure 6.18 Male subject caught in a significant negation behavior by blocking his mouth with both hands.

Two important issues should be addressed if the interviewer permits the subject to smoke. First, many people smoke as a means to relieve stress. The question the interviewer should consider is: does he want the subject to gain relief from his stress by smoking or by moving into the acceptance–response state and making an admission or confession?

The second issue is whether the subject's physical behaviors are normal smoking habits or indications of stress. The interviewer may find it difficult to determine if the way the lighter is handled, the length of the draw on the cigarette, the tapping of ashes, and so forth are a part of the subject's normal routine or if they are stress-induced symptoms. For an accurate determination, the interviewer may have to watch the subject smoking for an extended period of time under non-stress conditions to determine if smoking behaviors during the interview are a break from the normal pattern and therefore significant.

Figure 6.19 This subject is holding his bottom lip in his hand.

Figure 6.20 The subject is now occupying his mouth by chewing on the top of a pen.

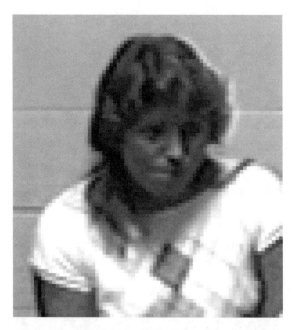

Figure 6.21 Subject who is pursing her lips. Also notice the "chin tuck" at the same time, suggesting some hostility.

Figure 6.22 Lip pursing by female subject under stress and attempting to control her mouth.

It can be hard to document whether allowing subjects to smoke strengthens their resolve to resist confession or, by allowing the subject to smoke, we will get any benefit from offering smoking as a "reward"-oriented response. An obvious factor in the smoking issue is the location of the interview. In many city, state, and federal buildings, smoking is not allowed indoors, and the same applies to a large majority of the correctional facilities around the U.S.

The Eyes

The most expressive part of the head is considered to be the eyes. If the observer can read and accurately decipher signals from the eyes, there is a wealth of information to be gained. We should be reminded, however, that there is no single body language symptom that indicates deception. The same is true of the eyes.

Eye Contact

The easiest eye behavior for anyone to spot is the level of eye contact. The easiest eye behavior for anyone to misinterpret is also the level of eye contact. The old folk wisdom says that a truthful person will always look you in the eye, but research has shown that this adage is not always correct (Ekman, 1992; Knapp, 1984). Diversion of eye contact, including the whole head movement, closing the eyes for extended periods, and blocking the eyes, does suggest some form of rejection of the issue, and in some cases, can indicate a certain degree of shame (Darwin, 1872; Darwin and Ekman, 1998; Ekman, 1992; Exline and Winters, 1965; Exline and Eldridge, 1967).

A more accurate method of analyzing the significance of eye contact level is to first determine the subject's normal pattern or level of eye contact and then look for changes in that pattern. There are numerous social, ethnic, psychological, and cultural reasons why even normal eye contact varies among individuals. In many Native American cultures, it is considered a sign of disrespect to look a person directly in the eye when talking to him. On the other hand, there are some European cultures that insist on eye contact as much as 90% of the time. In some male-dominated societies, it is inappropriate for a female to make strong eye contact with a male authority figure. Some cultures frown on a younger person making extended eye contact with his elders.

There are also some psychological reasons why eye contact may vary. It is known, for example, that introverted persons tend to have less direct eye contact under stressful situations or when they are being deceptive. Extraverted personalities, on the other hand, can show a dramatic increase in eye contact during conflict, particularly during deception (Knapp, 1982). Personal history and experience can have an impact on the normal level of eye contact, as can any personality flaws or disorders. The dynamic between the two individuals in the conversation also comes into play (Exline and Winters, 1965). If a person is discussing a topic that is embarrassing to him or to the person to whom he is speaking, there may be less eye contact. If a superior person is berating a subordinate, the subordinate person has less eye contact, while the person of a superior position is likely to have extensive eye contact (Exline and Eldridge, 1967). Should the listener in a conversation feel some form of contempt toward the speaker, the listener may have more extensive eye contact than normal. Some individuals who have difficulty hearing may also have greater eye contact because they are trying to decipher true emotional meaning while at the same time struggling to hear the spoken words. It is incumbent, therefore, on the observer to ascertain the individual's baseline behavior as opposed to assumed general standards for eye contact.

Because the normal level of eye contact varies among people, we need to establish another Practical Kinesic Principle:

Any change in a person's constant or normal level of eye contact, which is a timely response and part of a cluster, can be sign of stress and possible deception.

This principle reminds us that there is diversity in the level of eye contact and emphasizes the importance of establishing a constant before judging any apparent changes. Once a normal level of eye contact has been established, the interviewer should be suspicious of eye contact that may be too intense. This strong eye contact usually takes the form of an aggressive stare-down, and is an attempt to dominate the interviewer. This indicates the response state of anger in the subject.

In particular, the interviewer should note the eyelids and the muscles around the subject's eyes. When the subject is in an anger-response state, the muscles around the eyes will tighten and the eyelids will close slightly. The eyes will begin to look "hard" (see Figures 6.23 through 6.25). After you have established the subject's normal pattern of eye behavior, watch for increased incidents of excessive eye shifting at stress areas. This is not to say that a "shifty-eyed" person is not to be trusted or is being deceptive. Many physiological or environmental conditions could cause the shifting. However, if the shifting eye behavior increases at stress areas and is accompanied by other nonverbal symptoms, there may be deception.

The interviewer should also be suspicious of situations in which there is increased or prolonged eye contact. Part of this may be due to the subject's belief that he must look you in the eye so you will know he is being truthful.

Figure 6.23 Aggressive "hard eye" contact by subject. Notice the hand also blocking the mouth.

It is also done in an effort to watch for the interviewer's reactions; the subject is looking for an acceptance response from the interviewer. Both reactions indicate that the subject is in the bargaining state and is trying to establish some form of bond with the interviewer.

Subjects who suspect that their nervous eye behaviors are being observed by the interviewer may try to control these signals by disguising their breaks in eye contact. To mask their nervousness, subjects may look at their hands. They may look out a window, at pictures, up at the ceiling, or down at the floor (see Figures 6.26 through 6.33).

Suspects masking their nervous eye behaviors may verbally call attention to other objects in the room, thereby getting the interviewer to also break eye contact. They may read documents, point to evidence, inspect their clothing, or engage in other active eye-diverting behaviors.

Another form of eye behavior occurs frequently just before the suspect is ready to confess. The subject's eyes will roll back up into the head as the eyelids close. For some reason, the person has become susceptible to the voice of the interviewer. The interviewer should lower the pitch and volume of the voice and speak with a great deal of feeling and clear diction. The confession is often imminent. The interrogator should therefore watch for other signs of acceptance.

Figure 6.24 "Hard eyes" by female subject. Observe the V configuration of the eyebrows.

At the same time that the head drops onto the chest, the eyes will also drop (see Figure 6.34). This, along with other symptoms, indicates either a response state of depression or of acceptance. The most reliable method for determining which response state the subject is experiencing is to listen to the subject's verbal cues.

The interviewer should be alert for the subject whose eyes turn up to the ceiling, as with other preconfession behaviors. When this happens, the interviewer will note that the subject's blink rate slows down significantly. The reason the eyes turn upward is to prevent tears from flowing from the eyes. This form of eye contact behavior indicates the subject is in the response-state of acceptance. The movement also has been identified as indicating the person is giving rapt attention to the issue and is not absorbing much, if any, external information and is focused very much on himself (Darwin, 1872; Darwin and Ekman, 1998). His current frame of mind is the realization of the truth and the consequences now possibly associated with his involvement.

Neurolinguistic Programming (NLP), Eye Movement, and Deception

One of the most stubborn misconceptions in investigative interviewing concerns the ability to spot truthful and deceptive statements made by an

Figure 6.25 Male subject demonstrating aggressive "hard eyes." Notice the head position leaning away from the interviewer in an aversion behavior.

individual by merely watching eye movement. This misrepresentation of neurolinguistic programming proposes that when a person's eyes move to his left, the individual is most likely recalling information. Should the interviewer ask for information and observe a left eye movement from the subject, then the subject is most likely being truthful in his statements because he is recalling known information. On the other hand, movement of the eyes to a person's right is supposedly typical of a person who is creating information. If any response to an interviewer's inquiry elicits a verbal response along with right eye movement, it is believed the subject is being deceptive. Nothing could be further from the truth nor could a greater injustice be done to the practice of neurolinguistic programming, or NLP.

The concepts of NLP were developed in the mid-1970s by researchers Richard Bandler and John Grinder. Their basic hypothesis was that people access their thoughts through different methods. They proposed that this is, in part, due to the different means by which people unconsciously react to their world, which Bandler and Grinder referred to as "preferred referential systems," or PRS. Three preferred referential systems were

Figure 6.26 Female subject breaking eye contact by examining her fingernails with her hand up in front of her face.

identified — auditory, visual, or kinesthetic. The auditory system represents concepts and reactions to sounds, and in this phase, a person would communicate in terms indicating his reaction to sounds. "It sounds good to me," I'd like to hear your plan," and so forth. Visual preference involves responses and communication regarding the visual world, and verbal communication follows. "I see what you are saying," "I see how it can be done," and so forth. The kinesthetic system deals with the feelings of the person. Verbal statements portraying this preferred system might include "I didn't like the feel of the situation" or "It was rough going" or other feelings-oriented comments. If the listener pays attention to these cues, he can identify the preferred referential state of the speaker. Bandler and Grinder also proposed that a similar assessment of each person's preferred referential system can be diagnosed by observing eye movements. These eye movements indicate whether a person was actually remembering information or was constructing the information that he was communicating.

In a normally organized right-handed person "accessing" visual information, eye movement is up and to his left. If he is "creating" visual information, he will show eye movement up and to his right. Should the person

Figure 6.27 Male subject breaking eye contact by looking down at his fingers as he plays with them.

be accessing auditory information, he will exhibit eye movement laterally to his left, and if the subject is creating auditory information, he will exhibit eye movement laterally to his right. Should a person be dealing with the kinesthetic realm, his eye movements will move down and to his right. It is the "eye-accessing cues" that have been grossly misrepresented by investigative interviewers and trainers when NLP is being used as a method for detecting deception by victims, witnesses, and subjects.

Bandler and Grinder never proposed in any of their work that the eye-accessing cues were of value in detecting deception (Vrij, 1997, 2000; Walters, 1997, 1998). Their main goal in developing NLP was for use as a system for communication and therapy; it was not designed as an analytical tool. Bandler and Grinder suggested that communication between two people can be significantly improved if one of the two participants adapts his communication to the PRS of the other party. NLP theory does, in fact, teach good listening and communication skills, and those who diligently practice such skills are going to be successful interviewers.

Despite the fact that scientific evidence reports otherwise, some investigative interviewers have complete faith in their ability to spot deception

Figure 6.28 Male subject showing negation behavior by covering his face and eyes with his hands. At the same time, he shows aversion behavior by turning his head away from the interviewer.

merely by observing eye movement. In many cases, this has become the staple of interview and interrogation training in law enforcement academies and investigative interviewing programs, with instructors consistently citing Bandler and Grinder's work as the authoritative source of information. The use of eye-accessing cues to assess the truthful or deceptive responses of a subject is unreliable, and the correlation with deception is no better than chance. (Vrij, 1997, 2000; Dillingham, 1998).

Other studies have been conducted regarding various aspects of the NLP model and its consistency from person to person in communication situations. Again, in some investigative interview training, it has been proposed that, for example, when a subject demonstrates "visual" eye cues, but at the same time uses "auditory" verbal cues, then there must be some form of deception. Once again, research into this area has failed to substantiate reliability of any such analysis. In some studies (Elich, Thompson, et al., 1985; Farmer, Rooney, et al., 1985; Thomason, Arbuckle, et al., 1980; Poffel and Cross, 1985; Wertheim, Habib, et al., 1986), it was found to be common for

Figure 6.29 Subject showing negation behavior by covering his entire face, including the eyes, nose, and mouth.

Figure 6.30 Subject covering his eyes and part of the face by rubbing his eyebrows.

Figure 6.31 Negation and aversion behavior cluster. Subject covering her face and eyes while at the same time showing a major aversion behavior by turning her head away from the interviewer.

Figure 6.32 Subject demonstrating negation behavior by covering part of his face and nose with his hand. Notice the body angle and head angle away from the interviewer.

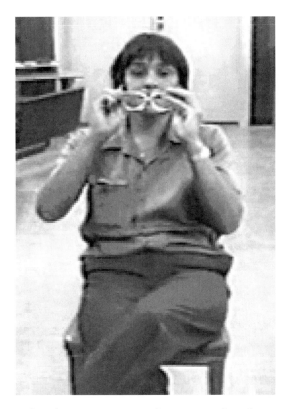

Figure 6.33 Female subject removing and examining her glasses. An interesting form of negation along with the stress behavior of playing with her glasses.

the subject to have eye movements inconsistent with speech cues. Those same studies also determined that eye cues were inconsistent with questions designed to elicit specific mental responses on the visual, auditory, or kinesthetic levels.

One of the arguments presented by those who continue to support the correlation between eye movement and deception is the connection between eye movement and hemispheres of the brain. The claim is that the right hemisphere of the brain is more involved in recalling information, hence the eye movement to the person's left when he is active in that portion of the brain. It is also held that the left hemisphere of the brain is the most actively involved in the creation of information, therefore, when that hemisphere of the brain is most active, the speaker presents right-eye movement. Since lies are "constructed," there will be right-eye movement, and when the truth is "recalled," there will be left-eye movement. This begs the question that if a person has memorized and rehearsed his lies, even for a short period of time, what type of eye movement will be observed during the recall of a memorized deception? Experts on memory, perception, and brain chemistry agree that

Figure 6.34 A strong example of a "body cascade." Notice the head and face turned down, as well as the shoulders rounded and rolled forward.

memory is, in fact, stored and retrieved from all over the geography of the brain (Walters, 2001a). It is also believed that created information may come from the vast stores of previously acquired experiences or the combinations of various individual experiences (Walters, 2001b).

In summary, the use of eye movements as a way to decipher deception has no more reliability than flipping a coin and guessing does. The same applies to making any credibility assessment by looking for an incongruent relationship between eye cues and any verbalized PRS cues. Perpetuation of this seriously flawed theory is bound to persist, and there will doubtless be many instructors and practitioners who continue to insist on the reliability of the concept. Most will continue to use it because it appears to be a quick method for determining deception in all subjects. Keep in mind, however, that there is no single universal, or even widely identifiable, symptom that consistently identifies deception in all people. To reiterate another one of our Practical Kinesic Principles: interview and interrogation is hard work.

Pupillary Responses

When asking a stress-related question, the observant interviewer may notice the subject's pupils constrict. This is often a sign that the person is experiencing fear (Darwin, 1872; Darwin and Ekman, 1998; Hess, 1975; Gray, 1971). In subjects experiencing anger or rage, the pupils may constrict to the point of looking like pinpricks (Darwin, 1872; Darwin and Ekman, 1998; Hess, 1975; Gray, 1971). These types of changes are, once again, the result of the changes occurring in the autonomic nervous system and, as such, are totally involuntary. They are excellent cues for defining a subject's stress responses. These changes are different from the eyes of subjects who are abusing drugs. Again, these two changes are merely indicators of general stress and are not by themselves to be construed as signs of deception. However, should the subject be attempting to persuade the observer that he is not upset or angry and at the same time demonstrate these types of pupil responses, then he is not being honest about his emotions.

With some subjects, there is another change that occurs to the eyes. Stress and certain intense emotional responses cause the eyes of some individuals to show changes of color (Gray, 1971). This is due, in part, to the chemical changes that occur, not only with fight-or-flight situations, but also with the change in body chemistry that occurs with all the emotional states.

The author's oldest daughter was born with blue eyes that eventually changed to gray as she got older. Now, under intense emotional conditions, her eyes regain strong streaks of blue in the iris. Her mother's eyes, which are hazel, also change under certain conditions, and show flecks of green.

Under most situations, the eye appears to have two white sections: one on each side of the iris. In high-stress situations, the eye opens wider to allow more light to enter. When this happens, another section of white may appear under one or both eyes. At times, white can be seen surrounding the iris (Darwin, 1872; Knapp, 1978; Gray, 1971; Darwin and Ekman, 1998). The phenomenon of showing extra white in the eyes is known in Japanese as "sanpaku" (see Figure 6.35). The literal translation is "three whites," as in three whites of the eye. The cultural meaning behind the term is "spiritually unwell." Japanese court physicians used the term to describe a person who was emotionally unstable.

Eye Blinking

Eye blinking is the "tachometer" for the brain, indicating how fast the brain is processing information. Eye blinking increases dramatically when a person is under stress, indicating rapid thought (Stern, 1988). The person is absorbing and evaluating the external information and processing response information at an extremely accelerated rate. Once again, should the person be trying to indicate that he is not under stress or appear to be trying nonverbally to appear relaxed, this high blink rate will be a contradictory signal. The high blink rate alone, however, does not indicate a deceptive person.

Figure 6.35 An example of "sanpaku." Notice the raised eyebrows of surprise and wide-open eyes along with the subtle appearance of "three whites" of the eyes.

At times, the blink rate may drop to nearly zero. This does not mean that the person has stopped thinking. It indicates that the subject is now involved in a complex internal conversation with himself. The subject is not consciously processing external information as efficiently as before. The interviewer may find that he has to call the person's name or ask for some form of response to interrupt this process and determine which response state the subject is experiencing.

Another near-zero blink rate often occurs when the subject is in the state of acceptance (Stern, 1988). The subject's eyes blink in near synchronization with the interviewer's verbal comments. Each of the synchronized blinks indicates that the subject has absorbed that small piece of information. The interviewer should make only short, brief comments that are easy for the person to understand and acknowledge. Asking for confirmation from the person about each factual piece of information will likely be successful and move the subject deeper into acceptance.

The average length of time the eyelids remain closed when blinking is about one-tenth of a second. At times, the interviewer will see subjects whose blinking eyes remain closed longer than this. This extended closure is a sign of stress and is a nonverbal form of denial on the part of the subject.

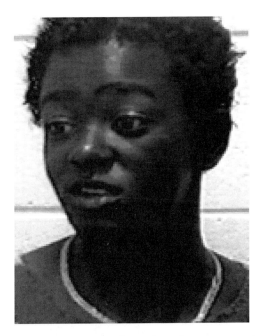

Figure 6.36 Raised eyebrows on the face of a subject, suggesting she is possibly stressed and surprised by the issue being discussed.

Eyebrows

If the eyes are the windows to the soul, then the eyebrows are the window dressing. They enhance the expressions demonstrated by the eyes and the rest of the face.

When the subject is responding with anger, the eyebrows assume a V shape (Darwin, 1872; Darwin and Ekman, 1998; Ekman and Friesen, 1975). The tips of the eyebrows point downward to the bridge of the nose (see Figures 6.23 through 6.25). A tightening or "hardening" of the eyes usually accompanies this. The depth of the other expression lines on the subject's face will be helpful in determining the degree of anger the subject is experiencing.

Should the interviewer notice that the subject has both eyebrows raised high along with the mouth slightly open, the subject is experiencing shock or surprise (Darwin, 1872; Darwin and Ekman, 1998; Ekman, 1992). This implies that the subject did not anticipate that particular area of inquiry and was caught off-guard (see Figures 6.35 and 6.36). The interviewer should pursue this area of inquiry vigorously due to the level of response by the subject. There may be some unresolved or high-stress issue surrounding this area that needs further attention. It is not at all uncommon for the observer to notice the occurrence of a sanpaku expression about the eyes at the same time.

Figure 6.37 Subject demonstrating skepticism. Notice one eyebrow raised higher than the other along with the tilt of the head away from the interviewer.

The advantage to observing nonverbal behavior is that it gives the interviewer some form of visual identification as to what the subject is experiencing emotionally and psychologically. Once an analysis has been made of the nonverbal and verbal behaviors, the interviewer is directed to the next appropriate step in the interview process. This means that the interview or interrogation process is driven by the subject's response behaviors and not by a preset or formatted interview. One of these many pieces of nonverbal feedback generated from a subject is an indication of disbelief or skepticism. Watch for the subject who raises only one eyebrow when listening to the interviewer. This facial expression suggests that the subject is not convinced by the interrogator's evidentiary argument (see Figure 6.37). This reaction of skepticism can indicate one of several factors. If the interviewer is trying to bluff the subject, it may be an indication that the interviewer has just been caught in his bluff. It may mean that the interviewer is taking an incorrect approach for the particular personality type of the subject. It can also indicate that the subject is in a strong denial-response state. Whatever the situation, the interviewer must change his approach because he is not being convincing and must overcome the subject's denial response.

The best nonverbal cues are those that a subject has little or no conscious control over. These are the best stress and emotion cues because they are

Figure 6.38 Subject demonstrating true emotion of depression and grief. Notice the eyebrows drawn together over the nose. Also notice "soft," round appearance of the eyes and facial features around the eyes.

unlikely to be censored by the subject. One good example of these involuntary or near-involuntary cues is an indication of strong emotional pain involving the eyebrows (Darwin, 1872; Darwin and Ekman, 1998; Ekman, 1992). In the majority of individuals, the eyebrows will pull inward toward each other over the bridge of the nose (see Figure 6.38). In some cases, depending on the individual, the investigative interviewer may notice small ridges of skin between the eyes and above the eyebrows that look like an upside-down horseshoe. At the same time, the eyebrows will be raised on the ends over the bridge of the nose and the corners of the mouth may also turn down. For the interviewer, therefore, the identification of this eyebrow behavior identifies strong emotional pain or suffering associated with the response state of depression. The interviewer should adjust his interview approach accordingly.

Case Study

Young parents reported to the police that early one morning, after rising to prepare to go to work, the father discovered that the couple's eight-month-old daughter was missing from their home. At the time of the report, the couple reported that they had found the back door to their apartment unlocked and standing ajar. The previous evening, the husband had returned home early from military maneuvers at a nearby military installation. Late that evening, before retiring for bed, the couple reported that they had allowed their daughter to play on their living room floor until she had gone to sleep. In order to avoid waking the child, they merely covered her with her blanket and let her sleep for the night on the living room floor on the first floor of their small apartment.

Twenty-four hours after the report of the kidnapping was made to the police, the parents appeared on several local television stations pleading for the return of their daughter. The author was asked to make some form of analysis of the television appearances of the two parents as well as an analysis of an audiotaped police interview. One of the remarkable cues of possible deception was observed during the father's television appearance. In the unedited tape, the parents are briefly discussing the written press release that had been prepared by the mother for their appearance on the television news. The couple showed no strong signs of grief or stress. As soon as the reporter announced that the camera was rolling, however, the demeanor of both parents immediately changed. The voice quality and verbal content of speech from the father was filled with grief and emotional pain, however, there was a total lack of any congruent nonverbal cues. In fact, instead of showing the depression configuration in the eyebrows, the father showed strong signs of fear in a remarkable display of sanpaku. This, along with a large number of clusters of other cues, caused investigators to conclude that the kidnapping may be a hoax. Within eight hours of reviewing the videotapes and audiotapes with the lead investigator, the parents were confronted, reinterviewed, and eventually confessed. The mother had been neglecting the child for about two weeks, and the child died of complications from lack of nutrition. The father had come home from maneuvers and found the child dead. In an effort to hide the crime, he transported the child's body onto the military base and disposed of the body in a large pond filled with turtles. Both parents were eventually charged with murder, destruction of evidence, filing a false police report, and abuse of a corpse.

The raised eyebrows seen in the demonstration of emotional pain and grief has been noted to be a regular feature in some individuals who are mentally ill (Darwin, 1872; Darwin and Ekman, 1998). This is also usually accompanied with a significantly and almost permanently wrinkled brow that suggests bouts of long-lasting depression. This is not to say that we can diagnose someone as being mentally ill or suffering from clinical depression merely by looking at his forehead for wrinkles or creases. However, it is an interesting phenomenon that can draw the investigator's attention to other elements of the subject's personality for some signs of mental and emotional disorder.

The Arms

Our study of the arms includes the shoulders, the arms, the elbows, and the hands. We will review such things as shoulder positions and crossing and touching behaviors by the hands. At the same time, we need to bear in mind that the symptoms we will explore must be changes from a normal pattern of behaviors and must be a timely response to stress-related areas. Remember, no single behavior by itself is proof of anything.

Shoulders

The interviewer should watch the position of the subject's shoulders during various phases of the interview for important insights. The movement and positioning of the shoulders tends to be an unconscious behavior generated by subjects and, at times, can give away telltale signs of strong emotional response. Some of these reactions can be quite obvious due to the range of movement and length of time over which they occur. Others are so brief they are called "microsignals," but they are significant "leaks" of emotional information.

For example, if the subject has one shoulder raised higher than the other and turned toward the interviewer, this is an "aversion" behavior. Coupled with other verbal and nonverbal cues, this can suggest that the subject may be responding with deception (Davis, Connors, et al., 1999, 2000; Ekman, 1992).

At the point of a relevant, or "hot," question, notice if the subject raises one or both shoulders (see Figures 6.39 and 6.40). This shoulder raise is going to be brief and would be classified as a microsignal. This is often described as a shrug, and suggests that the subject is nonverbally unsure of his answer and is looking for help or confirmation from the observer. As another form of aversion, it suggests that the response from the subject is likely to be deceptive. Other corresponding behaviors should be observed from the rest of the body and voice to confirm the deception cluster.

When the subject is experiencing either depression or the pre-confession state of acceptance, the shoulders may also show some change. When moving into either one of these states, the subject's shoulders may drop down and then hunch over or roll forward into what is referred to as a "body cascade" (see Figure 6.34). At the same time, the head and face may drop and the eyes may be cast downward. Once again, it is important to listen to the subject's verbal output in order to more accurately determine which response state the subject is experiencing.

When a subject is demonstrating defiance, which is typical of a person reacting with anger or aggression, watch for the subject to throw one or both shoulders backwards and stiffen the neck and back. The chin may also be raised in the defiance posture. This indicates that the subject is being defensive because of the "attack" the interviewer is making. We will discuss later how the interrogator should respond to anger and the other four response states of stress.

Figure 6.39 Notice the subject's head and shoulders in their normal, or "constant," position.

Figure 6.40 Notice the change in the subject's body position. His right shoulder is raised in a partial shrug. The head is also drawn to the right as part of the shrug.

Figure 6.41 A subject in a stress–response behavior with his elbows pulled tight against his body. Also note that he is controlling his behavior by sitting on his hands.

Elbows

When a person is relaxed and comfortable in a situation or with a particular topic of discussion, the position of the elbows in relation to the body is far different than when the person is under stress. When the subject is relaxed, the interviewer may observe the elbows hanging comfortably at the sides of the torso. By contrast, the stressed body takes on physical behaviors designed to protect vital areas of the body from attack or assault (see Figure 6.41). The primary area protected is the torso because this is the location of the heart, lungs, and vital organs. During stress, the elbows participate in these physical-protection behaviors as well. When the interviewer moves into what may be a stressful topic for the subject, he may see the elbows pull in close to the torso. There are usually other protective gestures being generated by the body at the same time.

Crossing Behaviors

Generally, crossing of any part of the body suggests that the person is defensive. This type of response from the subject can indicate general fear of the

Figure 6.42 Subject in a defensive posture of arm crossing along with a strong body position.

situation, or it can be generated by stress (see Figure 6.42). However, such crossing behavior alone does not indicate deception. They are simply signs of changing emotion and stress. They can help the interviewer decipher the subject's current emotional state. Once again, the keys to determining the significance of crossing is the timeliness of the behavior in relation to the stress question; is it part of a cluster of behaviors and is the behavior a change from the subject's normal pattern? There is a multitude of reasons a person may cross his arms that have nothing to do with being defensive or deceptive. For some, arm crossing occurs because the room temperature may be uncomfortably cold or breezy, or they can even be suffering from a slight fever. For those people who suffer back problems, crossing the arms at times relieves muscle strain on their backs. Similar causes could be emotional and social insecurity; circulation problems; or being self-conscious about weight, clothes, or some physical appearance. The overall lesson should be not to overread anything into arm crossing that is not really there. Some general body movements are simply part of the human "noise" of stress and communication (Davis, Connors, et al., 1999; Davis, Walters, et al., 2000).

When discussing "hot issue" areas, the interviewer may see the subject cross his arms with the fists clasped underneath. This indicates that the subject is probably going to be uncooperative to the point of even being

Figure 6.43 Subject in a comforting arm-crossing behavior of a body hug.

cocky. The stress–response state is anger. The key to decoding this behavior is to look for the clenched fists. At this point, the interviewer may notice the subject also has raised his chin in the defiant posture.

The position or height of the arms on the torso is similar to a barometer. The higher the arms are crossed on the body, the greater the defiant attitude of the subject. If, for example, the arms are crossed higher on the chest closer to the neck, the subject is going to be hostile and is experiencing a stronger anger response.

A subject may have his arms crossed, but they appear to have collapsed in on themselves. Other times, a subject will have his arms crossed while leaning over and in toward the interviewer. The subject is now showing some denial-response behavior, and the chances of cooperation with the interviewer are decreasing. These subjects tend to be more withdrawn, and it takes work to gain information from them.

Subjects who are responding to stress with depression may wrap their arms tightly around the torso (see Figure 6.43). The subject is probably also hunching over, the head has dropped down, and the subject will be making little, if any, eye contact. As with all other behaviors, not all arm-crossing behaviors are indicative of deception. Should the investigator be interviewing the victim of rape, sexual assault, or incest, he may observe arm-crossing behaviors when the subject is discussing the assault. The subject is demonstrating his emotional trauma through nonverbal means. Nor does the absence of such symptoms by these victims indicate they are being deceptive. These people may be dealing better with their victimization, or may still be in a significant state of denial. Should the interviewer in any way suspect the latter, extensive efforts should be made to obtain victim assistance and counseling for that person.

Hands

Most observers and researchers of body language and deception identify three basic types of behaviors that a person engages in that involve the hands (Ekman, 1992; Davis and Hadiks, 1995; Davis, Connors, et al., 1999; Davis, Walters, et al., 2000). Each of these behaviors has different functions and goals. Some of these same behaviors have long been recognized in the interview room as having significance. Some have been misinterpreted as being signs of deception when, in fact, they are only significant signs of stress and emotional change. Signs of stress do not mean that a person is being deceptive. Deception signals, however, are forms of stress because of the strong arousal response that occurs in the subject at the act of telling the lie.

The first of the hand behaviors is called "emblems." Emblems are hand gestures or signals that have broad universal meaning (Knapp, 1978; Ekman, 1992; Davis and Hadiks, 1995). For example, the index fingertip touching the tip of the thumb, forming a circle, is generally recognized as indicating that something is "okay." The upraised arm with only the index finger extended usually means "number one," as in signifying the best team or player. The raised middle finger has its obvious universal meaning. There are numerous other hand signals, some of them being only culturally or ethnically significant.

The second type of hand behaviors is called "manipulators." Manipulators create "busy work" for the hands and are also referred to as "adapters," in that they do nothing more than help a person deal with any built-up stress energy developed while reacting to the current environment (Knapp, 1978; Ekman, 1992; Davis, Connors, et al., 1999; Davis, Walters, et al., 2000). These actions serve little, if any, important function other than to give the hands something to do. They are the more recognizable nervous hand behaviors that people generate when they are under stress.

"Adapters" have an amazing number of variations that are often seen across a wide range of individuals. Yet other adapters are unique to specific

Figure 6.44 Subject showing general stress behavior of grooming by adjusting her clothes.

individuals as part of their defensive-demeanor profile. One general area would be grooming behaviors. Subjects may engage in extensive clothing inspections by brushing off lint, hair, or dandruff. They may be observed picking fabric "pills" from sweaters or socks. In a videotaped interview of a serial arsonist, the subject was concerned through the whole interview that his socks were pulled up and adjusted them constantly through the hour of conversation that was captured on tape. Other subjects are concerned with slips, pant cuffs, ties, or belts. Some subjects are observed buttoning and unbuttoning or zipping and unzipping their jackets, sweaters, coats, or shirts (see Figures 6.44 through 6.55).

Some subjects may participate in an active auditing of their fingers and jewelry. The interrogator will see increased efforts of checking the time or winding the watch. Individuals wearing other forms of jewelry will engage in twirling or twisting necklaces, spinning rings on their fingers, or fumbling with lockets or bracelets. Men find interviews to be the best time to peel calluses from their hands or clean their fingernails. Women may scratch or peel fingernail polish. These "manipulators" are great opportunities to disguise a break in eye contact with the interviewer.

The third form of hand behaviors is identified as "illustrators." These particular hand behaviors re-create various types of physical activity (Knapp, 1978; Ekman, 1992). For example, holding the hands and arms parallel straight out in front of the body with the fists clenched might indicate to the observer that the person is imitating driving a car. These types of behaviors are frequently associated with those demonstrated by street mimes (see Figures 6.56 through 6.61).

One interesting aspect of all hand behaviors is the general belief that certain ethnic or cultural groups tend to "talk" more with their hands than

Figure 6.45 This subject is busy grooming and cleaning his fingernails.

Figure 6.46 Subject engaged in adapter behavior by adjusting his jacket and clothing.

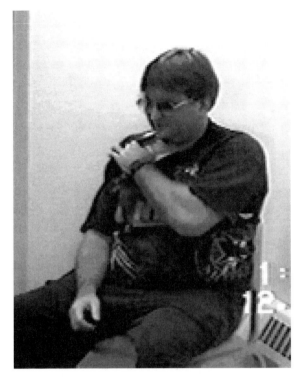

Figure 6.47 The subject is handling stress by scratching his shoulder.

other groups. There are several reasons for these observations, but we must first recognize that there is a distinct difference in the amount of hand signaling behaviors used by people based on their personal verbal skills. Studies in semiology, or the science of communicating with sign language, have helped to determine these conditions.

It has been determined that the level of hand signaling behaviors across societies and cultures can be charted on an inverted bell curve. On the opposite ends of the scale are those people who have extensive verbal communication skills and those with poor verbal skills. In the middle is the average population. Those individuals on the outside edges of the scale have far greater gesticulation or speech-gesturing behaviors vs. those of the average population. People with highly developed verbal skills enhance their verbal communication with a greater amount of gesturing. Those individuals with lower or poorly developed verbal skills, in order to express themselves and supplement their possible lack of developed verbal skills, must rely on extensive gesticulation.

A second consideration regarding the use of the hands in communication concerns the communication-learning environment. Should an individual

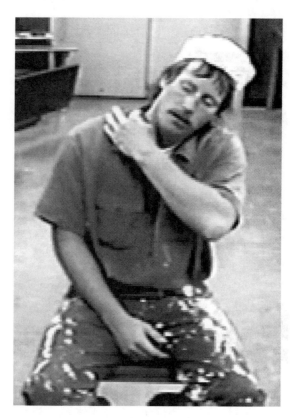

Figure 6.48 Male subject showing grooming behavior by scratching his neck and playing with his shirt collar.

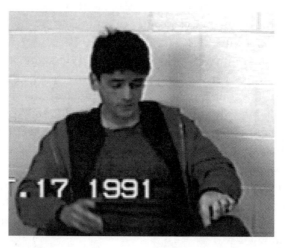

Figure 6.49 The subject is now busy with the important behavior of picking lint from his clothing.

Figure 6.50 During an important point in his interview, this subject found it necessary to remove cotton pills from his socks. Also notice the stress behavior of breaking eye contact and smiling or laughing at the same time.

be raised in a culture that puts a high value on communication, the subsequent social and educational conditions the person is exposed to will subliminally emphasize those gesticulation skills. Those cultures or ethnic groups that put less emphasis on verbal communication skills will thereby impart fewer skills in the same learning environment.

Personal experience, education level, parentage, and siblings also contribute to the verbal skills of the individual. An extensive educational background that focuses on verbal skills seems to encourage greater gesticulation. Skills or experience in public speaking, for example, seems to necessitate the development of such skills.

In any case, the interviewer is reminded not to make broad-based assumptions about nonverbal or verbal behaviors for either the general population or for specific groups. Each person is the essence of his own personality, personal experiences, education, and other conditions. The interviewer must accept each person as an individual study and look for behavior changes within the realm of that individual's normal and abnormal symptoms.

Figure 6.51 An adapter behavior by a subject who is examining and adjusting his ring. Notice the stress behavior of breaking eye contact at the same time.

The level of activity demonstrated by the hands and arms can be indicative of a change in the level of stress. The interviewer will recognize that the stress level for the subject has apparently changed if he sees an increase in gesturing behaviors as certain "hot issue" questions are asked.

There are subjects who engage in finger drumming or tapping when under stress. The interviewer may notice that the greater the stress level, the louder and faster the subject's finger tapping becomes. In some cases, the change in the norm may be the subject ceasing his drumming until out of the problem area. The investigator may also find that the drumming or tapping is not limited to just the fingers. Some individuals express stress by tapping a pen or pencil on a table, clicking the mechanism for a ballpoint pen, or other forms of rhythmic tapping.

An increase in activity of the hands can also include increased touching of areas around the head. For example, the subject may engage in all forms of preening behaviors, such as fixing the hair or retouching makeup. There may also be increased touching in the "facial-touch target" (see Figures 6.7 through 6.10, 6.15 through 6.17, and 6.28 through 6.32).

Other touches to the head include scratching, pulling, or rubbing of one or both ears (Davis, Connors, et al., 1999; Davis, Walters, et al., 1999; Davis,

Figure 6.52 This subject is dealing with stress by distracting himself by playing with a pen in his hands. Also notice the break in eye contact at the same time.

Walters, et al., 2000) (see Figures 6.63 and 6.64). The suspect may use the hands to partially or fully cover or block the eyes in a gesture that indicates he does not want to face the problem (see Figures 6.28 through 6.31). Such negation behaviors often have a significant link to moments of deception on the part of the subject. Touching in and around the head can also include the neck. Some subjects express increased stress by putting their hands to their throats as if protecting them from attack (see Figure 6.65). A woman during a stressful interview commonly demonstrates this type of behavior. It does not mean that she is being deceptive, but that she is experiencing the stress associated with fight-or-flight situations.

If a subject's hand goes to the back of the neck, particularly if the subject is rubbing and squeezing the neck, another emotion is implied. Rubbing, massaging, and, in particular, squeezing the neck indicates that the subject is becoming agitated and angry with the interviewer and the discussion (see Figure 6.66). The interviewer is definitely pursuing the correct area of sensitivity, but he may want to use a little less pressure to prevent the subject from driving headlong into full-blown anger, which will be counterproductive.

Occasionally, an interviewer may notice that a subject presents an air of superiority or authority by the way the hands are held in front of the body. A hand posture that is sometimes displayed by persons of position or power

Figure 6.53 Playing with and grooming the hair can also be a handy adapter behavior for dealing with stress.

is referred to as "steepling." Steepling occurs when the subject holds the hands together in front of the body. The hands will be open, with the fingertips touching lightly (see Figure 6.67). In some cases, the fingers may be lightly interlaced, with the hands held in front of the body. The hands may be held high in front of the body, in plain view, and level with the chest. At other times, the hands are steepled lower on the body near the stomach or waist.

The stress–response state of bargaining is indicated by several hand behaviors. Many of us have seen people hold their arms outstretched from the body with the palms open in a pleading gesture. This behavior is a form of bargaining by attempting to show openness and cooperation with the interviewer.

Bargaining behavior is also demonstrated when the subject holds one or both hands and arms up. This gesture should remind the interviewer of a person who is swearing an oath before the judge in court or of someone who is surrendering to a police officer. Religious statements made by the subject frequently accompany these two postures. They may also be seen when the subject is making statements about his personal moral code in an effort to add emphasis to his comments.

The interviewer should also look for other types of touching behaviors. In particular, the interviewer should take notice if the subject appears to be

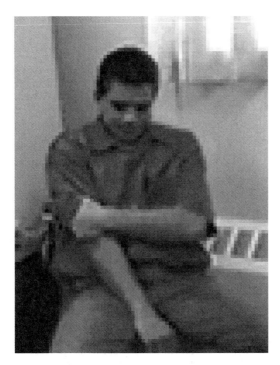

Figure 6.54 Scratching and grooming behavior by a subject may increase as the subject's stress increases.

using touching behaviors in order to comfort or soothe himself. These types of self-touching include wringing, rubbing, or stroking of the hands. The subject may also accomplish the same function by rubbing the forearms or the tops of the legs.

If the interviewer is the focus of touches from the subject, two totally different moods may exist. Should the touches appear to be gentle or light, they may be used as bargaining behaviors. Touching has been shown to be calming and relaxing. The subject uses these types of touches in an attempt to bond with the interviewer.

The other form of touching the interviewer is an attempt to control or dominate the interviewer. The subject may take the opportunity to reach out and touch the interviewer in an authoritative manner. This includes reaching over and squeezing the arm or shoulder of the interviewer. It may include placing a hand on the back of the interviewer's hand and pressing downward, squeezing the hand, or even holding the hand. This touching is a form of covert anger. A subject engaging in this type of touching behavior is attempting to gain some form of emotional or mental control over the interviewer. By being the initiator of strong or dominant touching behaviors, the subject is attempting to signal his control over the interviewer.

Figure 6.55 Watch-winding by a subject provides some relief from stress and may show some impatience on the part of a subject. It also provides a way to break eye contact.

Another form of hand behavior is indicative of denial. An individual who wishes to dismiss a problem or dispense with an issue may make a sweeping gesture away from the body (see Figure 6.68). Most frequently, this gesturing with the hand is toward a door or window, as if to throw the problem out. This behavior has also been classified as an "aversion" behavior and has been observed as being associated with deception (Darwin, 1872; Darwin and Ekman, 1998; Davis, Connors, et al., 1999; Davis, Walters, et al., 2000).

Memory Reanimation

The interrogator should be sure to keep an eye on the subject's hands when he begins to describe the crime, the crime scene, his alibi, or an alibi location. Some subjects at this point subconsciously demonstrate a variety of visual information with their hands (Knapp, 1978; Ekman, 1992; Davis, Walters, et al., 2002). The interviewer should not be surprised to see a subject inadvertently reenact what he did with a weapon during the commission of a crime. The interviewer may see the subject reenact the drawing of a gun, stabbing with a knife, choking actions with the hands, and other behaviors (see Figures 6.56 through 6.62).

Figure 6.56 This subject is describing and demonstrating how a victim received a defensive wound on his left hand while being stabbed in the heart.

Figure 6.57 The subject is describing shooting into the windows of a house when the homeowner was killed.

Figure 6.58 The subject is describing a knife fight and is demonstrating slashing at the victim with a knife.

Figure 6.59 The subject is now describing how the victim had his throat cut by the subject.

Figure 6.60 The subject is describing how the victim was also stabbed multiple times in and around the heart.

Case Study

A serial killer of gay men was interviewed about the murder of one of his victims. The subject insisted that one killing was really an accident and that he was not responsible for the victim's shooting death. The subject indicated that he had picked up the victim at a gay bar and convinced the man that he needed a place to stay for the night. Upon arriving at the victim's apartment, the suspect attempted to restrain the subject allegedly for the purpose of robbing him. The suspect contended that the victim managed to retrieve a revolver from an end table in the living room. The two men engaged in a struggle for the gun. The suspect said that during the struggle, he was twisting the man's arm behind his back in an effort to make him relinquish the weapon. During the struggle, the victim was shot in the back of the head. When describing the shooting, the subject reenacted grabbing the shoulders of a person from behind. He then held his hand in the shape of a gun, aimed, and fired at what would be the back of the subject's head.

Part of the subject's memory reanimation may be the retracing of a particular route that he took to a location. For example, the subject may say that he has never been at a particular location, but at the same time, you may see him using his hands to draw the location in the air, on his knee, or even on the tabletop.

Figure 6.61 The victim in this case was clubbed to death with a softball bat by the pictured subject.

Not only will subjects retrace routes that they followed to a crime scene, but subjects have also been known to draw schematics of the crime scene locations. Subjects have drawn the shape of a room or building; they have traced the location of objects in the room; and they have also indicated their locations in an area relative to other landmarks, suggesting intimate knowledge with the scene.

Reenacting gestures may include other physical movements. Subjects may use their hands, and occasionally other parts of the body, to re-create specific physical behaviors. The subject may mimic lifting, turning, or twisting behaviors similar to those noted in the case study. The subject may act out driving, wrapping, holding, or the moving of persons or objects. An accused burglar may subconsciously reenact opening a window or prying open a door. A car thief may act out lifting the hood, disabling an alarm, or defeating the locking mechanism on a steering column.

A suspect may use his hands to visually support his verbal descriptions of shapes or sizes. This may be to assist in describing the length of a knife, the thickness of a club, or the size of a hole. Visually demonstrating these characteristics can assist the subject as he tries to support his alibi or explanation, or to just express himself more efficiently.

There are some hand behaviors that are important to the interviewer because they provide critical information concerning the subject's internal emotional or mental state. Such gestures strongly suggest that the subject is experiencing depression. These depression behaviors frequently involve such symptoms as pointing a gun-shaped hand toward the chest or the head. The subject's verbal cues will also be filled with depression comments.

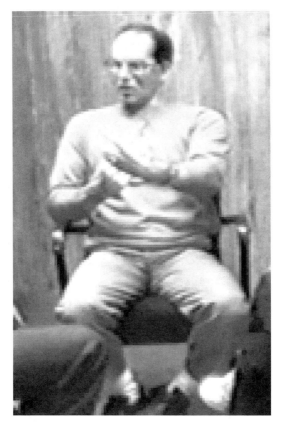

Figure 6.62 The male subject is describing how his victim was accidentally shot in the back of the head. The subject was behind the victim, holding him under the chin, when he pressed the muzzle to the back of the victim's head.

Case Study

Two investigators from a state board of nursing regulation were conducting an interview of a registered nurse suspected of stealing drugs from the wing of the hospital where she was assigned. During the interrogation, it was apparent to the investigators that the subject was suffering from depression. At a critical point in the interview, the subject broke down under the realization of her personal problems, drug use, the possibility of losing her job, and criminal prosecution. The investigators observed the subject then make the shape of a gun with her hand and put her finger into her ear in an obvious display of depression.

The nurse was removed from her job, and prosecution was diverted when the subject was admitted for extensive treatment for chemical abuse and depression.

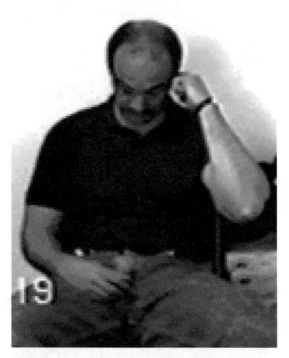

Figure 6.63 This subject is showing the negation behavior of rubbing and covering the ears. Notice the head position and aversive break in eye contact.

Conversely, an interviewer may notice that the subject uses a great deal of gesticulation when the interviewer is identifying the "constant" of his subject's analysis. If the interviewer notices a decrease in the level of activity of the hands at certain questions, the interviewer should suspect a change in the stress level for the subject.

Acceptance

Gestures of the subject's hands in combination with verbal cues can confirm that he is in the response state of acceptance. When he is in this response state, his state of mind is conducive to admission or confession. It is imperative that the interviewer recognize the subject's condition and capitalize on the opportunity.

The interviewer should be alert for moments when the subject's hands move to his chin. If he begins to rub or stroke the chin with the dominant hand, it indicates that he may be ready to confess (see Figures 6.69 through 6.73). This suggests agreement or acceptance and the subject resigning to the reality of the information. The touching behavior will be at the knob of the chin below the "facial-touch target" noted earlier.

Figure 6.64 Male subject showing negation behavior of ear rubbing. Notice the head aversion of turning away from the interviewer at the same time.

If the interviewer notices that the subject's hand has gone to the chin as well as the side of the face, the implication is entirely different than the acceptance response. The subject is demonstrating antagonism or anger if the thumb is placed under the chin and the finger is against the side of the face pointing to the eye in an L shape (see Figure 6.74).

A subject may also indicate he is in the response state of acceptance by using the hands in a demonstration of supplication. The interviewer should watch for moments when the subject opens his arms (if they have been crossed) and literally shows the interviewer his open hands or palms in a sign of resignation. The hands are usually held open, palms up, with the hands low, down near the lap and in front of the body, suggesting that the subject is in submission to the interviewer (see Figures 6.75 and 6.76). A display of open palms out to the sides of the body generally has another meaning, as noted earlier.

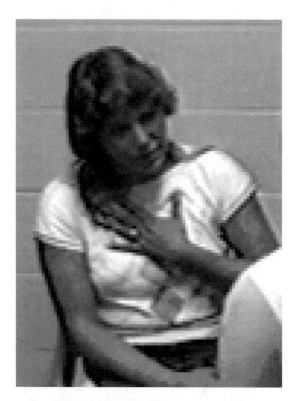

Figure 6.65 Female stress–response behavior demonstrated by the hand covering the chest. This is not a deception signal, but a sign of stress.

The Legs

The largest muscle group in the body is the legs. Anyone who exercises regularly knows that activities involving the legs are the best method for burning calories. By the same token, leg movements burn up greater amounts of the stored stress energy in the body. We already know that people are more aware of their speech symptoms than their body language and, therefore, are not conscious of most of the movements they make with their legs.

When a subject experiences the stress of probing, critical questions, the interviewer may observe an increase in the movement of the subject's legs. For example, the subject may cross his legs for the first time as if to create a barrier. This does not indicate deception, however, and is merely a form of adapting to the buildup of stress over the current situation or inquiry (see Figure 6.77).

Conversely, if the subject already has his legs crossed, he may engage in alternate movements. For example, if the right leg is crossed over the top of the left leg, the subject may reverse the cross by putting the left leg on top.

Figure 6.66 This subject, who is rubbing and squeezing the back of his neck, is exhibiting a strong stress and frustration behavior.

It is interesting to note that when the subject makes this change, the overall body alignment of the subject turns away from the interviewer in a nonverbal sign of rejection. Uncrossing of the legs, however, suggests that the subject is more at ease or feeling less threatened by the interviewer's questions or is becoming more accustomed to the interview setting or topics.

The use of the legs by the subject in the interview can be an attempt to create a physical barrier between himself and the interviewer. By erecting such a barrier, the subject helps to create a more comfortable and protected environment for himself.

A deceptive subject may stretch one leg far out in front of the other leg. The extended leg is usually aimed in the interviewer's general direction, acting like a barricade blocking the interviewer's progress in gathering inculpatory information. At other times, the leg is aimed toward a door or exit in what could be described as a sprinter's position. The subject is telegraphing that he would like to leave the interview room. In this case, the moment the movement occurs suggests aversion on the part of the subject and can be associated with deception. Other elements of the body will confirm this response. The torso may be leaning away, as are the shoulders and hips, from

Figure 6.67 A steepling behavior with the hands, as in the example shown here, can be a sign of the subject who has a sense of superiority in the interview.

Figure 6.68 An aversion behavior called "dismissal." Notice the subject gesturing away from the body as if to get rid of the issue.

Figure 6.69 Subject stroking the point of the chin in a typical submission behavior.

the interviewer. In some cases, the subject's head may be turned away from the interviewer (see Figures 6.78 through 6.80). Several of these aversion clues combined create an enormous cluster, and the deception probability is likely to be high.

Another form of barricading involves bringing the feet up into the chair. In one form, the subject may cross his legs with both feet in the chair. The other form has the feet in the chair, but with both knees pulled up towards the chest. Many times, the arms will be wrapped around the legs, holding them in place.

The action of crossing, uncrossing, or changing the crossing posture of the legs can enhance another denial behavior of the subject: stalling behaviors. The subject will listen to the question and then, before responding, delay his verbal response by breaking eye contact, uncrossing the legs, shifting the body position, crossing the legs, and resettling himself. Only after all this has occurred does he respond.

Knees

Movement of the legs can be an indication that the person may be under some degree of stress. These movements can be highlighted by the resulting exaggerated activities of the knees.

Figure 6.70 Male subject demonstrating submission behavior by stroking the point of his chin.

The practiced kinesic interviewer may notice that at certain questions the subject employs a wobbling of the knees as a means of dissipating stress. The more stress the person happens to be under, the faster the knees will wobble.

The subject can also demonstrate he is under considerable stress by moving the knees, but in a different plane than the one used to wobble the knees. The subject may begin to bounce the knees using a vertical motion. The knees may bounce in synchronization or one knee may be moving up while the other is moving down.

The Feet

As mentioned earlier, most of us are aware to a limited degree that our body language can demonstrate to those around us that we are nervous. This awareness of our nervous symptoms makes us want to try to control, if not suppress, their emergence. However, our bodies are so conditioned to automatically generate these cues that we are frequently unable to stop them. The

Figure 6.71 Female subject demonstrating submission or resignation by stroking her chin. This is a common pre-confession signal.

feet, because they are the farthest from the brain, is the least likely area we would consider as being the point for observing stress behaviors. To a lesser degree, the movement of the feet parallels the movements of the hands. The greatest portion of these movements can be classified as "adapters" — behaviors that occur as the person adjusts to the changing levels of stress that he may be experiencing.

There are two behaviors of the feet that are similar to the bouncing or wobbling of the knees mentioned earlier. First, when the subject's legs are crossed, watch for the foot that is suspended above the floor to wag or bounce when the subject begins to experience interview-related stress.

The second behavior also occurs when the legs are crossed. Pay particular attention to the leg and foot that is crossed and suspended above the floor. The interviewer may notice that when the subject gets agitated, the foot, and sometimes the entire leg, begins to swing. The faster and higher the leg swings, the greater the agitation of the subject.

There are some leg and foot behaviors that are evident with subjects who are feeling arrogant about the interview and the interviewer. For example, the interviewer may realize that at some point during the interview, the

Figure 6.72 Another example of a pre-confession cluster by a subject. Notice the stroking the point of the chin as well as the body-cascade posture of the shoulders.

Figure 6.73 Female subject showing submission cluster by stroking the point of the chin. Notice the eye contact is cast down.

Figure 6.74 Aggression response by a subject. Notice the L shape of the hand to the face. Also notice the V shape of the eyebrows and the "hard eyes" expression of aggression.

Figure 6.75 A submission signal in the form of a supplication gesture, with the arms out and the palms up.

Figure 6.76 Female subject showing a supplication pose with her palms out and turned up in resignation.

subject has put one or both feet on the interviewer's chair. A portion of this behavior can be attributed to the subject's attempt to encroach upon or dominate the interviewer's personal space. Another possible goal is to assist in developing a barrier between the subject and the interviewer.

While the subject is seated, he may demonstrate an air of confidence by assuming a sitting posture with the legs crossed in what looks like the figure 4. One foot will be on the floor, but the other leg will be crossed with the ankle resting on the knee. This, along with other supporting gestures with the arms, can suggest a powerful portrait of superiority.

When the subject has both feet on the floor, he sometimes gives the interviewer insight as to how he is coping with the interview. For some individuals who are under stress, they may have a tendency to pull both feet back up under their chair as if to hide them from the interviewer's view. When they relax, the feet slide back out from under the chair. For some subjects, crossing the feet at the ankles precedes the movement of the feet

Figure 6.77 Leg-crossing behavior can mean a person is being defensive. It can also occur when a person is under stress, but can also be merely a comfortable sitting posture.

under the chair. This suggests the subject may be under greater stress than when he merely pulled the feet under the chair (see Figure 6.5).

If the interviewer becomes aware that the subject is sitting with both feet on the floor and that the feet are turned in and pointing toward each other, the correct diagnosis is that the subject is rather timid and withdrawn. Conversely, if the feet are on the floor with the toes pointed outward, the subject's attitude is one of arrogance and self-confidence.

If the subject taps or even stomps the feet, two other emotional states are being presented. Gently tapping the foot is evidence of general fear, nervousness, or impatience with the situation, and is telegraphing the subject's desire to get on his feet and get away from the problem.

On the other hand, stomping of the feet has an entirely different implication. A person who is stomping one or both feet is highly agitated and hostile (Darwin, 1872; Darwin and Ekman, 1998). Stomping behavior is a common signal of hostility among animals. Horses, for example, will signal each other their defensive attitude by stomping their feet.

Figure 6.78 A remarkable example of aversion behavior by a subject. Notice the dramatic body-lean away from the interviewer as well as a pronounced aversive head movement at the same time. The stretched leg posture and turn of the body are also significant.

Sitting Postures

The sitting postures a subject assumes can provide information regarding the subject's past and current state of mind. Sitting postures are formed by a combination of cues known as clusters and may be further combined with other symptoms to create more complex postures, or they may present themselves as individual signals.

One of the easiest sitting postures to decode, as well as one that has been frequently seen by interviewers, is an "aversion" behavior (Davis, Connors, et al., 1999; Davis, Walters, et al., 2000) that we will call the "liar's lean." When an individual is uncomfortable or feels threatened, he experiences the survival instinct of fight-or-flight in various strengths. The "liar's lean" is a demonstration of the "flight" portion of that survival response. The interviewer may observe the subject leaning toward a door or window in an indication that he would like to leave or escape the threatening environment. This lean may be subtly discernable, or it may look like the person is going

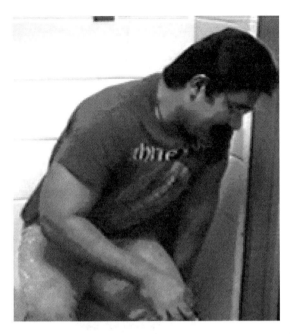

Figure 6.79 Significant aversion body movement by a subject who has turned his body, face, and head away from the interviewer.

to fall out of the chair sideways. The lean is significant to the interviewer when it occurs in response to a specific question or topic. It is with regards to his response that the subject could be deceptive. Should the subject maintain this posture during a specific topic area, there is a higher likelihood the subject is deceptive and may have, in fact, anticipated this particular discussion in advance of the interview, hence the strong reaction (see Figures 6.81 through 6.84).

The interviewer may notice other subtle variations on the theme of the liar's lean. For example, the interviewer may notice that the subject's entire body is turned toward an obvious exit. Frequently, the direction the body is pointing in is not always only toward an escape route, but, in fact, is turned away from the interviewer in rejection of him. In some cases, the subject may also have his hips, shoulders, and head turned away from the interviewer.

Should a leg be extended out and away from the body, the interviewer may notice that the leg is pointed toward or even aimed directly at the door. If the legs are spread apart, one of the subject's knees may point to the exit. If the investigator were transporting the subject as a prisoner, these types of body positions could be an obvious sign that the prisoner may be considering running. Should the subject be standing, as would occur during a traffic stop or taking a report on-scene, the interviewer might notice the subject's body weight positioned on the leg closest to the door or other escape route. At the

Figure 6.80 This subject is showing a more controlled aversive body posture. In this case, the subject has his body turned at a 90-degree angle to the interviewer.

same time, the subject may have his body turned toward the nearest escape route, or at least some portion of the body is telegraphing his thoughts and feelings of flight by pointing to some possible avenue of egress.

There are some sitting postures that suggest the subject is feeling superior. We noted one of these postures earlier when discussing the legs and the method of crossing the legs in a figure 4. This, as well as the other sitting positions, not only express confidence and even arrogance, but also serve the purpose of creating bodily barriers between the subject and the interviewer. They also permit the subject to take full advantage of the barrier of distance that is created between both parties.

A subject may assume a sitting pose that gives the interviewer the impression that the subject is ready for any action that comes his way. The person may sit in the chair with both legs spread wide apart. The hands will often be hooked into the belt by the thumbs, with the fingers pointing toward the groin. The implication is one of virility as the subject attempts to project an image of masculinity and power.

Another sitting pose reminds the observer of a person who is attempting to appear extremely cool and casual (see Figure 6.85). The subject will sit

Figure 6.81 This subject is showing an obvious body lean away from the interviewer and toward a door. Notice the turn of the body as well as the crossed legs and arms.

Figure 6.82 Subject in a subtle body-lean posture away from the interviewer.

Figure 6.83 Strong body-lean posture by a subject. Notice the angle and turn of the shoulders, as well as the angle of the head. Notice the crossed legs and the subject holding his legs with his hands.

Figure 6.84 Significant aversion behavior in this subject's upper body. The torso is also showing some body lean.

Figure 6.85 A rather cool rejection sitting posture, with the body turned and leaning away from the interviewer. This subject is usually quite confident and sarcastic.

slouched in the chair, once again with the legs spread out as far as possible. The upper torso of the subject will appear to be draped over the back and arms of the chair. The subject would have the interviewer believe that he is not at all impressed or bothered by the proceedings going on around him. Interestingly, the body will be away from the interviewer in a posture not too different from the liars lean.

Jailbird Seat

There are sitting postures commonly practiced by male subjects who have served a lengthy amount of time incarcerated. The postures, known as the "jailbird seat," are apparently learned by the subject either from force of habit or possibly from subconsciously observing other inmates.

Anyone who has sat in a classroom for a long period of time knows what will eventually happen to their backside. This "tired butt" syndrome arises from the person's weight being concentrated onto two small areas of the gluteus maximus. The blood is being squeezed out of these areas, creating discomfort and numbness.

If you have visited a state correctional facility or a county jail, you know that the inmates spend a great deal of the time sitting and waiting. They may be waiting for meals, counseling sessions, hearings, medical treatment, a turn on the weight pile, or just plain waiting. The end result is often a numb

Figure 6.86 An example of one of the jailbird-seat postures.

posterior. As a result, inmates have learned to adjust their body positions to alleviate this discomfort, and once outside the confines of the institution, may resort to the same habitual behavior when they find themselves once again sitting and waiting.

One of the "jailbird seat" positions finds the subject sitting forward with his back away from the back of the chair. His legs will be crossed, frequently at the knee, and his hands will be crossed and resting on his knee (see Figure 6.86). This sitting position moves the weight of the body from the two small areas on the bottom and redistributes the weight along the backs of the legs.

To realize the benefits of sitting this way, try both postures yourself. Sit normally, with your back straight and both feet on the floor. Imagine what it would feel like to sit in this position for an extended period of time. Pay particular attention to where your body weight is concentrated on the seat of the chair. Next, assume the "jailbird seat" and notice the change in pressure from your bottom to the backs of your legs.

The second "jailbird seat" also involves the subject sitting forward in his chair with his back away from the back of the chair. This time, however, the upper torso is positioned nearly over his legs. His forearms are resting on his thighs. Most importantly, the interviewer will notice that the arms and hands are flexed (see Figure 6.87).

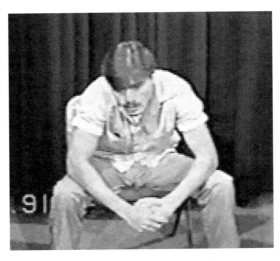

Figure 6.87 Jailbird-seat behavior by a subject. A strong and aggressive position.

Scared Rabbit

Up to this point, we have been discussing body language in terms of movements that are made when the subject is under stress. However, body movements are not the only indicators that a person is under stress. Stress also can be seen in a subject by the absence of any form of body motion, just as the rabbit, deer, or squirrel freezes in fear when they sense a threatening activity around them. This "frozen" behavior is classified as a "control" behavior (Davis, Connors, et al., 1999; Davis, Walters, et al., 2000). Depending on the extent to which the subject is trying to suppress his movement, he may be planning on disguising all possible emotional and other nonverbal responses from the interviewer. This obvious attempt at "control" suggests the subject is going to be deceptive regarding his true emotions. The observer is advised to pay close attention to the verbal cues for more accurate analysis.

When a subject is demonstrating a "scared rabbit" response to stress, the interviewer will notice that the subject sits for long periods of time without any body motion. Even an innocent person will have random body motions during the period of time that he is being interviewed. The deceptive subject may respond to the stress of a pointed and effective interrogation by freezing all body motion.

People are aware to varying degrees that their body language speaks volumes of information to the skilled observer. To stop this leak of critical information, they may try to suppress some of their bodily actions. The attempt to suppress symptoms requires the use of some form of control behavior or actions that abate the information leaks.

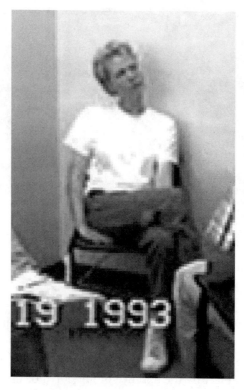

Figure 6.88 Female subject showing a lot of effort at "control behavior." She has her legs crossed, is sitting on one hand, and the other is clamped between her legs.

The interrogator may see the subject clench his hands together to stop the occurrence of nervous actions. Subjects have often been known to even sit on their hands to control symptoms (see Figure 6.41). Similar goals are accomplished by clenching the hands together, then holding the hands between the legs and clamping the legs together on them (see Figures 6.88 through 6.90). The crossing maneuvers of the arms and legs, discussed earlier, can also accomplish this goal.

Territorial Behavior

One of the characteristics common to all animals, including the human animal, is the exhibition of territoriality. We all tend to establish imaginary zones around us. We have different responses to actions that occur in each of those zones and classify other people around us into groups that are allowed to move within those zones. In 1959, Dr. Edward Hall studied this phenomenon demonstrated in human behavior which he called "proxemics."

Figure 6.89 "Control behaviors" exhibited by this subject include crossed legs, one arm holding the other, and the free arm clamped between the legs.

In police academies throughout the United States, officers are taught the critical concepts of street survival tactics. One of the primary concepts on which street-survival skills are based is the protection from threats to an officer's personal space. During any routine street interview, officers are careful not to allow a subject within much more than an arm's length, if not more, from the officer. The reason is that the officer is able to provide himself with a little extra time and distance to respond to any aggressive action that a suspect may take. In short, the officer is creating a defensible zone around himself for protection.

The same behavior also holds true for the deceptive subject during an interrogation. A subject, aware that the interviewer is going to be penetrating his innermost thoughts, feels the need to create a protective shell around himself. Many interviewers have noticed that subjects attempt to increase the distance between themselves and the interviewer. In the same manner that the legs and arms are used to create barriers, subjects may rely on desks, tables, purses, briefcases, file folders, and other objects to create some form of protective cover. The successful interrogator knows how to recognize and overcome these additional barriers to confession.

Figure 6.90 Female subject controlling her hand behaviors by keeping them in her pockets. One good way to keep down the nervous stress signals.

There are common zones that we have established around ourselves and there is social significance to each of them. The zone that is closest to us physically is labeled the "intimate zone." We permit only those people with whom we maintain an intimate relationship within the range of approximately 6 to 18 in. Those people often include our parents, spouses, lovers, children, and others with whom we are prepared to permit access to the most personal parts of our lives. This is the area that the subject of an interview does not want to share with the interviewer. The physical presence of the interviewer within this zone creates not only stress for the subject, but also distress.

The second zone of proxemic classification is the "personal zone." This area is approximately 18 in to about 4 ft. This is the range in which we permit our identified friends and close associates access. These are the people with whom we work and socialize with on a regular basis. The next zone is the "social zone" and is about 4 to 10 ft. This is the range reserved for people we are not familiar with. This is the distance we would like to keep between ourselves and the rest of the patrons in a bar or restaurant. The people who are moving in this range receive little attention from us unless their behaviors are specifically directed toward us.

The furthermost zone from us is the "public zone" and is from about 10 ft and outward. The people who move in this range receive little, if any, notice from us. We have little concern about their activities, and at times we will go to great lengths to avoid being conscious of others in this range. However, should we become interested in the activities of a person out in this area, we feel comfortable enough that we can openly watch these people without any negative social sanctions.

Realizing that all people subconsciously adhere to these zones, and that all people aspire to maintain a minimum zone of protection around themselves, it should be no surprise that the subject of an interrogation would want to maintain a protective zone between himself and the interviewer. Keeping arms and legs, as well as desks, tables, and other objects between himself and the interviewer assists the deceptive subject in maintaining that protective zone. The more protection the subject has, the safer he will feel, and the more difficulty the interviewer will have in controlling the subject's physical behaviors and keeping his attention.

The job of the interviewer is to reduce and overwhelm all the subject's efforts at resisting the truth about his actions. Overcoming the impediments to confession include reducing the physical barriers that may be used to assist in supporting the psychological barriers. The more barriers between the interviewer and his subject, the more barriers there are between the interviewer and the confession.

Attacking Proxemic Zones

Once the interviewer has determined that the subject is being deceptive, then the role of the investigator changes from interviewer to interrogator. The interviewer-turned-interrogator changes his method of dealing with the suspect's various stress–response states. One technique that is frequently used to improve the conditions for obtaining a confession from a subject is a concept called "attacking the zones." It should be noted that this method has been given undo credit for increasing the likelihood of confessions when, in fact, there is no evidence supporting that claim. What little research that has been done regarding successful interrogation techniques does not even earn rank in terms of the number of times it was successfully used to gain confessions (Leo, 1996).

We know that subjects have developed emotional and psychological barriers to revealing their guilt, and they often support this defensive nature by creating various types of physical barriers. The interrogator is already addressing the emotional and psychological aspects of the subject's rejection behavior with a verbal attack. "Attacking the zones" has been credited with increasing the effectiveness of the interrogator's attack, whereby the interrogator subtly defeats the subject's physical rejection behaviors. Since the subject is attempting to improve his defensive resistance to the exploratory efforts of the interrogator, the interrogator can take steps to neutralize those efforts. In fact, this is true not only in interview and interrogation situations, but also in many business, sales, counseling, therapy, and management settings. As the interrogator, you have probably already noticed that the subject is attempting to increase the distance between the two of you. Your goal, therefore, should be to deny the subject the sense of protection provided by developing these barriers.

To establish proxemic and kinesic control over the subject, the investigator should avoid having any physical objects between himself and the subject. Desks, tables, chairs, end tables, conference room tables, and even large expanses of open space inhibit the interrogator's ability to maintain such control. The concept of the old "eyeball to eyeball" interrogation approach can help accomplish that goal. However, there has been a great deal of misinterpretation of this approach along with the methods used by some investigative interviewers. There are many forms of stimuli that can also negatively affect a subject's behavior within the confines of an interview room. The behavior of the interviewer on a nonverbal level is also a source of major stimulus for the subject. It can have a negative, contaminating effect on the subject's nonverbal demeanor, and for the interviewer who is not conscious of this effect, the subject's responses can be misread and the subject's behavior, and even his admissions or confessions, can be contaminated.

In most cases, the interviewer is well advised to conduct the interrogation from a distance of approximately 24 to 36 inches from the suspect. Operating in this range inhibits the subject from feeling immune from the interrogator's exploratory efforts (see Figures 6.91 and 6.92). It is not and absolutely should not be used as a form of physical intimidation. Such behavior on the part of the investigative interviewer can easily create distress for the subject (Gudjonsson and MacKeith, 1982; Irving and Hilgendorf, 1980; Sommer, 1969). The interviewer should use the position as a method of indicating interest in the subject and as an exhibition of a desire to become intimate with the details of the subject's personal dilemma.

The interrogator should not start his interrogation from this position. Over time, as the interrogation progresses, the interrogator should move closer into the appropriate zone of 24 to 36 in. However, the process should not be used with the same intensity when interviewing a victim, cooperative witness, or similar subject who is not likely to be hostile to the interviewer's questions. In addition, the interviewer is well advised to be cautious when using "attacking the zones" methods beyond general environmental control and maintaining the subject's attention, due to the negative impact of misleading "distress" reactions that can be created in a subject's behaviors.

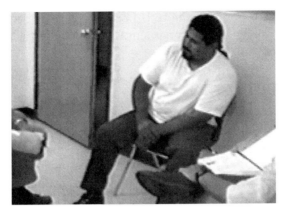

Figure 6.91 An example of using proxemic space in the interview room. Notice the interviewers are not too close to the subject, but still control the space and distance between themselves and the subject.

Figure 6.92 Good proxemic distance between the subject and the interviewers. Encroaching too close can contaminate the subject's behaviors with distress.

Body Language Clusters

Now that we have reviewed several individual body language signals, the interviewer-observer should begin to recognize the subject's behaviors as they occur in clusters. Remember our Practical Kinesic Principle stating that behaviors are identified in clusters rather than individually. We are now armed with the information necessary for us to determine if the subject's body language is supporting the verbal cues of truth or deception. If these body language gauges are not congruent with each other, as well as with the verbal cues, deception is indicated.

Negative Clusters

When a subject is experiencing one of the four negative stress–response states: anger, depression, denial, and bargaining, the subject generates clusters of behavior identifying the negative response. The interviewer needs to compare the verbal information with the nonverbal information for an accurate assessment. The majority of the signals, as well as their timeliness, leads the interrogator to his conclusion.

When the interviewer first enters the interview room, he may notice the subject sit down in a chair, almost dead center behind a desk or a table. By positioning himself with the table between him and the interviewer, the subject is using the table as a protective barrier.

The subject may not only abruptly sit down in the chair, but also may lean back in the chair or even rock the chair over on the back legs. This action assists the subject in creating distance between himself and the interrogator. Leaning back in the chair may also be accompanied by the subject crossing his hands behind his head, as if the hands are being used as a pillow. This posture is a typical sign of dominance or arrogance on the part of the subject.

A classic sign that the subject is in total dismissal of the interviewer is the presentation of a "cold shoulder." A subject may sit in the chair in front of the interviewer and then turn sideways in the chair. The final posture is with the body turned and a shoulder pointing at the interviewer.

When talking with the subject, the interviewer may note that the subject engages in activity that blocks or breaks normal eye contact. The subject may increase his blink rate when you are talking. He may put on a pair of glasses for no apparent reason or allow his hair to sweep across his face. The interviewer-observer may see the suspect start rubbing or pushing up the middle of the forehead with his finger. All of these actions assist in blocking or hiding the eyes.

We have already mentioned that subjects frequently show an increase in nervous hand activity in stress areas. These hand behaviors indicate impatience with the interviewer and the interview process and can indicate attempts to control the interrogator's aggressive inquiries. When moving into this general state of impatience or even anger, the interrogator may find himself in the suspect's "gun sights." The suspect may point at the interrogator with a finger or a pen or pencil, almost as if he is aiming at the interrogator (see Figure 6.93).

A variety of hand actions and body language can signal to the interviewer that the flow of conversation and information is acceptable in only one

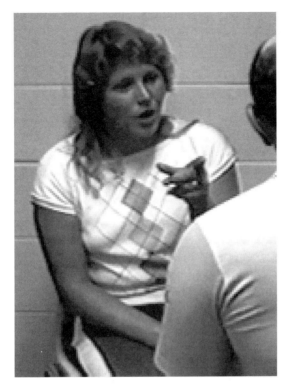

Figure 6.93 Female subject showing aggression by pointing her finger at the face of her interviewer.

direction. When the interviewer begins to speak, he may notice the subject lifting his hand or finger in a sign of disagreement. He may choose to turn his body to the side, presenting you with his "cold shoulder," but then, when he talks to you, he will turn and face you. The implication is that you must listen to him, but he is not obliged to listen to you.

A combination of facial expressions also contributes to the outward signs of negative response to the interviewer. The interviewer, therefore, may note that the subject never returns the interviewer's smile or even show a casual expression on his face during noncritical areas of the interview. The suspect maintains his "game face," or "war face," throughout the entire encounter. This "war face" can include indications that the subject is clenching his teeth, as is evident on one or both sides of the jaw as the muscles flex during the clenching. This in itself is strong evidence of anger and hostility.

A subject sitting in front of the investigator may show rejection and consternation by furrowing his forehead and knitting his eyebrows. At the same time, he may place his finger in the space just under the nose. If this gesture in the facial-touch target is observed while the interviewer is speaking, it suggests that the subject disbelieves the comments he is hearing. If it occurs while the subject is talking, it indicates that he does not really believe his own statements.

Another indication of this attitude of denial is exhibited through a behavior referred to as "nod service." Each of us as kids was subjected to a great deal of "preaching" from our parents. Some of these "sermons" were delivered with such regularity that the child "parishioner" had most of the words memorized. The child, already knowing what the rest of the sermon would be, would nod acknowledgment four, five, six, or more times, which is called "nod service." We were not agreeing with the sermon, but wanted the sermon to end because we had heard it all before and didn't want to hear it again. Subjects may use this same form of nodding in a silent expression of discomfort and displeasure with the content of the interviewer's comments.

Clusters of body language in the form of sitting postures alert the interviewer of general dissent. The subject may sit squarely in a chair with both feet planted on the floor. At the same time, he will lean forward with both palms resting on his thighs, his elbows pointed outward, and his thumbs pointed in toward each other. The interrogator senses that the subject is about to pounce on him.

Acceptance Clusters

Not all of the body language symptoms and verbal cues we have explored are limited to deceptive subjects. These same clusters are observed in reluctant witnesses, victims, sources of information, and informants. The same thing also applies to symptoms indicating those individuals who are being truthful and subjects who are ready to make an admission or confession.

When the subject is intellectually moving toward an acceptance response that can result in admission or confession, clusters of acceptance behaviors are generated. As with deceptive signals, there is no single symptom that indicates a subject is ready to confess. At the same time, it is important to remember that some of the individual symptoms seen when the subject is moving toward acceptance are also observed when the subject is responding with depression. The observer will make a more accurate analysis if he remembers to consider the verbal cues generated by the subject in conjunction with the nonverbal symptoms.

Early signs of acceptance generated by a subject include the phenomenon called "mirroring." When a subject begins to "tune in" to the interviewer's comments, the subject might copy the interviewer's facial expressions and physical behaviors. For example, should the interviewer nod his head while talking to the subject, he may notice the subject nodding at the same time. If the interviewer is talking and gesturing with his hands, he may see the subject respond using the same gestures. Should the interviewer tilt his head to one side while talking, he may notice the subject tilt his head to the same side as the interviewer. All of these are profoundly positive signs of movement toward acceptance by the subject.

Even some of the apparently trivial behaviors in which a subject engages are of great significance to the interviewer. Simple behaviors, such as loosening a tie or unbuttoning or even removing a jacket, coat, or sweater, suggest that the subject is at least more at ease and relaxed with the interviewer and thus in a state of acceptance. Other personal actions, such as loosening the belt or untying or even slipping off the shoes, have the same implication.

The interrogator may note that the subject is sitting relatively still as compared to previous sitting behaviors. In addition, the subject does not turn sideways, cover his eyes, or block his face. On the contrary, the interviewer notices the subject not only sitting still, but also turning to face the interviewer at all times, and may even lean forward toward the interviewer, indicating interest and agreement. The face is not obstructed and eye contact is more casual and focused on the interviewer.

The "nod service" behavior also changes. Instead of continuously nodding three, four, five, or more times while the interviewer is making a point, the subject gives a simple one or two nods in acknowledgment.

Pre-Confession Body Language Symptoms

Subjects who are finally moving to the point where they are ready to confess often give clear signals of their submissive state.

A subject who is in submission or acceptance literally opens himself to the interviewer. This openness is demonstrated not only verbally, but also nonverbally. The interviewer, for example, may observe the subject making comments while, at the same time, turning his palms up and leaning forward toward the interviewer. To be able to display the palms in such a manner, the subject must uncross his arms while leaning towards the interviewer, which suggests acceptance or even bonding with the interviewer. At this point, the subject has made up his mind about the evidence and has finally resigned himself to the inevitable (Darwin, 1872; Darwin and Ekman, 1998). The palms are presented in front of the body, reflecting an attitude of supplication, and the subject's defensive bearing subsides.

When in a submissive frame of mind, the subject may let his shoulders drop and roll forward, whereas previously, they may have been elevated in defiance. At the same time, the chin may drop down onto the chest and the eyes are downcast. The overall body language and verbal quality projected by the subject is that of submission.

Previous negative behavior signals demonstrated by the subject's eyes can change remarkably. The eyes may roll back into his head and the eyelids slowly close. The subject will look like he is ready to faint or even die. He may turn his eyes up toward the ceiling and start blinking slowly. He may also generate a stare similar to the San Paku stare. This stare, however, is accompanied with a slow blink rate that synchronizes with the interviewer's rate of speech.

Many interrogators and interviewers have often identified crying as a sure sign that the subject is guilty and undoubtedly is ready to confess. Crying can, in fact, occur at the point of submission, but in comparison with all the other submission behaviors, it is the least reliable. Crying can occur not only when the subject is being submissive, but also when the subject is responding with any of the negative moods of anger, depression, denial, and bargaining. Crying is triggered when the person is experiencing intense emotions. This emotional response triggers a tightening of the eyelids at the same time there is a physical contraction of the eyeballs (Darwin, 1872; Darwin and Ekman, 1998). The emotion experienced by the person is strong and so intense that he is unable to outwardly express the full depth of it. This creates "emotional back pressure," pushing the nonverbal and verbal expressions to their limit.

Crying when in the bargaining response state is a form of subtle manipulation and is an attempt to garner sympathy from the interrogator. Crying on demand, however, is not easy to do effectively when compared to genuine crying (Skinner, 1952, 1993; Ekman, 1992). When the subject attempts to cry on demand, the typical distress cues from the voice are not activated. Should the interrogator observe crying, he should make sure that the subject's verbal output is in one of the three verbal acceptance forms.

When the interrogator focuses on the suspect's face, he may see the subject stroke or rub his chin while smiling. The stroking will primarily be located below the facial-touch target. He may hear a deep sigh from the subject, indicating that he has ceased his efforts of denial and is prepared to surrender. In the meantime, his chin may begin to quiver, as if the subject is ready to cry, or he may rub his lips together for as long as 30 seconds as he searches for the initial remark with which to begin his confession.

When all the verbal symptoms and nonverbal cues present a cluster consistent with a subject who is ready to confess, the interviewer is either on the brink of accomplishing his goals or of driving the subject back into a frame of mind supporting further negative responses. When the interrogator observes a pre-confession cluster, it is time to stop talking because he has made his point. Further "selling" by the interrogator may result in him "buying" the confession back, or, in other words, talking the subject out of confessing. The interrogator should adhere to the following Practical Kinesic Principle:

> When the subject is demonstrating that he is in acceptance,
> the interrogator should stop talking and start listening.

The recommended course of action for the interrogator is to lower the pitch and volume of his voice. This quiet tone requires the subject to sit and listen carefully to the interrogator's comments. The interrogator should then provide the subject a way out of his dilemma that permits him to save face. This saving-face offer is one that allows the subject to maintain some form of self-esteem. No subject, under the majority of circumstances, will allow himself to be totally devastated and dehumanized by a confession. The human characteristic of self-preservation and survival is too strong and powerful. There always needs to be some seed of hope and self-respect from which the subject can rebuild.

Conclusion

After our extensive review of body language, you should have already noted that any person, either innocent or guilty, can generate a great deal of nonverbal information. Because of the large amount of body language behaviors that we constantly generate, keying in on one or two specific behaviors as a source of our analysis for determining if the individual is being truthful or deceptive would be severely flawed. Our two Practical Kinesic Principles regarding the identification of baseline behaviors and interpreting behaviors in clusters are extremely critical in assuring an accurate analysis.

Body language is more accurately viewed as a method of verifying that the speaker is comfortable with his own message. When the person is open and honest, his verbal and nonverbal cues are consistent with each other. When the subject is not convinced of his own remarks, those symptoms are incongruent and suggest deception. At the same time, those nonverbal behaviors provide the observer with information necessary to identify the subject's particular stress responses and his attitude regarding the interview and the interviewer and, in particular, when he is ready to confess.

II

THE PRACTICAL KINESIC INTERROGATION PHASE

The Stress–Response States

7

During the analysis phase, the goals of the investigator were to determine which individuals were being deceptive and in what specific areas those subjects were deceptive. Identification of those points of deception was ascertained by how the deceptive subject responded to direct questions or discussion about the issues of a case with the stress–response states. The presence of these responses, in and of themselves, are not indicators of deception, but rather how deceptive subjects use them differently than truthful individuals. These responses are an immediate indication of the subject's current mental and emotional responses. Once the deceptive subject has been isolated, along with the specific areas of deception, the investigator can focus his efforts on breaking the cycle of deception. The demonstration of each of these stress–response states is crucial to the interrogator's plan of attack. Recognition of each state permits the interrogator to take the actions necessary to disarm the four negative responses of anger, depression, denial, and bargaining.

These four negative reactions are self-perpetuating and self-sustaining. It is the person's internal cognitive and emotional responses to external stimuli that triggers them. If the interrogator permits the entire negative process to continue unabated, his goal of moving the subject toward admission or confession will be sidetracked and unproductive. The interrogator must be able to quickly and accurately identify the subject's specific response to each point of the interview and plan his subsequent interrogation attack. This requires the interrogator to have a deep understanding of each stress–response state, including the characteristics of each response, how it is defined, its goals, the results the subject hopes to attain by using the response, and how the interrogator should respond in order to control each response and facilitate the subject's movement toward acceptance and confession.

Anger

The anger response is the most destructive of all the negative-response states. Whether the subject is a suspect, a witness, the victim, or an informant, anger

209

can be and often is, the furthest from the response state of acceptance or any form of productive communication. Left unchecked, the gulf between the subject and the interviewer increases proportionally. The greater this gulf expands, the less control the interviewer has over the subject. It is critical to remember that the mere presence of anger does not mean the subject is going to be deceptive. Anger can be triggered in a subject for many reasons.

Characteristics

A person may express anger out of fear. The fear can have emotional origins, or be triggered by perceptions of possible physical harm. The professional investigative interviewer avoids triggering aggression in a subject because that subject fears that he will suffer physical harm at the hands or at the direction of the interviewer. Any information gained from a subject under such conditions will certainly be excluded in a court of law. Just as important, any information gained from the subject under such conditions is likely to be inaccurate and unreliable. A person on the emotional level can say the same for such a response, during which the subject fears he is under personal attack by the interviewer. The subject feels that he is at risk of extensive pain should the interviewer expose personal or relationship issues. In either case, the interviewer needs to examine his actions to be sure that they are not causing such an aggressive response and consider how he can modify his behaviors or the conditions of the interview setting.

When there is a major personal loss experienced by a person, it is not uncommon for those around him to see that person express anger as a way of coping with the loss. Such personal losses could include divorce, loss of a job, or break-up of a personal relationship. Nor is it unusual to see anger from a person going through the grieving process when a loved one has died or is suffering from a terminal illness. This response is a common sight for those officers, counselors, investigators, or interviewers who deal with the victims and family members of violent crime.

There are times in the interview setting in which a subject feels that the interviewer is attacking his personal image and self esteem. This is most easily triggered when the person suffers from some degree of insecurity. The subject now takes every question, suggestion, or inquiry to heart as if its sole objective is to humiliate him. In order to deal with this subject successfully, the interviewer has to address the subject's insecurities and spend time developing a degree of rapport and trust before proceeding successfully to the topic at hand.

Emotional sensitivity over former interpersonal relationships also triggers anger. This type of aggression response can cloud the investigative process for the interviewer. Should the sensitivity exist between the principles who are the focus of the investigation, the interviewer has to weed out what is truth and what is an attempt at getting even with the other subject. Is the victim inflating or even falsifying his victim status as way to exact revenge on the other person? The same can also happen with friends of victims who deliberately exaggerate their knowledge of events. Diligent follow-up interviewing eventually reveals what is fact and what is fiction. Invariably, the source of these aggressive responses is some "wrong," either real or imagined, that one individual has visited upon the other, and the primary goal is not necessarily a lie, but lying can help serve the purpose of "settling the score."

We have all experienced anger over a frustrating problem or situation: the car that won't start, traffic that won't move, people whose actions or behaviors irritate us and drive us to distraction. Similar conditions exist with the frustrated victim who feels no one is listening to his complaints or the witness who feels his important information is being paid little or no attention. Juvenile officers and domestic violence investigators frequently see this type of tension in the homes that are the scenes for their cases. Unfortunately, the aggression these individuals feel is visited upon the innocents around them. There are cases when inanimate objects and animals become the targets of anger. In all of these situations, it is the fact that the subject feels that he is not in control of the flow of events around him and perceives himself to be the victim of conditions not of his own making that triggers this reaction.

Another emotional anger trigger is the sense of failure that a subject may experience. For the subject, it may be the fact that his "foolproof plan" has fallen flat. It may be that he realizes that he made poor decisions and now must face the consequences of his actions. In cases where there are two or more individuals involved, anger may be triggered because the subject feels that he has let down the rest of his associates and thereby has failed in his commitment to them. This form of anger can be quite strong if the subject has placed high, or even almost impossible, standards for himself, only to see his plans collapse because of some personal flaw or mistake. This type of anger is often seen in highly intellectual subjects, those with overly abundant amounts of ego, people in highly visible or public positions, or the participants in complex white collar cases.

The subject who needs to exert control, whether over the interviewer or interrogation situation or the issue itself, uses anger. By gaining control, the subject can dominate the ebb and flow of the interrogation and the interrogator's ability to focus on critical issues. As long as the subject maintains this control, he can keep the interrogator on the defensive.

Anger is the behavior that is most akin to the animal mechanism of "fight" identified in the fight-or-flight survival response. The fight response is triggered first on the emotional level and then is supported by the subject's intellectual processes. Intellectually, the subject recognizes that the questioning process is a serious threat to his emotional and mental stability, as well as to his well being, and therefore he needs to fight for survival. As a result, the subject attacks that threat. The most important thing to remember about anger, however, is that by itself, anger is not a reliable tool for diagnosing deception in subjects. There are numerous situations during which anger is presented that have nothing to with deception. If the subject uses anger as a significant method of "avoidance," then the interviewer is justified in diagnosing that there is some "incriminating" value to the anger. "Incriminating cues" are those cues that both truthful and deceptive subjects generate, but deceptive subjects generate a greater number of these symptoms overall. In such cases, it is well worth the interviewer's time to uncover what information is being withheld or altered by the subject.

Anger facilitates the subject's ability to stave off the threat presented by the interrogator and is recognizable by the occurrence of confrontation behaviors on the part of the subject. The subject seeks the source of the greatest threat to him at any given moment and targets that source for his attack with the objective of overwhelming the issue. The attack comes in one of two forms. The attack may be covert, in which case, the "assault" is surreptitious and veiled.The second form is a focused attack that is of a far more personal, overt nature.

In the verbal section of the analysis process, we identified examples of each of the types of anger attacks. We noted that covert anger included such verbal symptoms as attacking minor details, trivial information, and case facts. Covert anger incidents also included general complaining by the subject, a change in the form or manner in which the subject addresses the interviewer, or even remarks about the interrogator's lack of skills or understanding in a specific area of business or a profession.

Verbal cues of focused anger on the part of the subject are expressed in the form of personal attacks. The focused attack is the most readily identifiable of the verbal cues of anger. For example, the suspect may blame the victim, suggesting that the victim was responsible for the occurrence of the crime. The suspect may make verbal attacks on the interrogator, his department, or even some of the witnesses.

At the same time that the subject's verbal cues of anger are demonstrated by the content of his speech, the intensity of the anger response can be measured by changes in the quality of the subject's speech. While experiencing anger, the subject may demonstrate increased volume, rapid speech, and higher pitch, or conversely may start talking softly in a lower pitch that resembles a growl. The key is the change in the normal voice characteristics that has occurred and the quality of the voice indicates the strength of the response the subject is experiencing.

The body language section of the analysis phase assisted the interrogator in determining that the subject was handling the interrogation through anger.

The interrogator may have noticed the subject's eyebrows form a V over the bridge of the nose or the face and the throat turn red. The subject may pound his fist as he tries to make a point, point a finger at the interrogator, or slap his leg. The legs, when crossed, may swing in the air like a field-goal kicker, or the suspect may tap or stamp his feet. All of these verbal and nonverbal behaviors assist the interrogator in correctly diagnosing that the subject is responding to the investigative inquiry with anger. Once anger has been correctly diagnosed, the interrogator can take the next step in controlling and diverting the anger to a more productive response.

Goals

The primary goal of the subject in using anger is to dominate the interrogator and the interrogation. By developing and maintaining dominance and control, the subject can keep the interrogator on the defensive. It is necessary for him to maintain this control in order to break the momentum of the "attack" he perceives as coming from the interrogator's questions. Breaking the momentum of the interrogator prevents the investigative interviewer from identifying and exploiting the suspect's vulnerabilities and, therefore, sustaining the assault on the subject's defenses.

When the suspect is in control of the interrogation, he can maintain his rejection of the interrogator's argument or presentation of case facts. At the same time the subject is gaining control of the interrogation, he also hopes to force the interrogator into tipping his hand and showing the negative information he hopes to use against the subject sooner than he had planned. By gaining forewarning of the interrogator's "game plan," the suspect can prepare some form of defense in anticipation of the interrogator's direct attack. In this manner, the suspect can prevent himself from having to accede to the interrogator's position, which would mean surrender or confession.

Results

The deceptive subject produces results that are in his favor, but there are disadvantages for the subject as well. One of the weaknesses in using anger as an approach is that while the subject is attacking, openings are presented for the interrogator to exploit. The interrogator should be alert for moments when the subject becomes consumed by his apparent control and unintentionally provides the interrogator with additional information that can be used against the subject in the ensuing interrogation. His anger can overtax the suspect's ability to use restraint in preventing those momentary mental lapses.

The interrogator is sure to realize that he has little, if any, chance of success in gaining a confession from an aggressive subject. The subject who is hostile and angry is frequently oblivious to the importance of the comments directed at him. Anger generates such an intense concentration on the part of the subject that all of his mental, physical, and emotional capacities are focused solely on survival and destroying the threat before him.

By remaining in a state of anger, the subject hopes to prevent himself from forming any type of bond with his perceived enemy, the interrogator. To allow such a bond to exist or even begin to develop puts the suspect at great risk. The risk is that the interrogator will gain control and the suspect may be forced to face the reality of his actions and deceptive behavior. The interrogator cannot allow the response of anger from the subject to continue. To do so results in the suspect's ability to derail any attempt on the part of the investigator to develop a communication bridge between himself and the suspect.

Interrogator/Interviewer Response

Once the interrogator recognizes that a subject is responding with anger and he has an understanding of its functions and goals, the interrogator is better equipped to deal with the attack. To allow a subject to remain in any negative-reaction state means that the negative behavior will continue to sustain itself in some form. The goal of the interrogator, therefore, is to find some way to defuse the anger and move the subject into another form of response.

The first step in defusing anger is for the interrogator to realize that the subject's anger is a sign of frustration. A football team that is thoroughly beaten by the opposing team and realizes that there are only a few minutes left in the fourth quarter will become frustrated with the position in which they find themselves. The team members recognize that part of the responsibility for the current dilemma lies with them because their own errors have partially defeated them. The result of this frustration is often reflected in the fights that break out between the players, especially in a high-stakes game. The deceptive subject feels the same type of frustration with his efforts.

One of the primary goals of the interrogator in dealing with anger from a suspect is to avoid being pulled into the whirlpool effect that anger creates. An angry subject tends to draw others into anger. When both the subject and interrogator are reacting to each other with anger, both parties are barricaded in their positions and become inflexible in their response to others who are trying to communicate with them.

During the career of any athlete, his coach has told him to avoid playing in anger because the athlete is more prone to mistakes. Such is the plight of the angry suspect, who will frequently make a mistake, providing an opening for the interrogator. The principle works both ways. An angry interrogator presents openings for the suspect, making himself vulnerable. Coaches have also warned their athletes that they often become the targets of attacks from their opponents. Although the athlete would be inclined to respond in kind, such a response is a mistake. The same applies for the interrogator. Although you may be inclined to respond in kind to the subject's verbal acts of aggression, to respond will inevitably cost the professional interrogator dearly and can cause irreparable damage.

An interesting characteristic of anger that the interviewer can utilize to his advantage is the normal life span of anger. Anger needs a great deal of energy to be sustained. If left alone and not fed by any outside source, anger can burn itself out. The total resources of the suspect are not sufficient to sustain anger for a period of time much longer than an average of about two minutes. Anger creates such tremendous and severe vascular-emotional strain on the individual that the human system cannot handle the demand. Simple patience and avoidance of anger on the part of the interviewer gives anger an opportunity to consume itself.

When individuals are hostile towards each other, they have, in reality, taken opposing views on one or more issues. In an attempt to defuse anger, the interrogator should avoid taking the opposite position of the subject, for this results in the anger being "fed." The answer, however, is not to take the subject's point of view because, first, it may be the wrong view, and second, the interrogator will be seen as trying to patronize or placate the subject, which can also feed his anger. It is imperative, therefore, that the interrogator try to remain neutral in the face of anger.

An example of avoiding taking sides in an argument is found in how police officers are trained to respond to domestic disturbances. These situations are highly emotional and volatile. The officer's first task is to separate the combatants in order to defuse the anger and prevent any physical harm. In his efforts to resolve the dispute, he is warned never to take the side of either of the two parties. No matter how right or wrong each party may be, the officer who takes one side or the other will find himself the target. Very often, he will be the target of both parties, who have now turned on this "meddler." The officer, as well as the interrogator, is well advised to remain as neutral as possible in any conflict.

Another tactic in defusing an angry subject is to take him back to a point in your conversation when the subject was under control. To find that point, you may have to go as far back as the beginning of the conversation. It would be ludicrous for the subject to develop anger over an area that has already been agreed upon. The best point of control, however, is if the interrogator can identify an area in which the subject was experiencing depression. The subject who is using depression as a response is attacking himself.

Also, consider that you may be focusing on too broad a range of issues with the subject. The subject's sense is that he is being overwhelmed with too much information or too many issues at one time. Try breaking down the information you want from the subject into smaller, more manageable parts. By dealing with the case in smaller elements or one element at a time, the interviewer allows the subject some sense of control, even though the interviewer is controlling the situation. This is not to imply that issues be ignored or minimized by the interviewer. We are only directing the subject's attention toward resolution of the issues in smaller, but more productive, steps.

A final comment regarding anger is an admonition to the interrogator. No one likes to be attacked verbally. No one likes to deal with hostile situations. No interrogator likes to be the focus of an attack by a guilty suspect. It can take a great deal of personal restraint and self-discipline to maintain control of your emotions in these types of situations. But remember, the suspect is the one who is under the gun and he is frustrated because he is having difficulty dealing with the reality of his behaviors and actions. When the interrogation is done and over with, the suspect is still guilty. The goal is for the interrogator to go home after the interrogation and for the subject to go to jail. You can take the abuse!

Depression

Depression shares the characteristic of aggression with anger. In anger, the subject is directing aggression outward toward those who are around him. Depression, on the other hand, is inverted aggression. In other words, the subject has turned on himself.

Like anger, the mere presence of depression does not mean that the subject is being deceptive, although it can create conditions that are not conducive to gaining a great deal of information. We should remember that we may also be dealing with victims, family members, and possibly witnesses, as well as suspects.

Definition

If anger is an expression of the "fight" side of the fight-or-flight survival response, then depression is the expression of the "flight" side. As with any of the stress–response states, the subject is having difficulty in dealing with the reality of the situation, but in this case, chooses to retreat from the reality by mentally and emotionally withdrawing into himself.

The response state of depression generates less outward activity on the part of the subject than does anger. The entire process of depression is a negative of anger. With the aggressive behavior internalized, the force of anger's destructive energy is consuming the subject. Since we know that anger is severely debilitating to a subject, then depression is twice as destructive for him. He is expending the cognitive and emotional energy normally generated when he is experiencing anger, however, he needs an equal amount of energy to defend himself against his own internal attack. As a result of this phenomenon, the response of depression is extremely debilitating to the subject's ability to respond to the threat of reality with which he has been confronted. Keep in mind that the response state of depression we are discussing in this section is not the same as clinical depression. Clinical depression, along with its characteristics and identification methods for the interrogator, are discussed later in the text.

Characteristics

The verbal symptoms of the depression response were discussed earlier in this text. Those verbal symptoms include comments from the subject about how depressed or "down" he is feeling because of the incident or the investigation. He may also comment about how his health has been suffering because of the investigation, including how he has not been eating well, sleeping well, or having other physical problems.

The subject who is reacting to the investigation with depression may find it necessary to mention how his life has been devastated or unalterably changed because of all the attention surrounding this case. He may mention that his career has been affected negatively, as has his family life, and even his relationships with friends, neighbors, and co-workers have been severely strained.

The interrogator may hear the subject blame a variety of other sources as being responsible for his current dilemma. Remarks may be made about how everyone has turned against him or has turned their backs on him. He may comment how other people don't really like him and only used him when they needed or wanted something from him. Now that he needs some support, those same individuals have abandoned him.

The depression comments may go as far as threatening to commit suicide or do physical harm to himself. Those remarks may include veiled threats, such as leaving town, quitting his job, or leaving his family, to outright remarks of how he is thinking of taking his own life. These types of comments should never be taken lightly or mistaken as nothing more than idle talk. If the subject is talking about it, then he is thinking about it. If a subject makes remarks that even hint at self-destruction, you should take all actions necessary to protect the subject from himself. This is not to say you immediately throw him to the ground and call for medication and a straitjacket. It does mean you should be sure that there is some form of professional analysis and intervention for the subject. It is extremely critical that this subject not be left alone without some form of regular supervision and care. Later in this text, we will discuss the profile of a suicidal personality.

The nonverbal symptoms of depression are easy for the interrogator to identify. The subject may begin to cry, although crying can appear in any of the other response states. Other nonverbal cues include bowed head and downcast eyes, slumping or hunched shoulders, and the body of the subject appearing to be wrapped up in itself. The observant interviewer may notice hand wringing, a hunched posture, and a significant decrease in eye contact. Keep in mind that the interrogator must make his diagnosis based not only physical symptoms, but also on the verbal cues a subject generates.

Goals

There are several goals that the subject is attempting to accomplish when he responds to the interrogation with depression. The primary goal is to evade reality. The subject must find some means by which he can withdraw from the unpleasant truth and reduce the chances of suffering more damage to his self-esteem.

This escape behavior allows the subject to search within himself for a place of safe haven. In this haven, he will try to weather the storm, with hopes of being able to survive the attack and emerge after it passes. The purpose of the withdrawal is not to fight the threat, but to retreat and hide from it.

Retreating within depression allows the subject to accomplish another goal. If he does not make himself open and available to the interrogator, he is not forced to make any emotional contact with the interrogator. This protective response further isolates the subject from the current questioning process.

Results

Since depression is one of the four negative-reaction behaviors a subject can use when encountering interrogation stress, the end results are not conducive to the facilitation of an admission or confession. Subjects responding with depression are rigid and reserved, both mentally and emotionally. The subject's withdrawal from the conflict and the ultimate isolation occurs because he prefers to suffer alone, out of the view of the interrogator and any other observers.

The investigator needs to remember that this subject's ultimate goal is to survive the attack with as little injury as possible. Thus, he rarely contributes much to the interrogation itself. Without such input, the interrogator has little to which he can respond. The suspect takes this approach, not only because it decreases his exposure and risk, but also because he is operating in an air of suspicion. The subject sees himself in a precarious position created by the interrogator. Thus, he will view all efforts of the investigator to help with extreme paranoia and will regard the interrogator's comments, actions, and motives with skepticism.

Depression in a subject has a way of seizing the entire operations of the mind, including its thought processes. The result is that the subject can only focus on one issue at a time, and that issue is the pain he is suffering because of the injury to his self-esteem. The issue of pain is such an all-consuming issue that little or no other information can be considered. While the subject is mentally fixated on his pain, he will be unable to devote much in the way of mental and emotional energy to other issues. Because of this, the subject will become single-minded and responds to all other outside stimulus slowly. The person will pay little attention to the evidence, warnings, and admonitions the interrogator presents. Each of the individual issues that the interrogator raises are considered only after their importance is weighed in comparison to the distress the subject is feeling. Inevitably, the anguish the suspect is experiencing is always more important an issue than anything the interrogator mentions.

The negative results of depression left untreated are extensive, both for the interrogator and the subject. The subject experiencing depression is providing the interrogator with his soft underbelly and is making himself vulnerable to attack, provided the interrogator knows what to do. This means that the subject is sacrificing a great deal of personal security in the hope of gaining some small form of survival. Left unattended, the subject's chances of recovery from depression diminish proportionally.

Interrogator/Interviewer Response

When a subject appears to be responding to the interrogation with depression, the investigator must be sure he knows which form of depression behavior the suspect is experiencing. Each form requires a specific response from the interrogator. If the suspect is feigning depression, then the real response is bargaining, and the subject should be treated accordingly. When a subject is experiencing genuine depression, the interviewer will see it in the subject's body language behaviors. He will hear it in the quality of the subject's voice and in the content of his speech. And he will feel the depression on an empathetic level. On an instinctive level, human beings are capable of sensing genuine pain in another human being. If these three elements are not present in the subject's presentation of depression, then we are most likely dealing with a bargaining response. We will discuss bargaining later in this section.

If the depression appears to be clinical depression, the interrogator is well advised not to attempt to address it. The chances of getting a confession from a truly clinically depressed subject are dramatically decreased. The rate of success in getting a confession is complicated by the fact that clinical depression is a far more complex problem than the interrogator is capable of handling during the limited time and circumstances of an interrogation. We will discuss the general characteristics and profile of clinical depression later in the text.

If the subject's depression appears to be the stress–response form, the interrogator should bond with, or "feed," the depression. The most important issue for the subject at this point is the pain he is suffering. If the interrogator ignores this pain, the subject will withdraw further within himself. Ignoring a subject's depression is to diminish the significance of the pain the subject is suffering. This rejection of the subject's depression by the interviewer can push the subject into a more entrenched and volatile form of behavior — paranoid depression. This is one of the most destructive of all human behaviors, not only for the subject, but also for those around him who he attempts to destroy — especially those who ignore his emotional pain. Since depression is debilitating for the subject, feeding the depression keeps the subject turned against himself. The result is that his defensive reserves are greatly diminished, leaving little energy to attack the interrogator and his case.

To feed the subject's depression, the interrogator must learn to be patient with the subject's slow progress. A subject experiencing depression is slow to respond and slow in his thinking. His verbal, nonverbal, emotional, and mental processes are slower than that of a person who is not in depression, and the interrogator's inclination will be to try to energize him in order to get a response.

The subject is going to be suspicious of the interrogator and is going to be cautious in developing any personal bond on his own initiative. The interrogator must be the one to reach out and offer to establish that relationship. The interrogator accomplishes this by providing the subject with all possible opportunities to openly discuss his pain without fear of rejection from the interrogator. It is only after he has totally vented all his personal anguish that the subject will address the real issue of his guilt.

On its surface, this recommendation sounds as if the interrogator is at the mercy of the subject. A closer look, however, reveals that this response causes the subject to play into the interrogator's hands. Once the subject has vented his pain, there is little energy left to attack the interrogator, which is a definite advantage to the interrogator.

Depression can create another advantage for the interviewer should the subject be guilty. A subject in depression is most concerned about his own pain and will be fully engaged in an internal examination of all his faults, failures, and shortcomings. The fixation, however, overrides a person's normal verbal editing and censoring systems. As a result of this critical self-analysis, deceptive subjects frequently expose information that is significant to the investigation. It is not uncommon to hear comments such as "I knew they were going to find out about this." "When I heard they were looking at the travel logs, I knew they would find out." "When my wife told me you had called the house, I was afraid this would come up." These are cues to the investigative interviewer to pursue a line of questioning that further explores these comments or topics; they are frequently significant elements to the investigation.

If the subject indicates that he is concerned about how the entire investigation is having a negative impact on his family, the interrogator should discuss that problem at length. If he is indicating he is depressed or is contemplating harming himself or taking his life, the issue also needs to be talked about at length with him.

In dealing with anger, one of the recommendations was to take the suspect back to a point where he was experiencing, or might be experiencing, depression. The interrogator should not randomly assume the areas in which the suspect is susceptible to depression. Those points should be carefully noted based on the subject's personality and previous veiled comments indicating possible points of weakness.

Denial

The subject who is using denial as his response is rejecting reality. It is from the negative-response state of denial that all other negative-response states have their origins. Without the presence of some portion of denial, the other three negative responses eventually collapse. For this reason, denial is the most critical of all the negative-response states for the subject because it enables him to build up and maintain his entire fortress of deceit. In essence, denial is where the greatest bulk of deception occurs — it is the heart of deception (Davis, Connors, et al., 1999; Davis, Walters, et al., 2000; Walters, 2000).

In order to create the rejection of reality necessary to build this fortress of deceit, the subject must convince himself and the listener of his lie. He cannot accept the event or acts in which he has engaged and which have brought him to this juncture, and he cannot afford to have the interrogator or anyone else accept their existence either. This double deception must be sustained so that he can defend himself against the anxiety created by the reality of his actions. But there is a major flaw in the subject's plan to use denial. First, in order to create a functional deception, the subject has to know what the truth is. The deception has to disable the strength of the evidence of the reality he wants to deny. This creates a major intellectual paradox. The deceiver has to call attention to the evidence of the very reality he is trying to discredit, and in doing so, calls attention to the possible existence of that very same evidence that is so damning to his argument.

Denial never succeeds for the subject, as he is fully aware that he is lying. Subjects are not forced, trapped, or tricked into lying; it is a conscious choice that he makes. The question the investigative interviewer should always keep in mind is what the subject stands to gain by lying and what is at stake if he chooses to tell the truth.

Definition

Denial, although it is the origin of the other three negative-reaction states, is different from the responses of anger and depression. Anger and depression are direct descendants of the animal survival instincts of fight-or-flight. Anger and depression are also found in the behaviors of both truthful and deceptive subjects and therefore are not reliable as indicators of deception. The response state of denial operates on a higher and more involved intellectual level. The fourth negative-response state of bargaining is also a defensive form of this intellectual protection system.

Denial is, by its very nature, the mechanism a subject uses to create his lies, and this is done for two main reasons. First, it helps him defend himself against the anxiety and stress that is created when he is forced to face the reality of the crime. Second, it is used to protect his ego. This dual protection system creates a barrier between him and reality, but reality always seems to find a way to creep back into the light of his awareness. To shield against it, he builds his fortress of deceit to hold the ever-invading truth at bay. It is from this response state, therefore, that 90% or more of lying occurs (Davis, Connors, et al., 1999; Davis, Walters, et al., 2000; Walters, 2000).

Characteristics

The interviewer will recognize verbal denial behavior in the subject by the presence of one or more of three primary characteristics. First, the subject may refuse to recognize the question and its direct or implied significance. Second, he may directly or indirectly refuse to answer a question. Finally, he may find some way in which to stall before responding to a question.

When the suspect is responding to a question with the behavior described earlier as "specific denials," he is failing to recognize the question. He has realized that there is an error in the question and responds only to the error as his means of escaping a response to the real inquiry made by the interrogator.

This failure in recognition is at work when the subject uses comments involving displacement, such as "they," "them," "those people," and so forth. The same phenomena occurs when he shifts pronouns or verbs or uses qualifiers in his responses. This permits him the opportunity to appear to give an answer without responding directly to the interrogator's question.

Refusing to answer the investigator's question is the most obvious method of avoidance that the subject can use. It is a straightforward rejection of the issue at hand. As we mentioned in the section on verbal behavior, the easiest and best method of maintaining avoidance is to claim to have a memory lapse. The failure of memory, no matter which type, gives him one of the safest havens of retreat from the allegation.

Other avoidance tools include the use of blocking statements, in which the subject avoids answering the interrogator by responding with a "why" question, requiring the interrogator to show proof of guilt. He can do the same thing, but with a different impact, by using denial-flag expressions, such as "honestly," "believe me," "truthfully," and similar expressions.

Comments involving "bridging phrases" permit the subject to maintain a posture of avoidance by helping him verbally step over critical areas of stress in his remarks. Guilt phrases and weighted expressions are also forms of avoidance. The simplest form of avoidance is the deceptive "no." That "no" answer, however, is a form of "no" that he has not used any other time he has chosen to respond with a truthful "no."

The third verbal characteristic is that of delaying a response. It should be no surprise that stalling tactics are at the heart of this segment of the denial response. The subject stalls before answering to give himself a chance to determine if he wants to lie or tell the truth, and, if he decides to lie, how big a lie should be told.

As a stalling mechanism, subjects use some forms of speech dysfunction. Frequent "ah," "err," "um," and "uh," as well as nervous laughs, grunts, groans, growls, moans, whistles, and other sounds assist in giving him a chance to recover and prepare a clear line of thought.

There are numerous body language symptoms that are seen in clusters and that support a subject's denial response. Such behaviors include hiding the eyes, closing the eyes, or breaking eye contact when responding to a "hot issue" question. Crossing behaviors involving the legs or arms, physical barriers of distances, objects, shoulders, and other symptoms create the impression of denial. These and other nonverbal behaviors further exhibit the subject's intention to reject reality.

Goals

There are a couple of goals that a subject hopes to achieve through his use of denial. The first is to totally reject the reality of the case facts in order to perpetuate his argument that he is not guilty. His second goal is to convince the interrogator, just as he is trying to convince himself, that those facts are erroneous, and therefore he is not guilty.

The subject accomplishes his first goal by intellectually trying to identify any possible weaknesses in the evidence presented against him. If the interrogator acts as if he is unsure of his comments or is not completely correct in his assessment of evidence, the deceptive subject utilizes that weakness to attack, hoping to widen the gap between himself and guilt.

The second goal is accomplished by lying to himself and to the interrogator. To do this, he must develop a line of reasoning that supports the concept that all the information is wrong. It is not easy, however, to make oneself believe that which exists really doesn't exist. The entire process is a paradox. To create that mental state, the subject must recognize the threat of reality in order to argue that it does not exist. If the interrogator continually attacks the subject's denial with evidence, the intellectual disharmony continues. To break this impasse, the suspect must now also convince the interrogator that there is no basis to the evidence.

Results

Denial is a self-sustaining process. The more that a deceptive individual maintains the intellectual exercise of denial, the more denial is necessary to keep the process going. The more denial occurs, the greater the subject's resistance against admission or confession. Denial provides the brick and mortar that a subject uses to build his fortress of deceit. Without denial there is no deception.

The presence of denial in the subject slows the interrogation. Each time the suspect presents his point of denial, the interrogator must recognize it, address it, and adequately overcome that point before he can address the next issue. The more points of denial the subject creates, the more effort the interrogator must use to overcome them.

Interrogator/Interviewer Response

The only way that the interrogator can deal with a subject who is reacting with denial is to attack. The interrogator must force the subject to face the reality he is trying to reject. This means that the interrogator must first of all recognize what the subject is attempting to deny. Second, the interviewer must know how the subject's personality's mental mechanism works in the perception and treatment of reality.

Denial, overall, is really several smaller acts of denial, all occurring at one time. Recognizing this, the interrogator can isolate the individual points of deceit the subject has presented. The interrogator then attacks each of those points with the truth and evidence of its existence. This must be done about every three to five minutes by the interrogator.

In that denial is self-sustaining, the interrogator must cut off the lifeblood of the process, which is the subject's continuing deception of himself and his attempt to deceive the interrogator. The interrogator must not let his case be stalled or diverted by allowing himself to be convinced that the subject's argument is legitimate. Instead, he must make a straightforward attack every few minutes with the specific evidence that contradicts the subject's denial.

The denial process is a mental procedure, and the procedure is unique for each of the two main personality types involved. Each of these two types perceives reality through different filters and then processes the information in different formats, just as different types of computers process information using different programs. The interrogator must know how each subject formats and processes that information.

The interrogator must be able to identify which personality type he is dealing with, and then he must attack the subject's denial in the same manner in which the subject's perssonality organizes his denial mechanism. We will discuss these two types in greater detail later. We will also discuss the most effective attack methods for each type. At that time, it will become apparent to the interviewer why he can have the "right subject," the "right evidence," and use the same standard attack method that has been successful on other subjects but why it won't work on a particular personality type. We must realize that it is not the subject that is the problem, it is the interrogator who has made the mistake.

Bargaining

Bargaining is the weakest of all the stress–response states. In this response system, the subject accepts reality and his involvement in it, but only in an altered state that limits the extent of his responsibility. From this point, the interrogation can move into a full acceptance phase, or it can revert to any of the negative-response reactions. The subject is vulnerable to the directions of the interrogator, although not to the same extent as he is when responding with acceptance.

Definition

Bargaining is the second form of mental response to stress. The other mental response system was that of denial. If more than 90% of lying occurs in the response state of denial, then the other 10% occurs in the state of bargaining. During this state, however, the subject is not rejecting reality outright. He is disguising reality to make it easier for him to live with and without giving up and going completely into acceptance. The subject may also be attempting to change our perception of him as the perpetrator in the events that have occurred. It is a "softening" of his participation and intent as the possible actor. In both cases, the altered images are less damaging than the reality of the facts would show.

Bargaining is found in both truthful and deceptive subjects. Victims will attempt to recast their role in the crime and their true behaviors for fear of embarrassment or for fear that no one will believe the true nature of the events. Witnesses have been known to engage in the same behaviors because they were someplace they shouldn't have been or saw something they weren't supposed to see. They also underplay their knowledge for fear of being wrong and mistakenly identifying a person as a suspect. In these cases, the individuals may have guilty knowledge that the interviewer needs to explore. We are not talking about the normal anomalies or flaws that occur in eyewitness testimony. Those are errors in "perception." We are talking about deliberate misrepresentation on the part of the subject. Bargaining is more accurately perceived as a form of evasion than the pure deception we see in denial.

Characteristics

In this state, the subject is still in the process of lying to himself and to the interviewer. This time, however, he has partially accepted at least some portion of the reality of his behavior. To able to accept a portion of reality, he must alter it into a more palatable form. To transform this reality into the more agreeable image, the suspect must attempt to cloak the severity of his actions, as well his failure to control himself and commit the act. He must also find a way to create an appearance for himself as more of a victim than a suspect, or at least as a person with good intentions that have gone wrong. At the same time, he is trying to convince himself of these reconstructed pictures and actions, and he must get the interrogator to agree with him for the disguise to succeed. The primary characteristic of bargaining is the creation of disguise. The subject must create, or at least suggest, a substitute characterization of himself or the crime.

Verbal cues of bargaining are those that accomplish the recharacterization of the subject and the crime. For example, he may describe the crime using "soft" or substitute terms. This is a psychological desire to avoid harsh reality. The subject may describe stealing as "borrowing," speeding as "keeping up with the flow of traffic," or rape was actually "just rough sex." We will find similar recharacterization throughout our subjects' conversations.

When responding with bargaining, the subject may attempt to improve his relationship with the interrogator by establishing some form of emotional bond. This is accomplished by being overly friendly with the interrogator. The hope is that the interrogator will be impressed with the subject's apparent nonthreatening behavior and show leniency. The subject may try to garner sympathy from the interrogator by discussing personal problems. He may bring up his health problems, financial difficulties, family troubles, and other personal dilemmas and tragedies. Deceptive subjects use these and other complaining behaviors in hopes that the investigator will identify with his tribulations and show him compassion.

Other bargaining symptoms include the use of "gray statements," as well as name-dropping comments, statements of subjects' firm moral codes, the swearing of religious or other oaths, or other assurances of their personal ability to resist deviant behaviors. These comments, along with confirming body language symptoms, such as broad smiles, passive eye contact, and other nonthreatening body cues, are designed to present the subject and the event in the best possible light.

Goals

The ultimate goal of bargaining is to identify and establish some form of bond with the interrogator. Finding that bond with the interrogator is nec- essary for the subject to maintain his disguise of reality. Like denial, the disguise is a deception of the interrogator as well as the subject himself.

The subject uses bargaining as a method of covertly assessing any possible danger that the interrogator may pose. It is essential for him to identify this risk in order to find some method to survive the eventual exposure of his deviant or negative behavior. Once that peril has been identified, the decep- tive subject attempts to overcome the danger by looking for common emo- tional and intellectual ground with the interrogator.

Finding that common ground permits the subject to become a chame- leon, changing colors in hopes of finding the perfect camouflage so that he can go unnoticed by the interviewer. The "colors" he chooses to disguise himself with are the intellectual, emotional, and mental characteristics of the interrogator. Once he has established that perfect or near-perfect reflection of the interrogator, the subject has a greater chance of success in altering the interrogator's opinion and mental vision of the subject.

Results

The ultimate result of bargaining is a generally diminished liability. By getting the interrogator to agree to substitute images, altered perceptions, and dis- guised reality, the subject's fragile self-esteem is salvaged. When these dis- guised images of reality are finally in place and appear to be accepted by the interrogator, the subject has a greater chance of surviving the interrogation with a reduced risk of emotional injury. At the same time, he can create at least the partial perception that he, too, is at least a quasi-victim. This posi- tion, however, does create several vulnerabilities for him.

Disguising reality requires the subject to make at least a partial acceptance of some of the aspects of reality. That partial acceptance alone puts him extremely close to total acceptance of his criminal actions. As a result, this partial-acceptance position is a precarious one, making him open to manipulation by the interrogator.

Responding with a bargaining approach also requires the subject to show the interviewer all of his possible weaknesses, which can be exploited. Once he has shown his "hand" and offered a bargain to the interrogator, the subject has no other control over his position of deceit if the interrogator rejects the offer.

Interrogator/Interviewer Response

When the interrogator recognizes that the subject is in the response state of bargaining, he needs to understand that the subject is already accepting at least some portion of reality. Then he needs to realize that the subject is prepared to meet the interrogator halfway on at least some issues. Furthermore, the subject is open to the interviewer's suggestions.

In order for the interrogator to control a subject who is responding with bargaining, he must first hear out the subject's bargaining comments. The content of those comments gives the interrogator the key to his attack on the subject's negative reaction by telling the interrogator which portions of the event or crime the subject is accepting, albeit it in an altered state. The information altered will either be the crime itself or the image of the subject.

If the subject is disguising the information concerning himself, he has left an opening for dealing with the reality of the crime. The interrogator should then work on getting the subject to agree to those facts of the case that will not totally jeopardize him. Too much of an attack at this point may drive the subject into a stronger negative reaction.

If the subject is camouflaging the crime, he is leaving himself open to attack regarding his personal image. The interrogator should now approach the reality of the subject's personal life and his actions. As before, too strong an attack can drive the subject away, but the opening cannot be ignored. The primary objective in either case is to make sure that the subject perceives that the interrogator is open to his comments.

Once the interrogator has identified the bargaining response, has heard and decoded the subject's remarks, and has identified which area to focus on first, he must make sure that he does not fall prey to the subject's persuasions. Instead, the interrogator should reverse the subject's comments, turning them against him. This is done by first accepting the subject's bargaining offers and then pinning him down on each of the elements using the suspect's terms, definitions, and characterizations. Now, the subject's reclassification of himself or the crime becomes the tool the interrogator uses to lead the subject toward acceptance. The end result is that the interrogator makes some form of emotional or intellectual tie with the subject. That tie assures the subject, by using his own bargaining comments, that the interrogator is not out to destroy him or his self-esteem.

Acceptance

Acceptance is the positive-reaction state in which confession occurs. The subject is no longer operating a mechanism that is designed to reject the reality of the crime. He is prepared to submit himself to the interrogator and his presentation of the case facts, although there is always a tiny amount of ego-protection measures in place.

Definition

When a subject is using the response state of acceptance, his resistance to facing reality has been depleted. The person has surrendered his efforts at denial and is ready to submit to the facts leveled against him. He sees acceptance as his only relief from the unrelenting and exhaustive process of denial, which has not provided him with the victory against the interrogator that he had hoped.

Characteristics

Mentally, the response of acceptance is the subject's surrender to the crime. The process of maintaining overall denial demands significant mental energy on the part of the deceptive subject. He has finally determined the process is too overwhelming and deserts the effort.

This surrender state is reflected in the subject's statements to the interrogator. Those statements can appear in any of three different forms. One form was that of a "buy-out" offer. The second one addressed the fantasy-reality of the crime and the subject's actions. The third was a statement inquiring about the punishment associated with his behavior. Each of these forms has slightly different characteristics, but all serve as indications of acceptance.

Once the subject has reached the mental state of acceptance, additional confirmation is provided by the presence of acceptance signals in his body language.

Goals

The goal of acceptance is simple — submit to reality. While submitting to reality, the subject hopes at the same time to save some semblance of self-esteem. He believes that if everything goes well, he can salvage a small vestige of control over the outcome by knowingly and willingly surrendering to the truth. The light of recovery exists in the hope the subject has that he will be afforded leniency in his punishment and will be given the chance to start over again. Confession or admission provides him with such an opportunity.

Results

The result of the subject's acceptance is his abandonment of the negative-reaction responses that have been generating deception. The deception process is no longer adequately protecting him from stress. Each of his negative responses has been dismantled or overcome by the interrogator. The only remaining option for dealing with the crime is to acknowledge it.

Once the subject is responding with acceptance, he allows himself to be open to the comments and requests of the interrogator. He is ready to follow the interrogator's instructions and is prepared to deal with his problem without rejection or delay. The interrogator is now in control of the flow of events.

Interrogator/Interviewer Response

Dealing with a subject who is in acceptance is the most critical moment for the interrogator. An overzealous response by the interrogator can destroy any gains that have been made up to this point. A frequent mistake made by many interrogators is to begin a continuous stream of chatter. The successful interrogator is the one who knows when to stop talking and start listening. At this point, the subject should be doing 95% of the talking and the interrogator should be doing 95% of the listening.

Upon recognizing that the subject is in the acceptance state, the interrogator should lower the pitch and volume of his voice, which forces the suspect to listen carefully. Then, the interrogator should offer the subject a way to give an admission or confession while still salvaging some of his self-esteem.

Confession Signals

Debt Service Comments:

1. I didn't do it, but I'll be glad to pay it back.
2. I didn't hurt him, but I'll pay the medical bills.
3. I know my kid wouldn't do it, but I'll pay his share of the damage.
4. I didn't take them, but I'll replace the missing equipment just to get this over with.
5. If the property were recovered, would the charges be dropped?

Fantasy/Reality Statements:

1. I didn't do it, but I'll take the blame until you find the guy who did it.
2. Do you want me to confess even though I didn't do it?
3. If I told you I did it, I'd be lying to myself.
4. What do you want me to say?
5. Do you want me to lie to you and confess to something I haven't done?

Punishment Statements:

1. What am I going to be charged with?
2. Could I get suspended from school?
3. Could a person be fired for this?
4. Is my mother, father, or wife going to find out?
5. How much time does the judge usually give for something like this?

Body Language Confession Signals

1. The body will open up by unfolding the arms and possibly the legs.
2. The palms may be turned up while in the subject's lap.
3. The shoulders may drop down and roll forward.
4. The subject rubs the knob of the chin while smiling.
5. The chin drops toward the chest or throat.
6. The subject leans forward into the interrogator's body space without touching him.
7. The subject gives a deep, cleansing sigh for the first time.
8. The subject's eyes turn up toward the ceiling and start blinking slowly.
9. The eyes roll up, exposing the whites of the eyes, and then the eyelids close.
10. The subject has a blank, sanpaku-like stare, with the eyes blinking in rhythm with the pauses in the interrogator's comments.
11. The subject rubs his lips together for about 30 seconds, as if trying to form the first words of confession.
12. The subject's chin quivers.
13. There is genuine crying that accompanies submission.
14. There is an overall look of submission, as if the subject has mentally and emotionally surrendered.

Kinesics of Excluded Subjects

8

Earlier in this text, we noted that there are groups of individuals that do not produce reliable results when interviewed. Those groups include children at puberty, the mentally deficient, the mentally ill or psychotic, and those subjects under the moderate to severe influence of drugs or alcohol at the time of the interview. Unfortunately, just by the mere nature of the work involved in the law enforcement community, we will find that a disproportionate number of these individuals are the victims, witnesses, and suspects interviewed. Recently, a study conducted by the National Institute of Justice determined that approximately 10 million people are processed or under supervision in the United States criminal justice system. This includes individuals who are under pretrial diversion, post-conviction supervision, or parole. Of that number, up to 13% of those individuals fall under the classifications of mentally ill, mentally deficient, or suffering from an organic brain syndrome, emotional disorder, or specific learning disability (Rubin and Campbell, 1995). More than half of that group suffers from severe mental disorders. The same group, however, only represents 1% or less of the general population of the United States. Such a high percentage of these types of subjects dictates that the investigative interviewer be able to recognize the various symptoms of these disorders and the impact they have on the subject's behavior as well as on the criminal act itself. The interviewer should adopt an interview strategy to successfully deal with subjects exhibiting such disorders, in that a standardized approach used with all subjects will be totally ineffective. The interviewer should also be able to recognize and document the subject's behaviors for later analysis should the subject be attempting to manipulate the criminal justice system by engaging in malingering or in an attempt to rationally avoid responsibility for his crime (Jaffe and Sharma, 1998).

When we identified those personalities that are excluded from the interrogation process, we discussed a brief profile of the mentally disturbed subject, enabling the interrogator to classify the subject as possibly being a psychotic. At this time, we are going to develop a more descriptive behavioral

233

analysis of not only the psychotic, but also subjects who may be suffering from brain disease, clinical depression, or who are possibly suicidal.

In this section, we do not intend to make the interrogator a psychologist or psychiatrist. We do hope, however, to give the interrogator more information about those personalities that he is likely to encounter in his career. In addition, these profiles are of those subjects who are suffering the severe to moderate effects of their particular malady. The importance of the investigative interviewer in being able to identify these characteristics is threefold. First, the subject's mental disorder will be (or should be) evident by the manner in which the crime was committed and is displayed in the characteristics of the scene. Second, the interviewer must make some form of field analysis of the subject's mental status in order to assign the correct level of credibility to the subject's statements and the effects his disability will have on the credibility of those statements. Third, it is incumbent upon the investigative interviewer to document the immediate behavioral symptoms that occur during the interview for any future evaluations that might be made by mental health professionals. These three actions will help ensure that those individuals who are identified as mentally disturbed or mentally deficient are handled properly by the criminal justice system. It also provides insurance against the games that streetwise subjects utilize to try and manipulate the criminal justice system by faking their disorders.

Schizophrenia

Schizophrenia tends to be a catchall description covering many mentally ill subjects. At times, these persons have been described as suffering from split personalities. In reality, that description is far from correct. This personality is best described as being a shattered, or fractured, personality. These people are perceiving the world in which they live from an irrational point of view. At the same time, they may have periods when they appear to move in and out of this irrational thought process, giving the appearance of having different "personalities."

Characteristics
The schizophrenic subject's description is divided into four main categories: bizarre behaviors, thought disorders, peculiar perceptions, and hallucinations. The ability of the interrogator to understand and recognize these symptoms gives him the ability to identify these subjects and therefore take appropriate action in the investigation and bring the subject to the attention of health care professionals.

Bizarre Behaviors

If there is one thing that will immediately catch the attention of an investigator, it is the peculiar physical behavior patterns of the schizophrenic. These peculiarities can include everything from unusual facial expressions to odd walking gaits or exaggerated hand and arm gestures. Such symptoms can be dramatic and bewildering for the person who is having his first encounter with a psychotic individual. Over a period of time, and after having contact with a significant number of individuals who are mentally ill, the investigative interviewer may notice that some subjects exhibit dramatic and overt symptoms and behaviors. At other times, he will observe subjects that are withdrawn, even to the point that the presence of the individual is barely noticed by those around him.

The schizophrenic subject may have unusual facial expressions. Some of these expressions are done for effect; that is, they are done deliberately to make a shocking impression on the interviewer or just to see how the interviewer will react to such bizarre behaviors. These include exaggerated facial expressions, glaring, or other forms of bizarre and extreme facial contortions. Common to this group is a long-distance stare, as if the person is not really seeing the speaker, but is staring at an object 1000 yards away. Other times, these expressions may be part of the subject's genuine confusion or a response to the other psychotic symptoms he is experiencing.

Strange gestures of the arms and legs include exaggerated waving or flailing of the arms. The subject may be observed sleeping flat on his back with his legs pulled up into his chest. The subject may engage in strange repetitive actions with his hands that serve no real function. The interviewer, for example, may see repeated touching of different areas of the body in the same sequence every few minutes. The subject may appear to grasp into the air as if he is catching flies, yet there are no flies. Another subject's limbs may be like a mannequin's. Someone may move the subject's arms as if to place the person in a pose, and the person will stay in that position for extended periods of time.

These individuals may also wear layers of clothing, including wool pants, sweatshirt, thermal underwear, a sweater vest, stocking cap, and an overcoat. This may not seem to be abnormal attire, except for the fact that it may be August in Arizona and the temperature is above 110 degrees, and this person does not appear to be hot. They may also be found with their bodies wrapped with plastic food wrap. They may have aluminum foil lining their coat or hat, or be carrying three large rocks in their right-front pants pocket. There is no consistency in the behaviors in which these subjects engage other than the fact that all are abnormal. When the interrogator discovers these oddities, the subject's explanations for these physical behaviors is just as strange as the behavior itself.

The overall lifestyle of the schizophrenic is as dysfunctional as the subject's observable behavior. These individuals generally have few, if any, real friends and little, if any, social skills that would assist them in developing and maintaining such relationships. They have trouble dating and probably have had trouble in school. These symptoms, in fact, may appear early in the person's life. It is not uncommon for some schizophrenics to exhibit their behaviors in their mid-teens, with the problem becoming full-blown by the time they hit their late teens or early twenties. They will have trouble getting and maintaining gainful employment.

This dysfunctional behavior can have a significant impact on normal daily behaviors. You may find that these subjects forgo normal personal hygiene and grooming behaviors. You may see the person wearing severely wrinkled or dirty, mismatched clothes. They may have tremendous body odor. Their homes may be filthy, with mountains of collected trash, rotting food, numerous animals kept in the home, or even animal carcasses that have been neglected and left to decompose in the yard or in the house.

The social interaction of the schizophrenic is often limited. This person avoids all forms of contact with other people and may go to great lengths to drive the concerned or curious away. What little contact he does have is quite traumatic for him and frequently for the person whom he comes in contact with as well. Eye contact is usually nonexistent, and if he shakes hands with someone, that person would describe the handshake like touching a dead fish or corpse.

Schizophrenic individuals frequently behave inappropriately in normal situations or when responding to stimuli. Those behaviors can include crass or cruel comments regarding the death of a family member or a disaster that has been reported in the news media. They may become severely agitated if someone simply asks them how their day is going. They may only speak if someone speaks to them, and then they may respond only in short, gruff tones; or, a person may have to go to enormous lengths to get any form of reaction from them.

Thought Disorders

When an investigator talks to the schizophrenic subject, it may not take long for him to realize that this person has some thought disorders. The initial impression the observer has is that the subject may be joking, teasing, or acting odd for his own amusement. That impression won't last long as the conversation continues. It normally does not take long for the moderately to severely affected schizophrenic subject's disordered mental processes to make themselves known. The content of the subject's speech, as well as the coherence of the ideas expressed, may be quite profound.

The listener may hear the subject engage in the creation of new words, which is a phenomenon called "neologism." These words have significance and meaning only to the subject, with no other normally understood interpretation. At the same time, the subject's recognized comments have no real purpose. Every idea is tossed into his speech with other ideas and concepts into a "word salad." The subject may initially have an idea that he wishes to communicate, but he never seems to get to the point where he has fully expressed himself.

Some subjects thoroughly enjoy the use of speech, particularly because of the way they can use the mechanism. For example, the interrogator may hear long narrations with a continuous string of words that are spoken only because they rhyme with each other, or the subject may have a certain special phrase that he uses again and again any time he communicates with someone.

Individuals suffering from this form of psychosis may see an ordinary event and assign a strange significance to it (see Figure 8.1). For example, a simple car accident may be explained as the result of contaminated brake fluid made from the oil criminally hoarded in the government's radiation-contaminated salt domes in the midwestern United States. All this is the result of a plot by illegal alien agents sent by the secret CIA-financed armies hiding in Belize waiting to storm the White House. The interviewer is well advised not to try to talk sense to these people or try to clear up their confusion, because they believe they are making perfect sense.

Several interesting things may characterize the schizophrenic subject's personal thoughts. These subjects may tell you that someone is stealing all their thoughts. They may claim that someone has access to their thoughts and is broadcasting those thoughts so that others can hear what they are thinking. Often, the thought stealing is accomplished through some form of electrical device that is used to broadcast the thoughts to other individuals who mean to do the subject harm in some way (see Figures 8.2 and 8.5).

The subjects may indicate that someone is placing unwanted thoughts or ideas into their heads and making them think certain programmed thoughts. These may be thoughts of disaster, severe doubts, unwanted urges, or even commands to carry out certain secret activities for some sinister purpose (see Figure 8.4).

Schizophrenic subjects may relate that they are experiencing unusual events surrounding their feelings or actions. Some may describe the way in which someone is making them engage in impulsive acts, such as screaming or throwing items, or that someone is controlling their movements. They may tell you that they are forced to experience emotions or feelings by some outside influence.

To: _____

From: Richard _____

Action Report on Electromagnetic Secret Weapon Attack

Action: _____

Location: _____   Time: March 17, 1989

Russia is bombarding the United States and other countries with a variety of electromagnetic electrogravitational warfare vibration wave frequencies.

These secret attacks cause or engineer weather distortion, airplane or spacecraft or missile crashes or explosions, earthquakes, electrical systems failures, wrecks, collisions, compass navigational errors, metal stress or cracks, building collapse, train derailments, oil spills, fires, explosions, ship sinkings and capsizings, gravity alteration, gas line disruptions, detonation of nuclear weapons or electricity generators, artificial lightning strikes, storms, droughts, forest fires, temperature extremes, jet stream stalls, tornados, hurricanes, typhoons, polar icecap melting, floods, human and animal behavior changes, shooting and wild behavior sprees, dog bite outbreaks, AIDS disease viral mutation, depletion of atmospheric ozone, earth magnetic field distortion, communications reception interference, immune system reduction, sudden death, sonic booms, and strange lighting effects.

All these attacks are designed to look like accidents or natural disasters. They are caused by the world's most powerful radio transmitters, sometimes disguised as radar, beaming infinitely magnified, continuously repeated extreme low frequency vibration waves to target areas. The waves follow the curvature of the earth by bouncing along and off the ionosphere and propagating downward to the center of the earth.

This electromagnetic technology, originally discovered by Nikola Tesla, has the power to destroy entire islands, continents, and planets. Its current secret usage, combined with lasers, microwaves, nuclear bomb explosions and radiation, and biological germ warfare, threatens to fulfill psychics' predictions by melting polar ice caps, raising ocean water levels, flooding the world, increasing earthquake warfare, throwing the earth off its axis, sinking half the earth's land surface into the ocean, and killing two thirds to three fourths of the world population between 1992 and 1999, unless a world awakening and public opinion backlash reaction stop it from happening.

Figure 8.1 Writings of a psychotic who has an unusual explanation for all the natural disasters that happen in the world.

Peculiar Perceptions

Schizophrenic subjects have reported that they and their world are somehow different from the one in which we live (see Figure 8.3). They may make remarks about how their bodies or talents are much different from the rest of the population. A killer may describe that he becomes 13 ft. tall after he eliminates the "harlots of Satan." He may describe how he can burn holes in the heads of his enemies with his thoughts. He may claim to be able to transport himself through time or to another realm of reality or a higher level of consciousness that no other person can achieve.

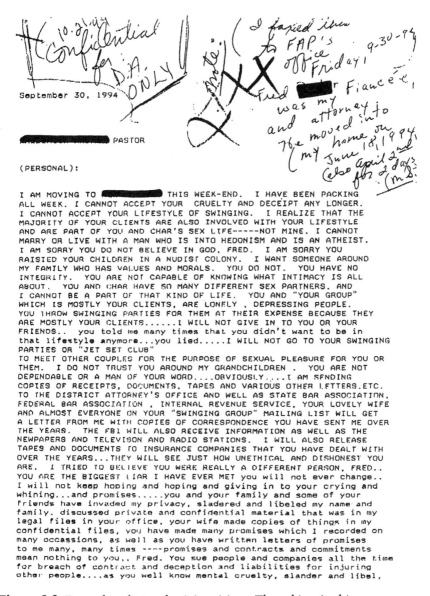

Figure 8.2 Examples of a psychotic's writings. The subject in this case sent more than 30 pages of material by fax to 17 different individuals, agencies, and news media.

These individuals may become obsessed with feelings they think they are experiencing because of the electromagnetic fields created by cellular phones or the Doppler radar owned by the local television station. They may think they smell gases being emitted from all the drug laboratories operating in the city. They may also discuss any number of problems indicating that they are extremely sensitive to sights, sounds, or smells.

captured pain   CAPTURED PAIN   captured   pain

Living life now is at it,s highest peak , I,ve   learned
that   life   is like   a   candle stick   just   waiting   to burn
out ; Life weve   been trained to know is not the   way we
should   always believe .

My new way   of thinking   is a harsh ⁄ but entertaining way
of thought   and   that is that there is no wrong things that
seem wrong are so very   right   for the system needs the
bad   or you wouldnt know what the meaning good meant

So   now I type away to tell   the story   of how I
captured pain if you have a weak   piss ant twitty little
mind you should stop reading now   before I   enter you mind
I have learned that there is over half the population out
there that are definatly fungus amung us..

Therefor for my research I didnt hurt any of you at all
that   actully have   a mind or   gut   1 meaning   a hair on
your   ass to live life like   every day   could be your
last. So we get   into the very heart of the matter and
ask ourselves   what are we planetters really doing here??

I tell you all we know nothing but we are here bidding
our time skipping along like little mice thinking that we
are really something and what we do today is really going
to matter tomorow well listen here little germs out there I
tell you all I know what the fucks going on .

You   all think that little jesus is going to save your
ass and your going to be good little germs, so you can go
to heven and be gods little pets well good luck little
germs, I bet your all thinking this guys really lost it..

Well I have I,m sick of being stuck here on
planet earth with all you retarded fucking dingdongs, I,ve
met in my whole entire life abought 10 thinkers out there
that I   could even comunicate with,

So sa   you go on here in my lttle notes I hope
you as I hope not a dingdong can understand my way of life
and dont hold it entirely against me I know your all
slightly wondering just a little just where the hell I,m
going with all this and I,m telling you all straight to
hell if so it exsistes . But I fucking doubt er

I"m really tring just to mislead you all into
giving up hope and mearly forgiveing me for my slight sins
for you are aboght to feel . I'm not entirely proud of what
I've done but what the hell who is we all wish we could of
changed a few things in our lives the only one thing I
would of changed is a secret that I may tell you all at
the end of my life, I am WRITTING to you all out thier

in hidding I hate ⋅to say   because what I   didnt think was
wrong at   all in the back, sides , and   front of my mind
most dingdong like   type germs wouldn't agree to.

I will give some of you out there creadit some
of you will agree to the way I found true exticy in my
pleasure of pain...................

I dont know of how long I will be able to type
My own brother caused me all this tormeant any ways,

You see he was always the good little fuck around the
house when we were kids , and put on a big front for the
whole god dam world , well the fake little basterd finally
took er in the shorts...... He was trying to tell on me
again just like he always told on all of us kids,

Figure 8.3 Example of a psychotic's writings. Note the delusions of power, control, and importance the subject believes he possesses.

Today I came into work and the radiation is heavily washing the "air" in
the building... my temples are irritated... and it is either affecting
others in the area, or they, as agents know what is going on....

I went to the gym last night, and I think that a sampling of anything I
did there, was used for todays effect on the environment. In other words,
my laughing and thoughts about the gay clones was taken back to the
surveillance administrators... and they've placed more agents into the
immediate area to watch when I leave the building and where I go...

the agency's basic intent is to modify my sexual preference, and to
monitor my sexual drives... it monitors the biological "aura" or
electrical properties of the body for the transmission of that energy to a
central site... the surface of the eye is monitored, as well is the
"psychic" aura... literally pictures or "ideas as vision" can be monitored
also... the device also manipulates emotion and can change the "comfort"
of an individual, by radiating waves that "irritate"... a masking can be
radiated that is a "holograph". This holograph passes through the
membranes of the body... I can imagine that it is more effective when
passing through the skull, and causes slight muscle tension in the face
and body... to change slightly the facial expressions and the emotions
assoicated with it.

So, as any normal man goes through out the normal day, thoughts of sexual
attraction, fantasies, ideas, etc... are monitored... the agency is most
interested in monitoring my sexual acts, and taking those ideas back to
the central agency for further analysis. Based on these archetypes they
then take the images they have stored, and match agents that would be
attractive or match the ideas I had 12 to 24 hours earlier.

I have found that the mind control system is most intent on manipulating
sexual urges, that are closely connected to the images seen in the eyes.
The system is real time, and basically, the people serving the system are
enumerated in the computer... on any given day, or a time, they are
allocated to certain "tasks" these "roles", so to speak, are presented to
me, the victim, in order to make a "reality"... I have risen above this
manipulation, and they know it...

Today, the agency decided to place masculine archetypes around the area to
monitor the building in which I work... either they have the building
steaked out remotely or they have certain "probable visit locations"
steaked out for an agent's entrance. This sounds paranoid, but it's been

Figure 8.4 Document posted on the Internet by a subject who appears to be
suffering thought disorders, mind control, and paranoia.

Hallucinations

One of the most common recognizable symptoms associated with the schizophrenic is the experiencing of hallucinations. A hallucination is a person's
perception of some sensory event — primarily in visual and auditory forms
— when in fact there is no sensory stimulation present. Of the two, auditory
hallucinations are more prevalent than visual hallucinations.

Visual hallucinations include the ability to see evil spirits or devils. The
person may be able to see the shadows of all his dead relatives, look beneath
the skin of a person and see the demon that possesses him, or observe a lizard

HELP DECLASSIFY: THE KNOWLEDGE OF: DECODING
THE BRAINSTEM RESPONSE SIGNAL
FOR LANGUAGE TO COMMUNICATE

MATERIAL SCANNING (SILICON)
MACHINERY TO DETECT TELEMETERING
HIGHLY SENSITIVE HEARING DEVICE
RADIO FREQUENCY JAMMERS (DEFINE RANGE)

(OVER)

OUR FEDERAL GOVERNMENT, IMPLANTED A
MULTICOMPONENT MICROSTRUCTURE ELECTRONIC
DEVICE, WHICH TRANSMITS ACOUSTIC AROUND ME
"EXTREMELY HIGH ACOUSTIC INSIDE" AND THE
SIGNAL OF THE BRAINSTEM, PLUS THEY CAN
COMMUNICATE BACK INTO MY IMPLANT "TWO WAY
COMMUNICATION" THE ACCOMPLISHMENT MADE; I
AM DECODED, THEY KNOW WHAT I AM THINKING.

Figure 8.5 Business card carried by a subject who appears to have problems with stolen thoughts, thought broadcasting, and paranoia.

turn into a human or vice versa. Approximately 20% of schizophrenics report having some form of visual hallucinations.

Auditory hallucinations almost always involve some type of voice. The person may indicate that he hears a voice giving him orders or always talking when he is watching television or when he is trying to talk to a friend on the telephone. Some subjects have indicated that they hear two or more voices and that these voices are always arguing between themselves, making it difficult for subjects to think clearly. Another auditory hallucination they may be experiencing is that of a commentator. The person believes that he is hearing the thoughts of another person or persons, who are always thinking about the subject and commenting on his activities. About 60% of those with schizophrenia report having auditory hallucinations.

Schizophrenic subjects are difficult to interview. If the investigator is able to carry on any form of communication with the person, the contents and quality of the information gained will be seriously flawed. The interviewer may not be able to tell the difference between the artifacts of some past hallucinations or paranoid thoughts or real experiences described by the subject. More importantly, the subject may not be able to tell the difference. Polygraph examiners have a great deal of difficulty in getting quality readings from these subjects during examinations.

For the officer who intends to take this person into custody, the risk of injury to one or both parties is high. This is not to say that all schizophrenics are violent and will attack an officer; however, these individuals, when they do become violent, can be extremely difficult to get under control. They have a source of strength and cunning that is phenomenal and in endless reserve. The officer should always take extra precautions, advise the subject of his intentions, and have plenty of assistance when trying to take him into custody.

It is also not inappropriate to agree with the subject's psychotic delusions, hallucinations, and perceptions because no amount of rational conversation will have a positive effect on this person. It may, in fact, act as a form of agitation to the psychotic and stimulate the subject's paranoid feelings about the officer.

Brain Disease

Schizophrenia is identified as a psychogenic disorder. To equate the opera-tions of the human brain with that of a computer, we would say that there is something wrong with the programming of the brain that is causing the disorder. Along with the psychogenic reactions that can cause mental distur-bances in subjects, there are other forms of mental disturbances, which are associated with organic changes in the brain or nervous system. Individuals suffering from the effects of these physical disorders have significant difficulty with mental stability during an interview.

There are two critical symptoms that typically render the statements of the brain-diseased subject incredible. First, these subjects have a great deal of difficulty maintaining any form of mental semblance of the passage of time. They frequently are unable to keep a consistent reference between themselves and any form of normal time line. Old memories are recent in the subject's mind, while recent events are not really registered.

The second problem is their ability to sort and store spatial information. Names of family members may escape their memory, while at the same time, they might mistake a young man who is a stranger for a former high school classmate who has been dead for two decades. In some severe cases, as with Alzheimer, they may begin to mislabel the names of household items or try to use their electric razor to cut their plate of ham. It is not unusual for them to begin a project and in mere moments totally forget what they were trying to do. Even normal day-to-day tasks that were once easily performed now elude them.

The possible causes of brain disease in individuals are numerous. These causes can include, but are not limited to, nutritional deficiencies; bacterial infections; alcohol abuse, possibly resulting in delirium tremors (DTs, or the "shakes"); Alzheimer's disease; physical head injury; brain tumors; syphilis; arteriosclerosis (hardening of the arteries); epilepsy; senile dementia (the mental confusion suffered by the very elderly); stroke; severe cocaine, crack or methamphetamine use; poisoning; toxic chemicals; neural damage; the abuse of chemical inhalants, or "huffing;" or even a lack of oxygen to the brain. The results of such damage to the brain can cause some psychotic-like behaviors, but they are in a more narrow or limited band of disorders than that of other full-blown psychoses.

Physical Symptoms

The first indications that may alert the investigator that the subject is experiencing some form of brain disease are the subject's altered physical behaviors and appearance. The nature of brain disease itself results in the interruption of the body's ability to maintain its normal healthy appearance and functions, and as a result, the subject may look unhealthy. The person may have a dulled complexion, and the way he carries himself may look like that of an ill person.

The observant interviewer may notice that the subject has an unusual taste in clothing. Individuals suffering from brain disease often lose many, if not most, of their normal social skills. They will frequently mix and match almost any style of clothing and may go to unusual extremes in the application of makeup. The interrogator may also realize that the subject has not bathed in a great while.

Behavior Symptoms

For the brain-diseased subject, the reality of his environment and interaction with it can be frightening and bewildering, and he will appear confused and disoriented to the interrogator. His resulting reaction to the interview may be at the extremes of the behavior scale. Some subjects appear to be lethargic and uninvolved. Nearly all individuals who are suffering from the moderate to severe effects of brain disease respond to other people with rambling thoughts and ideas. They may be withdrawn from other people and can act detached from their surroundings. The interrogator may find he has to go to great lengths to get any form of response from the subject.

The investigator may find that he can get the subject to respond to his surroundings, but has little success in getting the subject's cooperation

during questioning. Some subjects may indicate that they believe the interrogator and other individuals are actually trying to harm them or take
advantage of them by reason of some conspiracy. They will be extremely
defensive to any questions or requests by the investigator or other officers.
Other subjects are so totally disoriented that they do not know the current
day and date, and may not know where they are or even be able to recall
their own name.

Other subjects, however, can become agitated and excitable to the point
that the investigator may have significant problems in calming the subject.
These subjects can become combative and difficult for the officer to control
at the time of arrest or detention. Their emotions during that time can run
through the entire spectrum of behaviors, both appropriate and inappropriate
for the situation. Some of the subjects may be able to perform some of the
actions that the officer requests, but in the next moment, be unable to complete what may be a simple task. These apparent moments of ability and then
inability can be frustrating for the investigator who is dealing with this person.

Internal Mental Process

During any questioning process, the subject's severe mental problems will
become most apparent to the investigator. The interrogator is likely to notice
that the brain-diseased subject may make up information in order to give
the interrogator an answer. In the process, the brain-diseased subject exhibits
slow and disorganized thinking and has a short attention span. The interrogator may ask the same questions later in the interview and note that the
person dramatically changes or has no recollection of his previous responses.
The subject may discuss details from his past memories that are not even
related to the current situation. The brain-diseased subject may start conversations about his delusional thoughts, such as the conspiracy of the government, secret agents, poison gas, mind control, and so forth.

After a short time, it may become apparent to the interrogator that the
subject is having difficulty in understanding the interrogator's questions. He
may not be able to focus his attention on the interrogator's statements or is
unable to realize that he is involved in a continuing conversation or interview.
These individuals may not recognize normal symbols or objects by their
correct names. They will forget important facts and are unable to retain
previous parts of their conversations with the interviewer even after only a
few minutes have passed. Like the schizophrenic, they may also suffer from
visual and auditory hallucinations.

Interrogator Response

Once the interviewer recognizes that he is working with a brain-diseased
subject, he should remember that his chances of conducting a successful

interview are extremely low. At this point, the interrogator may be inclined to become frustrated and short-tempered. Working with this type of person takes time, patience, and understanding on the part of the interviewer. The difficulties presented by the subject in the interrogation room are not deliberate and are not intentionally meant to be disruptive, as in the case of a normally deceptive subject. This, however, does solve the interrogator's problems and presents an easy resolution to the case.

When dealing with the brain-diseased subject, the interrogator needs to remember that this person thinks and relates in a simplistic and maybe even childlike manner. The interrogator, therefore, needs to present information and questions in a short, easy-to-understand format. Facts and information are discussed in small pieces. He should speak slowly and in short, easy-to-understand sentences. Questions that involve any form of calculation or involved mental process are likely to be futile. It may be necessary to repeat questions frequently, and remember that the subject may become frustrated as he tries to follow the interviewer's train of thought. These subjects are also prone to strong bouts of depression, which can complicate the process even further.

The interrogator will find that he has an easier time associating with the subject if he focuses on the physical and mental skills that the subject can perform. He should allow the person to perform as many of those functions as he can without help. To diminish the subject's apprehensions and ward off combative behavior, it will help if the interrogator takes the time to carefully explain each step of the process. He should inform the subject about what is going to happen next and be certain that he makes at least face-to-face, if not eye-to-eye, contact with the subject. This will help ensure that he has the person's attention.

Above all, when dealing with the brain-diseased individual, the investigator should remain as calm as possible. To help reassure the subject, the interrogator should make sure that he tries to answer the subject's questions related to his confusion and disorientation. It will comfort the subject and provide greater stability if the subject is allowed to function in familiar surroundings with people he trusts, as well as with selected personal items, such as clothes, books, etc. The subject functions better if he is permitted to associate with an individual with whom he is familiar, or at least let him identify with one officer who will stay with him during the entire process to give him a sense of stability. The investigator should try to identify and notify the subject's physician, as well as any family members, as soon as possible for more background information.

The symptoms of the schizophrenic and the brain-diseased subject described are those of a subject who is under the moderate to severe effects of his illness. It is these groups that create the greatest difficulty for the investigator. Subjects who are not as severe can be interviewed, but will still present complications for the interrogator. A general knowledge of these conditions, how they progress, and their extreme symptoms will assist the interrogator in being more productive in the interview room.

Affective Disorders

Affective disorders are the most common of all the psychological disorders. They are the disorders that involve some form of serious or disruptive mood disturbances, which are more extreme than the common disturbances many of us experience at some point during our lives. The affective disorder that is of most concern to the interrogator and is the most common mood disorder suffered is depression.

Subjects suffering from clinical depression generally have a low confession rate, as do those persons who are suicidal. We will discuss a brief behavioral profile for the person experiencing depression or who may be suicidal. Again, we are not trying to train the interrogator in clinical psychology, but are only attempting to educate the interrogator as to the behavioral extremes that can have a negative impact on the interview process.

Depression

The depression discussed in this section is not the same form of depression discussed earlier when reviewing the five stress–response states. That particular form of depression is referred to as a "reactive mood." In other words, it is the response the person has to a particular situation, but is generally not so pervasive that it affects the person for a long period of time. All of us have felt "depressed" at different points in our lives, but without any major disruption. In those situations, we have a normal level of sadness and a general lack of energy.

The person suffering from clinical depression goes beyond the normal amount of sadness over life problems or experiences grief far above the normal amount expressed when someone encounters a normal tragedy of life. Severe depression, which creates difficulty in dealing with daily life and normal activities, has identifiable physical, behavioral, emotional, and cognitive changes. The ability to recognize and understand these phenomena will assist the interrogator in determining if the subject is suffering genuine depression or is using the behavior as a means of avoiding responsibility for his actions.

There are numerous theories as to why we suffer from clinical depression. One theory suggests that there are significant biological changes that can affect an individual's behavior. Such theories suggest that there may be a decrease in the production of serotonin, a chemical essential to the function of the brain. Social theories suggest that depression may be a result of an inability to cope with problems in a normal manner. Psychoanalytical theory suggests depression may be the result of a person's inability to appropriately handle anger and, as a result, he turns his anger on himself. Still other theories hypothesize that the person is unable to develop the fundamental skill of forming strong interpersonal relationships and create a sense of personal well-being.

Whatever the actual cause of clinical depression, it appears in various degrees of severity, from general gloominess and weeping to the point of being completely debilitated and unable to get out of bed. The causes for any particular individual's depression are as unique as the person himself, as is the treatment for that patient. At the same time, the development of depression from one person to the next can also have a wide range of deviation. For some people, the depression can rise quickly in a short period of time. For others, the development of depression grows gradually over a long period of time. The symptoms displayed from one individual to the next are also diverse. For our purposes, we will not focus on any one form, but will instead discuss a broad view of the disorder and some of the most common recognizable symptoms.

Behavioral Symptoms

The interviewer may observe several behavioral symptoms that are distinct from the behaviors of any other subject he may interview. Examples of such behaviors include the subject always dressing in dark or drab colors. These people generally have unhappy facial expressions anytime you see them. Their brows may be deeply furrowed, and their entire body slumps or slouches when they stand or walk.

The interrogator may notice when this person enters the interview room that he is moving slowly. In fact, nearly all of the depressed person's physical gestures and behaviors are lethargic. You may observe that the subject's sitting posture tends to be slumped. The person may be leaning forward with the shoulders rolled over forward and the head dropped down onto the chest and the eyes cast to the floor. At the same time, there is little or no movement from the subject, even during the rapport-building process. The person may appear to be frozen in the chair. Hand behaviors may be limited to slow, wringing movements. He may also sit with his arms wrapped around himself as if he were wrapped in a blanket.

People who are experiencing depression may have a lack of appetite, while other depressed individuals eat nearly all the time, as if food has become their only friend. Some subjects report suffering from marked bouts of insomnia, while others sleep for long periods of time — day and night. Other physical disorders include tremendous weight gain or loss, headaches, excessive crying, pacing the floor, loss of sexual appetite, constipation, or changes in health patterns, such as menstruation cycles.

Emotional and Mental Symptoms

Individuals suffering from depression characteristically have low self-esteem. In their own minds, they feel that they have no redeeming values and that there is no way anyone can love them because they are worthless. They blame themselves for all the bad events they suffer, and feel they bring unwanted suffering to those around them. They are often heard making critical or derogatory remarks about themselves and their lives.

The thinking process of depressed subjects tends to be slow and introspective. Their minds are totally consumed by the depression they are suffering. They have a tendency to block out all information that does not outweigh their current pain. Their concentration level is almost nonexistent, and they have a great deal of trouble paying attention to the interrogator for more than short periods of time.

Due to the problems with their mental processes, as well as the focus of attention on all the negatives in their lives, depressed persons rarely have an appreciation for the passage of time. These subjects often are not fully aware of what day it is, much less the month. They may not even be aware of what the current time is. This is due, in part, to their belief that they have nothing worth remembering and certainly have little to look forward to other than more pain and disappointment. They also do their best to block out any memory of stress-creating events in which they have been involved. This is particularly true of subjects in criminal investigations.

The interrogator who is working with a clinically depressed subject soon realizes that his chances of getting a confession are extremely low. Often, the interrogator has to fill out forms that require information from the subject because he is unable to complete them himself. These subjects are also more concerned about what is going to happen to them than about the facts of the case. When the interview gets to a critical point, the interrogator should not be surprised to hear the subject make either veiled or obvious threats concerning suicide.

Suicidal Subjects

One of the major risks of depression is suicide. It is interesting to note, however, that not everyone who commits suicide is suffering from depression, although most are. Again, the objective here is not to make some form of clinical diagnosis but to recognize and correctly identify any immediate signs of behavioral symptoms exhibited by the subject that may raise our concerns of the possible existence of suicidal thoughts or tendencies. This is a problem that knows no boundaries. It disregards age, race, gender, education, and economic conditions, as well as any criminal behaviors. It is a disorder the affects the person and his entire interactions with those with whom he has an intimate relationship, personal association, social interaction, and, in some cases, public figures.

Individuals who attempt to or do commit suicide have different motives for wanting to take their lives. Some may be suffering from the distorted thinking process that often accompanies depression. Other suicide victims believe there is no compelling reason for them to live any longer. Others feel like utter failures when they compare the successful lives of those around them with their assumed life of failure and disappointment. Some subjects take their lives as acts of revenge against those people whom they think have wronged them or taken advantage of them. Finally, there are those individuals who may be suffering from a terminal illness or excruciating pain from some physical ailment and take their own lives to end the pain they and their families are suffering. In any case, all these individuals believe their lives are unendurable and that suicide is the only solution to their suffering.

There is no real "suicidal type" of personality. There are signs, however, that an individual may be considering suicide. Observable behaviors include a lack of concern for personal appearance when it used to be important to the person. Look for the subject to start wearing darker clothing or clothing that is sloppy, dirty, or mismatched. A woman may no longer care about her makeup or clothing; a man is no longer concerned about his hobbies; or neither engages in their normal leisure activities.

During the interview, the interrogator may note that the subject is unable to maintain consistent eye contact or may demonstrate depressed behaviors. As with the depressed subject, the suicidal subject is also often unaware of times, dates, locations, or other critical information. He may also fidget constantly in the chair because he wants to get away from the interviewer.

There are many misconceptions regarding the suicidal person of which the interrogator needs to be aware. Full knowledge of suicide and its warning signs can ensure that an investigator recognizes the true threats and risks, which will allow him to take the appropriate actions necessary to ward off a devastating event.

"Suicidal Type"

Although there is no real "suicidal type," most people who commit suicide are over the age of 45. However, there is an ever-increasing number of suicides in much younger age groups, including teenagers. Some of the victims are isolated and lonely, and would appear to fit a high-risk category; however, there are plenty of suicide cases of individuals who are prosperous and popular. Some individuals are failures in school as well as in their personal and professional lives, while others can be perfectionists, self-critical, and highly intelligent. These two groups either commit suicide because they see no real future for themselves or they do not like the future that they perceive they will have.

Suicide Threats

Some investigators fail to take action when a subject talks about taking his own life. Others may believe the subject's particular comments about suicide, but don't believe he is capable of fulfilling the threat. A subject is most likely to commit suicide during some crisis event (see Figure 8.6). That event may be the subject's arrest, indictment, trial, dismissal from a job, an internal affairs or professional standards review board hearing, or similar event in which the investigator may be a part. Once the crisis has passed, usually so does the risk of suicide.

If an individual is talking about suicide, he is trying to communicate to others that he is seriously thinking of taking his own life. All threats should be taken seriously if other suicide factors are also present. Some of these threats are open, while others may not be so obvious. The interrogator must respond to any and all such statements. Do not adhere to the belief that if a person talks about suicide, he is not likely to take his own life. Getting the person to open up and talk about these self-destructive thoughts is extremely important.

Danger Signs

An awareness of certain danger signs will assist the interrogator in evaluating the level of risk of suicide by a particular subject. These symptoms, like other kinesic signals, usually appear in clusters:

1. Is there any evidence that the person has tried to commit suicide in the past? The subject has been in some form of crisis event in the past, has attempted or has been treated in order to prevent suicide, and may respond once again with suicidal tendencies in this crisis situation.
2. The individual may begin to withdraw into himself. Friends, relatives, or even correctional officers may note that this person is becoming more and more apathetic and isolates himself from those around him with whom he would normally associate.
3. The risk of suicide is greatest when the person is suffering a major stressor or some form of emotional trauma. That crisis event may be his arrest, impending arrest, or that he is the focus of an investigation. It may also include divorce, failure of a personal business, or financial

failure. In any case, it will be an event that shatters an important sense of well-being and stability for the person, from which the person may feel he is unable to recover.

4. If the person is revealing specific plans about how he will commit suicide, the interrogator should be cautious. This can include specific methods of death, how he plans to have his body found, or who he

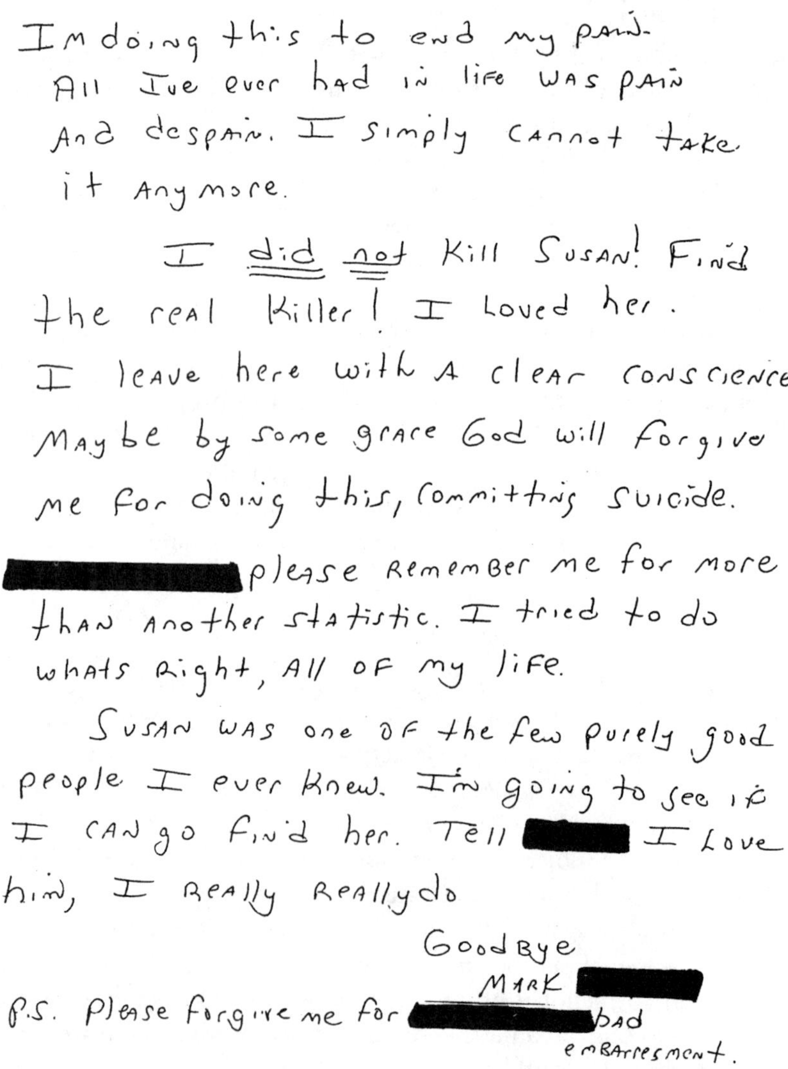

Im doing this to end my pain. All I've ever had in life was pain And despair. I simply cannot take it Anymore.

I did not kill Susan! Find the real killer! I loved her.

I leave here with A clear conscience. Maybe by some grace God will forgive me for doing this, committing suicide.

_____ please Remember me for more than Another statistic. I tried to do whats Right, All of my life.

Susan was one of the few purely good people I ever knew. I'm going to see if I can go find her. Tell ____ I Love him, I Really Really do

Good Bye

Mark ____

P.S. Please forgive me for ____ bad embaressment.

Figure 8.6 Suicide note of a homicide suspect. The suspect murdered his wife in the presence of their 4-year-old son. The suspect said a burglar who had slipped into their home early in the morning murdered her. The suspect leapt to his death head first from an interstate overpass

wants to find him. He may also include reasons why he wants to take his life. It is important to point out that not all cases of suicide involve some form of notice. In fact, it is estimated that less that 15% of those individuals who commit suicide actually leave a note (Geberth, 1996, 1997).

5. The person may express no concern for the usual deterrents to suicidal actions. For example, the person may not care about the amount of pain he may cause his family or the fact that he may be breaking the strong religious rules that he learned during his life. He may not be deterred in the least that suicide is such a final and irreversible action.

6. A strong sign is the giving away of personal items. Watch for subjects who give away jewelry, clothing, photographs, or other keepsakes. Teenagers may give away compact discs or tapes, stereos, or other important belongings. Adults may give away belongings that have great sentimental or monetary value.

7. An extreme danger sign is a sudden upswing in the person's behavior. The person may have been experiencing a long and troubling period of depression and doing a great deal of mental and emotional struggling with the suicidal thoughts. As the person appears to begin to recover from this deep depression, the rate of risk rises dramatically. What may have kept the person from taking his life was merely the inability to summon up the emotional energy to complete the act. Once he begins to recover, the emotional energy level necessary to commit suicide is available. It is also theorized that the final decision to take his own life may actually make the person feel and act better than he really is.

Be alert for the person who starts to speak in past tense. He may talk about how bad his life was or how good a friend a person has been to him. He may interact with family members using past-tense terms to describe their relationships and may have an air of finality to his comments.

Take Action

Once the interrogator has been alerted by the subject's behavior that there is a risk of suicide, he should choose actions necessary to decrease the risk to the subject. First, he must not be afraid to ask the subject if he is thinking about suicide. This will not put the idea of suicide in the person's head. If the subject is, in fact, considering suicide, he is more likely to be relieved to talk to someone about it. If the person will talk to you, sit quietly and listen to the subject and encourage him to openly express himself. The interrogator should not take a judgmental position in the matter, but only offer himself as someone who will listen. As with the subject who is ready to confess, the interrogator should also indicate to the subject that he is in the response state of acceptance. If the person refuses to elaborate on his suicidal thoughts, determine if there is another person with whom he would rather confer. This person may be a priest or minister, or the interrogator may suggest the subject talk to a counselor who is properly trained to assist him with his problems and help him through his crisis.

In all cases, should the interrogator feel that there is any possible risk of the person committing suicide, he should ensure that the subject is not left alone and gets immediate attention from a counselor, mental health care professional, the emergency room of a hospital, or some form of suicide intervention program.

Conclusion

When an interrogator encounters subjects who are suffering from some form of psychosis or affective disorder, he should recognize that, in general, his chances of success are greatly diminished. The reason for the decrease does not represent a failure on his part or mean that a particular subject is not guilty or may not be found guilty under the law. It does mean that extraordinary measures may be necessary to gain the information necessary to satisfactorily resolve the case at hand. This positive result may also be dependent upon the interrogator's ability to recognize the subject's particular mental or emotional problem.

Primary Dominant Personality Types

9

The analysis phase of Practical Kinesic Interview and Interrogation® supplies the interrogator with the information needed to determine if the subject is being truthful or deceptive. More specifically, it provides the interrogator with confirmation of what he has been feeling through his intuition. Clusters of deception behaviors generated in a timely fashion and changes from the subject's baseline behavior have given him that confirmation. In every case, the subject's unique behavior has been assessed for relevance to the issue at hand.

Once the assessment process is completed and the areas of deception isolated, the investigative interviewer now must overcome the subject's efforts at maintaining his negative responses of anger, depression, denial, and bargaining. As discussed earlier, the interrogator makes those attacks based on the particular response state the subject is demonstrating. Therefore, it is the subject's behavior that dictates the interrogator's response and not a set program of attack. This is especially true when the subject is responding to the interrogator through the use of denial and, in many cases, with bargaining.

We have already recognized that subjects can have different responses to any stress situation, such as those demonstrated by the five response states. We have taken great pains to identify the numerous verbal and nonverbal mechanisms subjects use to demonstrate each of these different response states. We now need to recognize that subjects have different mental operating systems and that the attack we make on denial and bargaining must be based on the person's unique personality type. It is through a custom-designed, subject-driven, narrative-based interrogation that we are going to get the most reliable and accurate information. A single-pattern approach to interviews that follows a rigid formula or predetermined set of questions has limited success with some subjects, and then only up to a certain point (Baldwin, 1993; Hess, 1989; Leo, 1996; Gudjonsson, 1992). The tactical interrogation process of Practical Kinesic Interview and Interrogation is designed to take into account the unique personality makeup and behavior of the interview subject.

Primary Dominant Personalities

Carl Jung and Hans Eysenck explored the uniqueness of human personality and advanced the concept of individuals being either introverted or extraverted in the early twentieth century. Jung, a former associate of Sigmund Freud, is credited with coining the terms "introvert" and "extravert," which he referred to as "attitude types" (Campbell, 1971). Jung's early theory and Eysenck's extensive research have contributed greatly to the understanding of the primary differences in humans based on personality type. Eysenck's work, in particular, attempted to identify the specific characteristics that delineate each type. He also was concerned with mapping each of these personalities when they deviated from the normal population and developed into psychoses or neuroses. Our first concern as interrogators, however, is to understand how these two primary "attitudes" of personality differ from each other. More specifically, the investigator needs to develop an understanding of the way these two distinct personalities think, react to other individuals, react to their environment, and solve problems through their particular reasoning systems.

For nearly 30 years, physicians, psychologists, and psychiatrists have recognized that the brain's two hemispheres have different operating systems (Gazzaniga, 1998). Though the two hemispheres are redundant systems, each accomplishes thought processes and resulting behaviors from two distinct perspectives. In general, the right hemisphere is that portion of the brain that operates using abstract thoughts and ideas. It understands the concepts of loyalty, love, honor, and so forth, and assigns meanings to words, such as house, cat, etc. It responds with emotion and evaluates things through an emotional reasoning process. The left hemisphere, on the other hand, operates through logic and sensory input. It is the portion of the brain where verbal expression of thoughts and ideas occurs. It works in a spatial manner and reacts to the environment through its tangible elements.

It is important to reiterate the individuality of each person. Even the phenomenon of which hemisphere is dominant in a person can have numerous exceptions, which is again confirmation that all subjects are exclusive unto themselves and must be recognized and treated as such.

The overall analysis of both hemispheres and the study of individual personality and the various theories of personality development are quite complex and are beyond the scope of this book. The significance to the interrogator, however, is that to use a single standardized approach to all interviews and interrogations may, in many cases, be flawed. Although a standardized interrogation process provides the interrogator a methodology by which to organize and approach any subject on a general basis, there will undoubtedly be times when the interrogator has all the right information, the right evidence, has spotted all the appropriate deception signals generated by the subject, but then proceeds to interrogate the subject incorrectly.

In order to be as effective as possible in the interview, the investigator must acknowledge that each subject has a personality that is as exclusive to him as his fingerprints. This distinction is based on the person's individual history, the personal coping mechanisms that he has developed and uses in these types of situations, and his primary dominant personality. The interrogator must learn to accept the individuality of each subject and approach the subject based on how he filters and processes information through his personality and its reasoning process. This is accomplished best when the interrogator understands the characteristics of each of the primary dominant personalities, how they reason, and the way they respond to the stress of an interview, and then develop an interrogation attack profile accordingly.

The primary dominant personalities discussed here are not meant to be representations of exact maps of any individual. We also do not imply that individuals can be neatly pigeonholed into nice little groups. Such a process runs the risk of stereotyping all subjects, which again increases the likelihood that the interrogator will use a generic approach to all subjects in the interview room. This is exactly the situation that we are trying to overcome by identifying the specific attributes of each subject. Personality types are, to some extent, an instinctive mechanism (Campbell, 1971; Stevens, 1982). They are instinctive in construction in that there is some form of consistent behavior and responses from each subject over a broad range of events and in different environments. These responses occur outside of the conscious awareness of the person, yet along with individual life experiences, they make each person unique. Because we all work from these unique characteristics, we often fail to understand the reactions and responses of those around us. This is due, in part, to the fact that we tend to impose our individual characteristics on those around us and assume that others interact with the immediate environment in the same manner we do. Therein lies the problem for the investigative interviewer. We cannot interview subjects as if we are interviewing ourselves, but must recognize and respond to the unique characteristics of each individual subject, whether suspect, victim, witness, informant, or source of information.

In addition, we are suggesting that specific subjects will commit specific crimes. Any subject can commit any crime under any condition without respect to his personality. The way a subject perpetuates a crime, however, is an outward characterization of the subject's unique personality and behavior type. Clues to the subject and his generally exclusive behaviors are apparent in the methodology used to commit the crime and are a psychological fingerprint of the subject. This psychological fingerprint is what can be used later to "profile" the crime by criminal behavioral scientists (Douglas, Burgess, et al., 1992).

Our goal in identifying the subject's personality and his particular reasoning process is to make the interrogator more efficient and productive. We are not attempting to train the interrogator to be an analytical psychologist. If, however, the interrogator has an in-depth understanding of his suspect and approaches that subject accordingly from the appropriate intellectual- and personality-based perspective, the chances of a successful interview are greatly improved.

Introvert-Oriented Personality

The introverted-oriented personality is typically understood to be the personality that is emotionally based. This is not to imply that this person will only commit emotional types of crimes. As noted, any subject can commit any crime under the right circumstances. What we are saying is that this person's mental process operates by using emotional input; in other words, his reasoning system is emotion-based.

Throughout this book, the introvert will be described as an emotional person. The observer may have difficulty in grasping such a description of the introvert at first. The use of the term "emotional" in conjunction with the subject is not meant to suggest that this person displays an entire spectrum of emotional behavior. On the contrary, the introvert displays as little emotional output as possible. The use of the term "emotional" in this sense implies that this person's behavior, decision making, and stress responses are driven "internally" by emotion.

The introvert, or emotional personality, is the person who tends to withdraw inside himself when he encounters a stress- or conflict-oriented event. The ability to survive in such situations comes from his capacity to draw on the strength that lies within him. He is typically not the type of individual who attacks either the problem or the new experience. He prefers to remain stable and allow the experience to wash over him, "absorbing" whatever the current carries to him — hence the term "introvert." The introvert, therefore, sees his environmental conditions to be hostile and foreboding and out of his control. He also sees himself as not having the skills necessary to alter the present conditions and extricate himself from danger.

Emotion-Dominant or "Feeler" Personality

Characteristics

The emotion-dominant, or "feeler," personality is the strongest in behaviors of the introvert-attitude personalities. The "feeler" personality has various behavior traits that differentiate it from the non-emotional, or extroverted, personalities. Each of these characteristics is an expression of the means by which the person deals with repeated stress and conflict situations, as well as dealing with everyday situations and people.

The "feeler" is frequently a serious person and takes life seriously. This is not to say that he never enjoys himself or engages in any activities for fun. He does, however, approach life from the viewpoint that every single decision is critical, and he is fearful of making any mistake that may jeopardize his stability.

For the emotion-dominant person, stability is the key to survival. It is so central to him, in fact, that he is unlikely to respond to anything in an impulsive manner because he needs his environment to be stable, orderly, and predictable (Campbell, 1971). To help maintain this stability, he often finds himself drawn to situations that appear to be orderly and controlled. The world, however, does not always provide him with the stability and order that he prefers, so he must find it on his own or create it around himself. To help maintain balance, the "feeler" approaches new situations by applying the knowledge from past experiences as a guide. To accomplish this, he must have a good memory from which to draw the vital information from past experiences, so it should be no surprise that, in general, the "feeler" personality has excellent long-term memory capabilities compared to the other personalities.

The emotion-dominant personality finds impulsiveness in others a threat and tries to avoid such people and the situations they create. To him, such behavior represents a person who is careless, prone to mistakes, and takes too many risks, thus putting himself and those around him at risk of discomfort from his disorder and randomness. Because of the balance he maintains in his life, other people often describe the "feeler" as steady and reliable to the point of being predictable in his behavior.

The emotion-dominant's predictability comes from his desire to always be organized. His dislike for impulsiveness is as strong as his commitment to having everything well planned. Such dedication to planning is also the result of the introvert feeling that he has little or no control over the hostile environment in which he believes he lives. To survive in the midst of such hostile elements, the introvert believes he can only control himself and, therefore, must be dedicated — occasionally to the point of obsession — with maintaining personal discipline and control over his life. He therefore strives to keep things organized so there is less chance of disruption and the uncomfortable situation of having to improvise on short notice.

This emotion-dominant or introverted person views his entire world in terms of emotional content and context. Each situation is carefully judged in terms of its emotional value or threat. What could possibly happen in a given situation to create an uncomfortable set of conditions for him? This filtering mechanism is the manner in which the introvert gains early detection of personally dangerous situations and people, both of which he feels he has little control over.

Emotion-dominant persons tend to be timid or withdrawn, and they do not readily open up to people. If another person gets too close to him, he runs the risk of that person knowing too much. As a result, that person may be able to manipulate him or take advantage of his generally compliant nature. In general, this person would rather deal with books than with people because there is a certain amount of safety and security within one's own thoughts. The exception to this characteristic, however, is if the introvert is dealing with someone he considers to be a close friend. This is a person with whom he has developed a certain amount of trust and whom he feels will not betray him or his privacy. Privacy is of extreme importance to the introverted personality, and he guards it jealously.

To the casual observer, this person may appear to be slow. However, the interviewer should never assume the introvert is dumb. They, in fact, can have a high level of intelligence.

When a confrontation arises (or appears to be arising) between the emotion-dominant personality and another person, the introvert tries to defuse the situation quickly. He does not perform well in the presence of aggression and will not demonstrate any strong aggression himself. He is more likely to withdraw from the hostile interaction and seek shelter and assurance within himself. Before he withdraws, however, he will try to negotiate some form of settlement. He would prefer to end the process on an upbeat note, rather than leave the problem unresolved and festering.

The "feeler's" tool against any developing conflict is to listen carefully. The emotion-dominant personality believes the answer to any developing problem is hidden somewhere in the verbal interaction between himself and others. This is based on two reasons. First, he hopes to learn that the other person has a good impression of him. He desperately needs to be liked and receive approval from those around him. If he has their general approval, he is less likely to encounter any friction in the relationship. Second, the "feeler" may be able to ascertain if the person is giving any sign that there can be a negotiated peace between them.

Along with the emotion-dominant's apparent retiring nature is a great deal of tolerance and patience with other people. This person desires to be left alone so that he can be who he wants to be without interference or influence from others. He frequently feels that he is always giving himself up to others and what they want, and is seldom allowed to be himself. For this reason, he extends the same courtesy to others around him, hoping that they will respond in kind in return for his tolerance and patience.

When the emotion-dominant subject does get into areas of stress, one of the first things an observer will notice is the way the "feeler" moves through his stress–response states. Remembering that the introvert is a controlled person who holds his emotions in check in most situations, it should be no surprise that the changes from one stress–response state to another are almost indistinguishable. The introvert changes so slowly and subtly that it is hard to determine at what point the introvert is changing from denial to depression, for example. The observer must watch and listen closely to the emotion-dominant in order to accurately diagnose a change in the stress–response states.

Part of the reason for the slow and almost imperceptible change is the way the "feeler" has conditioned himself for such stress-related events. Introverts are gifted with an excellent memory, particularly as it applies to the experiences of stress and conflict. He has learned from each and every situation he has encountered and has catalogued every one of them in terms of the mistakes he made or the response he used that turned out to be the best for him. The "feeler" moves slowly during stress as he reviews his catalogue of response data, looking for a similar situation from which he will extrapolate his next best move toward what he hopes is the road to survival.

This slow-response behavior makes the emotion-dominant appear to be passive. This occurs for two reasons. First, the subject is carefully weighing his response to the situation for the correct avenue of reaction. Second, the introvert shuns hostility and aggression, and his first reaction to hostility is to shut down and hopefully wait out the storm. He has also already decided that he is going to lose something in this conflict and is trying to ascertain what, specifically, he is going to lose or what he is willing to sacrifice.

The emotion-dominant goes to great lengths to guard his emotions from others unless they can help him survive a particular situation. The result of this protective process, however, is that in his attempt to withdraw and avoid confrontation, the emotion-dominant subject unwittingly generates a great deal of body language and speech cues, which, when decoded, give the observer excellent insight. If there were such a classification, the introvert would be labeled as the classic reacting person. His body language is easy to read as he moves through his stress–response behaviors. A careful observer is easily capable of deciphering nonverbal symptoms of anger, depression, denial, bargaining, and acceptance.

The verbal cues that an emotion-dominant generates are as equally discernible as his body language. The introvert is constantly reaching out to others in his attempt to find the middle ground of compromise. In hopes of finding that middle ground, he unwittingly provides verbal cues as to his current response to stress. Because both verbal and nonverbal symptoms are so apparent, the observer must be patient, listen carefully, and watch the display of body language responses from the introvert.

Reasoning Process

We have already alluded to the fact that the "feeler" operates on emotions. Every situation and person involved is screened, measured, and weighed on the basis of its emotional content. The "feeler" is more likely to see the emotions attached to a problem than the facts of the problem. Therefore, he internalizes information on an emotional basis, then externalizes, or shuns, what appear to be cold, hard facts if he can find no emotional content or significance in them. Too much reality can overload him; it is too harsh and impersonal for his liking.

The "feeler" likes for everything about himself and his environment to be orderly and predictable. The emotion-dominant does not like impulsiveness or random behavior. He also does not like for anything to be left undone, unsaid, or incomplete. Everything needs to have balance and a certain amount of finality.

This desire to have everything complete and balanced is seen in the way the "feeler" approaches any issue before him. These emotion-dominant personalities think in a circular thought pattern. First, individual points of an issue are explored to their fullest extent. After one point has been totally discussed and evaluated and laid to rest, the next point in the issue is raised. No point is explored until the current element has been dispatched. Once all of the important points have been considered and evaluated, then they are all considered as part of the whole issue. Then the decision is made (see Figure 8.1).

This tedious manner in which "feelers" deal with issues contributes to the perception that they are slow to come to a decision. This is not true. They are just being meticulous and are trying to avoid a mistake. In fact, they tend to be rational, but slow and careful thinkers. They view a problem from all possible angles and leave no questions unanswered, if at all possible.

Response to Interrogation

The most accurate reading of any person and his attending personality is gained when observing the individual as he responds to stress. In such situations, the subject is forced to deal with the issue using his personal strengths, while also avoiding any perceived weaknesses. As a means of determining how to react to the current dilemma he faces, he draws on a past history of experiences in how he either overcame the obstacle or how, in his mind, he failed to deal with the problem adequately. The catalogue of past experiences coupled with his personality creates a unique response to each new significant event.

When the emotion-dominant personality walks into the interview area, he is already pessimistic about the outcome. He feels that he does not have the skills or the ability to assert any control over what will happen during the interview. He believes that there is little or no chance of surviving this situation without suffering some form of personal loss. The introvert sees himself as a victim and attempts to have others perceive him in the same manner.

This person frequently becomes quiet and restrained during the interview process. He does this, not because he is unaffected, but exactly the opposite. Since he is pessimistic about the outcome of the interrogation, he feels that he is at the mercy of his world and has little or no ability to change it. His best option, therefore, is to withdraw and wait until the threat passes. In this manner, the subject hopes to avoid behavior that may further antagonize the interrogator.

From the onset, the emotion-dominant subject's major concern is what the interrogator thinks of him. He is so concerned at times about any negative impressions the interviewer may have about him, that he will give that issue more attention than the evidence presented. The subject attempts to assess the interrogator based on the personality and the aspects of this person that could be dangerous to him. He is also reading the interrogator's emotional output so he can determine how he should respond.

The interrogator will find that the emotion-dominant personality would much rather approach the entire issue from a defensive position. The "feeler" does not respond with and maintain a strong aggressive response under these conditions. In fact, he is likely to respond to the interrogator in a rather warm fashion, considering the current circumstances. The subject believes that if he can make an emotional bond with the interrogator, he has a greater chance of withstanding the inquisition.

The "feeler" readily complies with the interviewer's requests, especially if he feels it will help preserve stability. This attitude relates to the subject's attempt to find some aspect with which to create a bond with the interrogator, as well as his avoidance of hostility. Should the interrogation process begin to degrade into hostility from either or both sides, the introverted subject quickly shuts himself down and refuses to feed the aggression.

Once the interrogation begins, the emotion-dominant subject uses his well-developed listening skills as a method of dealing with the interrogator's "attack." First, he hopes that by listening carefully to the interrogator, he will be able to identify any possible signs of compassion. Any perceived sign is reassurance for the subject that he has a chance of survival. Second, the subject hopes there may be some subtle offer of amnesty. Finally, listening carefully may give him a clue as to how he can solve the entire issue and avoid any further unpleasantness. He is also hoping that the interrogator will respond in kind to his patience and focused attention.

When the subject does respond or initiate comments in the interrogation, they are designed to elicit some form of emotion from the interrogator. The introvert will, in fact, use this form of emotional response as a way to get the interrogator to identify with him and agree that the subject may be as much of a victim as a perpetrator.

Since the subject internalizes emotions and externalizes sensory data, he internalizes the guilt of his behavior. In short, the "feeler" suffers a great deal, emotionally, for the guilt of his behavior. This inverted emotional response is what significantly contributes to the suspect's easily diagnosed verbal and nonverbal kinesic symptoms.

Emotion-dominant subjects need approval and acceptance from the interrogator. They hope that the interrogator will reach out to them in an attempt to make some form of bond. In an effort to develop such a bond with the interrogator as quickly as possible, the subject frequently makes warm, open remarks to the interrogator, indicating his readiness to accept the interviewer. The interrogator should not be surprised to hear such soft, empathetic remarks early in the interrogation.

Overall, the interrogator will note that the emotion-dominant subject is stable and predictable in the interview room. Handled correctly, the interview should be easy to conduct, with some form of admission or confession occurring as early as 15 to 20 minutes into the interview.

Interrogation Strategy

In any interview, the first thing the interrogator must do is identify the subject's personality type as soon as possible. He must then think and react just as that person would; the subject should see himself reflected in the interrogator.

The first rule in dealing with the emotion-dominant subject is to avoid all overt forms of hostility or intimidation. Remember, the "feeler" does not handle intimidation well and will shut down when confronted with such aggression. It is a dire mistake to assume that the interrogation is moving too slowly and needs to be "speeded up" by the projection of hostility. Once faced with hostility, the emotion-dominant will only surrender as little information as is necessary to satisfy the interrogator and then will walk out of the room, never revealing the wealth of critical information the interrogator missed.

Case Study

The suspect in the serial murders of elderly women had been identified and located. Background information and his behavior assisted in the identification of the subject as an introverted primary-dominant personality, along with some personality disorder. Extensive preparation was made to conduct an interview of the subject. Part of the planning process included the development of a specific interrogation strategy based on the subject's personality type. During preparation, it was learned that the subject had an intense dislike for the FBI.

Primary and secondary interrogators were selected. Both were familiar with the subject's primary dominant personality profile, as well as the subject's personality disorder, and had gone to great lengths to be totally familiar with the interrogation plan.

The initial phases of the interrogation went as planned. The subject identified with the primary interrogator, and the interrogator was making good progress and gaining critical information.

A third investigator on the case made the decision that the interrogators were treating the subject too gently and that someone needed to get the suspect's attention. The investigator donned an FBI National Academy t-shirt and entered the interrogation room. His interrogation consisted of yelling at the subject, making numerous verbal threats about his failure to cooperate, and eventually resorting to off-color comments about the subject's homosexual orientation. The subject responded by saying "F___ you!" and left the room. The investigators have not been able to conduct any further productive interviews with the subject since that time.

Be sure to conduct the interview in a location that is considered safe and comfortable for the "feeler." They like their privacy and will guard it jealously. Don't deny them that comfort. An emotion-dominant subject sitting out in the middle of a squad room full of ears and eyes seriously inhibits the subject's desire to talk. In the same vein, an interview room with a crowd of people "participating in" or "just sitting in" on the interview will also have a detrimental impact on the quality of the results obtained.

A wise investment on the part of the interrogator would be to spend plenty of quality time developing rapport with the subject. Do not be afraid to develop a bond with him, but it must a sincere bond on your part. If it is not seen as honest and open by the "feeler," he will reject you as patronizing him or using him. The display of a cold, official, or bureaucratic manner quickly turns this subject off. The interrogator needs to find some way to develop a bond with the subject, just as the subject is attempting to do with the interrogator. Do not, however, allow the bond to prevent you from attaining your goal of admission or confession. You want the subject to feel assured that you are there to help him solve his problem. This is not to say that you should patronize the subject, but that he tends to be more open and cooperative with people he feels he can trust and who will not take advantage of him.

Work slowly. This person thinks and reasons slowly. This does not mean he is not intelligent, just that his mental efforts are slow, careful, methodical, and thorough. All too often, an interrogation of an emotion-dominant personality runs at breakneck speed. Be patient and slow down. You must give the "feeler" time to absorb and evaluate your comments and the evidence. Make sure you give him plenty of opportunity to respond without interruption, and you will get more information.

Once the interrogation begins, start with the pieces of information that will be easy for the subject to accept. Carefully select those aspects of the case that will be the least threatening to the subject. "Feelers" have difficulty in dealing with the cold facts of the crime. They view the specifics of the crime in a vague or abstract manner. They will be interested, however, in being specific about the minute facts of the peripheral details.

The way to organize and present the evidence of a case to the emotion-dominant personality is to think of constructing the information like a puzzle. When assembling a puzzle, most people usually begin with the outside border. All the pieces that create the border are isolated and assembled first. This would equate to the meticulous building of the peripheral details of the case. All the minor details are thoroughly discussed and in place before the more important aspects of the case are discussed.

The next step in assembling the puzzle is to isolate specific shapes, images, or colors contained in the puzzle picture, such as sky, trees, buildings, and so on. Each object is filled in until it is completed before starting on the next image. The interrogator does the same thing. He should pick out a few important parts of the case that he needs to prove. He should discuss each piece in its entirety before addressing the next issue. The whole process, to the introvert, appears to be well planned and structured; there is a sense of finality to each point. Emotion-dominant subjects must think in advance to avoid putting themselves in risky, threatening situations from which they may not be able to extract themselves. You want them to see the case "building" against them from a long way off.

When the interrogator has made the assessment that this subject is deceptive and then begins to make his move on the emotion-dominant personality in the form of interrogation, he should display all the confidence in the world that he has the subject. The process, however, should not be done in a harsh or hostile manner. The interrogator should take care to soften his tone, even to the point of lowering the pitch and volume of his voice, keeping the "threat-potential" factor low.

When the subject responds to the interrogator, he needs assurance that the interrogator is listening to him. The introvert is a careful listener and expects the same from those he is dealing with. A good technique for the interrogator is to repeat a portion of the comment just made by the subject. This echoing accomplishes two goals. First, it reassures the subject that you are listening to him. Second, it helps the interrogator to slow down and take the time to allow the emotion-dominant to absorb the information and respond.

When interrogating the emotion-dominant personality, the interrogator should remind the subject that it is important for him to give a full statement. If he does not, he may again fall victim to the whims of others around him. If the subject does not speak first, someone may twist the truth, take advantage of him, and lie about him. Suggest to the subject that he cannot afford to let things get out of control like that.

Remember that the "feeler" reasons using emotions and he thinks in abstract terms. The interrogator should therefore work in abstract emotional terms. Ask about how the person felt, what he was thinking about, if he told anyone what happened, how those people responded, and similar questions. All these comments work on the emotional content of the introvert's thinking process. They also address issues from an abstract point of view. .

Briefing: Interrogation Strategy for the Emotion-Dominant Subject

This section is a quick briefing on preparing for the emotion-dominant subject's interview.

1. Work slowly. Take your time. Emotion-dominant subjects think and react at a slow pace. Do not rush the interview.
2. Be subjective. The emotion-dominant subject views the world in an abstract manner. Build on the emotional elements of the case.
3. Personalize everything. The emotion-dominant subject needs to feel a personal connection to the case. He must "identify" with all the players and events.
4. Build your case one piece at a time — like a puzzle. Discuss one issue at a time, and follow it to conclusion before you bring up the next point.
5. Work in an orderly, organized fashion. This person likes order and structure. Work chronologically on the issues, following them step by step.
6. Use a soft approach. The subject will have a difficult time handling cold, harsh, facts. Keep the interview as low-key and nonthreatening as possible.
7. This type of subject will incriminate himself quickly. Pay close attention to emotion-dominant subjects from the start. You will see obvious signs of stress and deception quickly.
8. Be sure to listen. Repeat their remarks back to them. These subjects need to be assured that they are being heard and not ignored or dismissed. Give them your undivided attention.

9. Avoid aggression. These subjects will not respond well to aggressive, dominating behavior. They will talk only to those they trust. Spend time building rapport.

Extravert-Oriented Personality

The extraverted personality is based on non-emotional input. Again, this is not to imply that these persons only commit non-emotional types of crimes. Rather, this person's mental process operates using sensory data as opposed to using emotions in the manner the introvert-oriented person does.

Describing the extravert-oriented personality as "non-emotional" may initially sound contradictory. In general, this subject may display all the stress–response mechanisms openly, along with the entire upper and lower range of the emotions. This person does not, however, allow emotions to dictate his thinking or reasoning process. The extravert-oriented personality reasons using the sensory input gained from his environment. This person-ality is energized by non-emotional, or sensory and logical, information. He is pragmatic and needs large doses of reality input all the time, or he becomes bored and distracted.

The extravert-oriented personality is unlike the introvert-oriented per-sonality, who tends to withdraw into himself in times of stress or conflict. The extravert, by contrast, when he is under stress or is dealing with any form of conflict, tends to lose himself in his environment and among the people around him. The extravert sees his environment as exciting and stimulating, as are the people he finds there. It is also a place over which he thinks he can exert some influence and have an impact on the settings and outcome. He is drawn to it with interest, and wants to explore as much of this interesting stimuli as he can and what can he make it do if he exerts his own influence upon it (Stevens, 1982; Campbell, 1971). Hence, the term "extravert."

When considering the extravert-oriented personality, there are three types. One type uses a reasoning process centered on sensory information. This subject is demonstrative when it comes to the stress–response states. The second type uses a reasoning process based on the logic of the sensory information and how that information is linked together. This extravert, however, is controlled and does not demonstrate the stress–response states with the same level of intensity as do the other two types. The third type uses these same forms of sensory and logic input, but also utilizes his ego in an odd mix of subjective and objective thinking and behavior.

All of these personalities in their most concentrated forms are extravert-oriented, but operate using slightly different reasoning processes. As a result, the interrogation of these subjects also needs to be adjusted in order to improve the results gained from the interrogation. For the purposes of identification, the highly demonstrative extravert-oriented personality is labeled "sensory-dominant" and is recognized as being an "active" extravert personality. The second extravert, using a logic-based reasoning system, is labeled "logic-dominant" and is seen as an "inactive" extravert personality because of his almost total lack of observable stress–response behavior. The third form, using the mix of subjective and objective thinking dominated by ego, is the "ego-dominant" and is seen as a "unique-active" extravert.

Case Study

A convicted pedophile was the subject of an investigation regarding the molestations of three children living in a housing project. The subject's prior conviction was for molesting five girls in a housing project where he had lived previously. The subject was sentenced to 10 years in prison, of which he served approximately 18 months.

During the interrogation, the interviewer was attempting to use an emotional interrogation strategy on the subject. As with most molestation cases, the statements of the victims and medical examination were the only evidence. Approximately 2 hrs into the interrogation, the subject stopped the interviewer and said, "I know what you're trying to do. You're trying to get me to rationalize my behavior and minimize what I supposedly have done, and it's not going to work. You're just trying to make me feel guilty so I'll confess." The interrogation ended unproductively.

In a subsequent interrogation, an extraverted-personality interrogation strategy was used. The subject did not confess. However, he did make numerous verbal mistakes with which he was confronted. The subject decided to plead guilty because he said he didn't want the children to be traumatized by having to appear in court. The subject received a 65-year prison sentence for the molestations.

Characteristics

The extravert-oriented personality and its attending traits separate it from the introvert personality in that the extravert has no difficulty interacting with his surroundings and the people he encounters. Each of the characteristics demonstrated by the extravert in dealing with stress and conflict have been learned and reflect the extravert's innate desire to gain reward for his ability to interact.

The extraverted personality interacts with his environment and others through one of two primary mechanisms. He uses sensory information, or he processes data using logical analysis. He does not use an emotional filter to ascertain the data he needs to handle stress or conflict.

Being generally unaffected by emotional input, the extravert-oriented personality tends to internalize sensory information, also known as tangible information. At the same time, he may exhibit all the normal stress–response reactions. These demonstrated reactions, however, are not a representation of his thinking process. The "sensory dominant" exhibits the entire spectrum of stress responses and will actively engage another personality, while the "logic dominant" is controlled and disciplined and has a low-level output of stress–response behaviors. He engages another personality on an intellectual or logical plane. The "ego dominant" uses the subjective information he gains from the relationships he develops as "pawns" to be sacrificed for the overall goal of self-preservation, with no real feelings for the personal losses.

"Sensory-Dominant" or Active Extravert

Characteristics

The "sensory-dominant," or active extravert, personality usually demonstrates a great deal of energy in his actions and personality (Campbell, 1971). At times, he appears always "on," and people around him rarely miss noticing his presence. Nor will the sensory-dominant allow anyone to overlook him. Everything and everyone is met with vigor and high energy, including situations of stress or confrontation.

The sensory-dominant personality is impulsive. His thoughts and whims result in his changing direction within a heartbeat. When he goes through his stress–response states, he changes faster than any other personality. The adjective "active" is highly appropriate for this form of extravert.

Since extraverts in general do not allow their emotions to dictate their actions, they have no qualms about readily and openly displaying their responses to others. Very often, those around him find this aspect of the person hard to deal with, or at least difficult to understand, unless those people are also active extraverted personalities. Other people often view these open displays of stress reactions as exaggerated. The sensory-dominant has such energy and yet little or no fear of his actions, that to him, such reactions are just a normal method of expressing himself and are therefore quite acceptable.

Sensory-dominant personalities need a great deal of sensory stimulation. Should the extravert find himself in a "boring" situation, he will either walk away or try to stimulate some form of activity that will increase his personal sensory stimulation. It is not uncommon for such personalities to say or do something just to get a rise out of those around them.

The sensory-dominant personality is competitive and achievement-oriented. He sees himself as needing to win in all situations. In many cases, he will turn a seemingly passive event into a competition just to keep things lively and give himself the opportunity to win at a contrived contest. They often set high, almost unachievable, goals for themselves and those around them, and push others to meet the challenge.

The sensory-dominant personality is recognized by his constant interaction with those around him. He is regarded as a joker and enjoys teasing people. Because he is so direct, he is often considered to be abrupt, abrasive, and insensitive.

The energy of the sensory-dominant and his ability to stimulate people makes him a good candidate for leadership. At the same time, this active extravert will attempt to direct the thoughts and actions of those around him. He frequently believes that his way is the only way and will do his best to impress that point on everyone else.

This personality thrives on rewards and is always looking for the fulfillment of winning the competition (Campbell, 1971). When confronted with stress or conflict situations, the extravert responds with aggression. The individual who may be the source of that confrontation will find that he has locked into a battle with a worthy and capable opponent. At the same time, the extravert will give due credit to a worthy adversary, and appreciates a good fight.

Reasoning Process

The sensory-dominant personality focuses on sensory information as a means of analyzing and solving problems. Thus, he must find some form of tangible information in a sensory format to diagnose and focus upon (Stevens, 1982; Campbell, 1971). He does not work well when thinking about things in an abstract form. He will rely on past experiences in terms of what he personally observed or experienced as his foundation for addressing a current stress issue. Because of this reasoning process, emotionally based information and abstract ideas are of little or no value in his decision making.

When the active extravert finds himself confronted with a problem or stress issue, he attacks the problem in a lateral or tactical manner (see Figure 8.2). The problem is seen as a long wall of issues that impedes his aggressive forward progress toward a solution. The sensory-dominant will move along the "wall," probing for any weaknesses. The interrogator will observe this as the subject continually attacks a wide variety of issues, bouncing around the whole spectrum of issues or evidence. He is trying to find that one weak spot to attack and ultimately breach the wall.

Sensory-dominants are some of the most active thinkers that you will ever encounter. They undergo a constant rapid stream of thought and frequently have such a leap from one idea to the next and then back again that many people have difficulty keeping up with them.

In the interrogation room and other stress-related situations, this fast-thinking skill can be a disadvantage as well as an advantage. To their advantage, these subjects are often "ahead" of the interviewer, anticipating the rest of the question or the next step. They are also able to quickly figure out the strategy of the interviewer and try to anticipate all his moves. This quick thinking and fast stimulus-response process holds disadvantages, however. First of all, this person tends to get distracted easily and is not always capable of concentrating for long periods of time on a single issue. Because he is so easily attracted to each new stimulus, his thoughts, in response, can send him on an unrelated track. Supervisors, friends, and associates may find it difficult to keep him concentrating on a task and may accuse him of being undisciplined.

Second, his rapid-fire mind often overwhelms his efforts to carefully edit his remarks. When describing the characteristics of the active non-emotional personality, we indicated that this person often makes curt, direct remarks. His rapid-fire mind is to blame for this phenomenon. It is also to blame for his ability to regularly exaggerate almost any point. These subjects are often effective liars and make up information to make themselves look better and further make their point.

Interrogation Response

The active non-emotional personality is the most vigorous "opponent" any interrogator will ever encounter. This personality has an endless supply of energy, and the more intense the interrogation becomes, the stronger the subject becomes. He enjoys feeding off the interaction between himself and his interrogator.

The active extravert shows no fear of the interrogation or the interrogator. He believes that he is up to the challenge and can outlast anyone. He challenges the interviewer at almost every turn. First, he does it to test the interviewer and see if he really believes what he is saying. Second, the subject wants to find out if the interrogator has the guts and the stamina to be a worthy opponent and fight for his point of view to be heard. The subject also does it because he enjoys the stimulus of a spirited battle with a worthy opponent. The whole time the sensory-dominant is testing the interviewer, he knows that the interviewer is right. The active extravert enters the interview room optimistic and with no doubt in his mind that he can win this confrontation. In no way does he fear the possible outcome or punishment he may have to endure. He believes that he has the strength of character and the ability to survive anything.

The active extravert has an extremely high awareness of everything that is going on during an interrogation. He utilizes his fast-thinking skills to try to outtalk the interrogator, and frequently accomplishes that goal. His fast thinking permits him to quickly pick up the interrogator's train of thought and anticipate where the interrogator will attack next. That skill is then used to disarm the interrogator's attack.

When the active extravert makes an attack of his own, he will attack across a line of issues, just like the front line of a battlefield. This matches his thinking and reasoning process of dealing with sensory information and with several points at the same time. He will continually attack the interrogator along this "battlefront," looking for any sign of vulnerability and trying to make the interrogator prove his point. Once one or more of those points are identified, he will relentlessly attack the interrogator on those issues to show that the interrogator is wrong and that the subject is not guilty. Should the interrogator recover on a particular issue and show strength, the active extravert quickly jumps to another point and begins to probe it for weaknesses.

Left to his own devices, the sensory-dominant personality will take control of the interrogation quite quickly. He will try to direct the interrogator's train of thought and the direction of the argument. He will manipulate the interrogator, the evidence, and especially the interrogator's own words. This personality is notorious for taking great risks and will use the interrogator's words against him. The active extravert will always try to take the lead and put the interrogator into the submissive or defensive role.

Part of the active extravert's reason for being so aggressive with his "opponent," the interrogator, is because he enjoys the conflict. His use of anger in such a situation is merely a means of interaction and communication. And the use of intimidation by an interrogator is of little or no consequence to him because he thrives on the energy generated. Should the confrontation get to the point of a personal attack, however, all bets are off, and anything and everything is fair. As long as the contest is kept on a strictly "business" level, the sensory-dominant will stay the course.

Should the interrogation slow down, the active extravert may make a comment or do something that rebuilds the intensity. He is easily bored with a slow, plodding conversation. He may engage the interrogator in an argument over an issue, not because the interrogator is incorrect, but because he wants to test the interrogator and see if he really believes his own comments and will stick to his guns over an issue.

Interrogation Strategy

As noted previously, the sensory-dominant personality has a great deal of energy and will display a full range of physical and verbal activity when under stress. The first and most important rule for dealing with this personality is for the interrogator to develop a plan of action and stick to it. This subject is going to be attacking on all fronts at the same time. It is easy to get distracted by the active extraverted personality's dramatic shifts from topic to topic and his dynamic outward displays of stress response. A well-developed game plan will help the interrogator maintain control.

Remember that this is a person whose reasoning process is based on tangible, sensory information. It will be necessary, therefore, to have as much evidence on hand as possible, along with the supporting documentation. The more documentation you have, the more effective you will be in arguing your case. Each point you argue with the subject must be supported with specific details and examples. Without some form of backup to his claims, the interrogator will be dead in the water.

An effective approach in presenting your case to the active extravert is to deal with the entire matter chronologically. Bring up each point in the sequence it occurred, and then present the evidence to support your accusation, doing so in an open and frank manner. Do not worry about presenting damaging information in a soft, easy-to-digest form. This subject respects a direct approach and likes to get to the heart of the issue as soon as possible. Too much formality and prelude quickly bores him.

The interrogator should avoid "laying down the law" to the active extravert. He does not respond well to people who try to control him. The best approach is to allow this personality to have choices, but to control those choices. When this subject does decide to confess, it will happen quickly and with little forewarning.

Of all the mistakes that the interrogator could make when dealing with the active extravert, the one that must be avoided at all costs is to allow the attack to become personal. As long as the interview is approached in a professional, business-like manner, the interrogation should proceed without problem. If the interrogator allows himself to become frustrated and take things personally, or allows his frustrated attack to degrade into a personal attack, the interrogation can quickly spiral out of control.

Briefing: Interrogation Strategy for the Sensory-Dominant Subject

This section is a quick briefing on preparing for the sensory-dominant subject's interview.

1. Move quickly, and get to the point. This subject is easily bored and will wander off mentally. Don't drag things out.
2. Be objective. Sensory-dominant subjects are not swayed by the emotions of a situation.
3. Do not get personal. This is strictly "business." Using a personal attack is seen as a desperate move by an interviewer who has no proof and is losing the game.
4. Do not bring it up if you can't back it up. Always back up your argument with some form of supporting proof.

5. Do not bluff. The sensory-dominant is an expert at this game and will immediately see through a bluff and call you on it.

6. This subject will take chances with his answers. Pin him down. This subject is an active verbal deceiver and will make up things just to sound good. Make him back up his claims with proof.

7. Stand your ground — be aggressive. This subject senses hesitation and uncertainty. He is challenging you, not because you are wrong, but because he is testing your resolve and commitment.

8. Set a game plan and stick to it. Decide what you must get from this subject and don't quit until you get it. Your discussions with this subject will cover many topics. Do not forget why you are in there.

9. Use specifics. The more detailed you can be about your case, the more control you will have over your subject. Do not let him get away with denial.

"Logic-Dominant" or Inactive Extravert

Characteristics

The inactive extravert does not utilize or exert the same external energy as does the active extravert. He also does not demonstrate the wide range of stress–response reactions. The observer of the inactive extravert might describe him as extremely controlled, self-disciplined, cold, and unapproachable.

The logic-dominant is an extremely efficient personality. He uses no more energy than is necessary to express any particular emotion or idea or to get the job done. He exhibits the least amount of symptoms of each of the stress–response states. He demonstrates hardly any emotion at all, but does show maximum personal restraint and control. All of his energy is directed into logical thought (Campbell, 1971).

The inactive extravert is not a people-oriented personality like the sensory-dominant. The inactive extravert personality appears to not need anyone. He views people as a convenience rather than as a necessity. He passes through relationships with people contributing little to the relationships.

The characteristic that the inactive and active extraverts share is that they do not use emotions as a means of problem solving or in reaction to conflict. However, while the active extravert uses sensory data, the inactive extravert uses logic as his primary reasoning system (Stevens, 1982; Campbell, 1971). This logic process is perfectly matched for the mind of the inactive extravert, which is analytical and systematic. This highly logical and analytical system has no place for, and therefore does not recognize, emotions as a reasoning or response medium. This contributes to the cold and indifferent appearance many see in the inactive non-emotional person.

The inactive personality recognizes the significance of the sensory information and evidence that the active extravert identifies with. The inactive extravert, however, must organize that sensory data based on its logical progression and interrelated relationships (Campbell, 1971). The logic-dominant personality does not fully appreciate the significance that others give to emotion as a communication method. He sees the use of emotion, including the extreme displays of the active extravert, as inappropriate and a waste of energy. Anything that is perceived as emotional by the inactive extravert is rejected because it ignores logic or has no logical order to it.

The active extravert responds to stress events through the use of aggression and readily displays this reaction behavior in any conflict situation. The inactive extravert uses aggression only on an intellectual level. When in conflict or when dealing with stress, the non-emotional extravert responds with intellectual aggression. He systematically scans any issue for illogical weaknesses, and this analysis is unrelenting and merciless.

Reasoning Process

While the active extravert has a rapid thinking process that covers a lot of issues in a short period of time, the inactive extraverted person has an unrelenting, analytical thought process that carefully digests every issue (see Figure 8.3). All information is broken down into its most basic logical components and then is consumed. For the observer, the inactive extravert appears to be a slow thinker. What the inactive extravert lacks in quick mental processing is made up for in his tenacity, logic, and accuracy.

Like the active extravert, the inactive does not use emotions as a basis for addressing and solving conflict. The inactive extravert does, however, understand the significance of emotions displayed by another person and may use those outward displays as a means to diagnose that person. He does not find use for them in his communication with others.

Being the analytical thinker that he is, the inactive extravert sees only two sides of any situation. To him, there is no real right or wrong. Rather, this person breaks issues down into pros and cons, weighs the balance of the two, and then accedes to whichever side outweighs the other. Sometimes, he is so dominated by his logic that he traps himself. Once this happens, he follows the logical progression without regard to the consequences he may suffer because of it.

The inactive extravert is "inactive" only externally. Internally, he has a powerfully analytical mind. He is a careful and meticulous thinker and uses a great deal of discipline in handling any problem. This is also the standard by which he measures people around him. He expects and even subtly demands that people use the same disciplined logical mental process he uses to handle situations. If they do not, he dismisses them as being weak and a waste of his time.

Interrogation Response

The first thing that will catch the interrogator's attention with an inactive extravert is his extreme calm. It is almost as if the more intense and stressful the situation, the more controlled the logic-dominant is. He appears not to be the least bit concerned about the interrogation or its outcome. He may even appear amused at all the fuss over what he considers to be a matter of little or no consequence.

What the interrogator may find frustrating about the inactive extravert is the apparent lack of response he gives to any stress situation. In fact, he does not respond to stress like any other person the interrogator will encounter. He can take anything and everything that is thrown at him in the interrogation room and never appear stressed. This subject has the least amount of kinesic body language and verbal signals of all the primary dominant personalities.

Although the inactive extravert does not generate much in the way of body language and does not respond with emotions, he does understand emotional behavior. The inactive non-emotional personality understands that for some people, an emotional reasoning process is the only way they can interact in stress situations. He also knows that for those people, the emotion demonstrated is common to the situation at hand. In order to correctly diagnose those emotional persons around him, the inactive extravert watches people carefully for emotional output. He uses this information to gain insight on this person and as a means to gauge his own progress in controlling and eventually dominating that person. This is especially true in the interrogation room.

Because the inactive extravert's reasoning process is dominated by logic, he will analyze the interrogator's comments for content and attending logic. If the statements ignore logic in any manner, the inactive extravert will dismiss the interrogator's attack.

Not only does the inactive extravert use logic as his base for the reasoning process, he also takes things literally. There is a distinct exactness in the words he uses to express himself. Each word is selected for a specific reason and for its most literal definition. He takes the comments of others literally. If he senses that the interrogator's words are poorly chosen, he is likely to ask for clarification.

For all the inactive extravert's logical methods and his analytical mind, as well as his ability to see the absence of logic in another person's comments, he is not a good liar. He appears to lack the creative skills necessary to develop a good lie and convince others of it. This subject is likely to omit information and then observe whether the interrogator is "bright enough" to catch the flaw in the logic of his remark. He prefers to sit and listen rather than expose a weak position, and he is therefore an extremely good listener. He is listening, not so much to words, as for keys to understanding how the mind of the interviewer works . He lies in wait for an interrogator's accusation to show a lack of logic and then attacks an issue on those grounds, rather than try to lie and explain away his actions.

Interrogation Strategy

The interrogation approach for the inactive extravert is similar to that of the active extravert in one aspect. Both inactive and active extraverts are attacked using case facts and without a display of emotion. The demonstration of stress reactions by the inactive extravert, however, is suppressed to the point that they are barely visible. For the inactive extravert, the display of emotion in any form is considered inappropriate and a waste. The interrogator, therefore, would be ill-advised to use any energetic displays of emotion or hostility, because the logic-dominant will interpret this as a sign of personal weakness and will lose any respect he may have for his interrogator.

When the interrogator presents his case before the inactive extravert, he should classify the information into only two groups: the evidence weighing against the subject, and the facts that are in his favor. The interrogator should always be sure that the information he presents against the subject outweighs the points in his favor.

When you present your case facts to the inactive extravert, present them in a systematic and orderly manner. Avoid jumping from one idea to another when dealing with this personality. You should be direct and specific about each point in your attack of his denial. Use specific terms and avoid trying to "soft-sell" anything. This person does not need to have his sensitivities protected.

The logic-dominant personality uses a linear thought process to handle stress and conflict and to solve problems. He sees all things as having some form of logical, linear linkage. In order for one event to occur, he thinks in terms of the event that precipitated the subsequent action. The interrogator must do the same thing when presenting his interrogation argument. "If C occurs, then B and A must be present. Since C happened in this case, then there must be an A and B. D never occurs unless there has been an A, B, and C. E could never happen unless D is already present. Since we have C and D, we know that A and B exist, and since we have A, B, C, and D, we know that E exists." The entire process is clinical and analytical, which is generally the same process in which the inactive extravert thinks. All the evidence against the logic-dominant subject could be laid out on the table in front of him, and his response will be, "And this means what?" Until the logic correctly connects him to the evidence and the crime, there is no proof is his mind.

To the logic-dominant subject, there is no real "right" or "wrong" in a situation, or at least not in the same way that someone else sees "right" or "wrong." The inactive extravert assesses every event and action in terms of its logical and illogical components. Each attacking piece of evidence is presented to the subject in the correct sequence that it occurred. The interrogator then presents evidence to support his allegation against the subject. Each point is linked logically to the subject, holding the subject accountable because of his actions.

The interrogator must then get the subject to agree to the legitimacy of the interrogator's argument. Once agreement has been reached, the interrogator then moves to the next piece of information and uses the same line of attack before moving to the next issue.

When the interrogator makes his attack on the inactive extravert, he should not expect to see a lot of response from him. As noted, this subject generates the least amount of verbal and nonverbal kinesic symptoms when compared to the other personality types. He is disciplined when it comes to controlling himself, mentally, verbally, and physically. At the same time, he does not feel the stress of conflict in the same way others do. The interrogator must look for weaknesses in the person's logical comments, which is his attempt to lie, and then attack those areas.

Both the inactive extravert and the active extravert will attack the interrogator. Their methods of attack, however, are different. The active extravert attacks the interrogator to see if he will stand his ground on each point he attempts to make. The inactive extravert wants to debate the logic of the interrogator's comments, looking for any sign of weakness in his reasoning. Remember to avoid showing emotions of any kind during this debating process. Such display will turn the subject off and you will lose ground with him, and he will perceive you as intellectually weak.

To avoid giving the impression of any emotional response to the inactive extravert, speak slowly and distinctly, accentuating each critical point. Every aspect of the interrogator's presence should be cold, dry, drab, and emotionless. You might find you sound like a robot, but it is not your bearing that the subject is keying on, it is the clarity and logic of the content of your message.

A common mistake made by many interrogators in dealing with the inactive extravert is wanting to speed up the extravert or evoke some strong reaction. This is not in the extravert's nature and definitely not in the interrogator's best interest. You need to use a slow, steady pace. This person is a slow, careful, and methodical thinker. If you go too quickly, you will wind up "giving" the subject answers so he doesn't have to create any for his own defense. Make the subject defend himself by creating his own responses, not by getting them from you.

The final note regarding interrogating the inactive extravert is do not get excited or overaggressive. Display no emotions regarding the subject, the case, or the interrogation. Such displays disgust this subject, and he will not understand what all the fuss is about.

The inactive extrovert subject will confess when all the case facts are correctly presented and supported with a strong and complete logical argument by the interrogator. His confession is almost anticlimactic.

Briefing: Interrogation Strategy for the Logic-Dominant Subject

This section is a quick briefing on preparing for the logic-dominant subject's interview.

1. Be logical. There is a "reason" for everything.
2. Be logically objective. It is not just the evidence — it is what it means in terms of "proving" the argument.
3. Link each piece of evidence together. Show him how every piece is important and connected to the case, no matter how insignificant.
4. Be as accurate as possible. Don't "soften" up the argument or imply your meaning. Be direct and specific.
5. Show absolutely no emotions of any kind. Do not get frustrated. Do not try to "drive" the subject nor try to bond with him. To the subject, this is a sign of someone with no mental discipline.
6. Expect little feedback from him in the way of verbal and nonverbal behaviors. Look for "missing" pieces to his argument. He will withhold information as opposed to making up a deception.
7. Do not try to shock him or trick him. This subject is a cold, clinical, detached thinker, and the effort will be wasted.
8. Think of the case facts like a long math problem. Work the case step-by-step and be methodical to avoid missing a single step. Take nothing for granted.
9. Link everything to the subject. You want to eventually tie all evidence to him. You are arguing that a link exists between him and the crime and, therefore, he is responsible for the crime.

"Ego-Dominant" or Unique-Active Extravert

Characteristics

The unique-active extravert is similar to the active extravert in that he tends to be quite demonstrative in his behavior, particularly under stress situations. The difference, however, is that the unique-active extravert's behaviors are activated by the impact current conditions have on the subject's self-perception or ego. Overall, the unique-active extravert is a charismatic personality and tends to draw a great deal of attention due to the nature of his projected public image, upon which he thrives. This personality strives to gain and maintain recognition from those around him, and he sees others as being elitist.

The unique-active extraverted subject's ego-dominant personality frequently puts him at odds with those around him. This subject sees himself as gifted, special, or talented and that he is in a position above all others. As a result of this attitude, he regularly overestimates himself and his abilities. Also recognized for his ability to ververbalize and purposely talk over the heads of those around him, he is commonly described as talking a good game, but never really living up to his own billing.

Due to his highly cultivated and polished nature, people often find themselves drawn to him, but when they try to kindle a relationship, they often find the relationship one-sided and unfulfilling. At the same time, this subject is constantly lured by those people, things, and activities that fulfill his present needs. He attaches himself to people or activities he perceives as being currently in the limelight and moves from group to group or from one hot spot to another to stay in that limelight. When the limelight is gone, he quickly and without remorse dismisses the person or group and unceremoniously terminates the relationship as being beneath him or a waste of his time. He then chases down another relationship or activity that will supply his need for ego-stimulating attention. It is for this reason that people are drawn to him, but at the same time, put off by him. He is often described as aloof and superficial and never trustworthy or committed to any relationship.

When things collapse, this is most likely because this subject has never planned fully for the possible contingency of failure. He notoriously underestimates a problem, if he recognizes the problem at all. It is his perception that because he is involved in a situation, the problem either does not exist or it will not affect him. In short, he is unrealistic in the face of trouble and handles it in a totally impractical manner.

The stress of failure or the inability to face the negative impact of his actions frequently elicits the stress–response state of depression from him. This reactive depression marks the subject's belief that the whole problem was the result of the horrific failures of others, who have let him down. "They" are to blame because "they" would not listen to him or "they" deliberately let him down.

Reasoning Process

The term "unique" was deliberately chosen for this personality because, compared to the other three primary dominant personalities, this subject's reasoning and thinking process is truly unique. We described the emotion-dominant personality's thinking processes as governed and filtered through an emotional screen. His decision-making process is grounded in subjectivity. The active and inactive extraverts, on the other hand, use objective thinking methods for their reasoning processes. The active extravert uses sensory data for his objective process, while the inactive extravert uses logic.

The unique-active extravert uses a peculiar mix of both objective and subjective thinking. This subject has the uncanny gift to immediately identify the heart of any problem and does so with flair and exceptional precision. While the active and inactive extraverts use tactical and linear processes, respectively, the unique-active extraverts use a global thinking system.

However, when it comes to confronting issues and solving problems, this subject relies on questionable and highly impractical methods. The reason for this is that this extravert, once he has identified the heart of the issue, immediately takes everything personally and makes his decisions on a ego-dominated, subjective basis.

An opinionated subject, the unique-active extravert routinely underestimates most of the problems he encounters. He reads more into a situation than is really there, yet misses the essential elements. As a direct result of this overestimation, the subject frequently fails to see any pitfalls in his decision-making.

Interrogation Response

The first impression the interrogator will have of the unique-active extravert who has just entered his interview room is that, as far as the subject is concerned, the interrogation is a complete waste of his valuable time. This entire issue is beneath him, and he should not have to be bothered by these annoying little details.

Impatient and condescending, the unique-active extravert invariably treats the interrogator as being beneath his perceived station, and if he must deal with this "inconvenience," he should at least talk to someone of position or importance and not some subordinate. He perceives the interrogator as being beneath him and incapable of handling the problem. As a result, this extravert does not care for the interrogator's ideas or opinions and summarily dismisses them as having little or no value.

This subject, although extraverted and active, makes a poor liar. He will propose explanations and excuses for his actions that are totally unrealistic and impractical, but expects the interrogator to accept the remarks without question merely because it is "his" explanation. The amazing aspect of these types of responses is that no matter how bad these excuses and explanations are, and despite the fact that they may appear even more ludicrous in the face of the true facts, this subject never backs down.

The same global-thinking skills used when solving problems fail when the subject is at the heart of the problem. Unable to accept that he is wrong, he will overlook all of the important issues of the case that the interrogator suggests point to his guilt. At the same time, however, he will focus on one or two aspects of his actions where he botched the whole thing. But don't expect the subject to disclose this information to you.

Finally, because of his elitist, ego-dominated personality, the unique-active extravert believes he has the ability to actually "steer" all the negative evidence in his favor. Though his stress–response states should be easy to identify and the body language easy to read, the interrogation of this subject is difficult at best.

Interrogation Strategy

Of all the primary dominant personalities, the unique-active extravert personality is the most difficult to interrogate, and the overall success rate in interviews is correspondingly low. The primary barriers to successful interrogation of this subject lie in the subject's powerful ego and how it influences his use of subjective thinking, and the subject's global thinking and reasoning process.

As mentioned, a dominant factor in this subject's behavior is his ego. As a result, he invariably responds to the interviewer as an underling. The interrogator may be tempted to take this as a personal affront, especially in view of his position and responsibilities. If the interrogator is aware of the peculiarities of this personality, however, this ego-dominant behavior can be used against the subject. By showing a little deference, feeding this subject's ego will permit the interrogator to lead the subject into self-destruction.

The interrogation strategy that works most effectively on this subject is to first, not be intimidated by the subject's air of superiority. Show the subject a little respect, and allow his powerful ego to show through. It will be his ego that does him in. When things start to fail, he will turn to the paranoid side of depressive thought and blame everyone around him for the failure. This is a critical point for the interrogator. Assist the subject in assessing blame for his failure and particularly how he has been betrayed by others' incompetence. Capitalizing on the subject's depression will help generate incriminating statements.

To further facilitate the subject's out-of-control ego, place emphasis on the importance of him clearing the air as to who was really at fault. Have him outline specifically where everyone else failed because of weaknesses and lack of foresight. He will be happy to give you his opinion.

Present the case to the unique extravert from the perspective of an overview, or "big picture." The subject will respond to details as being tedious and bothersome. At the same time, this subject will not allow you to believe that you have the details correct, and he will attack you on your accuracy. Save the details for when the subject brings them up, and then impeach his remarks with the facts. However, don't expect the subject to admit that you are right and he is wrong.

During the impeachment process, have the subject "enlighten" you and correct your "misinterpretation" of the facts. This subject is notorious for solving problems using illogical reasoning and impractical methods. This is exactly the behavior you want to illicit. His overabundant ego and flawed excuses and explanations will be obvious to everyone except him.

The key mistake to avoid with the unique-extravert personality is to "pull rank." This will cause the subject to reject you and will create aggression. Do not assume that this subject cares about your opinion; he could not care less.

Briefing: Interrogation Strategy for the Ego-Dominant Subject

This section is a quick briefing on preparing for the ego-dominant subject's interview.

1. Feed the subject's ego. Play up his importance while playing down your own. You want to appear to be of little or no real threat to him.
2. These subjects often feel betrayed by people. The ego-dominant feels that others have used him and taken advantage of his good nature. Feed this weakness.
3. Blame everyone else for the ego-dominant's failures. Help him lay blame at the feet of everyone else. It will take him off his guard.
4. Use case facts only to impeach his answers. Let this subject make a false statement, and only then present proof he is wrong. He will not acknowledge the proof, but it will frustrate him.
5. Think of the case as one large event. Deal with everything at once. Getting too much into details is beneath this subject. He prefers to deal with the "big picture."
6. Do not give him your feelings or opinions. Do not talk about how he is wrong or praise him for what he did right. He does not care about your opinion because you are beneath him.
7. Keep him focused on problem areas. This subject will dismiss or ignore any damning evidence. Keep bringing these issues up to him so he can "clarify" the issue for you.
8. Lure him into speaking out to set the record straight. The more you get him to talk, the more he will incriminate himself.
9. It is hard to get a confession from this subject. You want this person to implode and self-destruct, but don't expect a confession. You want everyone around to see the truth whether he does or not.

Conclusion

All too frequently, an investigator will gather all his forensic evidence and complete all the necessary background information regarding a specific investigation. He will then organize that information in such a manner that it makes complete sense to him. He may be totally convinced that, armed with the information he has, any subject would crumble under the weight of the evidence and confess. The problem with this mind-set is that the subject and the interrogator may be of two distinctly different personalities. Until we learn to approach each individual subject according to his reasoning process and personality type, we will continue to have the same marginal results using neatly ordered, pre-programmed interviews.

Each individual is unique, and so is the interview of that person. The best interviewer is the person who first understands himself and his unique characteristics. He then understands the diverse nature of other personalities and how they relate to him. During interrogations, he must be able to "turn off" his personality and assume the nature of the subject, adopting that person's mental processes.

Interjection Phenomenon

Occasionally, there are behaviors or actions in which the subject may engage that have little or nothing to do with his personality type. Psychotics and normal personalities alike have been documented as engaging in what are known as "interjection phenomenon." This is often described in detective stories and mysteries as the guilty subject's propensity for returning to the scene of the crime. Though it sounds simplistic, numerous subjects do, in fact, engage in such activity.

You may recall at least one time when working a crime scene that there was a particular person who made a nuisance of himself. He may have asked you a million questions about what was going on. You may have had to eject him from the crime scene several times. He may have gone from officer to officer, gathering bits and pieces of gossip about the case. Some of these individuals may have been overly cooperative and helpful while around you. This type of behavior is done deliberately.

There are times when some individuals involved in an investigation will volunteer for everything. They volunteer to take the polygraph even before you ask them. They offer to be in a lineup or photo spread. Some subjects offer blood or hair samples for analysis. They may be willing to offer fingerprints, clothing, or other pieces of physical evidence for forensic analysis.

Other subjects have offered to undergo hypnosis, urine testing, powder residue tests, and other evidentiary testing measures.

Some investigators have had subjects visit them at their offices to discuss the status of the investigation. As you might expect, these visitors have not been invited and their visits are almost always at the most inconvenient time and definitely to the advantage of the subject. If the subject does not visit the case officer, detective, or agent, he may contact the investigator's supervisor or chief to get a report on the progress of the department's investigation. It is important to note that this kind of behavior does not usually come from the victim of a crime unless it is extreme.

There have been many reported cases of subjects that have gone back to the crime scene after the scene has been cleared by the investigating agency. These individuals have been known to "locate" evidence that was possibly overlooked during the original search. They have located and interviewed witnesses that were not previously identified. These individuals managed to develop new investigative leads that the investigator "should look into." They may discover fires before the fire department arrives. They may be the security officers that always find the burglaries or who always have fights with unknown assailants.

This type of behavior has been seen in many celebrated cases in law enforcement history. Edmund Kemper was murdering young women in Santa Cruz, California, in the early 1970s. At the same time the police were trying to identify the serial killer of these women, Kemper hung out at a bar frequented by sheriff's department employees and bought them beers and listened to their conversations about his case. Kemper later admitted that he did this on purpose because people who are friendly nuisances are often ignored in such investigations.

When an investigator sees these types of behavior, he should immediately focus on that individual. The investigator should not be surprised at how many times he may have just found his suspect. If it is not his prime suspect, this individual needs to be eliminated as soon as possible. The subject may possibly be just a "police groupie" or have some psychological problem that needs immediate attention so that his interfering behavior can be suppressed.

Understanding, Avoiding, and Reducing the Risk of False Confessions

10

Investigative interviewers have long been reluctant to acknowledge the fact that there is such a phenomenon as a false confession. Whenever asked about the possibility of a person falsely confessingd to a crime, invariably, the answer is always, "There's no way an innocent person would ever confess to a crime that he didn't commit." Unfortunately, there are still some extremely unethical and unprofessional investigators who have relied on outrageously abusive physical and psychological interrogation techniques to gain a confession from a subject. Even then, however, the attitude has almost always been that the subject was guilty anyway. Similarly, the possibility is rarely considered that, absent any form of physical or overtly abusive techniques, there is a form of subtle coercion or undue methods that would create a situation in which an innocent subject might unwittingly confess or make incriminating statements that could result in his wrongful conviction. Recently, highly publicized cases of exoneration have proved these beliefs to be grossly inaccurate and those who adhere to these ideas disparately misinformed.

There is little doubt that a confession carries a great deal of weight in the courtroom. The question remains, however, under what conditions was the confession obtained and should a confession be the ultimate goal in every case? There are three pillars to the investigative process: forensic, psychological, and interview. Each case presents different demands and emphasis on each of the three pillars. There are cases when the forensic pillar is the most important element leading to successful conclusion and prosecution of a case. At other times, the psychological pillar provides the most important keys to the investigation's conclusion. The risk to justice occurs when an investigator places value on one pillar to the exclusion of the other two. When he does this, he runs the risk of developing self-confirming preconceptions that can weaken the entire effort and put the whole case at risk. Such is the situation when the investigator puts the goal of confession above all else.

The Evidence

Over the last few years, the courts have reversed and vacated numerous convictions of prisoners in U.S. prisons that, it was determined, had been wrongfully convicted. Reasons for the courts' decisions have not always been the usual obscure procedural flaw or a major change in legal precedence or interpretation from the U.S. Supreme Court. A large number of these cases have brought to light instances of mishandled or missing evidence, mistaken identity, errors in eyewitness identification, and, more significantly, DNA evidence. Estimates as to the number of cases of wrongful convictions varies, depending on the type of study conducted, but the accepted estimate is that approximately 1% of the convictions for serious crimes are wrongful convictions (Huff and Rattner, 1986). Wrongful convictions of subjects for lesser crimes are estimated to run much higher. In a study of 62 individuals who were exonerated by DNA evidence, in 52 of those cases, the conviction was primarily based on what turned out to be mistaken eyewitness identification (Sheck and Neufeld, 2000). An additional study of 350 cases of wrongful conviction (Bedau and Radelet, 1987) found that one class of major contributing factors was errors that occurred during the investigation, of which the primary error was false confession.

With so much overwhelming evidence of cases of wrongful conviction, can we ignore the significant role that the initial investigation, and especially the interview, plays in the investigative process? We know through multiple research efforts and the study of human memory that, in general, people make poor eyewitnesses. At the same time, there should be other significant elements in the investigative process, including forensic and psychological evidence, that should neutralize or at least diminish the negative impact eyewitness testimony can have on the outcome of a case. More importantly, if there are wrongful convictions in which one of the contributing factors is a false confession, is it the interviewers' behaviors or the interview environment that results in a false confession? And what are those conditions and in what ways can the interviewer accomplish the goal of getting reliable critical information, as well as a confession, without compromising the quality of the case or the confession?

The Elements of Wrongful Conviction

In-depth analysis of multiple cases of wrongful conviction (Brandon and Davies, 1973; Bedau and Radelet, 1987) has identified four groups of errors that contribute to the prosecution and conviction of innocent subjects. One common finding in all the studies is that there is usually more than just one factor that contributes to the miscarriage of justice. Interestingly, just as the kinesic observer in an interview must watch for "clusters" of behaviors in order to make any form of reliable assessment regarding a subject's possible deception, there is usually a "cluster" of errors, as opposed to a single exclusive factor, that creates the conditions more likely to result in a wrongful conviction. The four general categories of errors include police errors, prosecution errors, errors by prosecution witnesses, and miscellaneous sources of error.

By far, the largest number of errors that occur are police errors. This in itself is not surprising due to the significance that the investigation has on the outcome of the prosecution of a case (Greenwood, 1979). With such a tremendous emphasis placed on the investigative process, and with multiple disciplines and skills coming into play, coupled with the number of individuals involved in the investigation of a case, the errors that are bound to be made are going to be magnified. The largest source of all police errors, however, is the false confession. Other contributing factors include negligent or overzealous efforts by officers to solve the case. A small area includes threatening or coercing witnesses.

The second source of error is attributed to the subject's prosecution, including events prior to trial. The greatest error in this category is the suppression of exculpatory evidence. It is not uncommon in a crime scene to find evidence whose origins, presence, or significance could not be explained. When this happens, sometimes the prosecution feels it is better to exclude or even ignore this information, especially if the evidence contradicts the prosecution's theory as to how the crime was committed. Contradictory evidence can be outweighed easily by a mountain of other valuable evidentiary assets, however, it would appear that in the fervor to successfully bring a case to trial, overzealous efforts and preconceptions can blind the court as to the real significance of some evidence.

Errors caused by prosecution witnesses fall into two primary areas. Somewhat surprisingly, one of these areas is perjury. In these cases, witnesses had a multitude of reasons for perjuring themselves on the witness stand. Some do it as a form of revenge against the suspect or victim; others do it to protect themselves from prosecution for the role they may have played in the criminal act. Other cases of perjury involve testimony in return for leniency in similar or other charges. The second area is errors in eyewitness identification of subjects.

Miscellaneous sources of error include such things as misleading circumstantial case evidence or failure to fully consider critical evidence supporting the suspect's alibi. Failure of or incompetent defense counsel contributed to only a small number of the cases. A large number of cases in this category was attributed to the impact made by public outrage and pressure to resolve the case, which eventually had a major impact on the outcome of the trial.

False Confessions

The purpose of this section is to address the issue of false confessions, their existence, under what conditions and with what type of subjects they are most likely to occur, and what actions the investigative interviewer can take to reduce the risk of their occurrence. At this point, we need to develop an understanding of what defines a false confession.

There are three specific elements to a false confession (Ofshe, 1989). First, it is a person's response to a demand for a confession. Second, the person confessing fabricates it intentionally. Third, it is not based on actual facts in order to form the content of the confession.

The demand for a confession can originate for any number of sources. In the case of a criminal investigation, the investigative interviewer initiates the demand. The interview location, environment, and time also contribute to the pressure to confess. We should not discount, however, that there are other sources that can create pressure on a subject to provide a confession. The obvious sources are external, such as family, associates, or criminal partners. Not to be discounted, however, is the pressure that the subject may place upon himself. When this happens, there is a high probability of some form of emotional or mental disorder.

The second and third characteristics are interrelated. In a false confession, significant parts of the confession are fabricated. The subject may invent a connection between himself and the evidence, location, or victims. Or the subject may invent evidence, links, victims, or connections that do not exist. This is compounded by the fact that the investigator will find it extremely difficult to prove or disprove the subject's claims; the subject's explanations are not usually outlandish or outside the realm of possibility.

Under normal interview and interrogation situations, a confession is usually elicited because one or more of three elements are in place. The first is the internal pressure that the subject puts upon himself. This is the result of either overwhelming guilt or a sense of remorse for his crime. Another is the external pressure that is associated with the actions and behaviors of the interviewer, the location of the interview, length, and so forth. The third factor is the subject's belief in the "proof" of the evidence and that he can find no reason to continue to deny what he believes is irrefutable. Based on the definition of a false confession and the normal factors present in any confession, it is apparent that there is a fine line separating the false confession from the genuine one. However, upon closer examination, the conditions that create both are dramatically different in terms of the interview setting, conditions, and techniques used by the interviewer.

Contributing Factors: Environment

The factors that contribute to the stresses caused by the interview environment are not ones that can always be controlled. The mere fact that the subject is at the police station, at a deposition in the courtroom, before a grand jury, a union grievance hearing, and so forth, is stressful in its own right. There is one consolation, however, in that the more times a person is subjected to those settings, the less likely he is going to react stressfully to that situation. Where the danger lies, however, is in deliberately abusing these environmental conditions for the purpose of putting the subject in a state of distress. For the subject who is suggestible or easy to manipulate, the location itself can be imposing (Irving and Hildendorf, 1980). He is already in the unfamiliar territory of the police station, for example, and is most likely confined without any contact with peers or relatives. Furthermore, he is forced to submit to the authority of a person who has total control over the situation. In fairness, this is the most amount of pressure we want to place on the subject who is in custody, or will be before too long, and is the very reason for the protections provided under the Bill of Rights and the U.S. Constitution.

Extremes created in the interview environment can easily contribute to making vulnerable subjects more prone to falsely confess, and in the severest of cases, force even the most emotionally and socially well-developed of subjects to give false statements of implication. In the majority of cases, it is hoped that any investigative interviewer will be aware of the dangers of these conditions and will avoid them or not allow them to persist because of the risks involved.

The extremes in the interview environment found in many cases of false confession have been isolated (Hinkle, 1961; Shallace, 1974). Each one, in and of itself, is a significant stress-creating condition, although some of these conditions would not normally appear to have such a devastating effect. One such element is the use of social isolation. In an interview, it is necessary to restrict the amount of distraction and interference that would occur with outside visitors participating in the process. However, many hours, or even days, of isolation can have detrimental effects on anyone's judgment. Other will-breaking methods include long periods of sensory deprivation, denial of or minimum amounts of food and water, and deliberately designed fatigue-inducing conditions, such as extremely long interviews or even tag-team interviewing.

Extended periods of time without sleep or deliberate sleep deprivation have been seen in false-confession cases. There are, unfortunately, still situations in which less-than-ethical interviewers have abused subjects, causing physical pain, emotional abuse bordering on torture, or fear through threats of abuse and torture.

The end results of these distress-creating environments, in the long run, are counterproductive. If the interviewer believes that he is going to get reliable information, he is sadly mistaken. Under these conditions, subjects have been known to say anything just to bring an end to the horrific conditions in which they find themselves. These subjects almost always show severe signs of impaired judgment and mental confusion. These subjects also suffer from significant emotional and sometimes physical disorientation. They do become highly suggestible, but in situations in which the interviewer has resorted to these types of techniques, he has achieved his goal. The interviewer has undoubtedly developed some preconceptions about his subject and the case. With the subject in this current state of mind, the interviewer will get the confession he wants, but its credibility will be severely diminished.

Contributing Factors: Interviewer's Technique

If an interviewer expects to be successful to any degree in the interview room, he must be able to accurately spot when a subject is lying and what, specifically, he is lying about. Then, he must be able to persuade the deceptive subject that there is overwhelming proof of his lies. Yet it is in exactly these two areas where most interviewers lack the proper training to accomplish the end goal of case solution (Walters, 2002; Greenwood, 1979; Fisher and Geilselmen, 1992; Walters, 1997a).

The main goals of the first half of this text were first, to teach the reader what has been scientifically determined to be the verbal and nonverbal behaviors most likely associated with deception. The second goal was to teach the reader how to improve those conditions under which those symptoms can be accurately identified and diagnosed. A great deal of time was spent identifying numerous Practical Kinesic Principles designed to improve the interviewer's ability to create the proper conditions necessary to elicit and then correctly identify the signs of deception. The second half of this work has focused on identifying the most productive interrogation strategies, which are custom-designed for each personality type. Great effort was spent on how to identify each personality type, the typical patterns of behavior, how these subjects respond to the interviewer and the interview, and the unique decision-making process for each. We will now learn to recognize the devastating results that can occur when these tools we have studied and developed are either ignored or misused.

Without a doubt, any investigative interview will have some form of stress. The interview will involve traumatized victims, who may or may not be cooperative, but who could be undergoing a great deal of stress. The interview may be that of witnesses to the event, who themselves may be traumatized, or individuals who are critical sources of information. All these people may or may not be cooperative. Our investigation might lead us to depend on the quantity and quality of the credibility of statements of informants, who invariably have different agendas and self-serving motives for their actions. For the suspect, the interview will contain stress due the environment of the interview location, the investigation of an event that requires he be interviewed, and the official role of the interviewer. These exchanges can be frank and may require the interviewer to be direct and forward. Without proper care and control, these very same conditions can and have been known to contribute to false statements by witnesses and false confessions by subjects (Zimbardo, 1967).

The techniques of interviewers have been scrutinized numerous times, and each study has provided insight into what methods interviewers use and which of those methods are the most productive (Baldwin, 1993). One of the consistent findings (Moston, 1990b) has been that there are two approaches that interviewers use when asking questions: inquisitorial and accusatorial. Each method has different characteristics and different objectives.

The inquisitorial approach is characterized by the effort to gain extensive, valid information from the subject, and has a higher rapport-development rate. The interviewer typically gains a great deal of information that may not be directly related to the crime, but that tends to fulfill many of the needs of the psychological pillar of investigative discipline. In the end, more information is gained about the subject's general behavior, lifestyle, habits, and other critical background information. Unfortunately, few interviewers use this approach, although it has proven valuable (Moston, 1990b).

The accusatorial approach is marked by frequent direct confrontation, with the focus being to obtain an admission or a confession (Moston, 1990b; Baldwin, 1993; Irving, 1980). There are three main ways in which the interviewer uses the confrontational style. First, he may use a "direct confrontation," in which, with little or no introductory period, the interrogator requires the subject to state his innocence or guilt of a specific crime. This direct confrontation is usually accomplished by asking a specific question, such as, "Did you rob the Ontario Bank last week?" Second, the interrogator presents the evidence against the subject, forcing him to give an explanation that must either be some form of admission or denial. The third method is a combination of the two, which first asks the subject a direct question and, as soon as the subject "lies," "attacks" the lie with the evidence. The risk with the last two methods is that, by their very nature, critical case information has been fed to the subject. Later, when this same information is repeated back to the interviewer in another form, he believes that he now has proof of the subject's guilt when, in fact, now it is impossible to determine the true source of the information (Moston, 1990b).

It is the accusatorial method that creates the greatest risk for and has the highest incidence of false confession (Moston, 1990b). The risk is greatest when the subject is classified as "suggestible" due to environmental conditions, or compliant due to preexisting mental or emotional conditions. These subjects are also more vulnerable to suggestibility because there is typically a great deal of negative feedback from the interviewer if he does not like the subject's response. There is also a higher occurrence of leading questions, which direct vulnerable subjects to the answers most desirable or acceptable to the interviewer. Finally, questions that are not answered to the interviewer's satisfaction are typically repeated until the desired response is obtained (Register and Kihlstrom, 1988). In all, the accusatorial style betrays the fact that the interviewer has developed significant preconceptions regarding the subject, his guilt, and the case, thereby disabling any possible objectivity on the interviewer's part. Sadly, two-thirds of the time, investigative interviewers are using an accusatorial method (Irving, 1980). Unfortunately, it is this method that is most frequently taught to new investigators as the primary interviewing strategy (Gudjonsson, 1992).

Types of False Confessions

There is, without a doubt, a multitude of different emotional and psychological reasons why individuals confess to crimes that they did not commit. All of them, however, can be classified into three different types based on common characteristics (Kassin and Wrightsman, 1985). They are the voluntary false confession, the coerced-compliant false confession, and the coerced internalized false confession.

Voluntary false confessions are peculiar in that they are given without any external pressure from the investigator or the agency. Of course, there are those times when a crime has been committed and the subject has turned himself in to the police and makes a spontaneous statement of guilt. What makes these cases unusual, however, is that the subject has not committed the crime to which he is confessing, but, because of some emotional or psychological flaw, is doing so because it brings him notoriety. As an interesting example, in the famous Lindbergh baby kidnapping, more than 200 people falsely claimed responsibility for the crime (Kassin and Wrightsman, 1985).

In some cases, these voluntary false confessions are for crimes that have never even occurred. In this case, the subject is most likely having severe problems in discriminating between fantasy and reality. In other cases, the subject enjoys the attention and his ability to control and confound the police as they struggle to investigate a nonexistent crime. Some of these voluntary false confessions are due to overwhelming feelings of guilt due to low self-esteem or extreme anxiety disorders. These subjects feel the need for some form of punishment for either their behaviors in general or for an unrelated event. In their minds, punishment for the "adopted" crime will hopefully be sufficient to rid them of their feelings of guilt.

The source of coerced-compliant false confessions can be directly traced to the pressures of coercion during the interrogation. The subject is not confessing voluntarily, but has succumbed to the demands of his interrogators for some immediate gain. What the subject hopes to gain is the escape from an extremely stressful situation that he feels he can no longer tolerate. At the point the subject confesses, he is typically not fully aware of the severe ramifications and consequences of his statement. The subject may believe that the truth will eventually come out during his hearing or trial, clearing him of any wrongdoing. There are four motives for this type of confession. One motive is that the subject believes that by complying with the interviewer's wishes and giving the statement requested, he will be allowed to go home. Second, by making his statement, the relentless pressure of the interrogation will cease and the interview will end. Third, by confessing, this subject is submitting to the demands of the situation and feels that this is the only option available to him. Finally, the subject is motivated to confess because, by doing so, he can avoid being held any longer in police custody. An excellent example of these types of false confessions are the high-pressure sales bonanzas that offer the customer a free gift, show tickets, weekend vacation, or similar incentive if he will sit and listen to a 90-minute sales presentation. How many people have walked away from those having purchased a service or product that they didn't really want or need and later regretted buying?

The coerced-internalized false confession is invariably the result of "memory distrust syndrome" (Gudjonsson, 1992). These subjects believe, as a result of the interrogation, that even though they have no memory committing the crime, they are convinced that they are guilty of the offense. These individuals, during the accusatorial questioning process, distrust their own recollections and memories (Ofshe, 1989). A common statement is, "They have the evidence and they say that proves I did it, so I must be guilty."

The subjects most likely to commit these types of false confessions generally already have problems with memory. This includes severe alcoholics; heavy and long-term drug abusers; older subjects suffering from brain disorders, such as the early stages of dementia or organic brain disease; the very young; or the mentally deficient. In these types of cases, the subject is forced to acknowledge that he may (or does) have memory problems. Once that is admitted to, the interviewer often asks the subject if it is not possible that he could have committed the crime and forgotten it.

The Admissible Confession: The Protection against False Confessions

There is no denying the weight a confession has before the court, because from the mouth of the defendant comes the very words that can seal his fate and that will affect all legal proceedings from that point forward. The existence of a confession can determine whether there will be a trial or if the case will be plea-bargained before the opening proceedings — sometimes even before the first preliminary hearing. Its presentation to a grand jury can make defending the subject an insurmountable task, even for the best of attorneys. Eyewitness testimony, forensic evidence, and the psychological elements gain credibility exponentially when a confession is obtained. The key to protecting against false confessions and wrongful convictions and protecting the rights of the subject, ultimately providing justice to the victim, is that the confession must not only be admitted in the record, but it must also be legal and valid.

The first step in the process of validating the confession is to begin with the court's definition of a legal confession. In *James v. State of Georgia*, App. 282, 71, S.E. two-dimensional 568 (1952), the court defined a confession as: "an accused person knowingly makes an acknowledgement that he or she committed or participated in the commission of the criminal act. This acknowledgement must be broad enough to comprehend every essential element necessary to make a case against the defendant." From this definition, we can define the goals and objectives of our interviews.

There are two primary elements that need to be present in the confessions we obtain from subjects. The first is the *actus reus*, or the evidence of the crime. Does the evidence support the argument that either the subject's action or inaction was a direct cause of the crime? The confession must contain information that can be corroborated by physical evidence. Therefore, two of our three pillars of investigation are dependent upon each other. There must be forensic information that, by its existence, confirms that a crime has been committed and that this subject, as the primary actor, accessory, or accomplice, participated in the criminal act. Second, the confession should provide the explanation for the creation of the evidence and how or why it is linked to the subject. A prematurely concluded interrogation denies us this information. The two elements are interdependent upon each other and one without the other weakens the one.

The second element is the evidence of criminal intent on the part of the subject called the *mens rea*. If the mind of the subject is innocent, then there is no crime. Two more pillars are interdependent upon each other. To a limited degree, we may be able to infer from the evidence of the crime that there was some intent on the part of the subject. There are psychological elements exhibited by the subject during the commission of the offense.

However, we may not be able to fully grasp the reasoning behind the subject's behaviors until the mind of the subject is exposed to us during the interview. Only then will we have confirmation of the subject's intent. Did the subject premeditate the act? Did he deliberate before the act, when there would have been an opportunity for him to pursue a different course of action? Was there any malice on the part of the subject? What were the subject's thoughts, habits, behavioral patterns, and feelings when he committed the crime or after it was over? We must have *actus reus* and *mens rea* or there is no crime.

The insurance against miscarriages of justice and the protection of the rights of victims lies in the hands of the investigative interviewer. It is the complete and credible information obtained from victims and witnesses and, eventually, the professionally, ethically, and legally obtained admissions and confessions from subjects.

The Practical Kinesic Interrogation

11

Once the investigator has completed the analysis phase, identifying which of the individuals that he has been interviewing is being deceptive, as well as the specific areas in which the subject is being deceptive, he must now begin the interrogation process. In order to be successful in his attack, the interrogator needs to make an assessment regarding the particular primary dominant personality that he is interrogating. The assessment of the subject's personality gives the interrogator the framework upon which to build his interrogatory argument. That argument is designed to break the subject's particular efforts at denial and to disguise his actions that are unacceptable or criminal. Those efforts of denial and disguise occur because the subject is attempting to exercise a stress-protection system that Sigmund Freud identified as an ego-defense mechanism (Campbell, 1971).

Ego-Defense Mechanisms

Throughout our lives, we are confronted with countless situations involving stress associated with conflict and anxiety. These events may challenge the internal image we have of ourselves. This is the image that we would like others to have of us and of our actions and behaviors. There are times, however, when the reality of who we are and the consequences of our behaviors threaten those images. In the process of dealing with these unsavory situations and images, we learn to make use of an ego-protection system designed to protect those images should they come under attack. This defense system assists us in dealing with the discomforting aspects of the realities that can create conflict and frustration, and it eventually becomes a habitual process for us. Over time, the process of ego protection becomes individualized, and its development is based on our particular primary dominant personality, along with our own personal history of life experiences. This ego-defense system makes itself evident whenever an individual is under stress, including in interrogation settings. This system is what assists the subject in maintaining his resistance to confession. It is, therefore, the mechanism that the interrogator must overcome in order to gain an admission or confession to the realities the subject wishes to deny.

Whenever an individual realizes there is an assault on his image of himself, the ego-protection system is engaged. Being forced to face the reality of his inappropriate behavior through interrogation is an assault on the delicate balance between the subject's image of himself and the real person. The ego-defense system is critical in helping the person maintain that delicate balance. Thus, the goal of the subject's ego-defense system is twofold. First, the individual is trying to protect his self esteem. Second, it is his method of defending against stress and anxiety when he is faced with continuing frustration of any type.

Maintaining or enhancing one's self esteem is critical to the one's emotional and mental balance. We all want to see ourselves and our behavior as commendable, admirable, and strong. We desire for others to also see us as people who are in full control of ourselves and our actions. Seeing ourselves in this light enhances our self respect. We do not want to acknowledge any part of ourselves or our actions that may be interpreted as belittling or degrading. We only wish to acknowledge or take credit for what is fine and noble in our actions and us.

The goal of defending against stress and anxiety is the mind's way of maintaining mental and emotional balance. Anxiety and stress are viewed as undesirable and unpleasant. By nature, we seek to avoid such conflict situations, or at least attempt to reduce the discomfort when they do occur. Avoiding stress and anxiety is a method of survival in the face of conflict.

All defense mechanisms have two qualities in common, both of which involve the use of deception. We are the first target of our deception. We cannot face the reality of our actions and we will try to deceive ourselves about the truth. The other targets of deception are those people who have knowledge of our actions. This double-edged deception process makes itself evident in two forms: denial and disguise. Sigmund Freud recognized that we used these behaviors and that they are demonstrated by several different methods (Campbell, 1971) The following are the different forms of ego-defense mechanisms and a brief description.

1. **Denial:** using various ways to reject the reality of one's actions or the events that have occurred
2. **Displacement:** using a substitute object or person as a target for blame for an unacceptable impulse or unacceptable behaviors
3. **Intellectualization:** dealing with problems in an intellectual rather than an overt behavioral or emotional manner
4. **Introjection:** taking on the more acceptable attributes of another person and making them part of oneself

5. **Projection:** attributing to someone else the negative impulses or characteristics one sees in oneself

6. **Rationalization:** dealing with an inappropriate event or activity by justifying the behavior with plausible reasoning

7. **Reaction formation:** an unconscious impulse deliberately expressed in behaviors that are exactly the opposite of the negative behavior in which the person has engaged

8. **Regression:** returning to an earlier, more childlike behavior when current adult or mature behaviors in the face of anxiety do not suffice

9. **Repression:** an attempt to force unpleasant or emotional thoughts or obsessions out of conscious thoughts

10. **Sublimation:** an attempt to transform frustrating behaviors and thoughts into those considered more socially acceptable

11. **Minimization:** diminishing the level of significance of one's unacceptable actions by describing them in more socially acceptable terms or with more acceptable explanations

The interviewer is not expected to remember all 11 of these defense mechanisms, their definitions, and how they work. We have, in fact, already discussed them in general terms when we discussed the stress–response states. Notice that each of these mechanisms is either a form of denial or disguise. The response state of denial, for example, was defined as the "rejection of reality." In this response state, the subject is engaged in the deception of himself and others, one of the principle aspects of the ego-defense system. It is one of the methods by which a subject helps to defend himself against any stress and anxiety he may encounter.

We also discussed a stress–response state described as the "disguise of reality." When using this response behavior, the subject is accepting only a small portion of reality, but to make it more palatable to himself and to others, he attempts to change the other person's perception of the crime and, thus, of the subject. Recognizing our unacceptable behaviors and perceiving ourselves in a better light is another form of deception. This "disguise of reality" was identified as the response state of bargaining.

The behaviors in which we have engaged that stimulate our ego-defense system are not random events. We are motivated by a set of triggering keys, which, when not adequately controlled by our regular methods of self-discipline, may cause us to act in ways considered inappropriate by ourselves and others. A working knowledge of these triggering keys and their effects on appropriate human behavior provides the investigator with the insight necessary to successfully identify and attack the interrogation subject's defensive shield against admission or confession.

Motivating Keys of Behavior

Once again, we refer to Sigmund Freud to understand the concepts of deviant or unacceptable behavior. Freud indicated that we are all constantly under the influence of three primary behavior-motivating keys (Campbell, 1971). For most people, most of the time, there is no difficulty in controlling the urge to respond to these keys in inappropriate ways. There are times, however, because of personality flaws or moments of stress, that we may succumb to the pressure of these motivators and act against the normal conventions of appropriate personal and socially acceptable codes of conduct. Some of those failures in controlling our responses result in criminal activity.

Freud identified the key motivating factors as being sexually oriented, revenge oriented, or psychological need. If the investigator would take a moment and look at all of the cases he has ever worked, he will realize that one or more of these factors was present when the subjects of those cases committed their criminal acts. It is these impulses that cause the activation of the subject's ego-defense mechanism.

When the interrogator has isolated the deceptive subject and his behavior, it is time to make the interrogation attack. When the interrogator accuses the subject and confronts him with the reality of his inappropriate behaviors, the subject will respond with one of the five stress–response states. Should the subject respond with one of the four negative-response states, the interrogator takes the actions necessary to break the subject's negative responses, which enable him to maintain his overall rejection of reality. If the subject responds with the positive reaction of acceptance, the interrogator provides the subject with the mental and emotional setting necessary to give an admission or confession.

If the subject responds to the interrogator in one of the two ego-defense system states, denial or bargaining, the interrogator must attack the subject based on his personality type, using the mirror image of the subject's reasoning and problem-solving process. If the interviewer will listen carefully to how the subject organizes his denial and disguises his comments, he can learn what is at the heart of the subject's motivation.

When in stress, the subject will provide a verbal "encryption" of the particular ego-defense technique he is using and what motivated him to act in an inappropriate or criminal manner. By identifying that code and then framing questions and comments appropriately will draw the interview subject closer to acceptance.

The content of the subject's verbal encryption is most evident when the person is under stress and can give the interrogator critical information about himself. The encryption will include information indicative of the subject's primary dominant personality. It will also alert the interrogator to any possible personality disorders the subject may have.

This same encrypted information also tells the interrogator which one of the three motivating factors was at work when the subject committed his crime. When the subject is discussing the crime, crime scene, or alibi, moments will occur when the subject inadvertently provides the interrogator with the information necessary to identify the motivational key to his behavior. The key will not always be identifiable with just one or two words, however. It may take the interrogator a period of time to determine what the key may be. Once the key is identified, the information is then played back to the subject within the framework of the interrogator's questions and comments.

When the subject is undergoing the interrogation process, he is actually engaging in two conversations: one with the interrogator and one with himself. It is the second conversation that helps the subject develop and maintain his ego-defense system. This is the conversation in which he is trying to cope with his criminal behavior. The contents of that conversation are often different from and contrary to the conversation he is having with the interrogator. Under stress, there are moments when the subject loses his ability to maintain the barrier between those two conversations. As a result, he experiences "subconscious mis-cues." When these mis-cues occur, the subject may allow critical elements of his self-conversation to be openly verbalized to the interrogator. Once the interrogator identifies those mis-cues, he will often have found the key that will break the subject's ability to maintain his continuing rejection of reality.

Once the interrogator has identified the content of those mis-cued verbal encryptions, he must phrase his questions with parts of those mis-cues embedded in the question. He should not, however, repeat the subject's exact words back to him. This action causes the subject to realize that the interrogator has identified his ego-defense process, and he will create a newer and stronger barrier. Instead, the interrogator needs to be creative, rewording the essence of the subject's comments. Those comments are combined to match the subject's dominant primary personality and the appropriate stress–response state the subject is demonstrating.

Verbal Encryption: The Interrogation

When the interviewer interrogates the subject using the verbal encrypted keys the subject has given him, he must be careful to adhere to several Practical Kinesic Principles that will enable him to make the final push for the most efficient and effective approach that will lead to confession.

First, the interrogator should never do anything that may make an inno-cent subject confess, such as making promises or threats. The principles that we have discussed in this text are not illegal in any form. In their energetic efforts to get the confession, interrogators have been known to take risks that jeopardize the case, the confession, and their professional careers. Such acts are usually ones of desperation. Should the interrogator find himself taking such risks, he is better off discontinuing the interrogation until he can main-tain greater control over the subject and the interrogation, thus the Practical Kinesic Principle:

> **An interrogator should never engage in any type of behavior that could force even the truthful subject to confess.**

Second, if the interrogator does follow all the legal principles and rules regarding appropriate interview behavior and gets a false confession, he has most likely been working with a subject who is young or of low intelligence and is easily lead. Such confessions are usually dismissed as having been gained from a mentally deficient subject and the statement, therefore, was not knowingly and intelligently rendered, leading to the Practical Kinesic Principle:

> **A false confession is most likely to have been gained from a subject who is mentally deficient or is highly suggestible.**

Third, in all cases, the interrogator should ask the subject how much alcohol he consumed or what drugs and how much he used on the day of the crime. Research by the U.S. Department of Justice and the National Institute of Justice in its Arrestee Drug Abuse Monitoring (ADAM) program has iden-tified the prevalence of drug and alcohol involvement in crimes. The odds are in the favor of the interrogator that his subject was under the influence at the time he committed his offense (see Figures 11.1 through 11.9).

The interrogator should act as if there is no question that the subject regularly uses drugs or alcohol. For example, the interrogator may ask the subject if the people he was with that day were forcing him to use drugs or alcohol. The subject may be asked if he felt pressured to use a new drug that he would normally stay away from or if he used more than he normally does. The interrogator may suggest that someone mixed the drugs incorrectly or that the drugs were "bad." The suggestion can be made that the subject drank more than he usually does or that he started mixing drinks. This gives the subject something to blame for his behavior, but it does not make him any less guilty. The efforts of the interrogator can be greatly reduced if he realizes

Male Arrestees Drug Positive - 1997

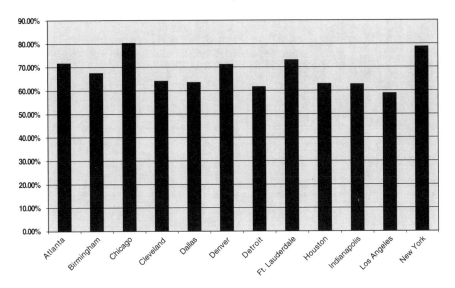

Figure 11.1 *Source:* Arrestee Drug Abuse Monitoring Program — National Institute of Justice, U.S. Department of Justice.

Male Arrestees Drug Positive - 1997

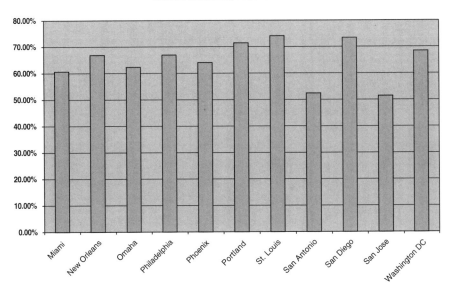

Figure 11.2 *Source:* Arrestee Drug Abuse Monitoring Program — National Institute of Justice, U.S. Department of Justice.

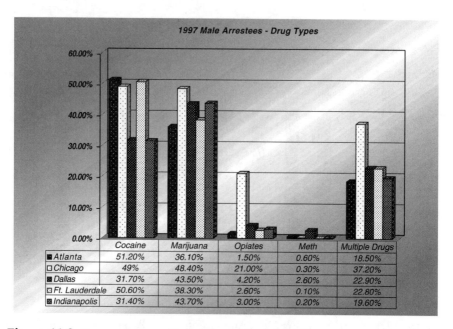

1997 Male Arrestees - Drug Types

	Cocaine	Marijuana	Opiates	Meth	Multiple Drugs
■ Atlanta	51.20%	36.10%	1.50%	0.60%	18.50%
☐ Chicago	49%	48.40%	21.00%	0.30%	37.20%
▨ Dallas	31.70%	43.50%	4.20%	2.60%	22.90%
▥ Ft. Lauderdale	50.60%	38.30%	2.60%	0.10%	22.80%
▩ Indianapolis	31.40%	43.70%	3.00%	0.20%	19.60%

Figure 11.3 *Source:* Arrestee Drug Abuse Monitoring Program — National Institute of Justice, U.S. Department of Justice.

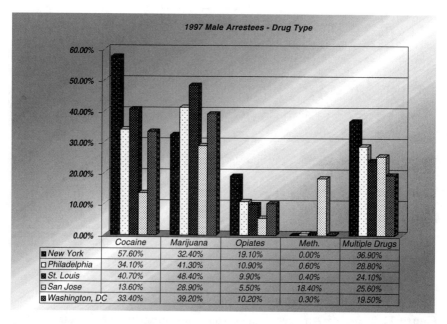

1997 Male Arrestees - Drug Type

	Cocaine	Marijuana	Opiates	Meth.	Multiple Drugs
■ New York	57.60%	32.40%	19.10%	0.00%	36.90%
☐ Philadelphia	34.10%	41.30%	10.90%	0.60%	28.80%
▨ St. Louis	40.70%	48.40%	9.90%	0.40%	24.10%
▥ San Jose	13.60%	28.90%	5.50%	18.40%	25.60%
▩ Washington, DC	33.40%	39.20%	10.20%	0.30%	19.50%

Figure 11.4 *Source:* Arrestee Drug Abuse Monitoring Program — National Institute of Justice, U.S. Department of Justice.

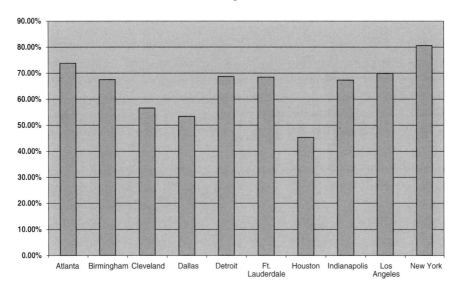

Figure 11.5 *Source:* Arrestee Drug Abuse Monitoring Program — National Institute of Justice, U.S. Department of Justice.

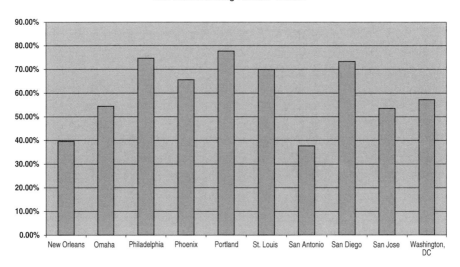

Figure 11.6 *Source:* Arrestee Drug Abuse Monitoring Program — National Institute of Justice, U.S. Department of Justice.

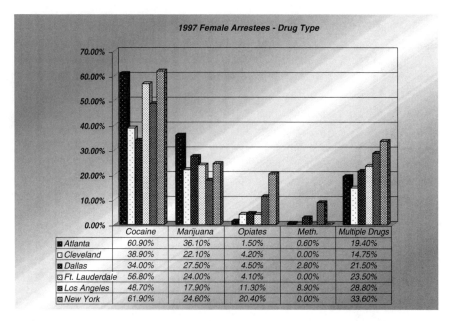

Figure 11.7 *Source*: Arrestee Drug Abuse Monitoring Program — National Institute of Justice, U.S. Department of Justice.

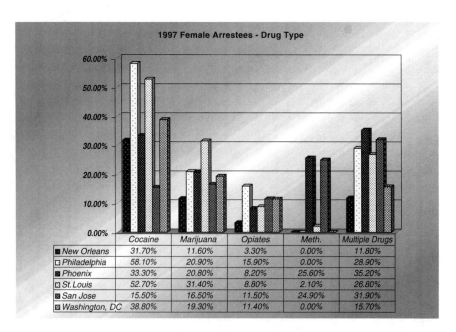

Figure 11.8 *Source*: Arrestee Drug Abuse Monitoring Program — National Institute of Justice, U.S. Department of Justice.

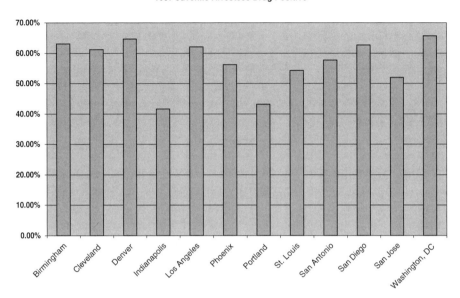

1997 Juvenile Arrestees Drug Positive

Figure 11.9 *Source:* Arrestee Drug Abuse Monitoring Program — National Institute of Justice, U.S. Department of Justice.

that the subject is looking for such a target of blame, and alcohol and drugs are a credible target, which leads to the Practical Kinesic Principle:

An interrogator will find that most subjects are prepared to blame alcohol or drugs for their behavior.

Fourth, the interrogator should remember to review the real or circumstantial evidence with the subject about every 5 min. This review of information is evidence to which the subject has already admitted, and is used to specifically attack the subject's further denials and disguise processes. In reviewing the evidence, however, the interrogator must be sure that he has organized that information to match the subject's reasoning format for his particular primary dominant personality, thus the Practical Kinesic Principle:

A successful attack on denial requires that the interrogator review the subject's previous admissions to proof about every 3 to 5 min.

Fifth, the interrogator should make sure that he has correctly identified the subject's primary dominant personality type. Once he has assured himself that he has made the correct assessment, he must follow those rules that have been outlined describing how each of the personality types are successfully interrogated, as stated in the following Practical Kinesic Principle:

A successful practical kinesic interrogation requires the appropriate assessment and attack of the subject's primary dominant personality.

It is critical to remember that the introverted, or emotional, personality operates through emotions and uses abstract ideas. Therefore, circumstantial evidence is used to attack his denial. The interrogator approaches the interrogation from the viewpoint that the subject is guilty and that the only question remaining is how the subject and interrogator will resolve the subject's particular problem. The interrogator must also find some way to establish a bond with the subject by complimenting the subject, sympathizing or identifying with his problem, or expressing friendship and understanding. He should avoid aggressive behavior with the subject because these subjects are generally pessimistic about the interrogation and the interrogator. Introverted subjects will withdraw in the face of aggression.

The extraverted, or nonemotional, personality operates in more tangible, sensory, and logic-based reasoning formats and, therefore, lots of evidence and documentation are used to attack his efforts at denial and disguise. The interrogator's attitude at this point is that the evidence against the subject stands on its own and there is not much reason to argue over its existence. This does not mean that the extravert will not attack the interrogator and his case. In most cases, the interrogator can expect such a reaction because the extraverted personality frequently uses aggression as a means of handling conflict or stress. The interrogator, however, should be prepared to stand his ground and stick to his belief in the facts of the case. He should present those facts in a formal, chronological, business-like manner. There is no need to develop a relationship with the extraverted personality. He sees such behavior as a sign of general weakness and will take advantage of the interrogation.

Sixth, the interrogator must correctly identify and respond to the stress–response states the subject is experiencing during the interrogation process. It is the subject's reactive behaviors of anger, depression, denial, bargaining, and eventually acceptance that dictate each of the interrogator's moves; it is not a formula that is followed without regard to the subject's personality type or response state. Gaining a confession from the subject requires the interrogator to identify and control the four negative-response behaviors and recognize the moment when he should capitalize on the subject's acceptance response, thus, the following Practical Kinesic Principle:

A successful practical kinesic interrogation requires the interrogator to correctly identify and respond to the subject's five basic stress–response states.

As mentioned early on in this text, those interviewers and interrogators who are the most successful at their craft have four easily recognizable elements to their interviews: orientation, narration, cross-examination, and resolution. These are used as the basis for the entire interview and interrogation approach, which is called a narrative-based interview. By fulfilling the requirements of these four elements, we will get the greatest amount of information from our subjects, make a more accurate analysis of their credibility, successfully attack their inconsistencies, and be more productive at gaining admissions and confessions. The orientation phase is the initial period of contact with our subject, during which we establish some form of dialogue. The objective is to obtain a grasp of the subject's baseline, or "constant," of behaviors. Establishing the constant is paramount to our ability to accurately diagnose any emotional and cognitive changes we may observe later from our subject. The narrative phase is designed to elicit as much information from the subject as possible by creating an atmosphere in which the subject feels he is in control of the conversation and can relate to the interviewer the information that he feels is most important regarding the events in question. It is during this period that the investigative interviewer be observant for signs of evasion and deception. The cross-examination phase is the period during which the interviewer conducts follow-up questioning of the subject and questions any inconsistencies in the subject's remarks or contradictions between the subject's explanation and the evidence. The subject may be permitted to clarify those inconsistencies. He will also be confronted with proof of evidence contrary to any of his denials. This is the tactical interrogation phase. As soon as the interrogator gets the subject to admit to small items of the case, he should turn on the subject and directly attack, moving toward confession The resolution phase occurs when the subject is in acceptance and provides statements that confirm the nature of his actions and acknowledges his responsibility for the events that occurred and the evidence of proof. It is time for the interrogator to start making reality-based statements and move for a complete confession. Remember, the subject will always need a little piece of self-esteem to fall back on. The interrogator cannot totally annihilate the subject in order to gain the admission or confession. Our Practical Kinesic Principle, therefore, states:

All successful and productive interviews will contain the elements of orientation, narration, cross-examination, and resolution.

Finally, the legally obtained admission or confession will also have key points in its content. An admission or confession is not simply the statement, "I did it." To fulfill all ethical and legal requirements, we must be sure it contains information that explains the vast majority of the physical evidence that the act or crime has occurred and that the subject, acting as principle or accessory, is responsible for the commission of those acts, known as the *actus reus*. Second, our admission or confession should reflect the subject's frame of mind and his intentions during the act, as well as the thoughts, actions, habits, and behaviors before and after the act, known as *mens rea*. By fulfilling these legal requirements, we will protect against the wrongful prosecution of innocent subjects. We will enable a productive and successful prosecution of guilty subjects and provide the degree of justice deserved by the victim and society. Our Practical Kinesic Principle states:

A legally obtained admission or confession will always meet the requirements of *actus reus* and *mens rea*.

Following are examples of how the interrogator may attack the denial and disguise processes of several common types of suspects. These are generic examples and are not intended as a script for interrogating each subject based on the type of crime he has committed. Any person is capable of committing any type of crime for a multitude of reasons. The distinction in crimes is based on the subject's personality type, key motivating factor, and personality flaws, if any.

These generic examples of attacks on denial are worded for approaches to both the introverted and extraverted personalities. This does not mean, however, that these are the only means by which to interrogate these subjects. They are meant only as a method to provide information as to the various methods of attack and reasoning that can be used in various cases.

Thief

Thieves are usually the easiest subjects to interrogate. The subject often believes that no one has been physically harmed and, therefore, his behavior is not too severe compared to other behaviors in which he could have engaged. The following are some suggestions and lines of reasoning that can be used when interrogating the thief.

The interrogator can suggest that the subject stole in order to meet some important personal needs. For example, he was stealing in order to put food on the table for his family or himself. Maybe there is an overdue utility bill and the utility company has been threatening to turn off the electricity or cut off the gas or water. Perhaps someone in his family is sick, such as a child, parent, or spouse, and needed medical attention. Perhaps the person who is ill has run out of sick leave and there was less money coming in to meet the family budget.

The interrogator can try to get the subject to talk about his current financial instability. Perhaps he has exceeded the credit limit on his credit cards and the bill collectors are calling relentlessly. Everyone knows how important it is to keep one's credit record in good standing, and perhaps the subject has never been in this tight of a financial situation before. Everyone, at some time or another, has needed a little room to catch up or get ahead. It is always helpful to indicate to the subject that you believe he had all the intentions in the world of paying the money back.

Indicate to the subject that what he did, in fact, was a noble deed. He has actually been prepared to sacrifice himself to meet the needs of his family. If the person happens to be a parent, suggest that he did not do this for himself, but for his spouse and children. The subject could not stand to see his family in need. Any parent or spouse who really cared would do the same thing for his family.

The interrogator may discuss how the company for which this person works could not care less about its employees. Perhaps he was passed over for a promotion for a less-qualified person. Maybe the job that should have been his was given to a person outside the company. The raises that the company gives employees are not fair to everyone. Other less-productive employees got a greater percentage of a pay increase while the subject got less. He has been there many more years and has a lot more invested in the company, but is shown little or no appreciation by the boss.

The owners of the company are getting rich off the hard work of their employees. The interrogator may suggest that everyone knows there is a certain amount of loss expected at any company and that all the other employees are doing the same thing. It is not like the company is going to go broke over what he has done.

The interrogator can make the observation that the subject has gotten caught up in an extravagant lifestyle and does not realize what has happened to him. The subject has fallen into a trap that is difficult for anyone to escape. He can suggest that this is the subject's first real offense (provided this is true). It was really just a case of bad judgment, or even a passing impulse, to which he submitted, and things would be better if he returned the property or money.

The interrogator can point out the lack of security measures the company has in place to help employees resist this type of incident. If those measures had been used, this would have never happened. Or the reverse argument can be used. Those measures are in place, and that is the reason the subject was caught and the company wants to help people avoid this type of mistake. At this point, the interrogator can point out the extensive nature of these prevention systems and how the person was identified.

The conversation can include how all people "take" things at various times. Everyone has done this type of thing. Even little children take toys or candy, maybe even money from their mother's purse or father's wallet. Now is the time for the person to erase this silly mistake and get this problem behind him. Returning the stolen goods or money would be an important step in proving he is genuinely sorry and knows he made an error in judgment.

As mentioned in one of our Practical Kinesic Principles, the interrogator can blame drugs and alcohol as the source of the person's real problems. The subject surely must realize he needs help, or this was, in fact, a cry for help. If he was not trapped by drugs and alcohol, he would never have done this, or the drugs and alcohol have changed him or clouded his mind and reasoning process. He would normally never do anything like this and has never done anything like this before. It was all just a big mistake.

Car Thief

In this situation, we are not discussing the interrogation of the professional car thief, therefore, the interrogator can suggest that the subject just borrowed the car to take it for a ride. Perhaps the car's owner would not have really cared if he had only known the subject borrowed the car in the first place. Maybe in the past the person has been permitted to borrow the car from the owner, and he felt the owner would have had no objection this time.

The interrogator can indicate that he believes the person was just out walking around and some friends came by in the car and invited him to join them. He really had no idea they had taken the car without the owner's permission. Maybe the reason he was caught was he realized the car was stolen and he was trying to figure out some way to return the car to the owner without anyone getting into trouble over the incident.

Perhaps the subject did this impulsively. The keys were already in the car, so the owner did not behave as if he cared if the car was used. This is really just his first offense (if this is the case), and he was acting stupid and did something wrong. He did not steal it to make money or to take the stereo or parts from the car.

Suggest that there have been a rash of car thefts or car-jackings in the area. The interrogator can indicate that the stolen cars are being used for armed robberies, rapes, arsons, drive-by shootings, acts of vandalism, or even murders. He can then ask the subject if this was what he was doing, or suggest that you believe he is not committing these crimes, but he might get blamed for them if he does not clear things up right away. The idea is to get the subject to try to talk his way down to a mere car theft or just a "joy ride."

Once again, we can suggest the subject was drunk at the time or maybe someone got him drunk and he did not realize what he was doing. Maybe someone gave him some drugs he does not normally take or more than he normally uses, and he took the car without really knowing what was going on.

The theft of the car was only for the purpose of taking the stereo, rims, or tires. The subject was not stealing the car for a robbery or rape, as previously noted. It is not like the subject is part of a chop-shop operation that is stealing cars all over town. Get the subject to break on one small part of the auto theft, and then turn on him.

Murderer

The first thing to consider regarding the suspect of a homicide is the possible existence of some form of personality, emotional, or psychological disorder. The presence of any one of these factors can further complicate the interrogation process. Included in these factors may be the presence of some form of psychosis or affective disorder, as noted earlier.

In any homicide case, never assume that the murder does not have some effect on the subject. The subject may act as if he is tough and that murder is easy. He may appear to be acting unaffected, but, in reality, the taking of a human life has a dramatic affect on any individual. There will always be some form of trauma to the subject's soul. Anybody can be a crook, be tough, or act bad. A criminal subject may be able to justify almost any crime, but no one can totally justify the taking of a life. The interrogator should make sure that he never falls into the trap of believing the subject incapable of committing homicide.

The subject who commits homicide will have the intensity of all his stress–response states increased by over a hundredfold. The interrogator must be keenly aware of each of the stress–response states that the subject experiences and control the interrogation with the appropriate reaction to each state. The most pronounced response state the subject is likely to first demonstrate is denial. Almost every subject that comes into the interrogation room after committing a homicide is in a powerful state of denial. He will have constructed a false, but plausible, explanation of how the homicide occurred. As noted previously, the process of denial involves the deception of ourselves as well as others. In the case of homicide, the subject will have the most difficult time developing an adequate denial mechanism.

Remember that in the majority of homicide cases, the killing probably occurred during the commission of another crime. Unless the death was plotted or was a "hit," the death was not the immediate goal. Explore the various explanations of all the possible things that were going on at the time the death occurred, and get the subject to discuss those options or possibilities.

Suggest to the subject that there was no real intent to kill the victim. Perhaps the victim was at fault in some way because of a wrong he committed, or he forced the subject to make a more hostile response. The suspect may have felt that his life was in jeopardy and he needed to stop the victim. This is also a good time to blame alcohol or drugs for this abnormal behavior. If not for the extra beers someone forced him to drink or the confusion caused by the cocaine or the crack, it would have never happened.

Making such comments to the subject does not mean that the interrogator believes what he is saying, but the subject will be trying to identify some method of denial and to minimize his actions that caused the death. The goal of the interrogator is to make some small breakthrough and then push toward the full truth. Homicide suspects always try to project blame on other things and other people for their actions. They are unable to accept the fact they have taken the life of another.

Another productive approach may be to ask the subject if he has ever been in a situation similar to the one in which the victim lost his life. You may ask him if he has ever lost his temper to the point that he feared he would harm someone. The subject may be asked if there was a time when he engaged in a similar activity that, if it had gone any further, someone could have been seriously hurt or died. Have the subject explain in detail what that situation was. Another alternative would be to ask the subject to theorize what such a situation would be like and how things could easily get out of hand. The suspect may also be asked to explain any event in which he felt it necessary to aggressively defend himself or needed to display a weapon.

The interrogator may find that he is able to gain extremely valuable information if he gets the subject to describe the crime from a third-person perspective. Have the subject imagine that he saw the homicide occurring and what he saw, heard, or felt as he watched. If the subject acknowledges that he knows the victim, have him assume the role of the victim, and ask him to reenact what he thinks the person would have said or done. A similar goal is accomplished if you have the subject imagine that he was the killer and describe that person's thoughts or why he responded the way he did. This third-person process allows the subject to temporarily isolate himself from the crime and discuss the events in a detached manner. The interrogator should be alert for any key information that the subject may inadvertently reveal.

One of the most powerful methods of dealing with the homicide subject is to take him back to the scene of the murder. If the subject has still not admitted to the crime, he can be asked to either describe what he thinks may have occurred or how the crime was committed, as if he were directing a play, television show, or movie. If the subject has made a partial admission, have him reenact his behaviors and describe the crime or his alibi in detail.

The purpose of taking the subject back to the crime and having him reenact or hypothesize about the crime has two purposes. First, it is designed to stimulate the tremendous memory tracings of the event that are stored in his cue- or state-dependent memory, discussed earlier. Being so intimately involved with the scene and the dynamics of reenacting the events creates such a tremendous conflict between reality and the subject's attempt at suppressing reality that the subject frequently produces dynamic revelations and insight into the case.

Second, if the subject has admitted to portions of the case and is acting out his behavior, the documentation of the reenactment by either witnesses or, preferably, videotaping provides powerful evidence for the judge or jury in a trial or grand jury proceeding.

As with any of the other criminal suspects and crimes we are discussing, do not forget to identify the suspect's primary dominant personality type and control his five stress–response states. The suspect must be attacked based on his particular reasoning process and the denial mechanism he is using.

Drug or Alcohol Abuser

If the particular subject is using cocaine or crack, there are generally only two ways the interrogation will go. First, the subject may be locked into total denial and, therefore, will be difficult, if not almost impossible, to interrogate. Second, the subject's ability to maintain denial has been completely devastated by his drug use, and he will confess easily.

The interrogator may find he can suggest that the person is just not the same after he has used drugs or abused alcohol. His abuse has totally taken over a fine person, and now that person is unable to overcome the powerful grip the drug has on him. The only chance the subject has is to reach out and accept help now before it is too late and something more horrible happens.

The interrogator will have success if he can find any outside factors that have influenced the subject's drug abuse. It may be that the problem runs in his family, or that he is surrounded by the drug at work, at home, or among friends, and got caught up in the abuse. The subject is just like any other; he needs to find someone or something to blame for his behavior.

Hit-and-Run Driver

When interviewing the hit-and-run subject, the method of blaming drugs or alcohol for the subject's actions is saved until the end of the process. In other words, the drugs and alcohol are not used as an excuse, as with other crimes.

An easy approach with the hit-and-run driver is to blame the human instinct of fight-or-flight. The interrogator can go on at great lengths, describing the nature of this normal survival response; the driver's fear, shock, and surprise; and how such frightening events cause the body and mind to react. All that happened was a simple accident, and the subject was frightened and scared, and reacted just as any other scared person would. Under any normal situation, he would have never responded like this, but he lost control of his functions and was not thinking rationally.

Blaming a variety of other factors also serves the interrogator's purpose. The victim can be blamed for wearing dark clothes, for not looking where he was going, or for stepping out too far from the curb. Perhaps the person would have been fine, but he froze in the street in front of the driver and the subject could not stop in time. The interrogator can also blame weather, a dirty windshield, bad wipers, rain, snow, slick streets, faulty brakes, bald tires, or being distracted by other cars or pedestrians. Suggest to the subject that no one will ever know the real truth about how the accident happened unless he tells you.

The subject may be ready to explain that he was fearful no one would believe him if he told them what really happened, as if the accident was a fluke. The interrogator might suggest that he feels the subject just needs someone to listen to his version of the story and understand the driver's point of view.

Arsonist (Sexual)

The sexual arsonist, or the pyromaniac, is hard to interrogate unless the interrogator fully understands that the subject's behavior is the result of some form of sexual dysfunction. He will be asexual, sexually immature, or frustrated; has been sexually traumatized; or is uncomfortable with his heterosexual or homosexual status. As a direct result of this sexual dysfunction, he acts out or vents his problems using fire.

First, get the subject to like you. Try to get him to feel that you are the only person who has or will ever really care about him. As long as you do not socially or mentally abuse him, he will keep talking to you. Be prepared to spend the time necessary to develop a close relationship with him. When the subject acts like he has "adopted" you, you are on the right track to getting information.

Be sure to do a lot of listening. This subject is crying out for some kind of attention. Stimulate him into talking about himself. You will soon discover he will give you information in order to keep you around and to maintain contact with you. Talk to him about his life and family. Act as if it is important to him to keep you as his real friend. Your goal is to stay with him and allow him to bond with you.

Once he has made you his "new friend," he will talk. At this point, you can suggest that he needs to get help before someone else gets hurt. Indicate to him that you know he is not trying to harm anyone personally, but it would be sad if that happened. If there has been an injury or death, play up the fact that no harm was intended or that he never suspected anyone was around who would get hurt or that he needs to make amends as soon as possible.

Arsonist (Fraud)

This person has burned his own business or home for profit. There is usually only be about a 5 to 10% chance of getting a confession from this subject. More than likely, you will have to get him on the forensic evidence and the abnormal paper trail he has left behind. If he has burned his home, the percentage of success is greatly increased. Do not use the drug- or alcohol-type interrogation with this suspect.

This is one of the smartest subjects you will ever interview. You will more than likely discover this person has a record of deception and fraud. He has had previous bankruptcies, failed businesses, questionable business dealings, or insurance claims. He is probably also cheating the IRS or state tax service, as well as banks and other financial institutions, entities, and investors. He more than likely has his home or business for sale because of financial problems, liens, or foreclosures. The same may apply to his vehicles.

Fires in these cases are frequently set on Sunday, late Friday night, or early Saturday or Monday mornings. This is done to reduce the chances of early discovery and possible personal injuries. You may also learn that the subject is out of town at the time of the fire.

Case Study

> A minister was the owner of a large religious retreat in the mountains. The facility was made largely of cedar and far removed from full-time firefighting services. The primary building burned under questionable circumstances. Because the lodge was empty and the site was remote, the fire was not discovered for quite some time. Investigation of the scene by an arson investigator revealed a delayed ignition device and the presence of several small propane tanks similar to those used for camping lanterns. At the time the fire was discovered and the volunteer fire service was responding, the minister was in his insurance agent's office with his policy in hand discussing his coverage. The fire was ruled an arson, and the minister withdrew his claim.

When chasing down the paper trail on the subject, the investigator is likely to learn there have been recent changes in the fire policy or that the subject has a sizable policy for business interruption and the loss of records.

The general interrogation approach should be low-key and nonaccusatory. The investigator will find he is more successful if he appears to be a little dumb regarding the subject and his business. The subject will be off-guard and more likely to make mistakes regarding his activities surrounding the time of the fire.

The interrogator's goal is to uncover anything the subject may regard as unusual. He may ask the subject if there is anything about the scene that is puzzling or confusing if someone else does not know the full story regarding the fire or the purpose of the subject's actions. Try to get the subject to point out things that appear to be illogical about the fire, or get him to admit to the things he did that he normally does not do; these are the pieces of information that will incriminate the subject.

The subject may offer a number of possible causes for the fire. He may suggest that he always had trouble with the furnace or hot water heater. He may pinpoint a particular piece of equipment as being old or having bad wiring. He may tell you stoves, air conditioners, humidifiers, or other equipment may have been overheating lately, as well as mentioning other diversionary targets.

If it is a business, the interrogator should not be surprised if he is not allowed to talk to the company employees. This can happen even after the business owner has acted cooperatively in all other matters.

Case Study

Arson was suspected in the fire of a horse barn, which was located on a prominent horse farm and contained several brood mares that were in foal to some top racing sires. All the mares were killed in the fire. Initially, the owner of the farm was cooperative with the state fire marshal's office investigation and indicated that he would permit an interview and polygraph of all his farm help. The following day, each employee arrived for his polygraph and interview with an attorney provided and paid for by the farm owner. Total losses in the fire reached approximately one million dollars.

The fraud arsonist will usually obtain an attorney early on during the investigation. He will file charges and countercharges against the investigator, including harassment or intimidation. He may also quickly check into the hospital or begin filing a flurry of lawsuits against the investigator and the insurance company.

Sexual Assault

When dealing with the suspect of a sexual assault, remember that the suspect is probably immature, socially inexperienced, or has poor social skills. This subject is likely to have had incidences of criminal, or at least inappropriate, social behavior.

The ultimate goal of the interrogator is to get the subject to admit to the sexual act. This is the hardest part of the entire interrogation. The subject will have a great deal of difficulty admitting to the fact that he succumbed to his animal instincts and lost control when the assault occurred.

The first objective is to get the subject to admit that he was at the scene and then with the victim. Do not begin with the assault. Get him to admit to having had a conversation with the victim, possibly at the period of time in which he was seen with her, the location or locations at which he and the victim were together, and similar pieces of information. It will be easier for him to admit to the little things; the critical information is gained in small portions.

The interrogator may exaggerate what the victim has said happened to her. The interrogator then forces the subject to convince the interrogator of something less than the exaggerated story. The interrogator may also do the reverse, and suggest that the victim was acting provocatively and that the subject did the only thing any other man would do. This, of course, is not really the case, but, as with other suspects, the subject is looking for someone to blame, and the victim is a ready target.

Suggest to the subject that the best thing he can do to protect his interests is to discuss what really happened before the whole story gets blown out of proportion. Remind him that if he goes into court without some form of explanation, the jury will have no other choice but to believe the victim's story. He needs to tell the interviewer if he was only committing a burglary and she surprised him, or he was just looking around the apartment, or that it was really just a game that he thought he was playing with the victim. Perhaps in the past, they had joked around and done things just like this, and now she is upset about her boyfriend or husband finding out.

The interrogator can also get the subject to imagine that he was present at the scene of the crime. He can have the subject project how the victim responded to the suspect or what he would have seen or heard if he had been in the area when the assault occurred. Once again, listen for pieces of information that the subject inadvertently provides indicating his participation in the assault.

If the case involves multiple offenders, suggest that the subject would be better off as a witness or a victim of circumstances. He should not have to take the full blame for what the other participants did to the victim.

Child Molester

There are two general forms of child molester. The first form is more likely to display his deviant behavior in a random manner; in other words, the molestations are more on an episodic basis. The second form is totally dedicated and consumed by his lust for children. Nearly his entire life is spent in the pursuit of children as objects of sexual desire.

The first form of pedophile is known as the "situational pedophile." The occurrence of child molestations by this subject is usually intermingled with near-normal sexual behavior. This subject will most likely have a problem with drugs or alcohol that partially contributes to his problem. For some reason, the subject is temporarily unable to satisfy himself in a normal adult sexual manner and will select a child of convenience for molestation. He will normally be overwhelmed by his behavior and believes he will not do this again. Of the two primary types of pedophile, this subject is more likely to respond to treatment.

The second form of pedophile is totally dedicated and fixated on children. He is known as the "pure pedophile." In a lifetime, a pure pedophile can easily victimize more than 1000 children. These subjects are generally considered incurable. The paradox, however, is less than 2% of these subjects spend any hard time in prison, yet they have the greatest number of victims.

If a child is of minor age and claims to be a victim of sexual abuse, you should take the child at his word. The next step is to immediately divert the child into some form of treatment program.

The key to dealing with pedophiles is to remember that they think like children in all their social relationships. They are so unsuccessful in dealing with adults on a regular social basis that they must find someone who will not reject them, and that person will be a child. Pure pedophiles will go as far as courting the child, just like men and women engage in courtship or dating rituals. These subjects will also align themselves in situations where they can have constant access to children, through work, play, or other situations in which they can be with and possibly isolate the child.

The interrogator must think on the pedophile's level. It can be extremely difficult for the interrogator to learn this process. He must remember that the pure pedophile is unable to stop his contact with children, and discuss this fact with the subject. The subject sees himself as someone who loves children and constantly tries to find ways to justify his actions.

The greatest fear of the child molester is that the child may cry out or alert someone nearby as to what is happening. In his fear, the subject may lose control and kill the child. Speak of this fear with the subject only when you get near the point when the subject appears to be the weakest.

If the child molester is a female, there is a high probability that she is psychotic, is unbalanced mentally, or is mentally deficient.

Conclusion

The purpose in presenting these suggestions in interviewing these selected criminals is to remind the interrogator that to be successful, he must think like the subject. To accomplish this, he must recognize, identify, and understand the five stress–response states and diagnose the subject's primary dominant personality type. He then must control the subject's movement through each of those response states and correctly attack the subject's denial process.

The correct attack on the subject's denial is based specifically on the subject's primary dominant personality and his concurrent reasoning process.

The final Practical Kinesic Principle involves the process of being good at practical kinesic interview and interrogation:

> **The successful interrogator is one who studies
> his interrogation method, practices his skills, and uses
> the techniques he has learned.**

APPENDICES

Appendix 1:
Selection, Use, and Training
of Interpreters

Dr. Art Powell

Dr. Powell has more than 30 years of experience in interview and interrogation, which includes several years in the intelligence community. During his tours as a counterintelligence expert, Dr. Powell identified and neutralized over 900 enemy agents in several foreign countries. He has also conducted interviews and interrogations in over 40 foreign languages. Dr. Powell prepared this section to assist interrogators who conduct interviews and interrogations using interpreters.

Introduction

There are numerous people in all types of businesses, including the entertainment field, who use interpreters to communicate with others; however, many of these will state, "I am not sure they understand." The key to ensuring the interview subject does understand is for the interviewer to make sure the interpreter has been properly selected, oriented, and prepared for the interview. Even in those emergency situations in which one gets the first person available who speaks the language, the interviewer can still control the information-gathering process if he knows beforehand what techniques to employ.

The information set forth in this section is of even greater value when employed with the Practical Kinesic Interview and Interrogation technique, which teaches self-initiated verbal behaviors, nonverbal behaviors, structured questions, and many other interrogation techniques.

Objective

To aid investigators, interrogators, personnel specialists, government agents, police officers, and others in the field of gathering information in the most effective way to utilize an interpreter to extract information from an individual.

Selection of Interpreters

Since the use of interpreters can be a planned effort or a spontaneous incident, this discussion will be on two areas: those selected on a spontaneous or temporary basis and those chosen for long-term, continued service with an individual investigator or within a department.

Temporary Basis

Sometimes during an interview, an interpreter is selected for his particular language ability and there is no time for background screening; however, there are certain critical areas that must be addressed.

> **Orientation** — The interpreter must be given an orientation on what the objective is in the interview, including a familiarization with tools and equipment (e.g., polygraph) to be used.
>
> **Question formulation** — As in all interviews or interrogations, the interviewer must ensure that the questions he wants to ask the subject can be properly translated with the same meaning into the subject's native language. Improperly asked questions could result in a total loss of information or might even insult the subject. Take time to go over as many questions as possible with the interpreter before the interview starts.
>
> **Technical terms** — Taking the time to review questions with the interpreter is especially important when using any form of equipment or asking questions regarding technical matters. The interpreter must be knowledgeable about these terms. The investigator and the interpreter may have to come up with some critical changes in the approach used.
>
> **Word meaning and translation ability** — This is a direct tie-in to the previous paragraph. The interpreter must know as much as possible about the case beforehand to ensure questions can be translated into the subject's native tongue. Many investigators are satisfied with a mere transliteration, which loses meaning, or an attempt is made to summarize a question, which also loses meaning on every issue.
>
> **Time element** — Always allow two to three times longer for an interview using an interpreter as you would for a normal one-on-one interview. Remember that things have to be repeated three to four times on every issue.

Long-Term Basis

All the criteria mentioned for interpreters used on a temporary basis, as well as the following, should be taken into account when using an interpreter for long-term consideration.

- **Languages** — How many different languages does this interpreter speak? How useful will he be? Will there be any cross-cultural problems in using those languages? These are questions that must be answered. It is possible one could be in a situation in which more than one language translation is needed in an individual interview.
- **Age** — This should not have a great effect on the younger interpreters. Older interpreters may have a greater problem with social or cultural barriers. They are so entrenched in their own customs that they will not want to violate these, even at risk of losing valuable information.
- **Social and cultural barriers** — During the gathering of information, especially from hostile subjects, one must consider the problem of violating certain social or cultural traditions. If a tradition is violated without some prior consideration, the entire interview could be lost. One of those areas of concern is age, as noted previously. Usually, an indigenous person who is older is more entrenched in his social traditions than a younger person, and it will be harder to get that older interpreter to understand why you are willing to violate these traditions simply to gain information.
- **Screening background and attitude toward objectives** — During the selection process, a thorough background check should be conducted on any long-term interpreter prospect. You must be especially careful to select a person whose ideals do not conflict with the objectives of the investigation; that is, getting the truth and eliminating crime, corruption, and even hostile agents.

During this selection process, you must ensure that the interpreter is loyal to your aims and not your subject's. You must be careful to ensure that your translations are what you have stated, not what your interpreter wants the subject to believe. In ethnic situations, the bloodline is sometimes a great power.

Training of Interpreters

The most important rule for the interpreter is to ask the proper question. If the question is not asked, no answer will be received.

Complete Orientation on Function of Equipment (Polygraph, etc.)

This is done so the interpreter will have a clear understanding of the equipment and its technical functions.

> **Explanation of various types of examinations (polygraph) to be used** — For example, general, specific, peak of tension, etc.
>
> **Question methodology** — Give the interpreter as much Practical Kinesic Interview and Interrogation technique training as you feel necessary for him to know.
>
> **Interrogation methodology** — Again, give the interpreter as much training in these areas as you want.
>
> **Cultural and social barriers** — This is a reversal of roles. Let the interpreter train you in some of the cultural and social traditions that may present a problem. Then both of you can work out a solution to getting around these, if required.
>
> **Use of interpreters** — All of those concepts employed in the selection process apply equally well in the ongoing use of the interpreter:
>
> > Orientation prior to interview
> > Question formulation
> > Technical terms
> > Translation of statements and questions
> > Word meanings
> > Time required
> > Cultural and social traditions
>
> **Equipment familiarization** — If special equipment, e.g., the polygraph, is to be used during the interview, the interpreter must be given a complete explanation in order to convey this to the subject during the explanation phase of the interview.
>
> **Methods of questioning** — All techniques learned during your Practical Kinesic Interview and Interrogation technique training should be employed, being careful to make those special provisions to eye contact. Discuss these areas with the interpreter to ensure you know how your subject may react in the nonverbal behavior responses. (Remember, the subject is watching you while you are watching him). During

the discussions, you may determine if your subject is understanding any of your language as opposed to hearing only what comes through the interpreter. Simply watch your subject's facial and eye movements while you are speaking. If, in fact, he understands you, you will get some emotion; if not, you should get no facial emotion until the interpreter speaks. (If you still think he understands, but is playing a game with you, insult him in your language and stop — watch for expressions. Tell your interpreter what you are doing beforehand.)

Seating — Whenever possible, employ those seating techniques taught in the Practical Kinesic Interview and Interrogation technique course, but always face your subject when asking questions. As you talk to the subject, let your interpreter translate what you said without ever looking at the interpreter. Continue looking at your subject, even when the interpreter gives the subject's reply. Most subjects will look at the interpreter when they are talking; therefore, the interpreter, if possible, should be directly to your right or left — no more than 12 in. either way. This gives you an opportunity to observe your subject during all questions and replies. Many interviewers (even on TV) will say to the interpreter, "Ask him this." Do not do this under any circumstances. You speak to your subject at all times. This will aid you in determining how much English (or language used) the subject understands. You will be able to see those nonverbal responses even before the translation is given to the subject. In the rare event that you need two interpreters in the same interview, the additional interpreter will need to be given the same considerations as your first one. The second interpreter should be seated no more the 12 in. to the left or right of the first one. Again, much more time must be allowed for this type of interview.

Methods of Questioning (Polygraph Testing)

All questions for the original interview should be translated and in numerical order prior to examination. This will reduce confusion and save time during the testing phase. The examiner and the interpreter use prearranged signals for the interpreter to ask questions. The examiner does not ask the questions during the running of the polygraph charts.

Repeating questions — In addition to prearranged signals for questions, these same signals must be set up for any question you want to repeat.

Other signals during test — Additional signals may be prearranged for beginning and ending the test. All prearranged motions must not be made in view of the subject. All questions must have a spacing of 25 to 30 sec. between them in order to allow ample time for responses.

Question changes after initial test (post-test) — If any questions or information are given after the original test, the questions must be rephrased and the information verified.

Statements obtained — If there are any admissions or changes in information that require a statement, get the statement in the subject's original language and have the interpreter translate it verbally on the spot and in writing later. If those statements are to be used as documentation in an investigation, make sure the English version has a copy of the original-language statement attached. Make sure that if statements are planned for use in court or other official hearings, the statements are translated by a person who has been certified by the court or some other certifying agency.

Summary

Your interpreter can make or break the interview. Some may wonder, "Why give them Practical Kinesic Interview and Interrogation technique training?" The answer is because two pairs of eyes looking for verbal and nonverbal signals increase the probability of a successful interview.

These guidelines are those learned and practiced by the author during more than 11 years in foreign countries conducting interviews of friendly and unfriendly personnel involved in intelligence, criminal, and terrorist activity.

Appendix 2:
Review of Practical Kinesic Principles

Chapter 1

No single kinesic behavior, verbal or nonverbal, proves a person
is truthful or deceptive.

Behaviors must be relatively consistent when the stimuli are repeated.

The interviewer must establish what is the normal, or "constant,"
of behavior for each subject. Accurate assessment of a person's behavior
can be made only after establishing this reference point.

Once the constant has been established, the observer then looks for
changes in the subject's constant of behavior.

Changes in a subject's behavior are reliable for diagnosing deception
only if they appear in clusters.

Behaviors that are significant must be timely.

The interviewer should monitor his own behaviors in order to avoid
contamination of the subject's behavior. The subjects are watching us while
we are watching them.

Observing and interpreting behaviors is hard work.

Kinesic interviewing is not as reliable with some groups as with
the general population.

Chapter 2

The investigative interviewer should never enter the interview room with
any preconceptions about the subject or the interview.

Chapter 3

People are better able to control their verbal kinesic signals than they
are able to control their nonverbal kinesic signals.

Verbal signals are usually the most productive kinesic cues and are the
easiest for the interviewer to identify, but they occur less frequently.

The observer should watch for contradictions in the subject's behavior,
as these are strong indicators of possible deception.

Tension can cause a change in the pitch of the voice, as well as in
the volume and rate of speech.

Deceptive subjects demonstrate more speech dysfunction
than truthful subjects do.

Speech dysfunction symptoms occur because the subject is being hit with
relevant questions and does not have a clear "thought line."

Chapter 4

Do not misinterpret depression as acceptance. Listen for the
verbal output and proceed with caution.

When discussing critical areas, deceptive subjects experience more
frequent occurrences of memory failure than do truthful subjects.

The liar will only admit to what can be proven to him, then will always
refuse to admit to items of the case that cannot be proved.
Liars frequently give less factual information that can be substantiated in
order to control information.

When the subject is demonstrating that he is in acceptance,
the interrogator should stop talking and start listening.

Chapter 6

A person is better able to control verbal signals than to conceal and monitor nonverbal symptoms.

Deceptive subjects generally tend to have a greater number of touches to the head than do truthful subjects.

Any obstruction of speech, whether physical or symbolic, is a sign of stress and possible deception.

Any change in a person's constant or normal level of eye contact, which is a timely response and part of a cluster, can be sign of stress and possible deception.

When the subject is demonstrating that he is in acceptance, the interrogator should stop talking and start listening.

Chapter 11

An interrogator should never engage in any type of behavior that could force even the truthful subject to confess.

A false confession is most likely to have been gained from a subject who is mentally deficient or is highly suggestible.

An interrogator will find that most subjects are prepared to blame alcohol or drugs for their behavior.

A successful attack on denial requires that the interrogator review the subject's previous admissions to proof about every 3 to 5 min.

A successful practical kinesic interrogation requires the appropriate assessment and attack of the subject's primary dominant personality.

A successful practical kinesic interrogation requires the interrogator to correctly identify and respond to the subject's five basic stress–response states.

All successful and productive interviews contain the elements of orientation, narration, cross-examination, and resolution.

A legally obtained admission or confession will always meet the
requirements of *actus reus* and *mens rea*.

The successful interrogator is one who studies
his interrogation method, practices his skills, and uses
the techniques he has learned.

BIBLIOGRAPHY
and
INDEX

Bibliography

American Psychiatric Association. (1994) *Diagnostic Statistical Manual-IV*, American Psychiatric Association, Washington, D.C.

Argyle, M. and Dean, J. (1965) Eye contact, *Sociometry*, Vol. 28, pp. 289–304.

Artingstall, K.A. (1995) Munchausen Syndrome by Proxy, *FBI Law Enforcement Bulletin*, August, pp. 5–11.

Artingstall, K. and Brubaker, L. (1995) Munchausen Syndrome-related offenses, *Law & Order*, October, pp. 83–90.

Artingstall, K. and Brubaker, L. (1995) Interview techniques for MSBP-related investigations, *Law & Order*, November, pp. 81–83.

Atkinson, R.C., Atkinson, R.L. and Hilgard, E.R. (1971) *Introduction to Psychology*, Harcourt, Brace, Jovanovich, New York.

Aubrey, A.S., Jr. and Randolph, R. (1972) *Criminal Interrogation*, Thomas Publishers, Springfield, IL.

Ayling, C.J. (1984) Corroborating confessions: an empirical analysis of legal safeguards against false confessions. *Wisconsin Law Review*, 4, pp. 1121–1204.

Baldwin, B. (1987) Emotional Misuses of Anger, *Piedmont*, January, pp. 13–17.

Baldwin, B. (1987) The stressed mind: pressure can produce thought disorders, *Piedmont*, November, pp. 18–22.

Baldwin, B. (1993) Keep your lid on, *USAir Magazine*, February, pp. 16–19.

Baldwin, J. (1993) Police interview techniques: establishing truth or proof? *The British Journal of Criminology*, Vol. 33, No. 3, Summer, pp. 325–352.

Bandler, R. and Grinder, J. (1975) *Structure of Magic I*, Palo Alto, CA; Science and Behavior Books.

Bandler, R. and Grinder, J. (1976) *Structure of Magic II*, Palo Alto, CA; Science and Behavior Books.

Bandler, R. and Grinder, J. (1979) *Frogs Into Princes: Neuro-Linguistic Programming*, Real People Press, Moab, UT.

Beattie, R.J. (1957) The Semantics of Question Preparation. Academy Lectures in Lie Detection.

Bedau, H.A. and Radelet, M.L. (1987) Miscarriages of justice in potentially capital cases, *Stanford Law Review*, Vol. 40, pp. 21–179.

Bem, D. J. (1966) Inducing belief in false confessions, *Journal of Personality and Social Psychology*, Vol. 3, No. 6, pp. 707–710.

Benjamin, L.T., Hopkins, J.R., Jr., and Nation, J.R. (1987) *Psychology*, McMillan, College Park, New York.

Bennet, P.J. (1996) Interviewing witnesses and victim for the purpose of obtaining a statement, *Journal of Forensic Identification*, Vol. 46, No. 3, pp. 349–366.

Bilodeau, L. (1994) *The Anger Workbook*, Hazelden Foundation, Center City, MN.

Birdwhitsell, R.L. (1952) *Introduction to Kinesics: An Annotation System for Analysis of Body Motion and Gestures*, University of Louisville Press, Louisville.

Birdwhitsell, R.L. (1970) *Kinesics and Context: Essays on Body Motion and Communication*, University of Philadelphia Press, Philadelphia.

Birge, A.C. (1996) Munchausen Syndrome by Proxy, *Law & Order*, March, pp. 91–96.

Bower, G.H. (1991) Mood and Memory, *American Psychologist*, Vol. 36, No. 2, pp. 129–148.

Bowman, C.G. and Mertz, E. (1996) What should the courts do about memories of sexual abuse? Toward a balanced approach, *The Judges Journal*, Fall.

Brandon, R. and Davies, C. (1973) *Wrongful Imprisonment*, George Allen & Unwin, London.

Brown, R. and Kulik, J. (1977) Flashbulb memories, *Cognition*, Vol. 5, pp. 73–79.

Buckwalter, A. (1983) *Interviews and Interrogations*, Butterworth, Boston.

Buffington, P. (1989) *Your Behavior is Showing*, Peachtree Publishers, Atlanta.

Buller, D.B., Strzyzewski, K.D., and Comstock, J. (1991) Interpersonal deception: deceiver's reactions to receivers' suspicions and probing, *Communication Monographs*, Vol. 58, March, pp.1–24.

Callum, M. (1972) *Body Talk*, Bantam Books, New York.

Campbell, J. (1971) *The Portable Jung*, Viking Press, New York.

Cassell, P.G. (1998) Protecting the innocent from false confessions and lost confessions — and from Miranda, *Journal of Criminal Law and Criminology*, Volume 88, Number 2, Winter, pp. 497—556.

Ceci, S.J. and Bruck, M. (1995) *Jeopardy in the courtroom: a scientific analysis of children's testimony*, American Psychological Association, Washington, D.C.

Cohen, H. (1980) *You Can Negotiate Anything*, L. Stuart Press, Secaucus, N.J.

Cleckly, H. (1988) *The Mask of Sanity*, Fifth Edition, C. V. Mosby Company, Augusta, GA.

Darwin, C. (1872) *The Expression of the Emotions in Man and Animals*, D. Appleton & Co., New York.

Darwin, C. and Ekman, P. (1998) *The Expression of the Emotions in Man and Animals: Definitive Edition*, Oxford University Press, New York.

Davidson, G.C. and Neale, J.M. (1982) *Abnormal Psychology*, John Wiley & Sons, New York.

Davis, F. (1987) *Inside Intuition: What We Know About Non-Verbal Communication*, New American Library, New York.

Davis, M. and Hadiks, D. (1995) Demeanor and credibility, *Semiotica*, Vol. 106 1/2, pp. 5–54.

Davis, M. (1998) *Credibility Analysis Nonverbal Micro-coding Guide*, unpublished guidebook.

Davis, M. (Principal Investigator), Connors, B. (Director), and Walters, S.B. (Research Consultant). (1999) Credibility analysis validity study: nonverbal communication project — final report, John Jay College of Criminal Justice.

Davis, M., Walters, S.B., Markus, K. (2002) Judging the credibility of criminal suspects' statements, in preparation.

Davis, M. et al. (1999) Demeanor cues to deception in criminal investigations, unpublished paper.

Davis, M. et al. (2000) Verbal and nonverbal cues to false testimony in criminal investigations, presented at the American Psychological Association Annual Convention, Washington, D.C.

Davis, M. et al. (2000) Defensive demeanor profiles, *American Journal of Dance Therapy*, Vol. 22, No. 2, pp. 103–121.

DeTurck, M.A. and Miller, G.R. (1985) Deception and arousal: isolating the behavioral correlates of deception, *Human Communication Research*, Vol. 12, No. 2, pp. 181–201.

Dillingham, C.R., II (1998) Would Pinocchio's eyes have revealed his lies? A research experiment using eye movements to detect deception, master thesis, University of Central Florida.

Douglas, J. et al. (1992) *Crime Classification Manual: A Standard System for Investigating and Classifying Violent Crimes*, Jossey-Bass, San Francisco.

Duncan, T.S. (1995) Death in the office: workplace homicides, *FBI Law Enforcement Bulletin*, April, pp. 20–25.

Ekman, P., Friesen, W., and Scherer, K.R. (1976) Body movement and voice pitch in deceptive interaction, *Semiotica*, Vol. 16, pp. 23–27.

Ekman, P. (1969) Nonverbal leakage and clues to deception, *Psychiatry*, Vol. 32, pp. 88–105.

Ekman, P. (1992) *Telling Lies: Clues to Deceit in the Marketplace, Politics and Marriage*, Norton, New York.

Ekman, P. and Friesen, W.V. (1975) *Unmasking The Face*, Lexington Books, Lexington, MA.

Ekman, P. and O'Sullivan, M. (1991) Who can catch a liar? *American Psychologist*, Vol. 46, pp. 913–920.

Elich, M., Thompson, R.W. and Miller, L. (1985). Mental imagery as revealed by eye movements and spoken predicates: a test of neurolinguistic programming, *Journal of Counseling Psychology*, 32, pp. 622–625.

Exline, R. and Eldridge, C. (1967) Effects of two patterns of a speaker's visual behavior upon the perception of the authority of his verbal message, paper presented to the Eastern Psychological Association, Boston.

Exline, R. and Winters, L. (1965) Affective relations and mutual glances in dyads, *Affect, Cognition, and Personality*, Springer, New York.

Farmer, A., Rooney, R., and Cunningham, J. R. (1985). Hypothesized eye movements of neurolinguistic programming: a statistical artifact, *Perceptual and Motor Skills*, 61, pp. 717–718.

Fast, J. (1970) *Body Language*, M. Evans & Co., New York.

Fast, J. (1970) *The Body Language of Sex, Power and Aggression*, M. Evans & Co., New York.

Fisher, R.P., Geiselman, R.E., and Raymond, D.S. (1987) Critical analysis of police interview techniques, *Journal for Police Science and Administration*, Vol. 13, No. 3, pp. 177–185.

Fisher, R.P. and Geiselman, R.E. (1992) *Memory-Enhancing Techniques For Investigative Interviewing: The Cognitive Interview*, Charles C. Thomas, Springfield, IL.

Foster, D.G. and Marshall, M. (1994) *How Can I Get Through To You*, Hyperion Press, New York.

Foster, D.G. and Marshall, M. (1994) How to tell if he is lying to you, *Good Housekeeping*, June.

Frith, U. (1997) Autism, *Scientific American: Mysteries of the Mind*, Vol. 7, No. 1, pp. 92–98.

Gazzaniga, M.S. (1998) The split brain revisited, *Scientific American*, July, pp. 50–55.

Gerber, S. (Ed.) and Schroeder, O., Jr. (1965) *Criminal Investigation and Interrogation*, W.H. Anderson, Cincinnati, OH.

Geberth, V. (1997) *Practical Homicide Investigation*, Third Edition, CRC Press, Boca Raton, FL.

Geberth, V. (1995) The signature aspect in criminal investigation: criminal personality profiling, *Law & Order*, November, pp. 45–49.

Geberth, V. (1994) Munchausen Syndrome by Proxy (MSBP): an investigative perspective, *Law & Order*, August, pp. 95–97.

Geberth, V. (1996) The staged crime scene, *Law & Order*, February, pp. 89–91.

Geberth, V. (1993) Final exit suicide investigations, *Law & Order*, December, pp. 67–70.

Geberth, V. (1996) The psychology of suicide, *Law & Order*, October, pp. 163–166.

Geller, W.A. (1993) Videotaping Interrogations and Confessions, *National Institute of Justice —Research in Brief*, Rockville, MD, March.

Gillen, J.J. and Thermer, C.E. (2000) DNA-based exonerations warrant a reexamination of the witness interview process, *The Police Chief*, December, pp. 52–57.

Gorden, R. (1975) *Interviewing: Strategy, Techniques and Tactics*, Dorsey Press, Homewood, IL.

Gray, J. (1971) *The Psychology of Fear and Stress*, McGraw-Hill, New York.

Greenwood, P.W. (1979) The Rand Corporation Study: Its Findings and Impacts to Date, The Rand Corporation, Santa Monica, CA, July.

Gudjonsson, G.H. (1992) *The Psychology of Interrogations, Confessions and Testimony*, John Wiley & Sons, New York.

Gudjonsson, G. and Lebeque, B. (1989) Psychological and psychiatric aspects of a coerced-internalized false confession, *Journal of Forensic Science and Sociology*, Vol. 29, pp. 261–269.

Gudjonsson, G. and MacKeith, J.A.C. (1988) Retracted confessions: legal, psychological and psychiatric aspects, *Medical Science and Law*, Vol. 28, pp. 187–194.

Gudjonsson, G.H. and Petrusson, H. (1991) Custodial interrogation: why do suspects confess and how does it relate to their crime, attitude and personality? *Personality & Individual Difference*, Vol. 12, pp. 295–306.

Hall, E.T. (1973) *The Silent Language*, Doubleday, Garden City, New York.

Hare, R.D. (1993) *Without Conscience: The Disturbing World of the Psychopaths Among Us*, Pocket Books, New York.

Hess, E.H. (1975) The role of pupil size in communication, *Scientific American*, Vol. 223, pp. 110–112.

Hess, J. (1989) The myths of interviewing, *FBI Law Enforcement Bulletin*, July, pp. 14–16.

Hinkle, L.E. (1961) The psychological state of the interrogation subject as it affects brain function, *The Manipulation of Human Behavior* (A.D. Biderman and H. Zimmer, Eds.). Wiley, New York, pp. 19–50.

Hocking, J. and Leathers, D. (1980) Nonverbal indicators of deception: a new theoretical perspective, *Communication Monograph*, Vol. 47, pp. 119–131.

Hocking, J.E. et al. (1979) Detecting deceptive communication from verbal, visual, and paralinguistic cues, *Human Communication Research*, Vol. 6, No. 1, Fall, pp. 33–46.

Holmes, R.M. and Deburger, J. (1988) *Serial Murder*, Sage Publications, Newbury, CA.

Holmes, R.M. (1989) *Profiling Violent Crime: An Investigative Tool*, Sage Publications, Thousand Oaks, CA.

Holmes, R.M. (1994) Stalking in America: types and methods of criminal stalkers, *Law & Order*, 1994, pp. 89–92.

Horvath, F.S. (1973) Verbal and nonverbal clues in truth and deception, *Journal of Police Science and Administration*, Vol. 1, No. 2, pp. 72–91.

Huff, C.R., Rattner, A., and Sagarin E. (1986) Guilty until proven innocent: wrongful conviction and public policy, *Crime and Delinquency*, Vol. 32, pp. 518–544.

Hurley, K. and Dobson, T. (1993) *My Best Self: Using the Enneagram to Free the Soul*, Harper, New York.

Irving, B. (1980) Police interrogation, a case study of current practice, *Research Studies* No. 2, HMSO, London.

Irving, B. and Hildenorf, L. (1980) Police interrogation: the psychological approach, *Research Studies*, No. 1, HMSO, London.

Irving, B.L. and McKenzie, I.K. (1989) Police interrogation: the effects of the police and criminal evidence act, *The Police Foundation*, London.

Jaffe, M.E. and Sharma, K.K. (1998) Malingering uncommon psychiatric symptoms among defendants charged under California's "Three Strikes and You're Out" law, *Journal of Forensic Sciences*, Vol. 43, pp. 549–550.

Johnson, R.N. (1972) *Aggression in Man and Animals*. W. B. Saunders, Philadelphia, PA.

Kalin, N.H. (1997) The neurobiology of fear, *Scientific American: Mysteries of the Mind*, Vol. 7, No. 1, pp. 76–83.

Kassin, S.M. and Wrightsman, L.S. (1985) Confession evidence. *The Psychology of Evidence and Trial Procedures*, (Kassin, S.M. and Wrightsman, L.S., Eds.). Sage, London, pp. 67–94.

Keirsey, D. and Bates, M. (1984) *Please Understand Me: Character and Temperament Types*, Promethian Nemesis, Delmar, CA.

Knapp, M.L. (1978) *Non-verbal Communication in Human Interaction*, Holt, Rinehart, Winston, New York.

Kroeger, O. and Thuesen, J.M. (1988) *Type Talk*, Delacourte Press, New York.

Kubler-Ross, E. (1969) *On Death and Dying*, McMillan, New York.

Lanning, K.V. (1987) *Child Molesters: A Behavioral Analysis*, National Center for Missing and Exploited Children, Washington, D.C.

LeDoux, J.E. (1997) Emotion, memory and the brain, *Scientific American: Mysteries of the Mind*, Vol. 7, No. 1, pp. 68–75.

Leo, R.A. (1996) Inside the interrogation room, *Journal of Criminal Law and Criminology*, Vol. 86, No. 2, February, pp. 266–303.

Leo, R. and Ofshe, R.J. (1988) The consequences of false confessions: deprivation of liberty and miscarriages of justice in the age of psychological interrogation, *Journal of Criminal Law and Criminology*, Vol. 88, No. 2, Winter, pp. 429–496.

Leo, R.A. and Ofshe, R.J. (1988) Using the innocent to scapegoat Miranda, *Journal of Criminal Law and Criminology*, Vol. 88, No. 2, Winter, pp. 557–578.

Leshner, A.I. (1998) Addiction is a brain disease — and it matters, *National Institute of Justice Journal*, October, pp. 2–6.

Leutwyler, K. (1997) Depression's double standard, *Scientific American: Mysteries of the Mind*, Vol. 7, No. 1, pp. 53–54.

Link, F.C. (1976) Behavior analysis in interrogation, *Military Police Law Enforcement Journal*, Winter.

Link, F.C. and Foster, D.G. (1980) *The Kinesic Interview Technique*, Atlanta.

Lykken, D.T. (1981) *A Tremor In The Blood*, McGraw-Hill, New York.

Marshal, K. (1985) Unmasking the truth, *Security Management*, Vol. 29, No. 1, pp. 34–36.

Marston, W.M. (1928) *Emotions of Normal People*, Paul, Trench, Trubriar & Co., New York.

McGough, L.S. (1994) *Child Witnesses: Fragile Voices in the American Legal System*, Yale University Press, New Haven, CT.

McGough, L.S. and Warren A.R. (1994) The all-important investigative interview, *Juvenile and Family Court Journal*, Vol. 45, pp. 13–29.

McNeil, E.B. (1974) *The Psychology of Being Human*, Harper Row Publishers, New York.

Mehrabian, A. (1972) *Nonverbal Communication*, Aldine, Atherton, Chicago.

Miller, G.R. and Stiff, J.B. (1993) *Deception Communication*, Sage Publications, Newbury Park.

Mobbs, N. (1968) Eye contact in relation to social introversion/extroversion, *British Journal of Social and Clinical Psychology*, Vol. 7, pp. 305–306.

Molloy, J.T. (1975) *Dress for Success*, P.H. Wyden, New York.

Molloy, J.T. (1981) *Live for Success*, P.H. Wyden, New York.

Monahan, J. (1996) *Mental Illness and Violent Crime*, National Institute of Justice, U.S. Department of Justice, Washington, D.C.

Moore, R.T. and Gilliland, A.R. (1921) The measurement of aggressiveness, *Journal of Applied Psychology*, Vol. 5, pp. 97–118.

Moston, S. (1995) The ever so gentle art of police interrogation, paper presented at the British Psychological Society Annual Conference.

Morris, D. (1967) *The Naked Ape: A Zoologist's Study of the Human Animal*, McGraw-Hill, New York.

Morris, D. (1977) *Manwatching: A Field Guide to Human Behavior*, Jonathan Cape, London.

Mullaney, R.C. (1977) Wanted! Performance standards for interrogation and interview, *The Police Chief*, June, pp. 77–80.

Myers, I.B. (1980) *Introduction to Type*, Consulting Psychologist Press, Palo Alto, CA.

Nierenberg, G.I. and Calero, H.H. (1971) *How to Read a Person Like a Book*, Hawthorn Books, New York.

Nierenberg, G.I. and Calero, H.H. (1973) *Meta-Talk*, Cornerstone Library, New York.

Nixon, R. (1979) *The Memoirs of Richard Nixon*, Grosset & Dunlap, New York.

Ofshe, R. (1989) Coerced confessions: the logic of seemingly irrational action, *Cultic Studies Journal*, Vol. 6, pp. 1–15.

Pease, A. (1984) *Signals: How to Use Body Language For Power, Success and Love*, Bantam Books, Toronto.

Poffel, S. and Cross, H.J. (1985) Neurolinguistic programming: a test of the eye-movements hypothesis, *Perceptual and Motor Skills*, Vol. 61, p. 1262.

Register, P.A. and Kihlstrom, J.F. (1988) Hypnosis and interrogative suggestibility, *Personality & Individual Differences*, Vol. 9, pp. 549–558.

Reid, J. and Inbau, F.E. (1966) *Truth and Deception: The Polygraph (Lie Detector) Technique*, Williams & Wilkins, Baltimore, MD.

Reid, J., Inbau, F.E., and Buckley, J.B.(1986) *Criminal Interrogation and Confessions*, Williams & Wilkins, Baltimore, MD.

Ressler, R.K., Burgess, A.W. and Douglas, J.E. (1988) *Sexual Homicide: Patterns and Motives*, Prentice Hall, Englewood Cliffs, N.J.

Royal, R.F. and Schutt, S.R (1976) *The Gentle Art of Interviewing and Interrogation*, Prentice Hall, Englewood Cliffs, N.J.

Rubin, B.D. (1984) *Communication and Human Behavior*, Collier, Macmillan, New York.

Rubin, P.N. and McCampbell, S.W. (1995) The Americans with Disabilities Act and Criminal Justice: Mental Disabilities and Corrections, National Institute of Justice, Washington, D.C.

Rudacille, W.C. (1994) *Identifying Lies in Disguise*, Kendall/Hunt Publishing, Dubuque, IA.

Samenow, S. (1984) *Inside The Criminal Mind*, Times Books, New York.

Shallice, T. (1974) The Ulster depth interrogation techniques and their relation to sensory deprivation research, *Cognition*, Vol. 1, pp. 385–405.

Sheck, B. and Neufeld, P. (2000) *Actual Innocence: Five Days to Executions and Other Dispatches from the Wrongly Convicted*, Doubleday, New York.

Skinner, B.F. (1952, 1992) *Verbal Behavior*, Copley Publishing Group, Acton, MA.

Sommer, R. (1969) *Personal Space*, Prentice-Hall, Englewood Cliffs, N.J.

Stern, J.A. (1989) In the blink of an eye, *Reader's Digest*, April, 1989, pp. 99–101, condensed from *The Sciences*, November/December, 1988.

Stevens, A. (1982) *Archetypes: A Natural History Of The Self*, Quill, New York.

Strachey, J. (1976) *Sigmund Freud: The Complete Psychological Works*, Hogarth Press, London.

Swidler, G.J. (1971) *Psychology For Interrogation*, Beverly, MA.

Thomason, T.C., Arbuckle, T., and Cady, D. (1980). Test of the eye-movement hypothesis of neurolinguistic programming, *Perceptual and Motor Skills*, Vol. 51, p. 230.

Trankell, A. (1972) *Reliability of Evidence*, Beckman (distrib.), Stockholm.

Trovillo, P. (1939) A history of lie detection, *Journal of Criminal Law and Criminology*, Vol. 29, pp. 848–881.

Vrij, A. and Lochun, S. (1997) Neuro-linguistic programming and the police: worthwhile or not?, *Journal of Police and Criminal Psychology*, Vol. 12, No. 1, pp. 25–31.

Vrij, A. (1997) Nonverbal communication and credibility, in A. Merton, A. Vrij, and R. Bull, Eds., *Accuracy and Perceived Credibility of Suspects, Victims and Witnesses*, McGraw-Hill, New York.

Vrij, A. (2000) *Detecting Lies and Deceit: The Psychology of Lying and the Implications for Professional Practice*, John Wiley & Sons, New York.

Wade, C. and Travis, C. (1987) *Psychology*, Harper & Row, New York.

Walters, S.B. (2000) *The Truth About Lying: How to Spot a Lie and Protect Yourself From Deception*, Sourcebooks, Chicago, IL.

Walters, S.B. (1996a) *Principles of Kinesic Interview and Interrogation*, CRC Press, New York.

Walters, S.B. (1996b) *Practical Kinesic Interview and Interrogation — Pocket Guide*, Lexington, KY, 1996.

Walters, S.B. (1994) *Practical Kinesic Interview and Interrogation — Overview*, Lexington, KY, 1994.

Walters, S.B. (2001a) *Practical Kinesic Interview and Interrogation - Student Workbook*, Lexington, KY, (1995, updated 1999 and 2001).

Walters, S.B. (1997a) *Principles and Techniques for Observing Verbal and Nonverbal Behavior to Determine Truth and Deception*, Laurel, M.D., Ed., Johns Hopkins University Press.

Walters, S.B. (1998) Personal communication with Dr. John LaValle, president of the Neuro-Linguistic Programming Society, March 1, 1998. La Valle confirmed that NLP teaching does not suggest that eye movement betrays truth or deception regarding an issue.

Walters, S.B. (1997b) Personal communication with Steven Robbins, Master Trainer in Neuro-Linguistic Programming, November, 11, 1997. Robbins states that both forms of eye-accessing cues, construct and recall, do occur when a person is remembering, and also cited this as a statement made by Bandler and Grinder in their various writings. Robbins conducted research at MIT on the eye-accessing phenomenon. His study determined that there is no consistent link between eye movement and preferred referential systems.

Walters, S.B. (2001b) Personal communication with Dr. John Ratey, Associate Professor of Psychiatry at Harvard Medical School. Ratey's study and research on the brain indicates multiple memory locations and retrieval mechanisms throughout the brain, and states that neither hemisphere is solely responsible for creation of nor the retrieval of information.

Walters, S.B. (2001c) Personal communication with Dr. Leonard Miller, Professor of Psychology and co-editor of the *Journal of Integrative Psychiatry*. Miller's studies indicate that in some cases, common or similar memories may, in fact, be stored together or possibly even overlap in the brain. Some points of memory may come from the combined experiences. At the same time, new or created information must come from events or stimuli previously experienced or stored.

Walters, S.B. (2002) Survey of interview and interrogation training in law enforcement training academies, in preparation.

Walters, S.B. (1989a) Videotaped interviews of inmates, Ashland Group Home — Kentucky Corrections Cabinet, Ashland, KY.

Walters, S.B. (1995) Videotaped interviews of inmates, Bexar County Jail, San Antonio, TX.

Walters, S.B. (1998) Videotaped interviews of inmates, Blackburn Correctional Complex, KY. Corrections Cabinet, Lexington, KY, 1989–1998.

Walters, S.B. (1999) Videotaped interview of Danny Bible, East Baton Rouge, LA, January.

Walters, S.B. (1990) Videotaped interview of Donald Lee Harvey, Lucasville, OH Correctional Facility, 1990.

Walters, S.B. (2001) Videotaped interviews of inmates, Fairfax County Jail, Fairfax, VA, Adult Detention Center, 1987–2001.

Walters, S.B. (1997) Videotaped interviews of inmates, Weld County Sheriff's Office, Weld County Jail, Greeley, CO.

Walters, S.B. (1993) Videotaped interviews of inmates, Eddyville State Penitentiary — Kentucky Corrections Cabinet, Eddyville, KY.

Walters, S.B. (1996) Videotaped interviews of inmates, Lebanon Correctional Institution — Ohio Department of Corrections and Rehabilitation, Lebanon, OH.

Walters, S.B. (1994) Videotaped interviews of inmates, London Correctional Institution — Department of Corrections and Rehabilitation, London, OH, 1988–1994.

Walters, S.B. (1997) Videotaped interviews of inmates, Lincoln Correctional Center — Nebraska Department of Corrections, Lincoln, NE, 1989–1997.

Walters, S. B. (1995) Videotaped interviews of inmates, North Dakota State Penitentiary — North Dakota Department of Corrections, Bismarck, N.D.

Walters, S.B. (1991) Videotaped interviews of inmates, St. Louis County Jail — Annex, St. Louis Municipal Police Academy.

Walters, S.B. (2000) Videotaped interviews of inmates, North Point Training Center — Kentucky Corrections Cabinet, Burgin, KY, 1987–1989, 1999–2000.

Walters, S.B. (1987) Videotaped interviews of inmates, Ogdensburg Correctional Facility — New York State Department Of Corrections, Ogdensburg, N.Y.

Walters, S.B. (1989) Videotaped interviews of inmates, Rankin County Jail, Rankin County Mississippi Sheriff's Office, Jackson, MI.

Walters, S.B., Vorus, N., and Davis, M. (1998) *Credibility Coding of Verbal Behaviors: Part I: Quality Coding from Tape,* and *Part II: Content Coding from Transcript,* unpublished guidebook adapted from Walters (1996).

Weisinger, H. (1995) *Anger At Work,* Quill, New York.

Wertheim, E.H., Habib, C., and Cumming, G. (1986) Test of the neurolinguistic programming hypothesis that eye movements relate to processing imagery. *Perceptual and Motor Skills,* Vol. 62, pp. 523–529.

Yuille, J.C., Ed. (1989) *Credibility Assessment,* Kluner Academic Publishers, London.

Yuille, J.C. and Cutshall, A case study of eyewitness memory of a crime, *Journal of Applied Psychology,* Vol. 71, No. 2, pp. 291–301.

Zimbardo, P.G. (1967) The psychology of police confessions, *Psychology Today,* 1967, Vol. 1, pp. 21–25.

Zuckerman, M., DePaulo, B.M., and Rosenthal, R. (1992) Verbal and nonverbal communications of deception, *Advances in Experimental Social Psychology,* Vol. 14, pp. 1–59.

Index

S

Sanpaku. *See* pupillary responses
Saywitz, Karen J., 19
scratching
    nose, 121
selection-oriented questions, 32. *See* open
        and closed questions
self-importance, 50
semantic memory, 55
sensory dominant personality
    characteristics, 270
    interrogation strategy, 273
    reasoning process, 271
    response to interrogation, 272
sexual assault
    interrogation dialogues, 320
shoulders. *See* arms
sigh, 42
sitting postures, 186
    figure four, 188
    jailbird seat, 191
    liar's lean, 186
    scared rabbit, 193
slurring, 40
smoking behavior, 131
social zone. *See* territorial behavior
soft words. *See* substitute words
specific denials. *See* surgical denial
speech dysfluency, 39. *See* speech
        dysfunction
speech dysfunction, 39, 40, 41, 43, 46. *See*
        stammering, stuttering
    Practical Kinesic Principle, 40
speech dysfunctions
    analysis of statements, 100
spittle
    corners of mouth. *See* mouth
stalling behavior. *See* stalling maneuvers
stalling maneuvers, 42, 43, 65
    analysis of statements, 98
    yawning, 126
stammering, 40, 41
staring. *See* eye contact
state-dependent memory, 56
statement analysis. *See* Practical Kinesic
        Information Recovery and
        Statement Credibility
        Assessment

statement samples
    analysis of statements, 90
stone face. *See* facial expressions
stress
    discriminating, 13
    discriminating, definition, 15
    general, 13
    general, definition, 13
    incriminating, 13
    incriminating, definition, 14
stress-response states, 20
stuttering, 40, 41
sublimation. *See* ego defense mechanism
substitute words, 73
sue, 48
suicidal comments, 54
suicidal subjects. *See* depression, suicidal
        subjects
suicide threats. *See* depression, suicidal
        threats
"surgical" denials, 67
swallowing, 41. *See* mouth
swear to God. *See* religious statements
swearing of oaths. *See* religious
        statements.
sympathy
    complaining for, 71

T

taking notes
    subject. *See* behavioral cues
tape recorder
    brought by subject. *See* behavioral cues
tearing up statements. *See* written cues
teenagers. *See* adolescence
territorial behavior, 194
    attacking proxemic zones, 197
    intimate zone, 196
    personal zone, 196
    public zone, 197
    social zone, 196
theft
    interrogation dialogues, 312
third person, 62, 65, 82, 95, 96, 101, 316
third person statements, 80
    defined and examples, 80
    verbal acceptance cues, 78, 80
thought disorders. *See* psychoses

thought line, 40, 41, 43, 44, 46
　Practical Kinesic Principle, 40
　speech dysfluency, 40
timely, 16, 36
　Pratical Kinesic Principle, 16
touching. *See* hands
　nose, 121
training, 23, 24, 25, 29
　in-service, 23
trivial details, 51

U

uh. *See* paralinguistic
um. *See* paralinguistic
underling passages. *See* written cues

V

value statements
　bargaining. *See* gray statements
verbal, 35, 36, 39, 42, 43
　Pratical Kinesic Principle, 35
　vs. nonverbal cues, 35. See
verbal acceptance cues
　debt service statements, 78
　punishment statements, 78
　third person statements, 78
verbal content, 47
verbs
　shifting of. *See* vocabulary shifting
victim, 23, 27, 32, 47, 48, 49, 51, 55, 58, 62,
　　　66, 70, 71, 82
　attacking, 48
　rape, 49
videotaping, 97
vocabulary shifting, 64
voice, 35, 36, 37, 38, 46
　clarity, 36, 46
　content, 35, 36, 41, 43, 45
　pitch, 37, 46. See
　quality, 35
　rate of speech, 36, 37, 38, 39, 46
　rate of speech increase, 39

　rate of speed decrease, 38
　volume, 36, 37
voice quality, 35, 36
　defined, 36
volume, 36, 37, 38, 46
　drop in, 38
　increase in voice, 38
　voice, 38

W

weighted expressions, 60
whistles. *See* paralinguistic
witnesses, 23, 24, 27, 32, 49
　attacking, 49
　blaming, 49
writing pressure. *See* written cues
written cues. *See* written statements
　adding phrases, 104
　adding words, 104
　capital letters, 102
　erasing words, 103
　letter size, changes in, 104
　retracing letters or words, 103
　scratching out words, 103
　tearing up statements, 103
　underlining passages, 102
　writing pressure changes, 104
written statement. *See* written cues
　analysis of statements, 102
wrongful conviction
　causal factors, 288
　cluster, 289
　elements of, 288

Y

yawn. *See* mouth
yes reponses, 33, 68
yes–no questions, 33. *See* open and closed
　　　questions